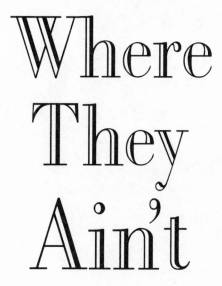

Where They Ain't

THE FABLED LIFE AND UNTIMELY DEATH
OF THE ORIGINAL BALTIMORE ORIOLES,
THE TEAM THAT GAVE BIRTH
TO MODERN BASEBALL

BURT SOLOMON

THE FREE PRESS

*f*P

THE FREE PRESS
A Division of Simon & Schuster Inc.
1230 Avenue of the Americas
New York, NY 10020

5 / 8 3 5 9 /

Copyright © 1999 by Burt Solomon

Design by Kim Llewellyn
Manufactured in the United States of America
1   3   5   7   9   10   8   6   4   2

Library of Congress Cataloging-in-Publication Data
Solomon, Burt.
Where they ain't : the fabled life and untimely death of the original Baltimore
Orioles, the team that gave birth to modern baseball / Burt Solomon.
p.   cm
1. Baltimore Orioles (American Association : Baseball team)—History.
2. Baseball—United States—History—19th century.   3. Baseball—United
States—History—20th century.   I. Title.
GV875.B2S65   1999
796.357'64'097526—dc21   98-51654   CIP

ISBN 0-684-85451-1

To Nancy, Anna, and Matt,

and to the memory of my grandfather, Myer Toor,
who was a boy then

CONTENTS

AUTHOR'S NOTE

Many of the baseball teams in this story, centered in the 1890s, carry names that modern readers may find unfamiliar. The Boston Beaneaters, the Cleveland Spiders, the Louisville Colonels—these belonged to the twelve-team National League of 1892–99, back when it was the only major league in the country. The team names were not as formal or enduring as they are today; the Brooklyn ballclub, for instance, was known as the Trolley Dodgers or the Bridegrooms or the Superbas at various times, or even at the same time. Adding to the confusion, when the American League began in 1901, it appropriated some of the team names the National League had abandoned—the St. Louis Browns, the Washington Senators, and the Baltimore Orioles. For Baltimore teams, the confusion over names did not end there. After the 1901–02 American League Orioles were moved to New York (and became known as the Highlanders and later the Yankees), Baltimore's minor league ballclub took the old moniker for the next fifty-one years, then passed it along in 1954 to the modern American League ballclub, which until then had been the St. Louis Browns.

I have tried to ground this story in the times it describes, in part by using the language and presentation of the period. Hence "crank" and "twirler" and other terms of a bygone age. I have left "street" and "avenue" in lower case, and kept the spellings of names as they were then—"Hughey" Jennings instead of "Hughie," and Ed "Delehanty" instead of "Delahanty" (as it later became after a birth certificate was found).

But in most ways, baseball has not changed very much from the end of the nineteenth century to the end of the twentieth. Owners still act like owners, and players like players. The following story should feel startlingly familiar.

PART ONE

Sentiment

In time it was made apparent to even the most casual
observer that baseball as a sport was playing second fiddle
to baseball as a business.

—FRANK HOUGH, sporting editor of
The Philadelphia Inquirer, 1900

Everything I have, except my family, is for sale at a price.

—NED HANLON, part owner of the
Baltimore Orioles, 1899

Keep your eye clear, and hit 'em where they ain't.

—"WEE WILLIE" KEELER,
peerless place-hitter, 1903

=1=
The Fields of Brooklyn

The weather in Brooklyn had been quirky since Christmas. The mercury had fallen the night before to thirteen degrees, the coldest of the winter so far, and snow had been predicted for this dying day of 1922. In its place came a heavy rain followed by hours of disarming sunshine and then a chilly wind.

"Wee Willie" Keeler, the famous old ballplayer, was propped up on pillows in his sickbed, looking wan and wasted. Though he was small, his features had been generous; now they seemed shriveled. The pain in his chest had been disabling at times, but his eyes still shone.

Charles Wuest, his doctor and friend, came by around noon. Willie invited him over for a quiet party that evening. "Well, I've got to have a New Year smoke and drink with old friends like you," Willie said. Even in illness and penury he seemed playful and kind. "I had a dream last night that we were all going to California to spend the winter."

He understood that he would never go. His brothers, Tom and Joe, and his closest friends had been told that the end was imminent. Willie had not: The patient never was. But surely he knew. No batsman had ever faced the twirlers with a keener eye.

He had already told Tom, his oldest brother, that he knew this was a fight he would lose. That night he spoke to his friends who had squeezed into his dim second-floor flat at 1010 Gates avenue. "You think that I am going to die," he said. "But I am not going to pass out this year. I am going to see the new year in."

Willie Keeler was only fifty, but what more was there to do? He had lost everything he loved when he left baseball. He had never married or fathered a child. He had been the first ballplayer to be paid

$10,000 a year. Known as the Brooklyn Millionaire when he retired, now he was a pauper. At last he had found Clara, but only when it was too late.

He fell asleep as midnight neared. His guests went into the street to listen to the bells of Brooklyn, the City of Churches, ring in the new year. Willie lived in a row house with bow windows, a half-block on the wrong side of Broadway. On the other side, beyond the loud grimy el, stood the Victorian mansions of Bushwick. Willie's side was crowded with the children of immigrants—from Russia, Austria, Germany, France, Alsace, and most of all Ireland, where his parents had been born.

All over Brooklyn, sirens and bells were sounded as 1923 arrived. An eight-year-old girl in Bushwick sat in the rear window of her home and was shot in the forehead by a rifle fired into the air. (Dr. Wuest, a coroner's physician, conducted the autopsy.) On Gates avenue, the muffled sounds of celebration penetrated inside.

Suddenly there was a sound in the sickroom. Tom, who had stayed behind, rushed to his brother's bedside. He found Willie sitting up. A smile creased Willie's face as he shook a miniature cowbell.

"You see," he said, "the new year is here and so am I—still."

He exchanged good wishes with the others once they returned. He took a short smoke and a drink—"really medicine for him," Dr. Wuest said later. Willie finished and said to his friends: "I'm pretty tired. I feel like taking a good, long sleep." He dozed off.

He never awakened.

Within an hour Willie Keeler had breathed his last. Dr. Wuest looked at his watch. It was a quarter past one.

On the death certificate the doctor described the cause of death as chronic endocarditis, an inflammation of the lining of the heart. Willie had suffered from it for five years. There was also a report of dropsy, an excess of fluid between the cells, the sign of a failing heart.

The reaction to his death was intense. WILLIE KEELER STRUCK OUT BY THE GREAT UMPIRE, the *Brooklyn Daily Times* grieved. WILLIE KEELER, GREATEST OF PLACE HITTERS, LEAVES BEHIND A BRILLIANT RECORD, ran the headline in the *Brooklyn Daily Eagle*. *The Sporting News* listed the records he still held. He had batted safely in forty-four consecutive games in a season. He had collected at least two hundred hits in each of eight straight seasons, and claimed to have once played an entire season without striking out. George Sisler had broken his record of 239 hits in a season only three years before. Willie's batting average of .424 back in 'ninety-seven was the second-highest ever (next to Hugh Duffy's .440), other than in 'eighty-seven, the year that four strikes made an out and bases on balls counted as hits.

Even more than his individual achievements, Willie Keeler had helped change the face of the national game. The newspapers in Baltimore mourned the passing of the first of the Big Four who had played for the celebrated Orioles a quarter-century earlier. At the time, baseball had been a game of power and thick-bodied men. Then came the Orioles, scrappy and swift. In 'ninety-four they won the first of three pennants in a row. They used the hit-and-run, the bunt, the squeeze play, the cutoff play, the Baltimore chop—whatever was unexpected and put their opponents on edge. They never stopped thinking. Scientific baseball, it was called, or inside baseball, or—more than occasionally—dirty baseball.

Whatever the name, the national game would never be the same. Before Willie broke in, ballplayers customarily held the bat at the very end; he choked almost halfway up and chopped and thrust and poked at the ball. By his success, he changed what was right. In place of the slugging came speed and strategy and smarts. Even now, Ty Cobb and Rabbit Maranville were still slicing up the basepaths in the old Orioles' footsteps.

It was after Willie Keeler had returned to Brooklyn from Baltimore that a baseball scribe asked him for his secret of hitting. Willie had been thinking about it for years. "Keep your eye clear," he replied, "and hit 'em where they ain't."

He could see the rotation on the ball from the instant the pitcher released it. He had to use every advantage, for he was not much bigger than a batboy. Willie claimed to be five feet, four and one-half inches tall—and would never consent to be measured. The others of the Big Four—John McGraw, Hughey Jennings, and even Swaggering Joe Kelley—were not all that much bigger. They were brainy at the bat and reckless on the basepaths and fearless in the field. Old-timers still talked of the afternoon in Washington that Willie had stuck his hand up through the barbed wire fence and prevented a home run. The great second baseman Johnny Evers, famed as a fielder himself, thought that no ballplayer had ever been a better judge of where a batter would drive a pitch.

Yet it was not only for his playing that Willie was eulogized. "The loveliest character in baseball," Brooklyn manager Wilbert Robinson, the catcher and captain of the old Orioles, murmured to a reporter on

New Year's night. Among teammates who sharpened their spikes, Willie was known for his decency and gentlemanly demeanor.

From the start he had been amazed he was paid to do something he would have done for free. "I like playing ball so much," he once told the Orioles in their clubhouse, "I'd pay them for the privilege if that was the only way I could get into a ballpark."

Yet even while he was on the diamond, the air of innocence was fading fast. Baseball was not what it had once been. Monopoly and greed had transformed the national game and at last it touched even Willie. "I am in baseball for all I can get out of it," he explained matter-of-factly when he jumped to the American League in 1903. "In baseball, as in any profession, business prevails over sentiment."

Ever since, things had only grown worse. The Black Sox scandal, when gamblers fixed the World Series of 1919, had shown baseball as something darker than a sport. In response—and panic—the ballclubs' owners had hired a tyrannical commissioner to save them from themselves. On the field the game was changing again. A borough away, a spindly legged strongman by the name of Babe Ruth was banging home runs and turning baseball into a game of sluggers again.

Nor was Brooklyn what it had been while Willie was growing up, just a dozen blocks from where he died. Brooklyn had never grown so fast. Where fields had been, now there were homes. Asphalt had replaced the cobblestones; the milk trucks no longer wakened the hard-of-hearing. A record number of new buildings had gone up in the previous year and more than a thousand miles of sewers twisted beneath its streets, instead of sixty, as just a decade before. Changes in zoning had spattered businesses among the narrow, unremitting homes. Willie had died beside a bank and over a branch office of the *Brooklyn Daily Eagle.* An undertaker labored a block away.

Willie Keeler's body lay in a plain oaken coffin by the bow window. He had died on a Monday and the funeral was arranged for Thursday morning. The mourners had started to gather by Wednesday. That night, two hundred members of the Brooklyn Lodge of the Elks, No. 22, passed through Willie's rooms to say their farewells to one of the lodge's most enduring members. Thomas Burns led the hymns and prayers, then every Elk filed silently past the casket and dropped a single red rose from his lapel.

Hundreds of people waited outside in the cold. In Willie's playing days they had been called "cranks" and were now known as "fans."

6

It snowed overnight, seven-and-a-half inches, the heaviest of the winter so far. It was also the prettiest. A covering of white concealed the grit of the streets. The plows had been out in the night so that by morning the trolleys could pass. In a full-page advertisement on page 12 of the *Eagle,* Abraham & Straus cajoled:

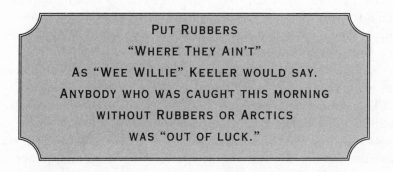

PUT RUBBERS
"WHERE THEY AIN'T"
AS "WEE WILLIE" KEELER WOULD SAY.
ANYBODY WHO WAS CAUGHT THIS MORNING
WITHOUT RUBBERS OR ARCTICS
WAS "OUT OF LUCK."

Several hundred people gathered again in the morning on Gates avenue and stood with their heads bared in the sun. Police reserves from the Ralph avenue station stood nearby.

Inside the tan brick house with the chocolate-colored cornice and the ornamental trim, the manager of the world champion New York Giants, one of the most celebrated men in America, stood by the open casket and stared at the face of his friend. John McGraw had known Willie Keeler for twenty-nine years. They had batted one-two in the Orioles' lineup. How many hundreds of times had Willie moved Mac along a base or more? They had wrestled with each other, the two bantams rolling around in the dirt. They had sat side by side at the vaudeville show and in church. After five glorious years as teammates they played on rival teams, then in rival leagues. When Willie's playing days were just about done, Mac hired him as a pinch hitter and a coach.

He gazed down on the casket for five minutes, which seemed an eternity. Mac was white-haired now. Once he had been the scrawny and fiery soul of a team. Now he was the Little Napoleon, stocky and imperious, who could never admit to a doubt that he was right. How he had changed from when they were young.

Willie had not changed. To be sure, he had compromised with the ways of the world. He had allowed his innocence to turn into something else. But he had never really changed.

Only now he was dead.

McGraw started to weep. The *Eagle* said he broke down. He wailed so loudly, the Keeler family recounted later, that Joe Kelley—always spoiling for a fight—barged in from a room away and threw him out.

Other ex-Orioles had come to pay their respects—Hughey Jennings and Steve Brodie and Kid Gleason and Jack Doyle and the man at the center of the team, their brilliant strategist of a manager, Ned Hanlon. Every year the old teammates still gathered for a reunion. Usually they went to Baltimore, but recently they had been coming to New York, so that Willie could attend.

Now they had learned, on a side street in Brooklyn, that the bonds between them would last until death.

The flowers kept arriving, as they had all night. Colonel Jacob Ruppert and Colonel T. L. Huston, the owners of the Yankees, sent an enormous cluster of roses and pink carnations. A casket bouquet came from the Giants—the first big league ballclub Willie had played for, and the last. Flowers arrived from almost every major league club and from the leaders of the national game and from celebrated players of yore. It took two open motorcars to carry them all the four blocks to the church.

The motorcars preceded the hearse, with its wide windows, the white curtains drawn. Joe and Sarah Keeler and their three children filled the first carriage in the cortege. Tom and Annie Keeler took the second. McGraw shared the third carriage with Hughey Jennings, now his assistant manager, and with Wid Conroy, who had roomed with Willie on the road when they were Yankees—the Highlanders then. Nine more automobiles carried Willie's friends. The crowd walked behind the procession, all the way to the church.

The neighborhood grew fancy. The row houses widened and had staircases with wrought-iron railings. The Gothic spire of the Church of Our Lady of Good Counsel, on Putnam avenue between Patchen and Ralph, rose like a guardian angel over a neighborhood in no evident need of one. Snow covered the steps of the brooding gray church; ice encased the bower of branches that wreathed the Crusader-arched doorway.

Inside, the rows of stone pillars soared toward gilded arches at the vaulted ceiling. Painted saints graced the cream-colored walls between the stained-glass windows made in Munich.

Hundreds of worshipers crowded inside. Charley Ebbets, the president of the Brooklyn ballclub, was traveling in Europe, and Wilbert Robinson, the portly Uncle Robbie, was at his winter home in Georgia (disappointing local sportswriters, who hoped to ask about the rumors of a trade). But many others had come. Charley Ebbets, Jr., and Ed McKeever represented the Brooklyn club. National League president John Heydler, concessionaire Harry Stevens, and Pat Powers, who had started Willie in the big leagues, sat in the pews. So did Abe Yager of the *Brooklyn Daily Eagle* and Joe Vila of the *New York Sun* and John B. Foster of *Sporting Life,* the expired weekly—the newspapermen who had become Willie's friends.

The ushers wore tuxedos. Father Donahue, in his fiddleback vestments, stood with his back to the mourners. He and two assistant priests conducted the requiem Mass.

A smaller crowd gathered again shortly before noon at Calvary Cemetery, just into Queens. Snow shrouded the hillside. Willie's father had purchased the plot when Willie was three years old, to bury a baby daughter and later a two-year-old son. He had come here again to bury his beloved wife. For the past eleven years he had rested beside her, facing east across the quiet landscape, toward Ireland.

Now Willie, sweet Willie, would join them. Three tender pink roses gently rested on his casket, and John McGraw and Hughey Jennings and Wid Conroy each tossed on a spadeful of earth as it was lowered into the ground. Tears came to their eyes, not only for a teammate but for a time.

It snowed fiercely on the first Saturday of March in eighteen seventy-two. The ferry boats found it hard to cross the East River from Manhattan island and they had to rely on the clanging of the bells more than on the lights to guide them into the docks of Brooklyn. The passengers huddled together for warmth, barely able to see the massive gray stone tower rising out of the water by the far Brooklyn shore. It was to be three times the height it was now, the loftiest thing on the horizon, to hold the grand unearthly bridge that would forever change Brooklyn.

The sun rose clear and bright the next morning, on the Sabbath, the third of March. Along the sunny side of Brooklyn's streets, the snow turned to slush. At the Plymouth Church, in the eminence of Brooklyn Heights, the lionlike Henry Ward Beecher shook his iron-gray mane, taking pains not to castigate sin so harshly as to discomfit the sinner. Even in Brooklyn, he roared in his nasal twang, wealth was becoming the measure of success.

Still, Brooklyn was nothing like New York, across the East River, where the incumbent mayor, a Tammany Hall man, was facing a jury and Boss Tweed was nine months away from being arrested. In New York, people lived in dark and crowded quarters, and murders had become unremarkable. Not in Brooklyn. It was the fourth most populous city in the nation, and just a ferry ride away from the largest. Yet the air felt fresh and the streets were calm and a man might gain title to a home of his own.

Pat Keleher had managed to do so, at 376 Pulaski street, at the edge of the Bedford section of Brooklyn. That was three years ago. Now he had something else to celebrate. His wife, Mary, gave birth this day to their third child, their third son. They named him William, which was Pat's Christian name.

Pat had arrived from Ireland a dozen years before, carrying the family name of O'Kelleher. As a boy he had worked on a farm in County Cork, until the absentee landlords had mismanaged the country's rich soil into ruin. At the age of twenty-six, still too poor to marry, Pat had walked the twenty miles over Watergrass Hill and down to the ocean. His shoes dangled from around his neck, to save the soles for when he reached his new home.

Pat was not one of the garrulous, talkative Irishmen, but a guttural sort, a compact man who spoke in grunts. His chin was strong and his skull looked squat, as if flattened by the weight of the world. Yet he had a wicked sense of humor. His eyes had a spark—a pugnaciousness—that lit up his face. He looked every inch the Irishman.

This was not bound to help his prospects in his new homeland. Even in Brooklyn, so heavy with immigrants, in many a workplace the Irish need not apply. The newspaper advertisements specified Protestant girls for housework.

But Pat was determined. In this blunt land of liberty, he was quick to make his way. He dropped the *O'* from his name and found a job, quite a good one, driving the horse-drawn trolleys that ran along DeKalb avenue. He took a wife, Mary Kiley, who had come from Ireland the same time he did. They saved every cent, and when they had accumulated $700 they bought a house. It was not much to look at—little more than a narrow two-story shack, with monotonous shingles and a tiny front porch. The slit of a doorway was sheltered by a desiccated porch roof resting on rococo joists, which were meant to show luxury but suggested the reverse. The only light-hearted touch was a white picket fence that protected a front yard barely spacious enough for a newborn. Still, it was theirs—Pat's and Mary's and little Tom's and then Joe's and now Willie's. Already Pat owned more than he could have imagined in the despairing land of his birth. Almost everyone else on the block between Lewis and Stuyvesant avenues rented.

He loved working for the trolley. The horse-drawn lines fanned out across the city of Brooklyn like splayed fingers. The DeKalb Avenue Railroad Company, an independent line, carried passengers east to Broadway and beyond, all the way to Coney Island. But it was forbidden to run its cars on the direct route to Fulton Ferry or to City Hall, because the City Railroad Company, by virtue of its influence in Albany, had been granted the rights to the public thoroughfares. "The power of this impudent monopoly," the *Eagle* wailed.

Pat had known since Ireland not to count on anyone else for his survival. He started a modest moving business on the side and bought a plot of land farther out in Brooklyn on which he raised a few cows and a couple of goats. The cow's milk he sold and the goat's milk he drank, though he never learned to like it.

"You never put out any garbage," the garbage collector told him one day.

"We ates it," Pat replied.

For Willie and his older brothers and every boy they knew, Brooklyn was a wonderful place to grow up. There were frogs to catch and snakes to put out of their misery. In every direction from Pulaski street lay open fields. Directly across the street, at the five-story brick buildings of H. B. Scharmann & Sons Brewery, the boys could steal past the vigilant watchman, into the imposing entranceway, to snatch handfuls of sweet malt from the end of the chute. Or they watched the husky men rolling the hogsheads up and down the street, back and forth across the cobblestones, to distribute the resin evenly inside.

For boys in knickers there were street games galore, such as tag and leapfrog and Red Rover and many others that involved a bat and a ball—One o' Cat, Kick the Wicket, Kick the Can, Hit the Stick, all the precursors to what was already coming to be regarded as the national game. For Willie, living in the smallest house on the block meant having the biggest backyard. The three brothers never seemed to stop playing and though Willie was the littlest, he held his own. One day Tom and Joe were boxing with gloves on behind their house. Willie, who had never boxed before, said it looked like fun. They invited him to try. He thrashed them both.

He was small for his age but never defenseless. He was strong, and he had a knack. He was clever with his dukes. When he wrestled he could throw someone twice his weight. Few of the boys around Brooklyn had anything on him.

He always seemed to be having fun, even when he was not supposed to. At P.S. 26, the gabled schoolhouse over on Gates avenue between Patchen and Ralph with windows shaped like colossal tombstones, Willie's mind was never on his books. A matronly teacher dressed him down for assuring her that a rhinoceros was a fine-feathered bird. And she had another thing on her mind. "I shall no longer tolerate," she told him, "the bringing of baseball bats into this schoolroom."

Willie sat serenely at his desk and smiled, his coat pockets bulging with baseballs.

For Willie, school became a place to play ball. "For four years we had a team that easily beat any school team in the Eastern District," he remembered years later with pride. "I was captain and first batter a good part of the time. When I was elected captain I got a red-and-white belt with the word 'Captain' on it. That belt I never took off, night or day, during the summer." Often he would skip out in the afternoon—or in the morning—to toss a blackened baseball around with his pals. His father complained to friends that Willie wanted only to play baseball.

Baseball was in the air in Brooklyn. Empty lots had been turned into ballfields. Less than a mile away from Pulaski street stood the Capitoline Grounds, where Candy Cummings was said to have pitched the first curveball and Eddie Cuthbert had stolen baseball's first base and Dicky Pearce had laid down the first bunt. Two years before Willie was born, the Cincinnati Red Stockings, the original all-professional team, had suffered their first defeat there, to the Brooklyn Atlantics, after eighty-four victories.

Willie's father had put a bat in his smallest son's hands at an early age and coached him to "hit it out." This was fun, the way the home-strung ball leapt off the thick, dark bat. Right away Willie loved it. "I guess it was just because I couldn't help it," he struggled to explain many years later. "People say that a man or boy must be pretty near a crank on any subject to be a success at it. I was a crank on baseball—so there you are. I have lived in the same neighborhood in Brooklyn all my life and the oldest inhabitant will tell you he never saw me without a ball or a bat, or both, in my hands when I was a kid."

Willie and Tom joined the Eclipse Bowling Club and Willie kept up his boxing but found he did not enjoy inflicting pain. His first love was baseball. It was right for him. Size did not matter so much. Speed counted as much as power, deftness more than heft. The game rewarded the player who tried his damndest and never gave up.

At fourteen he began to play for the Rivals, an amateur nine, with its home grounds at Greene and Broadway, a half-dozen blocks from Willie's house. He would arrive before seven each morning and spend the day. "We were only sandlot kids," he said, "but what fun we did have." He played pretty much every position, but his finest game came in the pitcher's box. The Rivals were playing the Star-Athletics, of Eagle's Nest, who had not lost a game all season and had a minor legend named Swifty twirling. Half of Brooklyn and all of Long Island turned out to watch. Swifty gave up twelve runs and Willie allowed none. It was the most gratifying performance of his career, Willie judged decades later.

Mainly he played at third base. Even on an amateur team, that was an odd position for a left-handed fielder, for it took him an extra step or two to pivot and throw. Willie, though, was more than quick enough. And there was no better attribute a third baseman could have than instinct.

"I got lots of practice with the Rivals," he remembered fondly, "and made quite a reputation among the boys."

At fifteen he made up his mind that school was not for him. Willie's father could not have been happy—or surprised. The point of school was to get ready for working, and Willie had no desire to work. "After I left school I tried hard to work like other boys," he said, "but somehow I could never get my mind down to it." He refused to study for a clerkship, for fear of ruining his eyes and his lungs. He was offered a decent wage to work in a factory in Brooklyn and a like amount to play for the company's nine, so he said yes to the baseball and no to the job. When he was sixteen his father got a summer job for him at a cheese factory out on Long Island at $15 a month. Willie was angry but made no kick. From Monday to Saturday he stuck to the job, then drew $2 from the foreman on the pretense of going home. He went to Staten Island instead and played in a ballgame for $3 and expenses, and never worked in the cheese factory again.

13

"My father said I didn't want to work, and predicted that I would become a professional ballplayer," Willie said. "He was right, as parents usually are."

Boys who play baseball as amateurs turn into men who must earn a living. All over Brooklyn and everywhere else, semipro teams had sprung up. Men paid to watch men and almost-men play the pastoral game of baseball. It helped the spectators remember how the world used to be—or how they wished it to be.

Willie was first paid to do what he loved at the age of sixteen. He got $1.50 to play on Sundays for a high-blown nine called the Acmes. Soon he was getting more than that, once the other semipro teams saw how he played. The Sylvans took him on and, late in the season, so did the Allertons, across the Hudson in Weehawken, New Jersey. He was living just as he wanted. He went wherever he liked by trolley and ferry. Hardly a day passed when his feet missed the diamond.

From the start he had a distinctive hitting stance. "About the first time a boy picks up a bat he acquires a style of batting," he wrote later, "and he holds it for the remainder of his life. You can't change a man's style and make him successful." He stood straight as a fence post, crowding the home base, so as not to betray any fear. He was too small to swing from the end of the bat, so he choked up instead, almost as much as halfway. That way he could stay in control. And control, he understood, was his best advantage.

He needed an advantage. When he was eighteen he still looked fourteen, with a foreshadowing of fuzz on his face and upper arms as thin as cheroots. To look his age he had started to smoke cigars—and never would see a need to stop. He was convinced that smoking would never hurt his batting eye as long as he did not inhale; quitting during the season would only jangle his nerves.

He also showed his age in his knowing glance. Among the bigger men, Willie held his own. He was sharp with the bat and swift in the field. He was in demand—and gloried in it. In New Jersey he played shortstop for the Allertons and right field for a team out in Rahway; in Brooklyn he played third base for the Flushings and the Ridgewoods.

He also found the time to sell scorecards at Eastern Park, where a Brooklyn major league nine had its home. He could watch the men on the diamond and dream. His employers had no fondness for the name of O'Kelleher or Keleher, as it had become. They preferred Keeler, which was easier to say and looked better on paper and had the advantage of often being mistaken for German or Dutch.

Willie obliged.

"My father was convinced that professional baseball was not so bad after all," Willie recalled. The invitation from the Plainfield club had accomplished that. Strictly speaking, it was still semipro. But the Crescents played in the Central New Jersey League, which sounded real, and would pay him $60 a month.

Plainfield was becoming home to more and more New Yorkers, who escaped the miseries of the city by commuting on the Jersey Central Railroad, and the bustling town of 11,000 was crazy about baseball. When the Crescents traveled to Connecticut to play, the newspapers used homing pigeons to fly the scores back home. New grounds had been built on Somerset street, and the Crescents drew more cranks than any other ballclub in New Jersey, as many as 1,200 a game.

When they were winning, that is. Let them lose two or three games in a row and the crowds would stay home.

From the first Willie helped bring the spectators in. He showed a knack at the bat. In almost every game he got a hit. One afternoon in August of 'ninety-one he hit safely three times. "Let them sneer at Keeler no more," the *Plainfield Press* advised. In a game the following week, he got five hits. He outraced ground balls and stole bases galore. He went to bat thirteen times in a doubleheader and collected twelve hits—"three of them two-baggers," he was to remember. "Of all the records I ever made in after years none gave me the keen pleasure that that one did." Willie won the batting championship, with an average of .376, as the Crescents took the pennant.

It was in the field that Willie struggled. When Plainfield's shortstop was found to have wagered $25 on the opposing team and committed four errors to protect his investment, Willie took his place. His teammates and the cranks forgave his early fumbles and muffs, yet he kept making them. He booted grounders and threw wildly to first base. Some of his mistakes had no effect on the game; others brought defeat.

But slowly, not easily noticeable to the casual rooter, his fielding improved. Within weeks he was blocking hard-bouncing balls and, amid the errors, making a fine running catch of a fly ball.

One day he learned a lesson of a different sort. The Crescents had won twice as many games as they had lost this season and knew they were one of the best teams around. One of the best white teams, that is. They might have benefited more had the drubbing by the dark-skinned Gorhams come earlier. The Crescents cared too much about their own heroics and about the heads they could turn in the grand-stand. Their opponents did not. "The Gorhams were not a nine," a scribe in Plainfield wrote—"they were a unit." They bunched their hits and turned eight double plays and licked the Crescents, 9 to 2.

When Willie returned to Plainfield the next spring he was the most popular man on the team. He batted fourth and played at short-stop or in right field or as the extra pitcher for a holiday double-header. The Crescents had just edged into first place in June of 'ninety-two when, for Willie, everything changed.

Herman Doescher was about to become the manager of the Bing-hamton ballclub in the Eastern League. The square-jawed, blond ex-umpire was a hard man. A decade earlier he had been banished from baseball for scouting players for one ballclub, then signing them for another he had secretly agreed to manage, and eventually was rein-stated. Baseball was all he knew.

He was stopping off to visit his son in New York when he was told of a ballplayer named Brennan with the Staten Island Athletic Club who would be playing that Sunday at Leo Park out on Long Island. As the ladies in their bonnets and the beaus in their strawboaters pic-nicked by the ballfield, the old baseball man kept his attention on the diamond. It was not Brennan but the third baseman with the opposing team who caught his eye. The fact that Keeler threw left-handed was a drawback, to be sure. "But he picked up the ball so easy that I was attracted to him, but that was nothing like his batting," Doescher said. "For seven innings every time he came to bat he made a base hit, and many of them were two- or three-baggers."

He went up to Willie and asked how much he was making. Then he asked if Willie wanted to play in the Eastern League, just a step below the major leagues, for $90 a month. Willie jumped at the chance. Doescher handed him $25 and they arranged to meet at the railroad station the following day.

16

That night, Willie sat at home in Brooklyn and penned a letter to his manager in Plainfield. His handwriting was meticulous, full of sharp points and artful loops. "I know you will not feel hard of me," he wrote, "for you know you would like to see your players advance themselves, and of course there was such a great difference in the money."

The manager's reply was unambiguous. He told the newspapers that he could easily fill Keeler's place and promised to do whatever he could to bar Willie from the Central New Jersey League.

The Binghamton Bingos had slipped into tenth place in the ten-team league. "The public is awake to the fact that there is a screw loose somewhere and it looks very much like mismanagement," the *Binghamton Republican* groused. The third baseman was injured and the shortstop, John Irwin, took his place.

Willie Keeler reported to the team in Syracuse and was immediately put in at shortstop. He got quite a workout. He made four putouts, including a circus catch, and threw four men out. (He also committed an error that gave up a run.) At the bat he hit safely and drew a walk, and Binghamton won, 4 to 2.

The next afternoon, a welcome sunny day in Syracuse, the Bingos—out of desperation—had Willie pitch. It was a game he would never forget. The Syracuse Stars, hardly a powerhouse, batted him all over the lot, smiting nineteen hits. Willie was left in the box to face his fate, as twirlers ordinarily were. Only the Stars' sloppy baserunning kept the game as close as 9 to 3.

Willie never pitched again.

The Bingos lost four more in a row, in Buffalo and Rochester, before going home. Binghamton was new to Willie. It called itself the Parlor City, this place of drab graciousness in upstate New York, where the inhabitants passed the summer on their spacious front porches and waited for the long winter to come. Binghamton was thriving. Its population had doubled in a decade, to more than 35,000. The narrow jutting streets in the center of the city had new brick buildings made fancy with cornices. Factories had sprouted on open land. More than two dozen of them crowded downtown, making shoes or men's clothing or furniture or carriages or—most of all—cigars. Out on Stow

Flats, where the Bingos played, the fairgrounds were being refurbished, behind an overdecorated archway that aspired to be elegant before it merely seemed worn.

Not until his fifth game with the Bingos did Willie make more hits than errors. Soon he was playing third base, after a slashing line drive broke John Irwin's leg. Willie found he was fast enough in pivoting to throw—sometimes too fast, so he was off-balance as he got the ball away. Once he lost the game by dropping a pop fly because he was doing the next thing first. He committed forty-eight errors in ninety-three games. "In the Eastern, I had been called 'the best left-handed third baseman in the league,'" Willie recounted. "All the others were right-handed."

Yet along with the errors came spectacular catches that brought cheers from the stands. Even before the team reached Binghamton, Willie showed he could handle a bat. In a doubleheader in Rochester he struck six hits. Soon he was getting two or three or five hits a game.

Once he had his batting eye, he kept it. When he struck out against Troy it was considered an event. At Stow Flats, he hit his first home run, inside the grounds. He would have had a second one a few innings later had he slid into home.

It was a mistake he would never make again.

The Eastern League split the 'ninety-two season into separate pennant races to wake up the cranks. During the first half, the Bingos came in last. But in the second "series" they finished first. In ninety-three games Willie hit safely 153 times and scored 109 runs. He led the league's batsmen with an average of .373.

On the diamond he noticed almost everything. But near the end of September he failed to notice Pat Powers in the grandstand.

The rotund, pleasantly balding man was well-known around the Eastern League, having managed the Trenton and Buffalo ballclubs. Now he was the manager of the New York Giants, in the National League. He had been watching the young infielder with a critical eye and liked what he saw. The Giants were not the only team to have sent an agent. The man from the Louisville Colonels also extended an offer. Pat Powers exceeded it. He offered $800 to the Bingos and a salary of $1,600 to Willie. Then he applied his persuasive manner and his oily tongue.

That was how Pat Powers "brought me into fast company," Willie would remember. "Then my troubles began."

=2=

The National Game

In more ways than one, baseball was already the national game. It had been, more or less, for decades. Oliver Wendell Holmes played it as a student at Harvard, where he graduated way back in 'twenty-nine. Lincoln was out playing baseball, or so it was said, when the committee of Republicans arrived in Springfield in 'sixty to tell him of his nomination. (He sent word for them "to wait a few minutes till I make another base hit.") Andrew Johnson, the martyred president's successor, declared baseball the national game. The National League was born in eighteen seventy-six, the year of the nation's centennial. Sixteen years later, Benjamin Harrison, that cold fish in the White House, became the first president to attend a major league game, at the Swampoodle Grounds in Washington, the day after Willie Keeler begged his Plainfield manager's indulgence.

Was this not God's work?

Indeed, it was more than that. Baseball had begun as a sport for gentlemen, when the Knickerbockers played the first organized game in the Elysian Fields over in Hoboken in 'forty-six. The Civil War made it a pastime for everyone, once the soldiers took the game home with them. When the immigrants came, they played too. (Soon the bulk of the ballplayers had parents born in Ireland or Germany.) Stalwarts of baseball made lavish claims about how the national game fit the American temperament—about how baseball *was* democracy, how it readied boys for the rough and tumble of life, how it required the pluck and endurance of English cricket along with the dash and speed and spirit of America (though complaints were mounting about games taking two hours that should have lasted ninety minutes).

The most remarkable thing about these claims is that they were true.

Maybe this was why the debate over baseball's origins grew so heated: The question went to the core of what (if anything) baseball meant to a nation that had lost its innocence. The evidence barely mattered. Baseball bore a striking resemblance to English rounders, which arranged four bases in a diamond and gave each striker three chances to swing at a ball the defense delivered. But if baseball was of English descent, how could it possibly embody all that America was? Surely then, or so any real patriot knew, baseball had its roots in the old-time American children's game of cat-ball. A "pitcher" would throw a "cat" whittled from a piece of wood at a "batter" who was given three misses with a bat. Just start using bases and choosing up sides, and cat-ball became baseball—"a fruit of the inventive genius of the American boy," a true believer wrote in 'eighty-eight.

The game kept changing as rapidly as the country did. Whatever the country needed, baseball could be. Years passed before the rules settled down. At first the baserunner might be put out by being soaked—that is, thrown at. Until 'sixty-five a batter was declared out if his hit was caught on one bounce. At first, bunts in fair territory that rolled foul were deemed fair. Originally the pitchers threw the ball underhanded and then no higher than the hip, then below the waist, then to the shoulder, and, starting in 'eighty-four, however they liked. The twirlers threw from a box located forty-five feet (and starting in 'eighty-one, fifty feet) from the diamond-shaped home base. Until 'eighty-seven the batter was allowed to ask for a high or a low pitch. In the course of the 'eighties the owners kept experimenting with balls and strikes. The number of balls that drew a base shifted from nine to eight to seven to six to seven to five and, in 'eighty-nine, to four, as the number of strikes that put a batter back on the bench changed from three to four and back to three. There had recently been talk of using a tenth player to bat for the pitcher. It took decades to get the balances right.

The customs of play kept changing as well. It was the practice but not yet a rule for the umpire to declare a batter automatically out on an infield fly. The twirlers, needing to outwit the rulemakers, kept learning new tricks. By the time everyone believed that a curveball actually curved, pitchers had conceived the inshoot and the drop ball and the change of pace. Into the 'eighties it was the twirler who signaled the catcher what he would pitch. The first baseman played with a foot on the bag until (or so the story had it) Charley Comiskey tried stepping away. Unless a runner had reached third base or the batter had only one more strike to go, the catcher stood ten feet or more behind the batter and bent forward from the hips, ready to snag a pitch on the bounce. The umpire, clad in blue since 'eighty-two, either stood behind the catcher or out by the pitcher's box.

The catcher bowed to self-preservation first. Life was hard, and the baseball was too. Any ball hit into the seats had to be thrown back, and it got lumpy and misshapen as the game went along. Still, the ball hurt if it struck you. The first catcher's mask, a wire cage like the one used in fencing, was tried in 'seventy-seven by an outfielder for the Harvard Law School nine who did not want to fill in as a catcher and lose his teeth. Then came chest protectors and thin leather gloves that, by 'eighty-nine, had become padded mitts. The other fielders, more sheepishly, also tried using gloves—fingerless at first—to ease the sting. The pioneers were ridiculed as men of soft flesh. But by the end of the 'eighties most of the fielders had succumbed, though many of the pitchers still resisted.

This improved the haphazard fielding only to a point. The close-fitting gloves did nothing to extend the fielders' reach. And there was the field itself. The narrow basepaths were dusty but smooth, as was the path from the pitcher's box to home base. But even on professional ballgrounds, the patchy grass of the infield concealed all manner of ruts, and the outfield was prone to troughs and slopes. Few balls rolled true.

The ballparks were rickety places that felt something like home. They could be built quickly if there was a need, out on a trolley route, away from the center of town. A grandstand could be slapped together in weeks, even a two-decked one, all lumber, prone to fire and termites. So could the bleacheries, which were becoming known as bleachers, the coarse raggedy boards unprotected from the summer sun. A ballgrounds was shaped like the lot it was on, ordinarily with a spacious and irregular outfield.

The rules on pitching put a premium on brute strength. Batsmen needed the same. What better way to score than to slash a hard pitch past the infielders and beyond the outfielders' reach? Strong men—big men, powerful men, even merciless men—prevailed. Was that not the way of the world? In commerce the Carnegies and the Vanderbilts were king. The same was so in the national game. In baseball it was such as Adrian Anson, the big blond first baseman and captain of the

Chicago White Stockings. Cap Anson was a slugger, the finest ball-player on the best team of the 'eighties—unimaginative, relentless, a household name. He had altered the customs of baseball when he refused to let the White Stockings take the field in 'eighty-seven against a team with a black ballplayer, thus setting a precedent. It was America's team, the old White Stockings, featuring Anson and the dashing Mike Kelly—King Kelly, the most famous ballplayer of all, who had inspired the popular song "Slide, Kelly, Slide"—and Ed Williamson, who hit the most home runs ever in a season (twenty-seven in 'eighty-four).

"A veritable team of Samsons, an aggregation of six-footers"—that was how a young angular catcher named Connie Mack described the Chicagoans. No wonder the vaudeville audiences found themselves drawn to recitations or dramatizations of "Casey at the Bat," a poem about a big man's disgrace.

Life was hard. People died before their time for no discernible reason. The ballplayers needed grit, for the all-night rides, the hasty meals, the casual accommodations. But most of them had had a trade—as a wheelwright, a railroad brakeman, a carpet weaver, an asylum attendant, a calico dyer, a piano maker—and now understood their good fortune. They meant not to lose it. The players donned spikes and made it a point of pride to play hurt. They got no pay otherwise. The twirlers pitched every day or two. On the diamond the umpire struggled to keep control.

John Montgomery Ward anxiously scanned the docks as he arrived back in New York after an around-the-world tour sponsored by Al Spalding.

No Helen. Helen Dauvray, the beautiful actress, had been the Giants' shortstop's wife for barely a year when she promised to meet him in San Francisco and sail with the two teams for Honolulu. Johnny Ward was the captain of the All-Americas, who were to play Cap Anson and the White Stockings in a series of exhibitions in New Zealand and Australia. She had wired her regrets from Omaha. The ballplayers had gone on to Ceylon and Egypt and England. Wherever they went, they had been enthusiastically received, but they failed to interest the world in America's national game. (Spalding caused a sensation when he tapped the Prince of Wales, Queen Victoria's eldest son, on the shoulder.) They made a name for themselves—and for Spalding's sporting goods.

That was seven months ago and now, in April of 'eighty-nine, she had stayed away again. By the following January they would be living apart and she would return to the stage.

Johnny Ward was not accustomed to being ignored. Nor was he an easy man to live with. Back in 'eighty he had pitched the second perfect game in baseball history (just five days after the first one) and became a sterling infielder when his arm gave out. He was smarter than most ballplayers and made sure they knew it. He was handsome in a mannered sort of way, with a waxy, well-shaped moustache. The muscles of his face seemed tight, as if he assumed that people were watching. He was a college man, and more. He had spent a year at Penn State and earned a law degree from Columbia in 'eighty-five, the year he became president of the Brotherhood of Professional Base ballplayers.

That was the source of the second jolt he experienced upon his return to New York, one he was probably better prepared for. While the travelers were in Egypt, playing by the Pyramids, word came from home that the National League owners had adopted the Brush Classification Plan. John T. Brush, the priggish owner of the Indianapolis Hoosiers, had proposed to assign every ballplayer to one of five categories, each with its own salary ceiling of $1,500 to $2,500, based on the quality not only of his play but also of his behavior, on and off the field. Johnny Ward was outraged—ballplayers had been earning as much as $4,000 or $5,000, occasionally higher—and made plans to quit the tour. Al Spalding dissuaded him. The National League cofounder, now the unsentimental president of the Chicago White Stockings, gave his assurance that he had had nothing to do with it. But when they got to England, the Brotherhood president sailed for New York in advance of the tour.

Even as his boat docked, Ward was met by angry ballplayers who wanted to declare a labor strike. He was cool-headed and argued against it. The season was just about to start, and the ballplayers, other than the illiterate ones, had signed their names to a contract. Backing out now, the lawyer-ballplayer knew, would put the ballplayers in bad odor with the public.

The Brotherhood had been benevolent at first, when nine of the Giants had started it as sort of a fraternal organization in 'eighty-five. A year passed before newsmen even learned of it.

It was only a matter of time, however, before the Brotherhood became something less benign. The tension between capital and labor had been festering. It could be traced back to 'seventy-nine, when the National League owners had adopted the reserve rule. Each ballclub could reserve the services of five of its ballplayers for the following season, to stanch the competition that had sent salaries spiraling and to stop the wealthy clubs from cornering all of the stars. Why should a ballclub spend good money to train a fellow and then lose him to a competitor for a few dollars more? The reserve rule was a brilliant solution devised by Art Soden, the penny-pinching owner of the Boston Beaneaters. It ended the movement of players from team to team at ever-higher salaries. When the American Association started up in 'eighty-two as a rival to the National League, it shunned the reserve rule—for all of one season. Then the younger league came to see the benefits too. Soon both leagues extended their reserve lists to eleven men, then to twelve, then fourteen—practically the entire team.

The Brotherhood's mission began to come clear the winter after its founding. The owners vowed to limit salaries to $2,000 and refused to give ballplayers an advance over the winter. Ballplayers with pregnant wives and not a cent to their name sent pitiful letters, which were routinely ignored. The next winter the bad feelings mounted, when the great King Kelly was sold to the Beaneaters for an unheard-of sum of $10,000. Al Spalding got all of it. Kelly got none.

"What was formerly a pastime has now become a business," Johnny Ward bemoaned in *Lippincott's Magazine* in the summer of 'eighty-six. A year later, he made his case in *Lippincott's* that "in the eye of the baseball 'magnate' the player has become a mere chattel." A ballclub had the contractual right to release a ballplayer on ten days' notice or, if it liked, reserve his services year after year and keep him for his entire career at whatever salary the club proposed. It was a form of servitude that had a precedent for the generation that had fought the Civil War. "Any such claim by one set of men of a right of property in another," Johnny Ward wrote, "is as unnatural to-day as it was a quarter of a century ago."

Within a year the Brotherhood had signed up more than a hundred players. Johnny Ward formed a committee of three ballplayers— himself and Ned Hanlon and Big Dan Brouthers, both of the Detroit Wolverines—and met with the National League owners. But the League, like any self-respecting business, refused to recognize the Brotherhood as a labor union.

It was Brush's Classification Plan that caused the final rupture. The Brotherhood committee sought another meeting with the magnates. "There is nothing to discuss," Al Spalding replied, putting off the request until fall.

The ballplayers responded by laying the groundwork for a new league. Johnny Ward was painstaking by nature, and Ned Hanlon, a center fielder with Pittsburgh now, was a shrewd, quiet man who could keep a secret. When his team played in Cleveland he sought out Al Johnson, the street railway magnate and the brother of the city's reform mayor. Hanlon wanted to know if Johnson had a place along one of his lines for a ballpark.

Yes, he did.

In the course of the 'eighty-nine season, as each League team passed through Cleveland, Al Johnson conferred in private with one or more of its players. They worked out plans. The moneymen would build the ballparks in each city and take the first $10,000 in profits; the ballplayers would split the next $10,000 among themselves and then half of the rest.

The League magnates knew that something was up but never suspected its magnitude.

On the fourth of November in 'eighty-nine, they learned. Thirty or forty members of the Brotherhood gathered at the Fifth Avenue Hotel in New York, a marble palace that the League magnates had long favored for their own meetings. The lobby, with its ornate molding and plush club chairs, hosted enough silk hats and gold-headed canes to indeed have been a gathering of magnates instead of laboring men who meant to pass as magnates. Just off the lobby, in the bar, Johnny Ward was nursing a highball, looking more like one of the magnates than the anarchist they imagined him to be.

The ballplayers issued a manifesto of 638 words and minced none of them. "There was a time when the League stood for integrity and fair dealing; to-day it stands for dollars and cents. Once it looked to the elevation of the game and an honest exhibition of the sport; to-day its eyes are upon the turnstile. Men have come into the business for no other motive than to exploit it for every dollar in sight." The reserve clause—for now it was part of every player's contract—was the instrument of the owners' greed. "Players have been bought, sold and exchanged as though they were sheep instead of American citizens."

The Players' League put teams in seven of the National League's eight cities. (It went into Buffalo instead of Cincinnati.) Eighty-one

National Leaguers and twenty-eight from the American Association jumped to the new league, to be rid of the reserve clause and gain a voice and also a cut of the profits. King Kelly, Dan Brouthers, Charley Comiskey, Tim Keefe—all of the stars jumped leagues, except for Cap Anson, who owned stock in the White Stockings and felt a primal loyalty to Al Spalding, the team's owner.

Spalding was put in charge of the League's three-man War Committee. He was a formidable man. He was no longer the lean and sinewy right-hander who had won forty-seven games for the White Stockings in 'seventy-six—a clever twirler, the first to use the change of pace, brilliant at keeping the batter off balance by quick-pitching him or letting him fidget. Except that he was never able to master the curve. He pitched one victory in 'seventy-seven and, at age twenty-seven, quit the diamond only to pursue, with athletic abandon, another side of baseball. He and his brother opened a sporting goods store and found immediate success. Soon Al Spalding became the Barnum of baseball, bringing energy and inventiveness to promoting the national game—and the equipment for playing it. As his success grew, so did his circumference. Gone was the slender face of schoolboy sullenness. Instead, his face had grown broad and stern. He had the imperturbable mien of a man who was certain he knew what was right.

The National League sent its lawyers to court to stop the ballplayers from jumping, to no avail. Al Spalding tried something else. Shortly after the 'ninety season started, with three major leagues now competing for the coins of the cranks, he invited King Kelly to his hotel room.

"How are things going with the game, Mike?" Spalding asked the high-living, hard-drinking catcher.

"Oh, the game's gone to hell," came the reply.

"Why, what's the matter?"

"Everything's the matter; everybody's disgusted—clubs all losing money. We made a damn foolish blunder when we went into it."

That was what Spalding had hoped to hear. He put a $10,000 check on the table. He asked the ballplayer if he would like it.

The answer: "Would Mike Kelly like $10,000? I should smile."

And there was more, Spalding assured him—a three-year contract, with Kelly to fill in the salary himself.

The ballplayer blanched. Did this mean he would have to quit the Brotherhood—"go back on the boys?"

"That's just what it means."

26

Kelly asked for time to think. He walked the streets of Chicago for an hour and a half. Then he returned and said, "I can't go back on the boys, and neither would you."

Of the three major leagues, the Players' League clearly had the best ballplayers and the most cranks at their games—though all sides routinely lied about their attendance. "If either party to this controversy ever furnished to the press one solitary truthful statement as to the progress of the war from his standpoint," Spalding wrote, "a monument should be erected to his memory."

And it *was* a war, at least to the generals. The American Association had seen its finest troops desert. Brooklyn and Philadelphia had teams in all three leagues. The National League scheduled its games head-to-head with those of the Players' League, turning the oldest league into the upstart's implacable enemy. How could there possibly be enough cranks with their afternoons free? Every one of the twenty-four ballclubs in the three leagues lost money.

Then Spalding made his bluff. Precisely how he managed it, behind closed doors, the public never learned. But this much was known: After the season he met with three of the Players' League's owners and soon enough had them believing that their financial losses were worse than the National League's own, though this was not the case. Capitalist to capitalist, they conferred. The Brotherhood, left out, was incensed, but agreements were reached. The Players' League franchise in New York was willing to merge with the financially floundering Giants, which several of the National League owners had already been forced to bail out. Then the Pittsburgh clubs merged and then the Chicago clubs and the ones in Brooklyn. It was every team for itself.

And thus the Players' League collapsed.

Its ballplayers were ordered to return to the teams they had forsaken. In Philadelphia the new owners of the American Association club, the Athletics, forgot to include two of their ex-players on the reserve list. The National League's Pittsburgh club swooped in and snatched one of them (and thereafter were known as the Pirates) and the Beaneaters signed the other.

Another war was on.

The American Association had always been different from the National League. The Beer and Whisky League, its detractors dubbed it, because so many of its magnates were brewers, mainly of German descent. The Association's clubs sold liquor at the ballpark and priced tickets at twenty-five cents (instead of fifty) and played games on Sundays, so the workingman might come.

When the National League refused to return the two purloined players, the Association withdrew from a National Agreement it had signed in 'eighty-three. "Spalding says he wants war and we will give it to him," one of the Association's leaders sniped. Each league raided players from the other (King Kelly signed with the Association and then jumped back to the National League) and said nasty things in the newspapers.

When twelve of the sixteen clubs lost money in 'ninety-one, something had to give. It was the Association, weakly capitalized, that sued for peace.

Not long before Christmas the owners from both leagues convened in Indianapolis. By then their course was clear, and with admirable dispatch a deal was struck. The four weakest Association franchises were to disappear, each owner to be paid for his loss. The stronger four—in Baltimore, Washington, St. Louis, and Louisville—were to merge with the National League, to form a single, twelve-team circuit. For stability's sake, the owners of all twelve teams signed an "ironclad" agreement: The new league could not alter its composition for ten years to come unless every club agreed. Baseball was a monopoly now.

The surviving magnates argued about what the new league should be called. The consolidation committee had suggested a blend of the two names, which the National League's owners summarily rejected: To call it the "American League" put the wrong league first. Nobody liked the "National Association," the name of the failed circuit that had preceded the National League in the early 'seventies. So a compromise was found: The new entity was named the National League and American Association of Professional Base Ball Clubs. Soon it was shortened to something more familiar: the National League.

Surely Willie Keeler was aware of the irony. Here he was, the size of a mascot, about to play for the Giants. The New York ballclub had carried the name for seven years now, ever since Jim Mutrie, then the ballclub's elegantly dressed manager and part-owner, had exclaimed to his beefy ballplayers in the thrill of a game: "My big fellows! My giants!"

The last day of September in 'ninety-two was sunny and warm. The sky was almost cloudless. Willie's dark eyes twinkled in the afternoon light as he made his way toward home base at the Polo Grounds. No grander sight could greet a twenty-year-old ballplayer than the Polo Grounds, a ballpark a man could know for a lifetime and never deserve. The diamond looked shockingly green so late in a dusty fall; center field seemed to go on forever. Over Willie's narrow shoulders rose the immensity of Coogan's Bluff. Its rough rock face seemed almost sheltering, and shrank the double-decked grandstand to mortal size. Each of the poles that propped up the roof was topped with a V, like a grudging flower.

Willie was in his baggy flannel uniform. He had almost a dimple in his chin. His nose had a sneaky prominence and his ears seemed a little too large for his face. Otherwise he had easygoing features—a ready smile, his hair parted down the center, his hairline looping down over his forehead, lending a jaunty air. Yet there was something about him that was unrepentantly self-contained.

Barely more than a thousand cranks had paid to watch the Giants and the Phillies tussle over fifth place. Despite the unseasonable warmth, it was too late in the year for strawboaters. The more daring of the men nudged their derbies to the backs of their heads and surreptitiously loosened their cravats.

The gong sounded to start the game. As the home team, the Giants had chosen to bat first. They would get the ball at its best that way, before it grew darker and harder to hit inning by inning.

The rookie third baseman led off. Willie was obviously nervous. That was the best thing about him, that he looked so anxious, a newspaperman remarked the next morning. He took his stance as close as he could to the left corner of the diamond-shaped plate. He stood flat-footed and stiffly erect, his slim body hiding his bat. He cocked his fists behind his left shoulder and grasped the bat far up the handle. He turned his head—only his head—toward the pitcher.

Willie's heart was pounding. The great Tim Keefe was roaming the pitcher's box. He was a wiry right-hander with a precise mind and a serious demeanor. He was thirty-five now, but he still had power and a sly curveball and a change of pace. He stepped on the back line of the pitcher's box, fifty-five-and-a-half feet away, took his step toward the batsman and opened the ballgame.

Too soon Willie returned to the bench.

Then he trotted out to third base. The League had seen only one left-handed third baseman before, and Hick Carpenter's record had little to recommend it. In eleven seasons he had committed 625 errors, counting the two he had made just this season in a comeback with the St. Louis Browns that lasted one game.

Willie had known to expect no mercy from his teammates. It was natural for the old-timers to be rough with the kids breaking in, who were after their jobs. That Pat Powers was intent on replacing costly veterans with cheap rookies made everything worse.

Willie could hardly expect anything nicer from his opponents, and the Phillies wasted no time in testing him. "Sliding Billy" Hamilton, the leadoff batter, had short chunky legs but was fast as a telegraph. He laid down a bunt and raced to first base and arrived before the ball did. Three batters later he scored.

The next two times Willie batted, he was stymied again. In the seventh inning, the score tied at 2, he faced Tim Keefe for a fourth time. With a teammate on first base he hit a slow roller to third and outran the throw. Before the inning was over both runners had scored.

But then the Phillies, with their sluggers, got to work. No batsman in the League was feared more than Big Ed Delehanty, who came to the plate in the eighth inning. He was a mountain of a man, a wild Irishman who hit the ball so hard he once split it in half. He stepped in to face the Giants' huge right-hander, Amos Rusie, the Hoosier Thunderbolt. Rusie's wild speed—year after year he led the League in issuing bases on balls—succeeded in frightening batsmen other twirlers could not faze.

Two men were on base and a run had already scored. Delehanty took two vicious swipes at the ball, then he let the next two pitches go by. Rusie hurled the ball in and suddenly there was a streak over Willie Keeler's head.

That was the game.

The newspapers gave Willie good notices. He had the only two stolen bases of the game. "He is a clever fielder and runner, and he handles the bat as if he were accustomed to hitting the ball," the *New York Tribune* reported. He was a lively third baseman who "jumped at once into popular favor," the *New York Press* judged. "Keeler is a fast young player, and plays 1892 ball."

And yet when Willie committed errors in four of the next five games, suddenly everyone wanted to know why Powers had robbed a kindergarten to assemble his team. Surely third basemen must be of a certain size—it seemed obvious, once you thought about it—so that they might have a longer reach and greater confidence in the face of reckless baserunners.

But he showed some gumption, for his fielding improved, and he showed a knack with the bat. His average at the plate came to .321, and he was asked to come back for the 'ninety-three season.

He did, but the ballclub's enthusiasm for him seemed to have waned over the winter. Almost two weeks passed before he was put into a game. Pat Powers was gone and a new manager had taken his place. It was Johnny Ward. The failure of the Players' League had traumatized him and he had returned to the National League, an owner's man. As if, in the real world, he had a choice. Johnny Ward believed in justice but he also believed in making his way.

His job was to remake the team. He had bought a beefy first baseman and traded for a fine new third baseman. So he thought about moving Willie to the outfield. The Giants were solid in right field and left, so Willie was tried in center, in place of Harry Lyons, who was fast in the field but suspect at the bat.

On a crisp day in May the Giants hosted the neighboring city's nine. Mike Griffin, the Brooklyn slugger, socked a long drive late in the game. Harry Lyons probably would have caught up with it. Willie did not. It went for a home run. In the bottom of the inning, with the Giants six runs behind, Willie tried to steal second base but got thrown out by yards.

The next morning the New York newspapers were merciless. Having Keeler in the lineup had "materially weakened" the team, Joe Vila judged in the *New York Sun*. "Here is the record of Keeler yesterday— no runs, no base hits, no put outs, no assists, no errors," *The New York Times* noted, commending Willie's misdeeds as "food for reflection" for the ballclub.

Willie was devastated. He came to Johnny Ward with tears in his eyes. How could he play, he wanted to know, after being roasted so?

"Don't you mind it a bit," the manager replied. "Go in today, and don't get nervous, and remember that I think you'll do."

In his first three times at the bat, he struck a double and a triple and a home run. He drove four of the Giants' ten runs across the plate and scored three himself. He also muffed a fly ball that allowed two runs to score. With the game tied at 10 in the last of the ninth, Mike

Griffin scorched a fly ball to left-center field. It was Willie's ball. He hesitated. So the left fielder sprinted for the ball and got there—and dropped it. The Giants lost.

"It was painful to watch little Keeler try to play center field," one of the newspapers jabbed.

"My field work was still ragged, but nobody disputed my ability to 'line them out,' and that kept me on the team," Willie said. Years later, he remembered the lesson he had learned. "Some folks tell a young player not to read the criticisms in the newspapers," he said, "but if you don't, somebody will come and tell you, so you might as well go on the field knowing the worst. There never was a good man who didn't get his belly full of criticism, and it never hurt any of them because they had the strength to turn it to their own advantage."

Johnny Ward put Willie in again the next afternoon. The Giants lost the lead, then tied the game in the eighth inning. With a runner at third base, Willie slapped a ground ball to the shortstop. The runner dashed for home. It was daring but foolish—he was nipped at the plate. Willie kept running toward second base and slid. He was safe.

And in agony. He had started to slide when he changed his mind. His foot caught the bag; his body slid past it.

He was carried off the field.

At first the doctors believed he had sprained an ankle. They were wrong: He had fractured it and would be out for eight weeks. "I took excellent care of myself," he said later, "because I knew that if I didn't, I would have to go to work."

When he returned, the Giants had no place for him. Johnny Ward had his eye on a Southern League twirler and needed some cash. He had an offer in hand—the young Keeler for $800. That was what the Giants had paid for him.

A deal was struck.

Around noon on the twenty-seventh of July, two unfamiliar faces emerged from the dressing room at Eastern Park, deep into Brooklyn. One belonged to an amateur pitcher named George Sharrott, who was there to practice with the team already known as the Trolley Dodgers because of the bewilderment of trolley lines every resident of Brooklyn had to dash across, and sometimes called the Bridegrooms ever since six of them had gone to the altar a few off-seasons earlier. The word quickly spread among the spectators that the other ballplayer, the wee fellow at third base, was Keeler of the Giants.

Even the cranks who considered themselves in the know were surprised. A delegation formed to learn what it meant. Its members went over to Willie, who was unable to explain. He had shown up at the Polo Grounds for practice that morning and learned of his fate. "I got orders to come over here and report at twelve o'clock," he said, "and was told that the Brooklyns had bought my release. I don't even know what position I am to play."

What he knew (though did not say) was that only three years ago he had been selling scorecards here, beneath the conical-spired roof over the double-decked grandstand. The owner of Brooklyn's Players' League franchise had insisted, after the contentious 'ninety season, that the merged club play at Eastern Park, in the East New York section of Brooklyn, so as to increase the value of the land he owned nearby. The field was too distant from the city's population centers for many cranks to come, and that suited Willie just fine. The idea of playing in front of your neighbors was less intimidating than actually doing it.

The Trolley Dodgers' recent play had done little to build up the crowds. They had lost a string of games of late. Charley Byrne, the real estate magnate and gambling hall operator who was the president of the Trolley Dodgers, felt humiliated by losing. He would exult when his ballclub was winning but was prone to panic when defeats piled up. He also liked to tell his managers what to do.

Byrne had grown tired of the rutty work of the generously paid veterans. He wanted young blood. "There will be a shaking up among the players of the Brooklyn club that will surprise them," he had warned just a week before.

Willie played third base that day against the Phillies, who were clinging to first place. The black smoke from the chair factory near Eastern Park sullied the air of East New York, but to Willie it felt pristine.

He was the smallest man on the field, yet in the fading afternoon light he got as many hits as Big Ed Delehanty and Big Sam Thompson and Sliding Billy Hamilton—Philadelphia's men among men—put together. Willie struck two singles and, in the sixth inning, a home run deep into the outfield that put the game out of reach. The Trolley Dodgers won, 20 to 2, and shoved the Phillies into second, behind the Boston Beaneaters. "I am glad to be able to play regularly," was all Willie said after the game. "I dislike to be idle."

He kept up the fast work. The next two afternoons, he smacked hard bounders and well-placed hits and stayed alert on the basepaths. He was cheered every time he came to bat.

Then the Giants swaggered into Eastern Park. Johnny Ward knew that Willie favored hitting toward left field, so when Willie came to bat in the fourth inning of a scoreless game, with two out and a man at third base, Johnny Ward waved his shortstop almost to third base and pulled his left fielder in.

Willie poked a pitch through the oversized gap that was left open, to the cheers of five thousand cranks.

So far his fielding had been, as the *Eagle* said of the hometown boy, "gilt-edged." Against Boston he handled the first six plays cleanly. Brooklyn was leading, 1 to 0, in the seventh inning when one of the Beaneaters laid down a bunt. Willie rushed in and scooped it up and pivoted fearfully to his left and sent the ball curving and cavorting across the diamond. Big Dan Brouthers, the Brooklyn first baseman, threw up his hands in horror. By the time the ball was retrieved at the edge of the fifty-cent stands, runners hugged second and third. Brooklyn's shaken twirler served up a fat pitch and the Beaneaters led.

One out later, another Beaneater bunted. Willie was determined not to repeat his mistake. He pounced on the ball and flung it so high that Big Dan would have needed a net.

Willie had given the game away.

The next day Willie made two errors, and he committed one in each of the following four games. The harder he tried, the worse he fielded, with his neighbors looking on.

His opponents kept killing him with bunts. Willie was not surprised. He would have done the same to them.

Now he knew why a left-handed infielder could never succeed— "no, not in the big league," he concluded. "A southpaw cannot get the ball to first fast enough nor accurately enough."

He had learned something even more painful. "The worst thing that could happen to a young player on the threshold of his professional career is to start in his native city," he came to believe. "His friends expect too much from him, and if he should be unfortunate enough to make an error, they want to know all about it. No allowance seems to be granted for nervousness."

Willie was reluctant to try the outfield again and soon he was riding the bench. By the end of August he was back in Binghamton.

There was talk that Willie was too little for the big league. Nobody knew for sure whose decision that was, but it was easy to guess that it was Charley Byrne's. The Brooklyn magnate was a gambler at heart, and when he lost a wager, he did not care to be reminded.

There was a feeling in the air that everything in America was changing. Not only in Brooklyn or New York, and not only in baseball. Everywhere, and in too many ways, the earth was shifting under Americans' feet.

The frontier had closed—that was one thing. The Census Bureau had said so in 'ninety, and an obscure historian named Frederick Jackson Turner made himself famous by explaining its significance at the grand Columbian Exposition in Chicago in 'ninety-three. Not that very many people were affected in a tangible way. But the country *felt* different when there was no place to escape to, when what passed for civilization was all there was.

That was the least of it. Material progress was lurching ahead. Every day, it seemed, something else was invented. People could now do things with the flick of a finger that their grandparents could not have imagined—read deep into the night by incandescent light or listen to a phonograph or talk on a telephone or watch a moving picture on the Kinetoscope, Thomas Edison's latest piece of genius. What a glorious age this was! The inventor was king. Look at the Chicago Exposition, with its gigantic Ferris wheel and its photographs and Kinetoscopes on display and the new confections—Shredded Wheat, Aunt Jemima's pancake mix, Pabst Blue Ribbon beer, Juicy Fruit gum.

The preachers lamented the materialism of the age, as preachers always had. Yet this time surely they were right. It was a Faustian bargain: In exchange for entertainment and communication and breakfast convenience and a slightly longer life span, Americans lost a measure of control over their lives. They became a cog in a machine. Evil became anonymous, without a name or face attached.

The divisions, in a way, were even uglier than thirty years earlier, in the horrors of a civil war. Then, it had been region against region and brother against brother, in bloody battle over awful principle. Now it was capital against labor. People were flocking to the cities, into their sweatshops and slums, and began to embrace baseball for its touch of green. A Gilded Age was giving way to something grimier. Economic warfare had its battles in the Haymarket riot in Chicago in 'eighty-six and the deadly Homestead strike on the outskirts of Pittsburgh in 'ninety-two. Nothing honorable was at stake—only survival and greed.

Willie Keeler had seen his share, not only through his father's eyes but also in Binghamton. With its rail connections and low rents and its supply of Slavic immigrants as cheap labor, Binghamton was second in the nation (to New York) in making cigars. When the market for cigars slumped, the city's sixteen manufacturers acted as one—the Ring, the workers called them, because of their web of relationships—in slashing wages. When the profits recovered but the companies refused to restore their pay, the nonunionized workers exploded into a strike that lasted all summer. After several of the companies crashed into bankruptcy came the mass arrests and the sight of women dragged off to jail. The companies' creative lawyers went to court and secured a ruling of conspiracy that was the grounds for a sweeping injunction that ended the long strike.

This had happened two years before Willie got to Binghamton, but the bitterness had barely abated, nor had the battle. Not long after Willie was returned to the Parlor City in 'ninety-three, the injunction was overturned, when it was too late to matter.

A man's fate was out of his hands. Impersonal forces had taken charge. Maybe it had always been thus. But beyond the caprices of illness and nature, at least a man had been able to see and smell the man who caused him wrong. Now, when wages were cut or a factory was closed or a railroad raised the price for carrying a farmer's grain, who could be blamed? J. P. Morgan, who held the livelihoods of millions in his hands? The trusts—in oil, steel, tobacco, cottonseed oil, sugar—that proved the truths of Social Darwinism? The invisible hand? Might as well blame an act of God.

How else to explain the financial panic that struck the country in 'ninety-three but as an act of God? Had the British investors provoked a run on American stores of gold? Was the Treasury fearful about meeting foreign creditors' demand for gold now that the prosperity of the 'eighties had ended? Had India joined the European powers in abandoning bimetallism? Whatever the reason, the value of a silver dollar dived in a single day from sixty-seven to sixty cents in gold. Ordinary people did not understand what was going on. There was nothing they could do—nothing anyone could do. The panic was just something that happened.

President Grover Cleveland insisted on returning to the gold standard and called on J. P. Morgan to assemble a syndicate to guarantee an offering of government bonds. That shored up the gold supply. But what the panic brought in its wake was far worse. Maybe it was that gold was diverted from trade and factories or that the banks called in their loans. By the end of 'ninety-three, 153 banks had failed along with 15,000 other businesses. A quarter of the nation's railroads collapsed. At least a fifth of the workforce was out of a job.

The nation, not a young one anymore, had never suffered a depression so severe. America was no stranger to tragedy, but this was something new.

=3=

Foxy Ned

Whenever the wind was wrong, the sweet smell of the hops mingled with the stench of the slaughterhouse across the lane too narrow for trees that was known as Dog Town alley.

Plenty of people lived nearby to notice. Immigrants and the children of immigrants lived in cramped row houses just north of North avenue, which had been the boundary of Baltimore until the city had tripled its size in 'eighty-eight. They were mainly of German stock—butchers and seamstresses and day laborers and grocers and drivers in the breweries close at hand. Breweries were big in Baltimore, along with oysters and marble steps.

The office of J. H. von der Horst & Son Brewing Co., in a three-story brick building, had two windows that faced out on Dog Town alley. Inside, on this spring day of 'ninety-four, Harry von der Horst was arguing with his father—again—over money.

"*Nein*," John von der Horst declared. "I won't let you have it"—that, in German as well. A stout man with imposing white whiskers, he spoke German unless he had no choice. With his sons, he could do as he liked.

Harry insisted that he was owed $6,000 if he was owed a cent—"and I must have it." His father had bestowed a third of the brewery upon him a dozen years earlier. Harry, forty-two now and the owner of the financially struggling Baltimore Orioles baseball team, was showing the artful desperation of middle age. At the moment he was in need of money to buy a piece of the ballgrounds, out by right field, which might give him some leverage with the Sadtler family, who owned the rest of the land beneath Union Park.

38

"I will never let you have any more money towards baseball," the old man snapped back at him. "I have sworn to that." Harry knew it was no bluff. John von der Horst had even gone to court once and obtained an injunction that blocked Harry from spending any more of the brewery's money on something as frivolous as baseball. Eventually Harry's lawyers succeeded in having the injunction lifted, but it had cut him off from his source of cash just when buying the right player or two might have turned the Orioles into a money-maker. The Baltimore nine had never come so close since.

The old man had had such hopes for his elder son. He had taken Harry out of school at the age of fourteen and sent him for apprenticeships in Philadelphia and Cincinnati and then to Germany for four months to learn how beer was made. Harry must have shown at least the minimal reverence after he got home, for the old man made him the general manager and then the brewer and then the maltster and at last, in 'eighty-one, when he was thirty, a partner. John Jr., the younger son, had already escaped to California.

What a long time ago that seemed. Last summer Harry had pleaded for a loan of $2,088.35 to pay his life insurance. His father laid down a condition: that Harry sign over a deed of trust to his one-third stake in the brewery, so that the old man could protect the assets in case the Orioles' losses continued to mount. The old man had insisted that Harry's prim wife, Emma, sign it too. Both of them did as he said.

Only when the old man was dying had he asked John Jr. to come home. The younger son had been making wooden and willow ware in San Francisco and then had worked as a banker. His wife and their three young children came with him to Baltimore. Starting on the first of July, the old man had promised, John Jr. would receive a third of the brewery's profits, though none of its assets.

Nothing mattered more to the old man than the Eagle Brewery. It was his life's work. He had arrived in Baltimore from Lower Saxony, poor and friendless, at the age of twenty-one. First he had worked for a grocer, before he opened a shop of his own. Then came a saloon. But there was only so much money, he quickly learned, to be made in selling beer, so he found a partner who knew how to produce it. They bought an oil cloth mill out on Belair road, just past North avenue— known then as Boundary avenue—and converted it into a brewery.

The neighborhood was crawling with breweries. Belair road, wide and calm, was a good wagon road with access to plenty of fresh water. It was also far enough from the places of power that the Germans could quaff their beer on Sundays without troubling the Presbyterians and Episcopalians who ruled the city. In the dance halls and beer gardens along North avenue, a goodly portion of what was brewed in the neighborhood was consumed.

Behind the Summer Garden, a beer garden where Belair road and North avenue crossed, John von der Horst had raised his family in a stucco house on the brewery grounds. A golden eagle—Horst was German for "eagle's nest"—adorned the roof of the five-story brew-house. The scattering of buildings housed perhaps the most modern of the two dozen breweries in Baltimore. It had been the first to install De La Vergne mechanical refrigeration (which improved the yield) and was the only brewery south of Philadelphia that made its own malt, in a six-story double malt-house. John von der Horst thus had eluded the brewer's customary fate of becoming mortgaged to his malt supplier.

That came of believing in science. He combined a shrewdness in marketing with his Old World ways. He kept a thoroughbred Angora goat in the stables of the brewery and claimed that its smell kept his horses—among the prettiest and strongest in the city—healthy. Every year at bock-beer time, on the wagon piled high with kegs of dark beer, the goat would ride beside the driver at the front of the parade.

Unfortunately for the Eagle Brewery, Harry did not have his father's mind. He was smart and energetic enough when he tried. That was the problem. He was too fond of living to keep his mind on hard, unpleasant things. That was how Harry thought of it. The old man saw it differently, as wasting time and money on nonsense.

Harry tried all sorts of arguments about why owning a baseball team made good business sense. There was no better place to sell lager than at a ballpark. Union Park's grounds had a beer garden and a restaurant that did a nice business. Liquor was sold around the corner of the grandstand, on the way to the bleachers.

"Well, we don't win many baseball games," Harry once said, "but we sell lots of beer."

His interest in baseball, of course, was about more than peddling beer—or even making money. That he had been a pretty good ballplayer in his youth was not the point either. As an adult, it was the conspicuous box in the grandstand and the luminaries who craved to share it that he relished. In the social circles of Baltimore, Harry became known for the lavishness of his parties, even as the ballclub languished in the red year after year.

The old man was aghast. "My connection with the baseball club caused him great annoyance," Harry acknowledged in a court deposition not much later, "as he didn't understand that business."

It was a measure of how well the old man understood his older son that he summoned John Jr. home once the spreading cancer made everything clear. He put his younger son on a salary and gave him a modest title, then conducted all of the brewery's business through him, using a letter of attorney.

The longer the old man lived, the more power his younger son would surely wield. As Harry kept arguing with their father over money, John Jr. looked on. "All I want is what is due me and nothing more," Harry shouted. "I have a right to demand what belongs to me."

He must have been right, for suddenly the old man said, "Well, I will make out the check to John."

And he did. He wrote a check and offered it to his unstained son, who handed it over to Harry.

The winter in Baltimore had been colder than usual. As 'ninety-three expired, a quarter of the city's cigarmakers were out of work. So were a third of the carpenters and bricklayers and can-makers and store clerks and three-fourths of the iron molders. The depression was not as bad in Baltimore as in the more industrial cities. But it was bad. Almost half the trade unionists were out of work. A rash of workers, Germans mainly, killed themselves.

There was much that was backward about Baltimore. The city's sewage system, for one. There was none. Open sewers ran along the curbs of almost every street, draining into Jones Falls or directly into the Chesapeake basin, leaving behind a miasma of summertime odors and the highest rate of typhoid fever of any big city in the country.

Baltimore was backward in another way. Its livelihood still depended more on commerce and the port than on factories. Baltimore was blessed with a fine natural harbor, protected from the ocean waves. More goods left from Baltimore than from any port in the nation other than New York or New Orleans. Because of the slant of the Eastern Seaboard, Baltimore was the most western of the eastern ports as well as the most southern of the northern ports, more than a hundred miles closer than New York was to Pittsburgh and Cleveland and Chicago. The Liverpool of America, it was called. The smell of the sea was never far distant.

Business was merely a part of life instead of life itself. The dirt and grime of an industrial age had not settled in, and civilized behavior still mattered. A lady with her parasol and a gentleman in his cutaway suit could be seen strolling in the gaslit evening along Charles street, now beneath a canopy of overhead wires. Baltimore was the seventh largest city in the country, with a population closing in on half a million, twice as many as a quarter-century before, but perhaps no major American city was so easy to live in. It was a bustling city but nobody seemed in a hurry. People gossiped on their stoops. The herringbone brick pavements along the maple-lined streets contrasted winningly with the creamy white steps made with the marble mined from quarries north of the city. The organ grinders and the hurdy-gurdies made a clamor on the streets, and iron wagon wheels noisily rattled over the cobblestones. The ample wildlife of Chesapeake Bay meant that partridge and canvasback duck were not only for the privileged, and even diamondback terrapin came at a reasonable price. Wages were moderate, yet the housing in Baltimore was unsurpassed. Tenements were unknown. The practice since colonial times of building houses on rented ground made it practical for people of modest means to own a home of their own. Ten or twenty dollars a month bought a two-story dwelling, with small wallpapered rooms and screenless windows that let the mosquitoes in on sticky nights. In the better homes the manners were formal and the ways were correct. Baltimore society showed some of the sophistication of New York or Philadelphia, but with a slower, less self-centered pace. Graciousness was a part of life, along with tolerance.

The tolerance was a natural consequence of the city's history and circumstance. From the beginning, Baltimore had been a crucible of colliding forces. Maryland had been founded by Catholics as a haven in a Protestant world and became a refuge for Quakers and others who knew persecution. The first Lord Baltimore had been an English Catholic, who had taken his name from lands the king had granted him in County Longford, near the center of Ireland. The city his son founded on the Patapsco River, shielded from the Chesapeake Bay, became the birthplace of America's Catholic hierarchy. It was the only city in the country besides New Orleans that permitted a prominent role for a Catholic elite.

Baltimore straddled the boundary not only between Catholic and Protestant but also, more virulently, between North and South. The issue of slavery had left the city fractured in despair. Baltimore had been the commercial capital of the South until the Civil War and was still a place of southern pace and sentiment. Poor whites kept streaming into the city from Virginia and Appalachia. No city to the north was home to so many black people; none to the south had so many immigrants. More and more, the rising numbers of Germans—nearly a quarter of the populace—and Irish and Russian Jews and such had lent an air of northern diligence.

These collisions of cultures might have brought conflict, and at times they had. But they had also fostered a willingness to get along. It was either that or self-destruction, and the good people of Baltimore were by and large too cautious, too conservative, too lackadaisical, to bother with slow suicide.

And yet there was no mistaking the fact that Baltimore was changing. Year by year, the screech of the railroad was drowning out the ghostly honk of the tugboat. A huge steel plant had gone up at Sparrows Point, complete with a company town. The oyster-catching closed down by Christmas because of the cold, bringing the oyster-canning business—the largest in the world—to a standstill. The hard times were stirring up an anger that felt vivid and new.

The land of pleasant living was turning into something more callous. Baltimore was becoming a brawling, ungentlemanly place. A golden age was showing signs of ending.

The Orioles had won one game and lost fourteen as the 'ninety-two season opened when Harry von der Horst put his top beer salesman in charge of the team. Jack Waltz was already the ballclub's traveling secretary, and as the new manager he wired Harry from the western trip that the Orioles kept losing because the men fielded badly and the pitchers were getting hit hard. "That would seem to cover the whole business," one of the newspapers lampooned.

Jack Waltz had a delicate moustache and a slightly comical look. But he was far from stupid. He knew enough to know how little he knew about baseball. He also knew enough to suggest to Harry a successor: Ned Hanlon.

Ned Hanlon was only thirty-four but he was big-time—a name. He had made a national reputation as the captain of the All-Americas team that Johnny Ward had managed and had become his right-hand man in the Players' League. Then, reinstated to the good graces of the National League, he had become the player-manager in Pittsburgh, until his hard-drinking teammates rebelled at his discipline the summer before. He kept playing center field, and not badly, until he slipped on a concrete walkway while chasing a fly ball in practice that spring and strained a tendon in his leg.

In other words, he was available.

Harry von der Horst liked the idea from the first. It appealed to the self-conscious boldness in him. He also saw the benefits. Undoubtedly the Orioles could use some discipline. Harry could use some too, of course, though he was less willing to acknowledge that, even to himself.

He asked the owners in Pittsburgh for permission to talk to Hanlon. They jumped at the chance to unload the aging star's $5,000 salary.

The Orioles were playing the Colts in Chicago when Hanlon met with Harry von der Horst and Jack Waltz at the Tremont House, at Lake and Dearborn. In the ornate building roofed with mansard crowns, Hanlon looked out of place. Physically he was less than imposing, his meek pompadour, flat cheeks, and handlebar moustache curled to perfection suggesting the countenance of a slightly bored bank clerk. His expression was bland; whatever he was feeling, he concealed. Sober in demeanor and spare with his words, he seemed to back away from the camera whenever he sat for a photograph. "Silent Ned," he was called.

Edward Hugh Hanlon was the son of a housebuilder in Montville, Connecticut, not far from New London. He had wanted to be a ballplayer since age ten, and he quit school at sixteen to pitch for the Norwich Arctics and then the New London Stars. But he was not joyful about it. That was not his way. He was determined, meticulous, assiduous—steely, more often than not. His Yankee reticence made other men want to please him. He seemed not to care what anyone thought of him and that was his strength, the quality that made him a natural leader. There was an apartness about him that lent him an air of mystery—and command. He was known to his intimates as Edward and to his ballplayers as Ed. To everyone else he was Ned.

He was a hard man to warm to, but there was plenty to admire. For one thing, he got the most out of what he had. He had never been the most dangerous of batsmen. What God had given him, he knew, would not suffice. So he was aggressive on the basepaths and graceful and swift in the outfield—and always, he used his head. He made singles into doubles and doubles into triples by watching the flick of an outfielder's wrist. He studied every opponent's habits and flaws. He seemed to notice everything and remember it all, at just the right instant. Above all, he was a man of precision and logic. At home he had a clock in every room. He was the sort who saw the pattern in the details, then found a way to rearrange them. Ned Hanlon was as smart in his own way as Edison, except that Edison was a show-off.

To a show-off like Harry von der Horst, Hanlon's understated air of assurance was bound to be impressive. How badly Harry wanted a winning team. He had gone far too many years without one. He was tired of losing money and having to fight with his father for every dollar. In Ned Hanlon, so comfortingly self-effacing, Harry could glimpse the prospect of some success at long last. It was a gamble, hiring a manager who would not be pushed around as if he was a beer salesman. But it was a chance Harry was willing to take. Harry was confident that he could push anyone around, with the exception of his father.

Hanlon understood how much Harry wanted him and turned it to his advantage. He insisted that he be given full authority to run the ballclub, including the signing and releasing of players. Harry agreed. Maybe he was secretly relieved to be rid of the responsibility.

The three men emerged from Harry's hotel room with a contract, which carried the crisp signature of Edward H. Hanlon.

The new manager was careful to lower the expectations among the newspapermen who had gathered. "A club that is demoralized by losses cannot be reorganized in a day or a week," he said, "but it can be steadily improved until the players are doing all that is possible for them to do."

The Orioles' players met Hanlon in Cincinnati four days later. The ballplayers knew that changes had to be made and could be forgiven for feeling apprehensive. Harry von der Horst introduced their somber new manager and sketched the scope of his powers. Hanlon, he said, would have charge of them on and off the field. From whatever he decreed, there would be no appeal.

Then Hanlon said a few words. Man by man, he assured them, the Orioles were one of the best teams in the land. If they worked as a unit and cared nothing for their individual glory, surely they could win more than half of their games for the rest of the season.

He insisted that the players never give up until the last man was out and that they play not only with their hands and feet but also with their heads. In a business sense, he told them, they and the ballclub were partners. Their remuneration would depend upon their efficiency.

"United we stand," he implored a team that was a collection of individuals, "and divided we fall." None of the players, he promised, would be released without a fair trial.

He had said the same thing, they remembered, on the day he was hired and had immediately sent home Pete Gilbert, the porous third baseman who was feeble at the bat. The lushers and the loafers were soon to be sent away. Still the Orioles would remain mired in twelfth place, the laughingstock of the League. The first baseman beat up the second baseman in a midseason fistfight. Sadie McMahon, the hard-throwing right-hander, went on a drunk on a day he was supposed to pitch, then he cursed Hanlon and Harry when he turned up. Another twirler, incensed about a cut in his pay, showed up soused and unable to pitch. Hanlon suspended them both.

The Orioles won barely a third of their remaining games. For the season they had by far the sorriest record in the National League, losing more than a hundred games. Of the seventeen players on the team when Hanlon arrived, he determined to keep just three.

One was Sadie McMahon, whose Christian name was John. He had acquired his nickname when a teammate called out to a girl on a street corner he shared and he answered instead, and he was sufficiently sure of himself to enjoy the ribbing he took forever after. He had a potbelly but was a man's man, with a bulldog face and his short blond hair brushed straight up. Indeed, he had apparently murdered a man four years before, at the circus grounds in Wilmington, Delaware, his hometown. He had been the twirler for a local ballclub and one of a dozen Irish-American toughs who had ambled up to Carmine Malascalza's peanut and fruit stand and started to help themselves. When the Italian immigrant and his brother protested, a strong blond roughneck punched Carmine and knocked him to the ground. When he was getting up, the same fellow, ten feet away, hurled a rock as hard as he could, and it crushed the side of the immigrant's skull.

The dead man's brother identified the assailant as John McMahon.

At the murder trial the victim's brother, testifying through an interpreter, was certain. Then came three English-speaking witnesses who remembered the Malascalza brothers as the assailants and who had no recollection of the twirler being closer than 200 yards away. When they were finished even the prosecutor asked for an acquittal. The crowd of spectators applauded, and the jury complied.

But if the rough right-hander lost control of himself off the ballfield, in the pitcher's box he was unshakable. He was stocky but his movements were easy and graceful. His pitches went where he wanted them to go. Later he claimed never to have been knocked out of the box or to have issued an intentional base on balls. He was nervy; the more urgent the circumstance, the better he pitched. He had command of his shoots—his speediest pitches—and his curves and his changes of pace and his own version of an overhand drop ball. He thrived on work. He had won thirty-six games back in 'ninety and thirty-five in 'ninety-one.

McMahon had come to the Orioles in 'ninety after the Philadelphia Athletics of the old American Association had gone bankrupt, as half of what the newspapers dubbed the "Dumpling Battery." The other half, catcher Wilbert Robinson, was known universally as Robbie. He was portly and perennially cheerful, even in the most trying of times. "Come, boys, ginger up!" he would jolly his teammates along. The son of the town butcher in Hudson, Massachusetts, Robinson had married early and fathered two sons and stepfathered two daughters. He had a natural dignity about him, a settledness that calmed the pitchers he caught. He was unafraid of hard work; during practices, he was ordinarily the heaviest man on the field (all 215 pounds of him) but the last to leave it. When the ballplayers circled the ballgrounds, Robbie ran in front.

He was not the most reliable of hitters: He had batted just .216 in 'ninety-one and had never broken .250. Yet he was dangerous with a bat in his hands. A month after Hanlon took over, in a game against the St. Louis Browns, Robbie hit six singles and a double in seven times at bat. It was a record for batsmen that would stand unequalled for eighty-three years.

Behind home plate Robbie was a veritable brick wall. He had a strong arm and proved something of a pioneer. With the Athletics he had been among the first catchers to signal the pitcher, instead of the other way around, and thus he was among the first to move up and squat close to the batter—even with no opponent on base—so that his signals might be seen. Everyone said how reckless he was, and injuries cost him dozens of games each year.

Only one other Oriole met Ned Hanlon's specifications, and he was as different from McMahon and Robbie—and Hanlon—as anyone could be. John J. McGraw was a scrawny hothead who had just turned nineteen and looked two or three years younger. He was the littlest man on the team but the fiercest. He had left his home in Truxton, New York, at age twelve after his mother and four of his siblings had died of diphtheria and his father had beaten him once too often. His face, in rare repose, was as lean and taut as a panther's. He was a force of nature.

He had joined the Orioles the season before. One day he was sitting on the bench when a brawny tobacco-chewing veteran shifted his hips so that McGraw fell off. The ballplayers laughed and then looked on in amazement as the five-foot-seven-inch rookie lunged at his tormentor with his fists and his spikes. He was reaching for a bat when his new teammates pinned his arms until he calmed down.

"You'll do, kid," said a teammate who had never talked to him before.

McGraw played baseball the same way. It was never a game to him. It was life and death. When the gong sounded, all that mattered was winning. The fastest pitching never backed him away from the plate. He slid into bases headfirst. Nothing scared him. "A ballgame—any ballgame—was something to fight for," he believed. He would say anything or do anything to win.

That included showing self-control, if that meant an advantage. Rarely did McGraw swing at a bad pitch. His patience brought him better pitches and more bases on balls. His mastery at fouling off pitches had fueled talk about changing the rules to count the first two fouls as strikes. As a left-handed batter he had learned as a boy to avoid his father's wrath at his breaking church windows in right-center field by hitting to the opposite field. He mainly played shortstop and was sharp in the field.

Hanlon saw that McGraw's value to the Orioles came less from his agility than from his intensity. He never let up and he had contempt for anyone who did. John McGraw could drive his teammates to another level of play. So he was to serve as the soul of a team that was about to be born.

*   *   *

By the closing days of the 'ninety-two season it was obvious to Ned Hanlon that George Van Haltren had to go. The hard-hitting young center fielder had started the season as the manager, before Harry's beer salesman took his place. He had been fired after the Orioles had forfeited a game because he had neglected to tell the umpire they would have to leave early to catch their train. Now his playing had lost its edge. He lost tight ballgames by dropping lazy fly balls or foolishly getting thrown out at third base. As Hanlon knew from personal experience, it was hard to be the manager and then not to be.

Hanlon made a deal with his old ballclub. In exchange for Van Haltren, who was batting .302, Pittsburgh gave the Orioles $2,000 and—at Hanlon's behest—a weak-hitting young outfielder named Joe Kelly. "I had my eye on Kelly for a long time," Hanlon explained to a scribe. "I think it is better to have a good, steady ballplayer than to have a great player who, for some reason, does not play as well as he should."

Not everyone saw steadiness in Joe Kelly. He was twenty years old and handsome as hell. He was an inch short of six feet and looked bigger. He was powerfully built, and his broad face had a cleft chin and surprisingly delicate features, topped by dirty blond hair that was parted in the middle and plastered to his head. He had a gift for repartee. The ladies loved him, almost as much as he loved himself.

Kel had gone through the parochial schools of Cambridge, Massachusetts, and learned to play baseball in the public parks around Boston. He was as fast as he was strong and could run like a sharp breeze in the outfield. He was aggressive at the bat and daring on the basepaths. Hanlon liked that. On the rare occasions he hit the ball, it kept going. Hanlon saw a ballplayer with power and a compulsion to win, who needed only to be taught the fundamentals.

Hanlon learned right away that Joe Kelly had another compulsion—to have his own way. The young outfielder refused at first to sign a contract, for fear that the last-place Orioles were not long for the League. Then he said he would sign but that first he needed to go home for a few days. He went home and stayed, until Hanlon persuaded him to sign.

It was not long before the Baltimore sportswriters paid the robust new fellow a compliment: They added an "e" to his surname. "Kelly" was shanty Irish, but "Kelley"—that was lace-curtain Irish. The higher status suited him, and Joe Kelley he would be.

Hanlon made Kelley his project in 'ninety-three. Every morning at eight o'clock he dragged the youngster to Union Park to work on his fielding and to learn the finer points of hitting and bunting.

For Hanlon, acquiring Kelley was just the first step, but it would be no easy thing to remake a team without money. The $2,000 from the Van Haltren deal would not be enough, and Harry von der Horst had no money to speak of—his father had made sure of it. Maybe ticket receipts would grow, but not until the ballclub improved. So how could Hanlon afford to improve the club without selling more tickets?

He would have to be clever. Hanlon looked for smart young ballplayers he could get on the cheap, with qualities that everyone else had overlooked. He had insisted on full authority when he was hired, but whether he would have it was something else. No matter what Harry von der Horst had promised, almost every owner sought to meddle from time to time. Why else be an owner?

Hanlon saw a solution to all of the problems at once.

It happened that he had amassed some money of his own. He had invested his salary in Pittsburgh real estate and then sold it, along with his $3,000 of stock in the Pirates. He and Harry struck a deal. Hanlon loaned $7,000 to the club in exchange for a quarter of the stock in the Orioles—and full control over the team. He would have a free hand.

When the Orioles' directors met in March of 'ninety-three, they elected Ned Hanlon as the ballclub's president. Harry von der Horst, at his own request, was made the treasurer. Soon he was sporting a button that instructed anyone who approached him with a question: ASK HANLON.

From now on it would be Hanlon's job to summon up the answers.

The horse carriages were lined up outside the Fifth Avenue Hotel. It was one of the classiest, priciest hotels in New York. Situated at the corner of Twenty-third street and Fifth avenue, the hotel faced Madison Square. Its white marble facade and Greek-columned entranceways insinuated the weight of a bank. For years it had served as the city's Republican headquarters, and the National League magnates had made it their own. It was everything they aspired to be.

They were to convene in Parlor F at noon, on the seventh of March in 'ninety-three. What with all the private buttonholing and corner lobbying, it was two o'clock before Nick Young, the League's mild-mannered president, managed to herd a quorum of owners into the grand gilded chamber on the second floor. At three-thirty they recessed for lunch.

It was past four when they gathered again, to take up the most consequential issue they faced.

Amos Rusie was considered to have been the proximate reason for action. It was not only him, however. Other hard-throwing pitchers overwhelmed the batsmen from so close in. Batting averages had been dropping all over the League, by as many as ten points from season to season, to a woeful .245 in 'ninety-two. That caused havoc at the turnstiles. It was hitting and scoring, after all, that drew the customers in. Nothing drove them off to vaudeville or the racetrack or the pool hall faster than quiet bats.

Nobody was surprised that Charley Byrne, the league's leading politician—the Napoleon of Baseball, he enjoyed being called—was in the forefront. To the Brooklyn owner, anything that stymied Amos Rusie and the Giants was to the good. It might even entice a few rooters across the bridge from New York. Byrne's proposed solution had a geometric appeal, the notion of moving the pitcher to the precise center of the diamond. That would put him eight feet farther from the batter, at a distance of sixty-three feet and six inches. Byrne and Harry von der Horst and the other member of the Playing Rules Committee also suggested replacing the pitcher's box with a slab of white rubber, to give the twirler less room to roam.

Some of the magnates saw these changes as too drastic. Frank Robison of Cleveland was the most antagonistic. His reason was simple: Denton True Young, the rawboned Ohio farmboy whose teammates had nicknamed "Cy"—short for "Cyclone." The closer to the quaking batsman the big young right-hander stood, the more the Cleveland owner liked it. Robison growled that Byrne would move the pitcher back to second base if he could.

Behind locked doors, amid the chandeliers and velvet, the owners argued. All of them were used to getting their way. Half of them liked the idea of moving the pitcher back eight feet and half opposed it. Soon a compromise appeared, as foreseen from the first. Why not move the pitcher back five feet instead of eight?

It was almost nine o'clock that night before the question was put to a vote. It passed 11 to 1. Frank Robison voted alone.

Sixty feet and six inches from the closest corner of the diamond-shaped plate—that was the new distance. No longer would the pitcher start anywhere he liked along the back edge of the pitcher's box. Instead he would be confined to the foot-wide pitcher's rubber, five feet farther from the batsman than before.

The owners flung open the doors of the parlor and invited the waiting newspapermen and ballplayers in. Not everyone was impressed with what they had done. "The change will not materially advantage the batsmen or lessen the speed of the pitching," the baseball states-man Henry Chadwick, the august sporting editor of the *Eagle* and the inventor of the box score, prophesied in print the next afternoon. *The Sporting News* predicted that the change "will possibly have the effect of increasing batting for a month or so after the season begins."

They were laughably wrong. Baseball would never be the same.

As the 'ninety-three season got under way, Hanlon continued to rebuild the Orioles. Over the winter an old friend had suggested two swell prospects he had spotted in the California League. Hanlon invited them east. Henny Reitz was a second baseman who was short and squat and silent, but lightning fast with his hands. "He'd say maybe three sentences a season, but all of them funny," a teammate said of him. Bill Clarke was a slender catcher with sunken cheeks and a spectral look. Hanlon was happy with both of them, in the ledger and on the diamond alike.

In June the wretched Louisville Colonels, on their way to an eleventh-place finish, came to Union Park. They had a beanpole of a first baseman, Harry Taylor, who smacked a multitude of singles and wanted to play near his home in the East. Hanlon offered to buy him, but the Colonels declined. They wanted a player in exchange, and a good one—Voiceless Tim O'Rourke, Baltimore's quiet shortstop, who was batting .363.

Ridiculous, Hanlon replied. Unless, perhaps, the Colonels wanted to throw in that sickly shortstop of theirs.

Hughey Jennings had been suffering from malaria and had batted .136 when he was able to play, and his freckled face and startlingly red hair looked sallow. Hughey was twenty-four but seemed younger. He looked even skinnier than usual and somehow shorter than five feet, eight-and-a-half inches. He was in his third year with Louisville and was popular with the local cranks—because he tried so hard, not because he played so well. He had a habit of bailing out whenever a pitch came inside. The twirlers knew that and pitched as any sane man would—high and tight.

The Colonels gave him up.

Hanlon had seen something more in him. Beneath the sunny disposition and the pall of illness, there was a drive to Hughey Jennings, a desperation to succeed. Hanlon figured that Jennings's flaws at the bat could be repaired; it was his brilliance in the field that revealed the kind of player he was. He lunged at the rope of a liner, dove for the hard ground ball.

Hughey Jennings had grown up, the ninth of twelve children, in the worn hills outside Scranton, Pennsylvania. His Irish-born father was a coal miner and too many of Hughey's eight brothers were miners as well. Hughey had left school when he was twelve to work as a breaker boy, sorting out the slate as the coal slid down the chutes. It was dangerous work for a boy, even for a man. Then for three years he drove a mule car deep underground. His grin had marked him from boyhood, but he was fast becoming a man before his time.

He wanted more and dreamed of being a lawyer. Baseball was what he did after work. Hughey had never been strong, but he was wiry and tough; by nature he was competitive and high-strung. Hoping to strengthen his arm, he baked it in a brickyard kiln. Soon he was making five dollars on Sunday, playing semipro ball. He joined an amateur nine in Lehighton and then a minor league team in Allentown before the Colonels signed him as a catcher in 'ninety-one. They gave him a uniform that fit his ascetic frame like a pillowcase.

To Hughey, it beat working underground.

Baseball was always a game to him. There was a tilt to his gaze; he perpetually seemed a little surprised. He was uncomplaining and persistent. He smiled, but he never let up. The previous winter he had taken a commercial course at a business college in Scranton. He could not help but try his damndest. "A ballplayer, to be successful," he understood, "must devote his time to his work. He must breathe baseball, eat baseball, play baseball, think baseball and sleep baseball."

The day after the swap between Baltimore and Louisville was announced, but before the players switched teams, Hughey made one of the most phenomenal stops ever seen on a Baltimore ballfield. In the fifth inning Wilbert Robinson scorched a pitch over second base. Hughey, playing shortstop, threw himself in front of the ball and, while lying on his back, snapped it between his legs to first base.

He practiced with the Orioles once he joined the ballclub. But for week after week he was sick, then Hanlon kept him out of games, so he could get his proper training. It was Hanlon's way. He would let the men mingle in practice, as he watched the newcomer and listened for the other players' spontaneous remarks. Even if the spectators clamored for the new man to be put in, Hanlon would resist, until he was sure that the men would work as one.

Hanlon arranged and rearranged—in his mind and on the diamond—until the chemistry felt just right. He imagined using Henny Reitz at second base and Hughey Jennings at shortstop and shifting John McGraw from shortstop to third. He liked the idea.

The outfield, however, was feeble, other than Joe Kelley, who was batting around .300. Hanlon had his eye on a flashy center fielder with the Browns. Walter Scott Brodie, a proud Virginian, the son of a Confederate cavalry officer, was known to his teammates as Steve, after the famous bartender on the Bowery who had leaped from the Brooklyn Bridge and survived (though there was a school of thought that he had flung a dummy over). The ballplaying Steve Brodie was every bit as gymnastic—and reckless. He was impressively intuitive in the field; at the crack of the bat, he would turn his back and rush to the spot where the ball would land before it did. His huge hands would gather it in.

Hanlon liked his hustle and his pluck. Not since 'ninety-one had Brodie missed a game. But at the bat his success depended on which week it was. Not that there was anything predictable, except that since he had started in the League in 'ninety, every season his average had fallen—until this year. What he was doing differently no one could say, and Hanlon knew enough not to ask. Surely it was not because Brodie had grown less eccentric. He still conducted soliloquies in center field. When he muffed a fly ball he would scream at himself and pound his head with his fist. During practices he would catch fly balls with his back to the plate.

He was quick to drive his managers to distraction. In St. Louis the owner and the manager were nearly as dissatisfied with Brodie as he was with them.

Hanlon bought him cheaply.

*   *   *

In Ned Hanlon's mind a plan was taking shape. "I decided early in the game that there was money to be made in baseball if it was studied seriously," he said years later, "and after I took hold of the Orioles I often got out of bed in the night to jot down a play that might be worked out."

The 'ninety-three season, coming to a close, was not quite as disappointing as 'ninety-two had been. Still, the Orioles, mired in eighth place, had little to lose. Hanlon started working out some new plays he had been thinking about for years. Even in his playing days on the Detroit Wolverines, heavy with sluggers, Hanlon had studied bunting and place-hitting—known as "sissy" tactics, seldom practiced. The older and larger men had scoffed at him for not hitting the ball as hard as he could. But he had held his own.

Others had tried before him. In the mid-'eighties King Kelly had employed the hit-and-run play. The run-and-hit is what it was. The runner on first base would bluff a steal of second, to see which infielder was going to take the throw. Subsequently the runner would go and the batter would poke the ball through the place the infielder had abandoned.

King Kelly taught it to the Beaneaters after he was sold to Boston. Frank Selee, Boston's easygoing manager, had a keen strategic mind and adopted the hit-and-run and had his players master the intricate teamwork of the double steal. He shifted his infielders pitch by pitch and devised the double play that went from the first baseman to the shortstop and back again. The Beaneaters were known to win games with twice as many runs as hits. Relying on speed and tactics, the Beaneaters dashed to their third consecutive pennant in 'ninety-three.

Baltimore was an even more promising place than Boston for a scampering style of baseball. Compared with the South End Grounds, with its close fences in left and right field, Union Park went on and on. The fence in right field stood 335 feet from home plate, and in center field an impossible 393 feet away, beyond the flagpole. There was plenty of space for a ball to squirt away or sneak past.

Hanlon had started to understand something else—the significance of the new pitching distance. Putting the twirler five feet farther away shifted the balance of things. The curveball became harder to control. The batter got another instant to react to the pitch, which had slowed ever so slightly by the time it arrived, and he had a molecule of additional control over how he handled it. Batting averages across the League leapt by thirty-five percentage points, to .280, in 'ninety-three, and the strikeouts dropped almost by half. The extra distance gave a runner a better jump to steal a base, and the hit-and-run another instant to succeed. More balls were put into play, so the quickness and the range of the fielders counted for more. A pitcher needed an extra moment to field a bunt. Being confined to the rubber gave him less room to maneuver. Raw power was giving way, at least a little, to cunning. More than ever before, headwork won ballgames.

"Scientific baseball," the newspapermen called it. And was this not the age of science? The newspapers were crammed with advertisements for modern cures, such as an electric belt to cure impotence and Carter's Little Liver Pills to relieve dyspepsia, torpid liver, and other maladies, and so-called nerve seeds that came "with a written guarantee to cure all nervous diseases, such as Weak Memory, Loss of Brain Power, Headache, Wakefulness, Lost Manhood, Nightly Emissions, Quickness, Evil Dreams, Lack of Confidence." Science was becoming America's new common faith. Progress was relentless. All it required was a man who questioned an assumption or explored an unexamined possibility or noticed something that everyone else had missed. There was nothing that a man with a brain and a will to succeed and a supply of capital could not accomplish.

When it came to science, inventions, and progress, Baltimore could hold its head high. The first telegraph message—"What hath God wrought"—which Samuel Morse had tapped out at the Supreme Court Chamber in the Capitol Building in Washington was received at a Baltimore & Ohio station out Pratt street in Baltimore. The city had seen the first umbrella manufacturing and the earliest use of illuminating gas and the first ice cream factory. The linotype machine had been invented in Baltimore and, just recently, so had the crown cork stopper that made it practical to bottle beer.

Hanlon saw that science had a place in baseball. "The game, like all things, has progressed, and it is today more scientific," he came to explain. "It is in some respects like checkers and chess, and must be played upon systematic plans. Modern baseball, as played by the Baltimores, is based upon the idea to keep opposing teams guessing. It is a case of dealing out uncertainties at all times. Against some teams the Baltimores adopt one style of play—against others they shift. They study the weak points of all teams and try to take advantage of those points accordingly."

Such clarity, however, was yet to come. Hanlon was still groping. He was trying tactics and discarding them. He was scrutinizing what worked and what failed. He was testing opponents' reactions. He was pondering the players he owned and what they could do.

Only after he struck one more deal would the patterns fall into place.

It was Big Dan Brouthers, the Brooklyn first baseman, that Hanlon had in mind. They had known each other for years, since their days as teammates in Detroit, where Brouthers had been a quarter of the famed Big Four, and they had worked shoulder to shoulder in the Brotherhood. Hanlon knew that the outsized first baseman might have just a year left in him. He was thirty-five now and his bulk—six-foot-two, more than 200 pounds—was not as firm as it had been.

Big Dan was a slugger of the old school. He had batted over .300 for the past thirteen seasons. Five times he had been the champion batsman and twice he had led in home runs (with eight and eleven). Ballparks all over the League had marked the landing places of his monumental four-baggers.

None of that, really, was what Hanlon was after. Brouthers was too old to be counted on to play his best. Hanlon wanted him more as a source of stability. His broad unemotional face, his slashing moustache, his legs like cannons upended, his air of assurance, his wife and four children, a big man's magnanimity toward smaller creatures—a team of youngsters needed someone to look up to.

Hanlon approached Charley Byrne. He suggested a trade of Brouthers for George Treadway. The Orioles' right fielder was a pretty good batsman and had the best throwing arm of any outfielder in the League, but Hanlon had a cold and calculating reason for offering him up. Treadway's dark complexion had prompted the word to spread around Baltimore that he was a black man. The ballplayers said he was, and the cranks would not let him alone. What a southern city it was in that regard. He was jeered at, until the strain made its mark and his batting fell off. Hanlon wanted him gone.

Byrne was interested, and he was happy to unload Brouthers, known for his devotion to the bottle. But what Brooklyn really needed was a third baseman. With McGraw to be moved to third base, the Orioles had one to spare. Billy Shindle was a fair hitter and a tolerably good fielder. He owned a business in Philadelphia and for two seasons had sought to gain his release. He had even been talking of quitting the game.

Byrne insisted on Treadway and Shindle for Brouthers.

Hanlon refused. He wanted man for man.

Johnny Ward had recommended a ballplayer to Hanlon, the little fellow, Willie Keeler. Brooklyn had "loaned" him to Binghamton and planned to release him. Hanlon had seen something in the 130-pound infielder. But he later acknowledged that even he had not seen all that was there.

Two days before 'ninety-three came to a close, the four-man trade was made.

Charley Byrne assured himself that he had gotten the better of the deal. He was wrong. It was for good reason that Hanlon was coming to be known as "Foxy Ned."

Willie Keeler trudged in from right field on the hard scraggly spring-practice ballgrounds in Macon, Georgia, and flung down his glove. He plopped down on the bench with an angry hummingbird's force.

"What's the matter?" Hanlon demanded.

"I'm not going to play the outfield," Willie snapped.

"Why not? What's the matter with the outfield?" Hanlon, having no patience with the inefficiency of a left-handed third baseman, had put Willie in right field instead. Willie had been unenthusiastic and had taken no pains to hide it. Every time a fly ball had come anywhere near him, Hanlon had watched him shy away, toward the foul line. Steve Brodie, the center fielder, would catch it instead.

"Oh, the outfield's all right, but it's that guy Brodie out there," Willie replied. "He's got it in for me."

"What's Brodie got it in for you for?" Hanlon asked.

"I don't know, but he keeps on yelling, 'I'll get *you*, you dirty dog! I'll get *you*, you dirty dog!'"

The other players on the bench roared with laughter. That was what Brodie screamed at every ball that came his way.

Even as the B&O had chugged its way south from Baltimore, the Orioles had started to become a team. Dan Brouthers found himself surrounded by the young colts, who listened with open mouths as he reminisced about the old days in the game. Joe Kelley's baritone anchored an impromptu glee club. Hughey Jennings and Bill Clarke, the tenors, trilled solos.

None of the other teams had gone south for spring practice in 'ninety-four. The White Stockings had pioneered the practice in the 'seventies, but no one could afford it anymore. The Orioles had tried it in 'ninety-three and finished in eighth place. Harry von der Horst, short of money as usual, had been reluctant to send them again, but Hanlon insisted.

It was a good thing he did. "The Macon camp was one of the most interesting training camps ever held in baseball," a scribe-turned-historian judged decades later. "History was made there."

A blizzard that devastated the local peach and strawberry crops greeted the Orioles in Macon. Hanlon paid no mind. The Orioles started practicing anyway.

Ned Hanlon was a man who believed in routines. When he was at home he insisted on soup before every meal. In Macon he had the players waken at seven o'clock every morning and had them on the field by nine-thirty, for three hours of running and drills. They would run back to the hotel for a midday dinner and a rest in bed, and return to the ballgrounds for an afternoon game. Then came a run of a mile or two at a nearby horse track, followed—at last—by a bath and a rubdown.

"This is a devil of an occupation for a man worth $30,000," Dan Brouthers huffed to Robbie as they sweated their way around the track—"and some of it bringing in ten percent."

Hanlon had the ballplayers work the hardest on whatever they were worst at. "Work, work, work, work, all the time"—that was how Hughey Jennings described Hanlon's method. None of the Orioles had the instinct for running the bases of a John Montgomery Ward, so Hanlon gave all of them daily instruction. They perfected the meticulously timed deception of the hit-and-run. He drilled them on placing bunts for hits, not for sacrifices. They practiced fouling off pitch after pitch. The infielders refined a cutoff play to prevent a double steal. The pitchers practiced picking off runners and covering first base on ground balls. The batsmen worked on a tactic that would become known as the Baltimore chop. George Van Haltren had first tried it— swinging down on the ball, at an angle, to bounce it so high off a sun-baked infield that the batter could scamper to first base by the time it came down. Now that Van Haltren was gone, it was Willie Keeler who showed a particular knack for it.

The Baltimore chop was an absurdity, but there was no rule against it—and it worked. Better yet, it was unexpected. That was the foundation of Hanlon's system—whatever was least expected was what should be done. He kept pushing his ballplayers to think. Every evening and any day it rained, Hanlon gathered his ballplayers in his hotel room at the handsome mansard-roofed Brown House and quizzed them on strategy and rules. He handed each of them a copy of the *Spalding Guide,* to learn the ins and outs of the rules. He devised a complicated system of hand signals—for batters, fielders, and runners—that one of the newspapers said "would put the Princeton football eleven to shame." Control over the ball—that was the highest good.

Hanlon noticed everything. He also knew how to command a ballplayer's attention. He refused to say for certain where—or if—anyone would play. He did not hesitate to call his ballplayers down for loose work. (He had fined several of them for sloppy play during 'ninety-three.) He seemed like a hard man, who held others to account. Yet he was every bit as hard on himself.

"He is eminently a just man, and a newcomer feels that he will get a good chance to show his ability if he has any," Willie Keeler found. "He does not rebuke a man in the hearing of spectators, and thereby take the heart out of a man when he makes a misplay, but points out the mistake next morning in the practice hour and makes a suggestion or two."

Hanlon had every reason to be delighted with the Brooklyn trade. "All wool and a yard wide," he chuckled a dozen times a day, watching the newcomers.

Dan Brouthers showed that he knew baseball from head to toe, and with sweet authority he swung his thick-barreled "wagon-tongue" bat. But it was Willie Keeler who was the wonder of Macon. Right field, when properly played, is the hardest of the outfield positions—or so John Montgomery Ward believed—for the balls hit by a right-handed batsman curve away in a trajectory that is hard to divine. Willie had started playing right field without using a glove, but after he dropped a fly ball and a Baltimore newspaperman got on him, he changed his ways. He was so quick on his feet that nothing got away from him. His arm was not as strong as Treadway's, but he got to balls that Treadway would have let by him for hits. When he took in a long hard-hit fly ball, Hanlon's face lit up with a gorgeous smile. "I will make those Brooklyn people think they have lost a $10,000 beauty," he boasted to a scribe standing nearby.

At the bat, Willie was every bit as pleasing. He had a good eye and could connect with any kind of pitch. He pushed or chopped his bat at the ball. His hits were sharp and clean. The hardest pitch did not back him off the plate.

Amazingly, that was the case with Hughey Jennings as well. He had batted .182 the previous season, because he could not stop himself from stepping away from inside pitches. In Macon he stepped straight into each pitch and blasted it to the outfield. He had John McGraw to thank. The two of them had spent the winter coaching baseball and taking classes at St. Bonaventure's College in upstate New York. In a corner of the dimly lit cellar of Alumnus Hall, McGraw had jury-rigged a batting cage out of scrap lumber and chicken wire. Hour after hour, week after week, he backed Hughey against the side of the cage and hurled high, tight pitches at him so that he could not pull away. It took weeks until Hughey had no need to.

"At first it was an awkward manner of swinging for me, and I thought I'd never conquer it," Hughey said. "But McGraw was a true friend and stuck with me. After many hours of practice I was forced to get the knack of hitting correctly."

The two small-town Irishmen were becoming the closest of friends. Their temperaments were vividly distinct. Hughey always seemed cheerful, while Mac never lost his edge of anger. Yet they shared an intensity, a seriousness of purpose, a luminous intelligence, which set the tone for the team.

Something about the Orioles was starting to be more than the sum of the pieces. Except for Sunday mornings, when Hanlon led the ballplayers to church, they thought only about baseball. Joe Kelley even dreamed about it. "Why, he never touched me!" he shouted one night in his sleep. He was sliding into second base and Silk O'Loughlin, the flaxen-haired umpire, had been calling him out.

Sadie McMahon pitched the first game of the spring, against Macon's minor league team. By now, Hanlon had settled on a lineup. McGraw was to lead off, meaning his job was to get on base, and Willie would bat second, to move Mac along.

Right away they showed themselves suited. McGraw struck four singles and drew a base on balls. Willie hit two singles, a triple, and a home run that stayed inside the ballgrounds. Fourteen Orioles crossed the plate in the seven-inning game.

It was a casual game but a revealing one. Hanlon, acting as the umpire, called McGraw out at second base when he was obviously safe.

McGraw, his face as smooth as an altar boy's, charged in a fury at Hanlon. Only when Hanlon smiled did McGraw see the joke and slink away.

"Baseball, like everything else, is constantly moving forward," a scribe wired back to Baltimore. "It is eminently a case of the survival of the fittest. It is one of the most gratifying signs of the times that the men are beginning to realize this. No more loafing, drinking and carousing. Only sober, hard-working men have any chance in *fin de siècle* baseball."

Willie Keeler was batting .523 when the Orioles got home.

= 4 =

Baltimore's
Grandest Parade

The Eutaw House was already past its prime. The lazy southern charm that had so enchanted Charles Dickens and Henry Clay and Ulysses S. Grant (while he was still a general) and had enticed Mary Todd Lincoln to stop off for a light meal on her way to New York after her husband was killed had become a little seedy. Maybe that was why the visiting ballclubs could afford it.

The rooms upstairs, moderately priced at $2.50 to $4.50 a night, each had a wooden bed, a straight-backed chair, and a marble-topped dresser with a washstand, but no private bath.

The six-story hotel of yellow brick was ponderous in its presence at the corner of Eutaw and Baltimore streets. Nothing stood taller on Baltimore's skyline than the steeples, and the hotel commanded a view of the bustling harbor a half-dozen blocks to the southeast and, beyond, of Federal Hill, which controlled the entrance to the Inner Harbor and thus to the heart of the city. Around the hotel, a jumble of horsecarts and drays jammed the streets. In the daytime the streets were always noisy—the shouts of humans and the snorts of animals and, more every day, the squeal of metal.

Cranks crammed the lobby and even the corridors of the Eutaw House on this cloudy April morning. They came to gaze with awe upon the New York Giants. They *were* giants. Amos Rusie measured six-foot-one and 210 pounds. Roger Connor, the aging first baseman, was two inches taller and ten pounds heavier and had hit more home runs as a ballplayer than anyone ever had. Duke Farrell, the catcher just acquired from the Washington Senators, was six-two. Jouett Meekin, whose pitching almost rivaled Rusie's, was six-one. Except for Yale

Murphy, the tiny new shortstop, the smallest man on the team was Johnny Ward, the second baseman and manager, who was a lithe, dapper five-nine.

He and his bigger boys had arrived at Camden Station the previous evening. They had gone immediately to the Eutaw House, for a good night's rest before the opening game of the 'ninety-four season. Johnny Ward paid for a shave and sauntered off to find Ned Hanlon and Harry von der Horst. Ward and Hanlon, old comrades from the Brotherhood, now notables in the League they had battled, good-naturedly wished each other misfortune for the three games to come.

"The Southern trip benefited the Baltimores, but we are still with them," Johnny Ward told the scribes who had gathered, pencils in hand. "What do we expect to do in this series? Well, we will be satisfied with two games, and let you down easy." He had really expected, it was reported afterward, to win all three.

Many of the sporting pundits favored the Giants to take the 'ninety-four pennant. The Orioles were known to be considerably improved, possibly enough to finish fifth or sixth in the twelve-team League.

The men from both teams fraternized in the crowded lobby and rocked in the oversized chairs. By late morning they had donned their uniforms, in anticipation of the one o'clock parade. The Maryland Naval Reserve Band had been playing since ten. Outside the Eutaw House, five thousand Baltimoreans buzzed around the forty open carriages. The musicians, packed uncomfortably onto a barge, played popular tunes as small black boys danced.

In bad times and in good times, Baltimore loved its parades. Sauerwald's Band and Drum Corps rode at the head in a six-horse wagon. After the carriage of newspapermen, Ned Hanlon and Johnny Ward shared a barouche, its driver at the reins on the high front seat. The two catchers, Wilbert Robinson of Baltimore and Duke Farrell of the Giants, occupied the next carriage, with a pair of Orioles and a pair of Giants in each carriage behind. Then came the personages of every description—the politicians and the men of affairs who were only too happy to associate themselves with the city's finest sportsmen.

The parade took an intricate circuit of the principal avenues, from Eutaw street to Lombard to Sharp to Camden to Charles to Pratt and so on, past the harbor. How pretty the city looked, even as the sun played hide-and-seek. The iron-fronted buildings glistened. All the cornices and ornamental molding were no fancier than the day deserved. Even the plainest of the gray-faced buildings looked revived when they were swathed in orange and black bunting. (Nobody before Hanlon had thought to identify the ballclub with the colors of the Baltimore oriole.) Ladies waved from arched windows on the upper stories of the finest commercial establishments. On the crowded brick sidewalks, throngs of people cheered the players as they passed—the businessmen in their silk hats and cravats, the street brats who darted from lamppost to lamppost, even the matrons with their parasols and fruited hats. The opposing buildings lining the narrow streets blurred the noise into a din.

At the harbor the tugboats tooted their good wishes. The carriages rattled over the cobblestones, as the parade passed saloons and social clubs, coal dealers and grand hotels, hosiery shops and toy stores. The city's lethargic pace had quickened.

The parade wound back again to Charles street and turned north along the spine of the city. Charles street was too narrow for such an elegant thoroughfare. The three-story buildings bore down on one another; even in early afternoon they blocked out the sun. Yet how glorious an avenue it was, home to jewelers and importers and the city's most eminent clothiers. Men lifted their derbies from their heads and shouted as the carriages rolled by. The parade passed the sixty-five-year-old grand marble shaft that was the nation's original Washington Monument. (The obelisk in the nation's capital, thirty-some miles away, was less than ten years old.) The ballplayers rolled by the city's loveliest residences, its most elaborate churches, and felt at home.

Beyond North avenue, Charles street widened. Scattered houses and fruit trees bordered the drowsy, dusty road. Even there, rooters lined the route and cheered the rebirth of baseball.

Dozens and scores and hundreds of cranks followed the parade all the way to Union Park. Electric streetcars had recently supplanted the old horse-drawn cars, and all of the extra streetcars that had been put on along the York road, a block east of Union Park, were filled to overflowing. Many a venturesome crank risked life and limb to hang by a strap from the doorway, but the nickels kept rolling into the till.

Others came by cable car or by horse-drawn conveyance of every class and description. The livery stables had done a lively business in hiring out rigs. When the carriage yard beside Union Park filled up, nearby residents made some money by using front yards as impromptu stables. Safety bicycles, all the rage with their low wheels and air-filled tires, swooshed along the streets, seeking out the slot rails the cable cars used. The bicycle racks beyond the left-field fence, along Barclay street, found their purpose.

The crowd had swelled around the ticket windows in front of Union Park, a ballpark that looked every bit as unprepossessing as the residential neighborhood in which it sat, with brick row houses on all sides. The front of it was a broad wooden wall twelve feet high, with ornamental lettering, opposite vendors' stands that the crowd swallowed up.

The game was set for four o'clock, but by three the management ceased selling tickets for the grandstand. And still the chimes of the silver quarters never let up. The green eyeshades in the box office grew tired of counting the money, and the gatekeepers were grateful for the turnstiles that kept out the ticketless cranks. As it was, 15,235 ticket-holders passed through—the mightiest crowd ever to watch baseball on a Baltimore grounds. It was thousands more than when Union Park opened in 'ninety-one and even more than for the game against the St. Louis Browns back in 'eighty-seven as the two nines battled for the American Association lead.

So great was the crush that the management opened a gate that sent a torrent of ticket-holders pouring into the farther reaches of the outfield, where two hundred policemen corralled them behind hand-held ropes. Maybe a thousand other rooters watched the proceedings for free—boys clustered around the knotholes or high up on telegraph poles or sedentary cranks who claimed a few square feet on a nearby rooftop. A row of houses lay just beyond the center field fence and others alongside each foul line. Students from the Woman's College of Baltimore (renamed in later years for the Rev. John F. Goucher, its second president) huddled with their teachers on the roof of the Latin Building to ogle the boys of spring. Even the distant rooters could catch the languorous strains of the orchestra in the ballpark, playing "Be Kind, for They Are Orphans."

Inside, Union Park looked fancier than ever, having been gussied up over the winter. The balcony of the double-decked grandstand was yet to be finished, but orange and black bunting was strung along the upper tier. Lines of flags connected the poles overhead. The grandstand was a profusion of black and white, the men in their frock coats and derbies. The unusually large contingent of ladies showed off their spring millinery, their silks and satins, their bustle skirts and their hourglass dresses with billowy sleeves.

Harry von der Horst had lavished complimentary tickets on the men who mattered in the city—the mayor, the governor, a congressman or two, the state's attorney, judges and capitalists and preachers and politicians—thirteen hundred altogether, each for admission of the holder and a guest. Baltimore was stratified by class and calling, as any city was, but not so much in the ballpark. Judges sat by mechanics, merchants by laborers, bosses by clerks. Out by the bleachers, on a rough pine fence only two inches wide, a Charles street swell in a top hat and a Prince Albert coat perched next to an urchin whose shoes needed new uppers and soles. On the sun-bleached benches along the right field line, ragamuffins squeezed next to Fauntleroys in velvet, the sons of Africa by the scions of Europe.

"For the time being, caste was forgotten," the city's Republican newspaper rhapsodized the next morning, "and all were sons of one father."

The cranks had matters more mundane on their minds. "Beer, ginger ale, lemonade, cigars, peanuts, cigarettes," the vendors in the bleachers cried. "What is it, gents? Wet your throats so ye kin holler." Only soft drinks were sold in the grandstand, but in the bleachers the brewed stuff flowed. Or the rooters could buy the sausage-like sandwiches that the city's German-Americans had known as *Weckers* and had bought at the Baltimore ballgrounds for years. The stands were filled as well with the harsh smell of strong tobacco, as almost everyone seemed to be puffing on a cigar or a meerschaum or a thin cheroot or a cigarette. Out by the flagpole inside the center field fence, the black scoreboard for the other League games still had nothing to say.

Umpire Tom Lynch, austere and firm, tore the red cover off the new white ball. He took on a practiced air of importance. There was no other arbiter on the diamond but he.

The gong rang out. It was really a big bell on the front of the upper stands, with a cord to the Orioles' bench. The Giants, in their baggy flannel uniforms, trotted out to their positions in the field. The Orioles had chosen to bat first. They collected on the bench, at the crook of the grandstand. The Baltimore ballplayers' new uniforms, antiseptically white, had black stockings almost to the knee and flat-topped white caps sheathed by double black rings.

"Play ball!" Umpire Lynch yelled out.

The huge crowd cheered as John McGraw—zealous, on edge, as always—strode to the plate. The field was lush, except for the basepaths and the runway of dirt from the rubber to home plate. The grass, painstakingly tended, was thicker along the first and third base lines, the better to keep bunts from rolling foul. Out beyond the diamond, spectators as many as thirty deep concealed where right field sloped away. By ground rules, anything hit into the crowd was a two-bagger.

John McGraw seemed very small, at Amos Rusie's mercy. The longer distance had not troubled the Giant twirler much, nor being confined to the rubber. He was in better shape than ever for the start of the season and flung an assortment of his hard-thrown shoots and nerve-wracking curves. McGraw was patient at the plate. At last he picked out a pitch and drove it on a line into left field. The outfielder ran hard and got to the ball—and muffed it.

McGraw danced at first base. The crowd shrieked with glee.

Now Willie Keeler, the littlest man on the team, came to the plate. His short, stubby bat was just thirty inches long and weighed only twenty-nine ounces. The League had never seen a bat so small. The folds of the plain white flannel hung from his skimpy frame. The black stockings reached up over his calves.

"The only way I have ever managed to hit Amos," Willie was learning, "is by standing well up to the plate and meeting the ball squarely. If I should swing hard at the ball I would lose my balance and the curve would fool me."

Willie slammed a pitch so hard at Yale Murphy that the Giants' rookie shortstop fumbled it.

Amos Rusie bore down when he had to, rendering Joe Kelley and Dan Brouthers and Steve Brodie harmless. Sadie McMahon was every bit as wizardly. The Orioles' ace threw with heat and worked his curves with subtle distinction, and his teammates backed him up in the field. Brodie was a streak of lightning. Willie was too. In the second inning, when one of the Giants' smaller sluggers drove a pitch deep into right field, Willie turned and ran at the crack of the bat and leaped the rope, scattering the spectators in a detonation of derbies. He caught the ball on the dead run.

By the eighth inning the Orioles had built a promising though hardly impregnable lead of 5 to 1. When Wilbert Robinson led off, a delegation of rooters presented the team's captain with a silver-handed umbrella engraved ROBBIE. In such situations, the honored batsman typically hit two long fouls and then struck out. Robbie whipped a pitch past the shortstop instead. After McMahon flied out, McGraw lined a beauty into center field. With two men on base, Willie came to bat. He had struck out—twice. Nerves, no doubt. Again, Rusie got two strikes on him, but this time he would not get a third. Willie drove the pitch out to left field, into the crowd, for two bases. Robbie scored.

With two outs Big Dan Brouthers came to bat. The barrel-chested slugger was cheered to the echo as he lumbered to the plate. He let several of Rusie's pitches go by. The next pitch leapt from his heavy bat, into distant center field. It soared over the heads of the awestruck crowd. The ball struck the center field fence three feet from the top and bounced back. By the ground rules, a two-bagger. Union Park had never witnessed as long a hit.

In the bleachers, the cranks rose as one and surged from side to side in a wave.

The game ended with the Orioles ahead, 8 to 3. Strangers hugged in the stands. In the outfield the crowd burst its ropes and turned the ballgrounds into a writhing mass of running men and boys. One of the Baltimore newspapers delivered its taunt the next morning:

> *And somewhere there is laughter,*
> *And somewhere children shout,*
> *But there is no joy in Gotham,*
> *The Giants are laid out.*

The Orioles won the next game, as Willie scored the winning run. The following afternoon, he came to bat in the seventh inning with the score 3 to 3. The tie was McGraw's doing: He had just slashed a single that sent Hughey and Robbie across home plate. The crowd went wild. Willie stood erect at the plate, utterly alert. As the pitcher threw McGraw started to steal. Johnny Ward dashed to second base and Willie poked the ball through the hole Ward had left vacant. Willie kicked up the dust on the basepath as McGraw slammed into third base. On Steve Brodie's fly ball, Mac scored the winning run.

So much for New York's high-blown pride.

Harry von der Horst declared that he would buy each of his ballplayers a hat. "None of the boys will require larger sizes than usual," *The Sun* presumed.

Or might they? "That one series made the Orioles," McGraw recounted later. "Seeing that our stuff had worked, we were full of confidence and cockiness."

*   *   *

Out along the York road, a ten-minute walk from the ballpark, most of the Orioles had taken rooms at the Oxford House, a quaint and comfortable wood-frame hotel with a spacious lawn and prints of fox hunts and horseraces decorating the rooms. The proprietor was an elderly Englishman with bushy side-whiskers and no interest in baseball.

Willie Keeler had a room. John McGraw had another. So did Hughey Jennings and Steve Brodie and Dan Brouthers and Sadie McMahon and two other pitchers and both utility men. The players enjoyed one another's company. They sang on the porch in the evenings. After breakfast they scrambled for the hammock on the back porch, as a place to skim the newspapers. Every morning for a week it was claimed by John McGraw. Soon the others stopped trying.

"Aggressiveness," McGraw said later, "is the main thing in baseball."

He showed it every day on the diamond. He dived into bases and blocked the hard hits that Billy Shindle would have let by for two-baggers. "Little Mac at third was a whole team and a dog under the wagon," the *Morning Herald* in Baltimore said as the Giants skulked out of town. "His skin is full of baseball, and when he starts into a game he forgets everything else and thinks only of winning. He is absolutely fearless, and will not get out of the way of anything or anybody." He pursued every advantage. In the third game against the Giants, when a wild pitch nicked his bat, he clutched the back of his head and started for first base. When the umpire refused to be fooled, even Mac cracked a smile.

His teammates both loved and feared him. He could inspire them—or ridicule them—to new levels of intensity. He made sure that they kept one another in line. "Woe betide the player who failed us!" McGraw said. "His life on the bench was not a pleasant one. He never forgot the roasting and never failed to deliver one if somebody else failed."

The Orioles were as lively as crickets. The champion Beaneaters, who followed the Giants into Union Park, led by two runs going into the ninth inning, when the Orioles rose up and scored fourteen. Every afternoon saw a different hero. Willie beat out grounders to first base. He and Mac worked the hit-and-run once or twice—even three times—a game. Robbie, the stout catcher, stole bases. Dan Brouthers unleashed his wagon-tongue bat and once even drove a pitch *over* the right-center field fence, so that a sign was put up boasting, HERE.

(Legend later had it that the ball bounced over to Calvert street and landed in a coal car at Union Station, winding up in Philadelphia.) The next day it was Joe Kelley's home run, on top of his triple and two acrobatic catches. Hughey Jennings was learning to tighten the muscles in his torso to brace himself for getting hit by the pitch. "Oh yes it takes nerve," he confided, "but you can't play ball without nerve."

Nerve was what the Orioles had—and smarts. They were too young and too full of themselves to know they could not invent whatever they wished. Night after night, in the viscous heat of the Baltimore summer, McGraw and Keeler and Kelley and Jennings sat up and puzzled out schemes to win ballgames. Who needed Hanlon? "Then we'd go out to the ballpark the next day and try them out, practicing them till we got them letter perfect," McGraw recollected. For hours they calibrated the chances of a runner's scoring from third base on a sacrifice bunt if he dashed for the plate at the pitcher's first motion. On the diamond they discovered that, on a bunt anywhere inside the foul lines, the runner could not be thrown out if he left instantly. And thus, as McGraw remembered it, the squeeze play was born.

The Orioles thrived on speed and surprise. Taking the extra base became the rule. (For the season they would hit 150 triples in 128 games and steal 324 bases.) There was nothing they would not try. Everything was game, if no rule stood against it—or even if one did. Science decreed it: No possibility was to be overlooked.

This made Tom Murphy important. He was the groundskeeper at Union Park, an understated man with dark regular features and the longest, thickest, droopiest moustache at the ballgrounds. Murph knew his business. As a groundskeeper in Indianapolis he had discovered a hard-throwing amateur named Amos Rusie. In Baltimore he made the field to his liking. He built up the ground just outside the third base line so that bunts might stay fair. He packed the path to first base ever so slightly downhill, to help the Orioles' speedsters. He mingled soap flakes with the soil around the pitcher's rubber, to cause the unwary perspiring twirlers to lose their grip. (The Orioles' pitchers carried dirt in their pockets.) The infield dirt was mixed with clay, to formulate a soil almost as hard as concrete. All summer long the infield remained unwatered, as a boon to the baserunners and the Baltimore chop. Willie once chopped down at the ball and made a two-bagger.

The Orioles hit the ball hard and often, and also with judgment. Even when the opposing teams suspected what was coming, often there was little they could do. Defending against the hit-and-run required letting McGraw steal a base or pitching wide to Willie or vary-ing who would cover second base so that Willie guessed wrong in plac-ing the ball. But he usually guessed right. Against the Cleveland Spiders one afternoon in June, Willie punched the ball through the second baseman's spot and, a few innings later, through the shortstop's. He was liable to get four hits in one game and three in the next.

When the League issued the averages for the batsmen a few days later, Joe Kelley, who rammed the ball and raced down the basepaths, ranked third, at .391. Willie Keeler was fifth, at .372. "Batters of the new school," Hanlon called them. "Most of the men have been edu-cated to call for a high or low ball, but these players hit at anything, high or low, equally well, and they keep a pitcher guessing."

That was the key: Keep them guessing. That took teamwork. Get a man on first base and his teammates would bring him home. Hanlon meant to build a machine of interlocking pieces. "In addition to supe-rior physical qualities," one of the Baltimore newspapers noted, "the *fin de siècle* players must possess a high order of brains, must be of cor-rect habits, have plenty of ambition and be possessed of a certain docility and evenness of temperament such as will insure proper disci-pline and the frictionless working together of the whole team."

Forget the docility. But the rest was in evidence. The last-place team of 'ninety-two and the eighth-place team of 'ninety-three fin-ished June of 'ninety-four in first place. The League had never seen such an emergence.

The Orioles split a doubleheader in Louisville, where the cranks bestowed a floral horseshoe on Hughey Jennings, their lost favorite. The Fourth of July was hot back in Baltimore, as it always was, though certainly the heat was easier to endure in pursuing pleasure than at work. The bicyclists made their own breeze. The air stirred now and again among the picnickers on the manicured slopes of Druid Hill Park. All over the city, the flags on homes occasionally unfurled.

Patriotism was a little harder to come by, however, what with the savage strikes and the deepening depression. On the Fourth, President Cleveland dispatched troops to Chicago to break the Pullman strike, which had halted most of the rail traffic coming into the city and in much of the nation. That provoked three days of riots in which thirty men died. The nation had started to feel old; nobody was left who remembered its beginnings.

When John von der Horst awoke on the Fourth, he was expected to live another month. He had resided for sixty-nine years on this earth, forty-nine of them in an adopted land. He had come home from White Sulphur Springs in West Virginia a month before, still uncured, and had already built a mausoleum near the front gate of Baltimore Cemetery, within sight of his beloved brewery. Made of Italian marble, with a copper roof and a door of solid bronze, it was worthy of him. But he was not ready to move in. With his iron will, he had survived past the first of July, to see his second son become a partner in the brewery's profits. To his first son, that meant ballplayers he could not buy.

At ten in the morning the old man seemed in no danger. By midafternoon he was dead.

John Jr. found the will in his father's vest pocket. Lena, a family member of mysterious origin, had put it there—at the old man's direction, she testified later—two days before he died. She was twenty now, an auburn-haired young gentlewoman, short but elegant, who harbored hopes of becoming a concert organist. Lena had married Henry Wilkins, who was charming enough but had no head for business. Yet she was still a member of the household, as confusingly as ever. When she was a little girl, John von der Horst had described her to the census-takers as his granddaughter. She was barely older than Harry's two daughters, who shared the stucco house. But in his will he named her as his daughter, which was apparently the truth. Whether he had formally adopted her no one could say for sure. It was assumed that he was her natural father, by someone other than his upstanding wife, Johanna.

But whatever he was to Lena, she was devoted to him, and to Johanna, ministering to them in their declining years. After Johanna died, in the summer of 'ninety-three, the old man needed Lena more than ever. Now he made his appreciation known, with a third of his estate.

Harry and John wasted no time. They were both twice her age and viewed her with contempt. Harry renounced his position as a co-executor (appointed along with John Jr.) of his father's estate, so that he might challenge the provisions of the will.

Lena was quicker into court. Barely two weeks after the old man died she swore in Orphans' Court that Harry and John Jr. "have conspired to do all in their power" to break the will and deprive her of what was rightfully hers. She asked the judge to name someone other than John Jr. to administer an estate that she estimated to be worth an astonishing $300,000.

The brothers and their lawyers scoffed at Lena's "disordered imagination." She was no sister of theirs, they said—no relation at all.

They need not have worried. Under Maryland law, even a conspiracy was no reason to disqualify an executor. A panel of judges dismissed her petition. The legal wrangling, however, had only begun.

For a while it seemed as if the Orioles would be stranded in Chicago because of the rail strike, but Hanlon had an idea. He and Harry von der Horst draped banners—*Baltimore Base Ball Club*—from both sides of the Orioles' railway car, in hopes that the strikers would let them pass through. The ballplayers were labor, were they not? Evidently they were, for the strikers allowed them to escape to Cleveland.

They should have stayed in Chicago. The trip brought an awful slump. They lost two of three to Louisville—the godforsaken Colonels!—and got thrashed in Cincinnati. Their hitting fell off—Mac's and Willie's and Kelley's and pretty much everyone but Brodie's. What a batsman Brodie could be. On the ninth of July he got six hits (and Willie got five) as the Orioles came from behind, 0 to 9, to beat the Pittsburgh Pirates, 14 to 10. The Virginian would swing at anything, and often he hit it. Halfway through the season his batting average soared as high as .382. That was nothing like his spirit in the field. Once when he muffed a fly ball, he pounded his head and shouted at himself: "You ought to go home and pick blackberries; you ain't worth seven dollars a year; you would muff an apple dumpling if you were hungry!" He once stopped as he rounded third base to cheer his teammates on and got tagged out. Another time he leaned a ladder against the right field fence to go after a heckler in the stands, until his teammates dissuaded him. He played with an abandon that served his teammates well.

But it was not enough. Not only had the batting fallen off; the pitching was worse. Sadie McMahon pitched beautifully, sometimes invincibly, with his sharp curves and his new slow teaser, but his arm was getting tired from so much use. The other twirlers, Hanlon said, "seem to think they are doing quite well enough and are content with that." Bert Inks, the tall undisciplined left-hander, had been overweight and smoked too much down in Macon, so that Hanlon sent him to a Turkish bath to get in condition. Tony Mullane, the ambidextrous veteran, was despised by his teammates. ("Yes, those are the bruises he got when I hit him with a potato roller," his wife testified in the divorce trial in a crowded Cincinnati courtroom on the seventh of July, "after he had cut me with a knife and smashed a water pitcher over my head.") Hanlon's three-man rotation kept changing. As soon as the Orioles got back to Baltimore, three of the pitchers went out on a drunk.

Hanlon called his players together and talked to them like a father. He told them he knew what the trouble was and had every man promise faithfully he would abstain from drinking for the rest of the season. Willie Keeler and John McGraw were teetotalers already. Now they all vowed to be. Hanlon imposed no fines, and even lifted one he had inflicted on Inks.

The Orioles lost three straight to New York and three more to Boston. They fell out of first place for a day, then regained it. Before long the Beaneaters overtook them once more. The critics brayed that the Orioles had been playing out of their class.

Hanlon went to work. He needed pitching the most. Whatever Hanlon wanted, Harry von der Horst was happy to oblige. Hanlon had his eye on Kid Gleason, a gutty right-hander from the Camden, New Jersey, waterfront who had won ninety-nine games the past four seasons and was known to be unhappy in St. Louis. He joined the Orioles in July. Soon Hanlon bought a big left-handed workhorse, Charley Esper of the Senators, who had lost more games—twenty-eight—than anyone in the League the previous season.

More was to come. By season's end the Orioles had spent more to strengthen their team than had the other eleven ballclubs combined.

The Orioles stood two games behind the Beaneaters and one ahead of the Giants when the New Yorkers came to Baltimore in the searing days of August. Sadie McMahon was supposed to pitch, but his arm hurt, so Kid Gleason went to the rubber instead. He had a pleasant clean-shaven face and a boyish blond forelock. Not much bigger than McGraw, he was almost as tough. He never ducked a fight and could lick a man who was fifty pounds heavier.

As the game went on, the Orioles seemed different somehow. Maybe it was something Hanlon had said or the sense of helplessness that came in facing Amos Rusie. They stopped trying to knock the ball out of the lot, as when they had been losing, but returned to their strength, resting content with a succession of sharply hit singles. Willie Keeler got three of them, breaking out of a slump. (He had gone through four games in a row without hitting safely.) It seemed like ages since the Orioles had displayed such clean, scientific hitting. They showed ginger.

They won by 12 to 9 that day and by 20 to 1 the next afternoon, when Willie and Joe Kelley struck four hits apiece and Hughey Jennings got five. Sadie McMahon's arm ached but he pitched anyway, and exceedingly well. What glorious fun they were having. This, every Baltimorean knew, was why God had made baseball.

Harry von der Horst dined that evening with Eddie Talcott, the treasurer of the Giants, who had made his fortune on Wall Street. An old black man stationed himself beneath the open window of the restaurant. As Harry exhorted his friend from New York not to feel glum, a warbling came from the sidewalk below, to the tune of "Titwillow":

> *A young man from New York, silent sat at his plate*
> *Singing Oriole, Oriole, Oriole.*
> *Why am I consigned to this awful hard fate?*
> *Oh! Oriole, Oriole, Oriole.*
> *Is it weakness of pitching or muffing, he cried;*
> *Or a great run of base hits all on the wrong side?*
> *Then he swallowed his napkin and slowly he died,*
> *Singing . . .*

Right field at Union Park was the terror of visiting ballplayers. It was rough and weedy and sloped down to the fence. The fence itself, of uneven pine boards, was slanted on the inside at something like sixty-five degrees (so that the advertising might be seen from the grandstands). The field was often spongy, because of the stream on the other side of the fence. It was a rotten field to play.

Willie loved it. Its vastness lent him an advantage, with his speed and his unerring sense of where the ball would land. He made hard catches look easy. No longer did Steve Brodie intimidate him; they never got balled up chasing fly balls. "He knew his territory like a child its ABCs," the center fielder said of Willie.

When Willie was near the fence, the incline of the ground meant that he could not be seen from home plate. This offered opportunities. Murph had kept the distant grass thick and tangled, so that things might be concealed. Once, Willie and Brodie both went tearing after a ball into right-center field. Brodie threw it back in to Robbie just as Willie flung a planted ball in. When the umpire reproved him, Willie stood there and grinned.

On the field Willie was ordinarily quiet and serious. His voice was rarely heard, other than, "I've got it." But baseball was a rough game, and the ballplayers—any ballplayer—took every advantage. Willie was impish about it. His teammates were less so. Each of them had his own way at the umpires. Willie was apologetic. Robbie would smile and kid them. Hughey would try to reason with them. Joe Kelley would scream. John McGraw would tread on toes and use vile language that Harry von der Horst worried the ladies might hear, which sometimes they did.

In the eighth inning of the last game of the season between the Orioles and the Giants, Mac was easily put out as he ran to first base. Yet he managed, as he crossed the bag, to veer several feet out of his way to gash the first baseman's leg. McGraw had taken to sharpening his spikes for his opponents to see.

"It was all done for its psychologic effect on the ballgame," McGraw explained. "But to make it good we'd go tearing into a bag with flying spikes as though with murderous intent. We were a cocky, swashbuckling crew and we wanted everybody to know it—and as a result we won a lot of our games before the first ball was ever pitched."

And win they did. They edged back into first place.

Labor Day had never been celebrated as a national holiday before, but in 'ninety-four, to help regain the workingman's trust in the depths of the depression, President Cleveland signed legislation that made the first Monday in September an official day off. The unions around Baltimore competed for the biggest delegation in the parade—the cigarmakers, the granite cutters, the glassblowers, the bakers, the blacksmiths, the Lithuanian tailors, and dozens more.

Labor's holiday, however, was as much for diversion as demonstration. The crowd was the largest ever to watch baseball in Baltimore. A seething mass of more than 24,000 cranks, not counting the unwashed who tore boards off the fence and sneaked in, overran Union Park to watch the Orioles host the Cleveland Spiders for a doubleheader. Fashion dictated that this was the last day that men might wear straw hats, and quite a few got knocked off in the mob. But their owners remained good-natured. They watched the Orioles overwhelm the Spiders, by 13 to 2 and (against the rosy-cheeked Cy Young) by 16 to 3. Willie struck six singles and a double in the two games. Joe Kelley came to bat nine times and got nine hits, five of them two-baggers. There was no stopping him. Kel was strong and swift and brimming with self-confidence. He was none too brilliant and he liked to imbibe from time to time. But scientific baseball did not really need intellectual firepower. It took quickness and competitiveness and a willingness to think and a passion for surprise. Those he had. Kel hit with power and could outrun an insult. In left field, the easiest of the outfield positions, he was deft as a unicyclist.

The Orioles went west. They had won thirteen in a row, the last twelve without Sadie McMahon, whose arm had gone lame. Still they kept winning, behind Kid Gleason and Charley Esper and now George Hemming, the former Louisville right-hander, with his thin face and his sly moustache and the unself-consciously arrogant look that Hanlon favored in his twirlers.

Everything clicked. The Orioles had speed, Willie and Kel most of all. "Why, he is so fast you can hardly follow him!" a young lady in the stands was heard to say of Willie. No one in the League could beat the left-handed batsman from home to first base. The team was running second in the League in stolen bases. In the field, they sparkled. Hughey Jennings was quickly coming to be considered the premier shortstop in the land. He got to grounders that no one else would have bothered to try for. Willie ranked second among the League's right fielders. Not since 'seventy-eight, when League ballclubs played half as many games, had a team made so few errors in a full season.

Even better was the batting. McGraw's had fallen off but Kelley's never flagged. The heaviest hitter on the ballclub, he batted .541 in the last thirty games of the season. Willie's average was climbing, too, as he often got three or four hits in a game. "Keeler had the best batting eye I have ever seen," McGraw judged many years later. "He held his bat away up in the middle with only about a foot of it extending beyond his hands and he could slap the ball to either field. It was impossible to play for him. I have seen the outfield come in behind the infield and the infielders close up till you'd think you couldn't have dropped the ball into an open spot if you had it in your hand—

but Keeler would invariably punch a base hit in there somewhere." Before the season was finished, the cranks speculated, Willie would overtake Kel as the team's top batsman.

Best of all was the Orioles' snap and ginger—"Get at 'em!" was Robbie's cry—and the way the ballplayers worked as one. When the season was over the same three outfielders had played side by side in all 129 games. McGraw claimed that he and Willie had practically revolutionized the style of hitting, so that advancing the runner became the new style of attack. The hit-and-run, the squeeze play, the Baltimore chop—base by base, they went at it, patiently, relentlessly, until they succeeded.

Willie had never had so much fun. "Say, I think I'm the luckiest guy in the world," he told his teammates. "I get paid for doing what I'd rather do than anything else—play ball."

As captain and catcher, Robbie ran the team on the field. But it was Hanlon's team. Every so often the manager called the ballplayers together and painstakingly pointed out each of their faults and offered pointers on some tactic of the game—how to execute a double steal, how to back one another up. In his remote and understated way, he could be heavy-handed. His attention to detail could get on his ballplayers' nerves. But more often than not, he applied just the right touch. He steadied Hughey's temperament and kept Steve Brodie's high spirits aimed not at the management or at his teammates but at the Orioles' opponents. The workouts with Joe Kelley had borne fruit as well.

The Orioles won their eighteenth consecutive game on the sixteenth of September, in the first of a Sunday doubleheader in Cincinnati. (Only in the West did baseball share the Lord's day.) In the second game, the Reds filled the bases in the first inning when the runners on first and second started to steal. Robbie ran the ball out into the infield—either man was a sure out. The runner on third base broke for home. Robbie did too—and slipped on the wet grass. Everybody was safe, and a run was home.

Two innings later, Reds on second and third tried again to steal. Robbie ran the ball toward third base, for an easy toss, and flung the ball into the mud at John McGraw's feet. Later in the inning the runner at third put the Reds ahead, 4 to 3.

With two outs in the last inning, the score unchanged, Joe Kelley hit his second two-bagger of the game. Willie Keeler came to bat. He had already hit a single and a double. Three thousand cranks squealed. On the Baltimore bench, hopes ran high. Willie stood with perfect attention, his bat concealed behind his thin, determined frame. He swung. A grounder dribbled ingloriously to the second baseman. The winning streak ended.

The next six games, the Orioles won.

The Giants, every bit as adamant, passed the Beaneaters and kept in the Orioles' shadow. The Orioles were undeterred. They went to Cleveland needing one more victory to clinch the pennant. They lost the first game, then prepared to face Cy Young the next afternoon. He remembered everyone's weakness and calmly, undemonstratively, took advantage.

Back in Baltimore the excitement ran high. "The success of the Baltimores is the greatest advertisement the town ever had," a grain merchant informed a wandering scribe. At Ford's Grand Opera House, at Fayette and Eutaw streets, where Horace Greeley had been nominated for the presidency back in 'seventy-two, hundreds of cranks crowded beneath the frescoes and chandeliers of the recently modernized theater to watch the Compton Electric Base-Ball Game Impersonator. Using an ingeniously constructed curtain that featured a diamond, movable figures and bells of different tones, the game from Cleveland was played out on Ford's eminent stage as the news of it flowed in by telegraph.

The game was a crackerjack. Though Cy Young had won two dozen games, all season the Orioles had found him an easy mark. Charley Esper, reluctant to throw his slow pitch, was hardly better. Going into the fourth inning the score stood 5 to 5. With one man out and another on base, Willie Keeler came to bat. In the first inning he had bunted and scored. This time Young threw just what Willie wanted. He drove the pitch to the farthest reach of right-center field. He raced around to home plate, and beat the throw.

When the twenty-seventh Spider was dispensed with, and the score stood 14 to 9, the Orioles flung themselves into one another's arms. They danced around the bat bags and howled. Hanlon cast his dilapidated straw hat, which he had promised to wear until the championship was won, to the winds.

At Ford's Grand Opera House pandemonium broke loose. Hats were flung toward the rafters. Harry von der Horst pranced across the stage, waving an orange-and-black pennant. In silver letters it proclaimed: *Champions, 1894.*

*   *   *

The shouts awakened the ballplayers, asleep on the train. It was five in the morning but a crowd had gathered at the railway station in Grafton, in the dour hills of West Virginia.

"Jennings! Jennings!" the men chanted. They were coal miners, as Hughey had been.

The train was not permitted to continue on its way to Baltimore until the finest shortstop on earth popped his sunburnt, carrot-topped head out through a window, into the dawning day.

Farther east along the Baltimore & Ohio track, past the rocky cliffs, in the hamlets of Oakland and Piedmont, the throngs of cranks called Oriole after Oriole to the platform.

The pennant winners stopped for breakfast in Cumberland, in the mountains of western Maryland. It seemed as if every man, woman, and child in the town had turned out. Shout after shout went up as the Orioles descended from the train. Everything was decorated in black and orange. The ballplayers wore their sharp new black sweaters with orange piping as they forced their way through the crowd. At the Queen City Hotel, a banner over the porch declared: "Cumberland Welcomes the Champions. Get at 'em!"

A thirty-piece band struck up "Maryland, My Maryland." Inside the hotel, as the Orioles ate, the ladies of Cumberland filed in to watch. They marveled at what a handsome fellow McMahon was and wondered which one was Brouthers and which was Robinson. The prying eyes made Willie and McGraw, the youngest of the Orioles, lose a little of their appetites.

As the team re-emerged into the morning, the cranks of Cumberland outside the hotel hollered: "Hanlon! Hanlon!" And then: "Speech! Speech!"

The quiet manager removed his hat. "Ladies and gentlemen of Cumberland," he began. "In behalf of the Baltimore baseball club I thank you for this hearty and unexpected greeting." He promised that the Orioles would play a game in Cumberland, once they had defeated the Giants for the Temple Cup, in the postseason series to come. He was presented with a colossal glass bat filled with ten-year-old rye, which Hanlon vowed not to drink for another ten years.

The ballplayers crooned a ballad written for them, "We'll Hang Johnny Ward from a Sour Apple Tree." The crowd went wild.

An escort committee of twenty distinguished Baltimoreans—ten had not sufficed—met the train in Washington. The crowd was already gathering in Baltimore, at Camden Station, the turreted brick terminus of the B&O, the nation's oldest commercial railroad.

The train was due in at 6:35 on a Tuesday evening, the second of October. By five o'clock some five thousand cranks had gathered. This had grown to twenty-five thousand by five-thirty and to fifty thousand by half past six. Darkness had fallen. When the rooters realized that buying a ticket to any destination earned a place on the railway platform, there was a surge of interest in short trips to the suburbs. Young men climbed the poles in the station and out along the rafters over the track.

Cheers went up when the headlight of a locomotive came into sight. The train arrived three minutes early—snap and ginger, indeed. Fireworks went off inside the station. Outside, the throngs heard it and set off a din such as the city had never known.

The new champions could barely edge their way onto the platform. A fife and drum corps of forty boys led the Orioles, in their uniforms, through the station. The crowds parted to let the players through to their carriages, then immediately closed up again, stranding the reception committee and the newspapermen. It took the policemen an hour to untangle the mob and get the parade moving toward the Fifth Regiment Armory.

It was the grandest parade that Baltimore had ever seen. More than two hundred thousand people came out for it—almost half the city. The route was impassable, until cops on horseback cleared a lane through the pulsating crowd. In front of City Hall, a father lugged his baby boy up a tall lamppost to peer down on the Orioles as they passed.

"The procession itself was part parade, part masquerade, part a mounted cavalcade and part a show of celebrities," *The Sun* discerned. Sauerwald's Band and Drum Corps marched in front, followed by the carriages bearing the ballplayers and the reception committee. Small boys swarmed twenty deep around their heroes, ignoring the danger from hoofs and carriage wheels to gaze with unutterable admiration into the face of whichever Oriole they worshiped. The last carriage bore the ball used in the pennant-clinching game.

The majesty of the parade came from what followed the carriages. Anyone who wanted to could march. Two hundred groups had signed up, including the Married and Single Men Base-Ball Club, the Baltimore City College class of 'ninety-seven, the Fifth-Ward Jolly Six Rooters (on a decorated float), the Mercantile Club (with three floats), the

Night Owls' Union, the Adonis Pleasure Club (with a band), the East Branch YMCA barrel wagon, the Station B letter-carriers (in evening dress), the William H. Newmyer Yacht Club, the Madison Square 'Cycle Club, and so on. The parade included sophisticated men in silk hats and hogs wrapped in orange and black. Participants rode on decorated wagons, hired hacks, drays, glossy barouches, sand-carts, and the backs of horses. A precocious fourteen-year-old named Henry L. Mencken rode in the parade with his brother Charlie and the Lürssen boys next door.

The parade went on for miles. The tail end of it was just uncoiling at Camden Station as the ballplayers completed their circuitous route around downtown and out Howard street to the armory. The arched metal roof surrounded by medieval stone sheltered the largest hall in the city. The mayor and the governor and almost twenty thousand rooters waited.

The pennant, five feet high at the pole and twenty-five feet wide, hung across the front of the cavernous hall. "Champion Base Ball Club of the United States," it announced in red, white, and blue. "BALTIMORE 1894."

Ferdinand Latrobe, the portly seven-term mayor, declared, "We have always had the most beautiful women and the finest oysters in the world, and now we have the best baseball club."

The Orioles survived the speeches and went on to a banquet at the Hotel Rennert, at Saratoga and Liberty streets. Ugly on the outside and charming within, the Rennert was Baltimore's finest hotel. Three hundred fanatics filled the airy, elegant dining room, to fete the champions by indulging in the Rennert's oysters—famed worldwide—along with duck and crab croquettes and champagne.

The ballplayers, at the center table, looked less than comfortable: They had donned evening dress, which many of them had borrowed. Captain Robbie rose from his seat and raised his empty champagne flute into the air. "Glasses up," he ordered, looking around at his men—"and now glasses down!"

Mindful of the Temple Cup Series ahead, he placed his glass upside down on the table. His teammates did the same, and the crowd hailed them.

As the bottles of champagne passed from table to table, too many of the ballplayers cast a longing glance.

*   *   *

The two messengers reverently carried a tin copy of the Temple Cup onto the floor of the low, domed Corn and Flour Exchange. The real Temple Cup, made of silver on an onyx base, was on display in New York. Still, the grain merchants stopped their trading for a moment and cheered. The overdecorated trophy had a fluted spout and ornately wrought handles and the embossed figure of a ballplayer ready to throw. William Temple, the urbane owner of the Pittsburgh Pirates, had donated the cup for a seven-game postseason series between the pennant winners and the runners-up. The idea had come to him after Pittsburgh had finished second in 'ninety-three.

The series was to start at Union Park two days after the Orioles returned. But by then they were in no shape to play, as the players soon failed to heed Robbie's injunction at the Rennert dinner. Invitations poured in from admirers; few were turned down. The ballplayers were wined and dined to exhaustion. "If I could only get five minutes' rest," one of the more popular Orioles was heard to complain.

Spirits, the liquid sort, was not what had thrown the series into doubt, however. It was money—how to divide the receipts. William Temple understood what motivated men. He had allotted 65 percent of the ticket receipts (after expenses) to the winning team and 35 percent to the losers—all of it for the ballplayers, he pointed out, and none for the owners.

To the Orioles, such proportions would not do. Temple had once been quoted—or misquoted—in a Pittsburgh newspaper saying that the pennant winners, not the series winners, would get 65 percent. The Orioles had spent six arduous months capturing the pennant. Why should they get so little if they lost four games? They insisted on at least an even split. Fifty-fifty was fine with the Giants: Ned Hanlon and Johnny Ward shook hands on it.

William Temple refused. He feared that a series with no incentive would prove a farce. The money must be divided as he wanted, he warned, or "Baltimore has forfeited the right to play for the cup." The ballplayers murmured about making private arangements, pairing up to split the money evenly.

When the teams took the field, nobody knew if it was for the opening of the Temple Cup Series or for an exhibition game. That was part of the reason barely ten thousand cranks showed up—that and the ominous clouds and the decision by Baltimore's management to double the ticket prices.

John McGraw was the last holdout. Five minutes before the game was to start, Robbie and a half-dozen Orioles surrounded him fifteen feet behind the pitching rubber. The Giants' quietly spectacular third baseman, George Davis, had approached him at the Eutaw House that morning with a private offer of a fifty-fifty split. Keeler and Kelley and Gleason had agreed to the same arrangement, but Mac still refused. He broke away from the huddle and crossed to third base. As a lucrative series was on the brink of becoming a single exhibition, Robbie shot him a look of disgust that no one who saw it would ever forget.

They coaxed Mac back and just as the gong was sounding he gave in. He called George Davis over.

"That agreement goes, George," McGraw said.

"It does."

Mac invited Joe Kelley in from left field as a witness. Dirty Jack Doyle, the Giants' first baseman, came over and offered Kel the same deal. Kel said he had already paired up with Amos Rusie but would get Willie Keeler to go in with Doyle, which he did.

Robbie strode to the grandstand. "We play the series," he announced.

The Orioles batted first, against Amos Rusie. Willie Keeler poked a pitch to left field. Two batters later he was thrown out at home plate.

Then Rusie shut Baltimore down. The dampness of the day helped his grip, so he made the most of his speed. The Giants, with something to prove, played with determination. In four consecutive innings, they scored a run.

The Orioles looked sharp in black and orange, but they were listless. Nary a Baltimore runner had crossed the plate when John McGraw opened the ninth with a single past third base. Two batters later, his daring baserunning found him crossing the plate. Then Hughey Jennings hit a slow roller to third and, as everyone could see, beat the throw to first.

The umpire called him out.

The Orioles kicked and kicked, to no avail. They were certain that the umpires—two, for such a series—favored New York. Even a Giants coach confided his amazement.

One batsman later, the Giants had won the first game.

Clearly this series was a matchup between pitching and hitting. Every regular in Baltimore's lineup had batted better than .300 for the season. The Giants' pitchers, Rusie and Meekin, were the best pair in the League.

Yet that was not the matchup that mattered the most. One team had a reason to win. The other one—its three best players, especially—did not.

The tension erupted before the second game began. The Giants were warming up at Union Park as the cranks wandered around the outfield when Eddie Burke, the little left fielder, suddenly hurled a baseball—as hard as he could, a witness said afterward—at a young man's face. A hundred men and boys crowded in on the outfielder until the police drove them off.

The game had its thrills. For the Orioles some of the vigor was back. As the ninth inning started, with the score 5 to 5, the Giants' leadoff batter tapped a good-natured ground ball to Hughey Jennings. As he made ready to scoop it up, the ball struck a pebble and bounced over his head. After another Giant got on base, Eddie Burke hit an easy bounder to Hughey. The shortstop needed only to touch second base, a step away, and throw to first. But he started to move before the ball was in his hand.

A moment later another Giant cleared the bases with a triple. The Temple Cup Series suddenly stood at two games to none.

As the Giants climbed onto their horse-drawn omnibus, with its wagon wheels and open sides, Eddie Burke was nearly hit by a flying piece of brick.

More than twenty thousand New Yorkers thronged the Polo Grounds two afternoons later. Amos Rusie pitched. Neither team scored an earned run. The Orioles made more errors and lost again, 4 to 1.

The Orioles took an early lead the next afternoon. Suddenly the game became a burlesque. Joe Kelley made three errors, and the twirlers were mutton pie. The Giants ran the bases at will. The pennant winners looked like tailenders. To lose 16 to 3—it was humiliating.

"Baltimore's in the Cold, Cold Ground," the crowd of ten thousand sang. The Temple Cup was New York's.

Each Giant's share came to $768, each Oriole's to $360. Amos Rusie was a gentleman. Before leaving for Indiana he left $200 for Joe Kelley. The other Giants welshed. Jack Doyle denied that he and Willie Keeler had agreed to anything.

Nick Young, the League's president, assured anyone who asked that the Orioles, having won the pennant, were truly the champions. But he had to keep saying so.

= 5 =

The Big Four

Shortly before midnight someone shouted, "Fire!" The cry awakened Murph, the groundskeeper, in his cottage on the Union Park grounds. He opened his eyes and saw a dazzling sheet of flame.

The wind was so still on the bitter cold night that the flames shot straight up. They came from the corner of the double-deck grandstand, out the first base line. People popped out of their beds on Huntingdon avenue and on Barclay street and even along Calvert street, a block away. The fire's glow could be seen all over the city.

Murph tried frantically to halt the march of the flames. He shouted for help. A policeman ran to a corner and called in an alarm.

By the time the fire engines galloped through the acrid smell of the smoke, there was little to be saved. In less than twenty minutes the grandstand had become a smoking ruin that creaked and crackled and fell to the ground. The firemen sprayed the third base end of the stands, to protect the row houses across Barclay street. Only the bleachers and the ticket office were spared.

Murph, his face dirtied by the flames, growled in the dark to a newspaperman, "The stands were burned as the result of a conspiracy." The day before he had turned out some tramps seeking shelter under the grandstand. Later he found a smoldering fire of newspapers and kindling and straw. After extinguishing them he had gone to tell Hanlon, who lived in a narrow brick row house on Calvert street, close enough to the ballpark for his young children to lie in bed on a humid night and listen to the crowd. Hanlon had not been at home.

He and Wilbert Robinson had gone to the theater. On their way home they saw the fire. They looked on in despair. "We were about to put more insurance on," Hanlon moaned. It was not the first time he had seen a ballpark reduced to ashes. The stands in Boston had burned to the ground while the Orioles were playing there the previous spring. Then the stands in Chicago and Philadelphia burned down on consecutive summer days.

The loss at Union Park was put at $12,000, of which $7,500 was insured. Hanlon and Harry von der Horst made it known that they were willing to rebuild someplace else in Baltimore, if a streetcar company happened to see an attractive investment.

The Orioles had finished the sort of season most owners only dream of. The new 'ninety-five season was getting off to an ominous start.

It was human nature to want a piece of such conspicuous success. The first hint showed up in Willie Keeler's letter to the *Morning Herald*. It came after he described how he was keeping in condition over the winter, first by hunting and skating out on Long Island for a few weeks and then, back in Brooklyn, working with light dumbbells and going for long walks. "So you see it won't take very much training to get me in condition to 'Get at 'em,'" he wrote. "I never felt better in my life."

And, oh yes, he had heard from Joe Kelley, "stating he was doing a big business, and that he did not know whether he would play baseball this coming season or not."

Then Joe Kelley wrote. He was in business with his brother in Cambridge, moving goods by horse-drawn dray. "We have had a prosperous winter when everyone else was yelling for work, and I am, to use a baseball phrase, on Easy Street at present." As to his plans for next season, he professed not to know.

The purpose behind the artful ambivalence soon became clear. By the middle of February, Ned Hanlon's mail started filling up with contracts, signatures affixed. Bill Clarke and Henny Reitz signed, then three of the twirlers. So did Robbie, who was practically part of the management. Dan Brouthers, almost thirty-seven, fell in line after Hanlon showed him a photograph of George Carey, the strapping young first baseman the Orioles had discovered in Ohio.

But four contracts had not arrived, from the players the newspapers were starting to call the Big Four. Twice before, baseball had known a Big Four. The first one included Al Spalding, on the White Stockings in

'seventy-six. Late in the 'eighties came the quartet of Detroit Wolverines, featuring Dan Brouthers. Both Spalding and Brouthers were big,
but in neither case had the reference been to size. It had connoted the
core of a team that had arrived as a unit from another ballclub.

None of this latest Big Four had come to the Baltimore ballclub
with any other. Nor did any of them stand very tall. Joe Kelley, the only
one with any real heft, was just five-eleven. Hughey Jennings was five
feet, eight-and-a-half inches, John McGraw was five-seven, and Willie
was five-four and perhaps a smidgen more. Yet they were the core of the
team. All four were Irish and scrappy and ready to laugh. They were
friends, who all played the same way. On the diamond and off, they had
learned to work as one. They prayed together every Sunday at St. Ann's
Church, a somber stone house of God on the York road, three blocks
south of Union Park. On the road, they would gather after supper and
visit some of the girls they knew in most of the cities around the
League. (Willie and Hughey would double-date.) All of them, and Robbie and Brodie too, belonged to the Maryland Yacht Club.

None of the Big Four had signed a contract, and Hanlon had not
heard a word. He suspected it was purposeful, that they were working
as a combine, with McGraw (as usual) at the center of things. McGraw,
back at St. Bonaventure's with Hughey, denied it. But surely Hanlon
was right. "The question that is always uppermost in a ballplayer's
mind after winning a pennant arose," McGraw confessed decades later.
"We wanted more money."

And why not? The Orioles had made as much as $50,000 in win-
ning the pennant. The attendance had more than doubled—tripled,
since 'ninety-two. Had the cranks come to see Harry von der Horst?
Or Ned Hanlon? The ballplayers wanted what they were worth.

How could they not think well of themselves? Joe Kelley had batted an astonishing .393. Kel could do anything—hit with power, drop a
beautiful bunt, speed along the basepaths, chase down a fly ball. Willie
batted a sparkling .371, scoring 165 runs in 129 games. An amateur
nine in Baltimore called themselves the Young Keelers. Jennings had
had a cigar named after him—Our Hughey.

Hanlon had offered each of them a raise of something like $500,
on top of the $1,500 they had been paid in 'ninety-four, and he was
not about to budge. Would they not be earning five times as much in
six months as a factory worker made in a year? To the scribes Hanlon
professed unconcern. He made it plain that he would take a team of
amateurs to Macon before he paid a penny more to the Big Four.

The Baltimore newspapermen saw it his way. With Hanlon they always did, apparently the price of securing the inside skinny. "Players should remember that the profits of last season by no means recouped the magnates for the losses of the years before," one of the scribes opined in a news article. "Baseball is a business, and must be carried on on business principles."

The holdout continued into March. When Hanlon arrived at the Fifth Avenue Hotel for the meeting of the magnates, Willie came over from Brooklyn and Kel took a train down from Boston. They haggled with Hanlon over another $100 or $200. He reminded them he had offered raises without being asked and had no intention of paying them more.

Afterward, Joe Kelley was seen downing thirteen drinks at the grand hotel's long mahogany bar.

The struggle between Hanlon and his four stars was all the talk in the saloons and barbershops around Baltimore. Over many a lager the argument raged. Losing the Big Four would leave a sickening hole in the team. But why should they be paid so handsomely for playing a game?

Just before the team left for Macon, Hanlon issued an ultimatum. The night before the scheduled departure, a letter from Hughey arrived. He and McGraw had agreed to the manager's terms. Mac had wired Kelley already.

Willie and Kelley got to Baltimore the next afternoon and went to confer with Hanlon. He made them wait.

"Players always hold out at this time of the year and try to get all they can," Hanlon had started to learn. "There isn't one case out of one hundred where players fail to report when the time comes."

A hundred cranks sledded that night through the snow and mud to watch the Orioles off at Camden Station. As the champions poured onto the platform and boarded their Pullman, the crowd pressed toward the railing. Nary a cheer went up, not even the semblance of one.

Ned Hanlon caught a train back to Baltimore as soon as the League magnates adjourned. He understood that Harry von der Horst would do a little business in New York and then come home.

That was on Saturday. Harry failed to show up on Monday or on Tuesday or for the rest of the week. Nor did he send word. His family and his friends became alarmed. He had given his address as the St. James' Hotel but he had never registered there. They wired him at his usual haunts around New York, to no reply.

A second week found him still missing. A search party set out, made up of three men who needed him. His brother John had some urgent business regarding their father's estate. John Waltz had decisions to make about the brewery. Hanlon, preparing for a baseball season, needed Harry's signature and money.

It was no surprise that Ned Hanlon and Harry von der Horst had been on difficult terms. They were vastly different men. Harry was a man of luxury and impulse, who treated others as his private preserve. Hanlon calculated to the penny. But it was more than that. Hanlon had ample reason for wrath. The money he had invested in the ballclub in exchange for a fourth of the stock had been structured as a loan but understood to be a sale. When the value of the stock was thought to have doubled in 'ninety-four because of the success that Hanlon had wrought, Harry insisted on repaying the money and reclaiming his stock. That Hanlon stayed (and succeeded in regaining a share in the ballclub) was a measure of his ambition.

But Harry was every bit as greedy with his own family—or whatever Lena was. A judge in Baltimore had named Harry and his two lawyers as receivers, to run the brewery for the estate, and in their wisdom they agreed to sell the brewery and its belongings—to Harry and his brother, for $75,000. Harry might have found it a propitious time to make himself scarce.

"Colluded . . . fraud . . . their own personal benefit"—Lena and her lawyers flung these accusations in court. Lena also waved around the deed of trust that Harry and his wife, Emma, had signed, as evidence that neither brother had been a partner in the brewery when their father died.

The battle kept getting more bitter. Harry sued Lena over jewelry and a sealskin coat that had belonged to his mother. Lena produced a lawyer with an unidentified client willing to pay $100,000 for the brewery and the land. Evidently the offer was genuine, because it was only two or three days later that Harry was found.

He would say only that he had been visiting friends in New York and Newark and that he had not known he was missing until the newspapers said so. Days after his return to Baltimore, he and his brother agreed to pay Lena $100,000 for her third of the estate.

Then he vanished again.

And then he got sued again, this time by his wife. Emma had been beautiful once and in her high-collared way she still was. When she set her mind to something she would not be deterred. She had given her husband every opportunity but he had deserted her again, she petitioned the court, without making "any provision whatever" for the financial support of his wife and two daughters. "He is of convivial habits and unfortunately given to dissipation and lavish expenditures," she charged. "Since upon the death of his late father, he came into possession of his estate, he has spent and wasted large sums of money." Without prompt action, she feared, "his large patrimony will be squandered."

The court issued a subpoena for Harry to appear. He ignored it. A second subpoena carried a deadline of the second Monday in March.

But a few days before that, tragedy struck, among the innocents. John's wife, Mary, had been stricken with pneumonia, as had John and one of their young sons. The son recovered, but Mary grew worse. She had been sick for fourteen days when she died.

John was too sick to be told. Six hours after her burial, he too succumbed, at the age of forty-one. In the course of a few days, their children—thirteen, twelve, and nine—had become orphans.

Suddenly Harry was back. He and his lawyers were named as the administrators of John's estate. A bank was appointed as the orphans' guardian.

They would need one.

Harry had one more problem to fix. He and his lawyers dickered with Emma and her lawyers. At last they agreed to a financial settlement. Soon Emma delivered a four-word demand to the clerk of the court: "Enter this case dismissed."

Harry's father was dead. His brother was dead. He had bought off his half-sister. Harry would soon be living in New York, apart from his wife. At last he was free to do whatever he liked.

Union Park was rebuilt, in the same location. But the 'ninety-five season started poorly enough, as if the Orioles' cockiness had turned in on them. For one thing, resentment lingered against the Big Four. Even Henny Reitz, who hardly ever said anything, had told the newspapers the holdout was a mistake. There were accusations that the foursome was hampering the team. The newspapers suggested a diagnosis: swelled heads.

Soon the Orioles sank into seventh place, then into eighth. The pitching was awful. It had been almost April before Sadie McMahon could even raise his right arm above his shoulder. How could the Orioles win without him? The other twirlers were duds. They showed little ambition without being pushed. Instead of using them in regular rotation, Hanlon waited until he watched the twirlers practice in the morning before deciding who would pitch.

All spring the Orioles mixed brilliant baseball with sudden, unaccountable lapses. Injuries hurt. Reitz broke his collarbone and Kid Gleason took his place at second base. John McGraw split his hand and was stricken with malaria. Dan Brouthers was not what he had been. On three occasions in an early game against the Trolley Dodgers, Willie Keeler stood on third base with Brouthers at the bat and three times finished the inning there.

When Big Dan's wife fell sick back in Wappingers Falls, up the Hudson from New York, the burly first baseman went home. He was barely gone when the newspapers started speculating he was not coming back. It was obvious who had planted the story. One of Hanlon's secrets was his preternatural feel for when a ballplayer was about to blossom—or wilt.

It was not in Hanlon's nature to wait. Within days he had sold the veteran—his longtime teammate in Detroit, his compatriot in the Brotherhood and the Players' League—to the Louisville Colonels for $500. Only belatedly, and bitterly, did Brouthers report.

The simple wood-planked dressing room at Union Park was squeezed between the right field foul line and the fence, across the two-plank bridge that spanned the drainage ditch. Inside, it was dimly lit. Two clotheslines stretched the length of it, with uniforms and sweaters bringing them low. Along the benches in front of the lockers, sweaty men peeled off padded uniforms. Willie Keeler and Joe Kelley helped each other out of their bloomers.

The Big Four was more like two large twos. Keeler and Kelley could always be found in each other's company. They were an unlikely looking pair, so brawny and so small, like a protector and an innocent, who formed a whole. Both were city boys, and happy with their lot.

Not that Hughey Jennings and John McGraw were gloomy. They were from isolated towns and had led hard lives. They were driven— desperate—in a way that Willie and Kel were not. Mac and Hughey had taken rooms together on Twenty-fourth street, in a dingy brick row house the first block west of Charles street. That was where the Big Four now put their heads together at night. McGraw was not easy to live with. Everything had to be his way. That was fine with Hughey. He was so cheerful, so accommodating, evidently so loved as a child, he could get along with practically anyone. Because of their dissimilar temperaments they could share quarters.

McGraw was throwing water over himself in the vast bathtub that stood to the left of the dressing room door. He shared it with Robbie and Steve Brodie and Kid Gleason.

"Talk about your porpoises," Robbie shouted—"watch me!" Then with a splash he disappeared.

When the fat captain resurfaced he sloshed water at Willie and Kel, who had wandered over. "Just look pleasant awhile," Robbie yelled out with a laugh. "It's 'you're next.' The bases are full."

The camaraderie had salvaged the 'ninety-five season. "A band of comrades, all fond of one another and working in a game like one man"—that was what Hughey called the Orioles. "There have been— and are—stronger individual players, but such teamwork will probably never be seen again."

"Teamwork was our middle name; everything had to give way to that," John McGraw remembered. "The great thing about that team was that every one of us, individually, felt that it belonged to us."

The Big Four had improved in their play by a third since the 'ninety-four season. Or so Hanlon said at one of the team meetings. That would hardly have endeared the foursome further to their team-mates, except that they knew Hanlon was speaking the truth.

Willie Keeler was hard not to root for, because in a way he was the heart of the team. He ran perceptibly faster than last year and could place the ball (or so it seemed) wherever he liked. He would take a short quick chop at the ball or occasionally swing with his forearms. If the infielders stayed back, he could bunt; if they came in, he could poke it over their heads. He practiced constantly and probed any pitcher he faced. "Every boxman has a weakness just as every batsman has," he noted, "and when you know what that weakness is you can generally get good results from it."

And he was wise enough to believe not only in science but also in luck. "I have never been able to find out what is the cause of a weak batting streak," he told a newspaperman in the wake of a slump. "There have been times when I could not hit the ball safe to save my life. My eye was clear and I picked out good balls just the same as when I was hitting safely, but no matter how hard I hit the ball, it went straight to some fielder.

"Then, after a spell of this sort, lasting two or three days, I would again get the ball safe, although I did not change my method of hitting it."

When the League published the batting averages near the end of June, Willie led the list, at .418. "To think that so small a man as Keeler should lead all the League sluggers!" *Sporting Life* marveled. "Truly it is the eye and not the size." The newspapers had started to call him "Wee Willie," with the rhythm and sound of the nursery rhyme:

Wee Willie Winkie ran through the town,
Upstairs, downstairs, in his nightgown.

If Willie was the heart of the Orioles, John McGraw was the family jewels. He was pugnacious; once he asked the umpire if he could see the ball and rolled it under the grandstand. He hated it when opponents and needling scribes called him "Muggsy"—the name of a tramp on the funny pages—and so, of course, they did. His intensity could be alarming. In an important game against the Senators, with the Orioles behind 6 to 5 in the ninth inning, Mac came to the plate with runners on second and third and two men out. He faced the pitcher with a confident air, waited for the right pitch, met it firmly, and drove both men home. Only after the game, as he stepped up into the omnibus, did he start to tremble. He cried bitterly and shook as if he were suffering from the ague. His nerves had snapped.

The Orioles were hard on themselves and harder on their opponents. "Even when the ball beat him to second by twenty feet," backup catcher Bill Clarke said of McGraw, "his mind would be sorting over arguments to give the umpire—while his feet aimed for the ball in the baseman's hand."

The Baltimore boys had been getting a name for themselves. The times were rough-and-tumble and the national game was, too. In 'ninety-four and again in 'ninety-five, the Orioles competed with Cleveland and Boston for recognition as the rowdiest nine in the League. They gloried in it. McGraw became known for holding baserunners by the belt (until one of them unloosened it and ran home). Or when *he* was a baserunner, he would cut in front of second base when the umpire's back was turned. One afternoon, when Tim Keefe, now an umpire, ejected Hughey from a ballgame, McGraw shouted, "Look here, old man, you sent out for a bottle yesterday."

"I was sick," Keefe yelled back.

"Drunk, you mean."

Steve Brodie once pulled off an umpire's mask and cap. McGraw and Jennings and Kelley would surround a man in blue and walk him backward all over the diamond. One afternoon, playing in Boston, Joe Kelley became incensed at an umpire who had called him out at second base. The umpire ejected him, then pulled out a pocketwatch and gave him one minute to leave the field. Kelley slapped the watch out of the umpire's hand and kicked it around.

"Now that will cost you twenty-five dollars, and the watch will cost you a hundred dollars," the umpire said.

"You're crazy if you think that three-dollar Waterbury of yours is worth anything like that," Kel shot back.

"It's not my watch—it's yours." For it was the pocketwatch that Kelley's admirers from Cambridge had given him before the game, which Kel had put in the keep of a clubhouse attendant who had gone on an errand and left it in the umpire's care.

"I think Mr. Kelley is the handsomest man on the Baltimore team," a sweet young thing in a red bonnet cooed before a game in Boston. But after he had kicked once or twice at the umpire, she changed her mind.

In Louisville, Hanlon met with his players and warned them to stop kicking so much, in hopes of stanching the flow of expulsions and twenty-five-dollar fines. But he exerted only so much influence over the strong personalities he had painstakingly assembled. Hanlon let the players set their own curfews on the road and run their own plays on the diamond. He had sought ballplayers with opinions of their own, and they liked playing for him.

And in truth, the rowdiness worked. The Orioles got runs that way. McGraw was right about how to intimidate opponents. It also filled up the grandstands—the bleachers, at least.

All during July and into August the Orioles bounced in and out of first place, often trading places with the Cleveland Spiders. Having Sadie McMahon back helped. Hanlon had run into him on a street corner downtown.

"What's the matter, Ed, you look downhearted," the winged right-hander said.

"I am, Mac," Hanlon replied. "I'm afraid they've got us licked."

"Don't worry. I'm ready to go to work now and I'll win you that championship."

"Mac, that's the best news I've heard."

And it was. A magician with his curveball and his change of pace, Sadie McMahon twirled three shutouts in a row. And the Orioles kept winning. They had swept fourteen straight games when they edged the Spiders from first place.

Baltimore was barely two games ahead when the Spiders came into Union Park the second week of September. The team had earned its name from the players' spindly physiques, and they were a mean match for the Orioles—rowdy, with a dirtier edge. Patsy Tebeau, the manager and first baseman, set the tone. At the bat he held his own—he batted .318 for the 'ninety-five season—but he was a brawler and a bully. His cartoonishly round, almost featureless face bore an intimidating glare. More than once, he had been arrested for his antics on the field.

"Show me a team of fighters," Tebeau said, "and I'll show you a team that has a chance."

The Orioles were on edge—they had everything to lose. Hughey lost the first game when he let a ground ball hit his knee. He had a hand in winning the second game when he and Willie slashed pitches from Cy Young past Tebeau at first.

Hanlon had said that Charley Esper would probably pitch the next afternoon, with the season on the line. But when he entered the club-house before the game and the men asked him who would pitch, Hanlon replied, "The best man we've got. This game is very important and we need it."

Sadie McMahon was sitting over in the corner. "Want me to pitch?" he said quietly.

"Yes," Hanlon answered, "if you feel like it."

"Well, then," the twirler said, "I'll pitch." Since his return he had pitched just about every second game.

Eighteen more nervous ballplayers had never taken the field. Seventeen, that is. Sadie McMahon, for all his fierceness, was calm as a dreamless sleep. In eight innings, before darkness fell, he gave up just a solitary hit.

In the sixth inning Patsy Tebeau blew apart. He went into a rage at an umpire's call to award an Oriole an extra base, until he was unceremoniously hustled from the diamond. The strain on the Orioles showed up in the field—McGraw could hardly throw across the diamond from third base—but they were their most scientific at the bat. McGraw's base on balls and stolen base inspired Willie's single, then Hughey's, followed by Joe Kelley's immaculate sacrifice bunt. Steve Brodie's fly ball sent Willie rushing home.

The victory was clinched. So was the season.

Before the Temple Cup Series started at League Park, in the rowdiest section of Cleveland, the local newspapers ripped into Hanlon for suggesting that the western clubs had thrown games to the Spiders. The Cleveland cranks came prepared. With tin horns and cow bells they kept up a frightful din. The respectable people were not to be found. Young toughs from the city of smokestacks seated themselves all over the stands. In their pockets they carried potatoes and stones.

For the Orioles, losing the Temple Cup the previous October still rankled. It had brought them nothing but ridicule, and tarnished the glory of having captured the pennant. The cup itself, on its onyx stand, had rested all season in the oversized safe that belonged to Andrew Freedman, the Tammany Hall man who had bought a controlling interest in the Giants. The Orioles wanted it.

So did the Clevelanders, who had the means at hand. While catching a high foul fly, Robbie got pelted. Flying vegetables and minerals hit McGraw in the head and dealt Kid Gleason a lump the size of a hen's egg. The few policemen in the stands stood by.

Anything went. When Sadie McMahon faced Cy Young, every advantage counted. In the eighth inning, with the Orioles a run ahead, one of the Spiders lofted a fly ball out to Joe Kelley. Patsy Tebeau, on second base, had been egging the crowd on. Suddenly a dozen cranks leapt from their seats and rushed onto the field, straight at Kelley. He evaded them and caught the ball. His pursuers surrounded him and flung their coats in his face, to stop him from throwing to third base. As the policemen serenely looked on, Tebeau scored.

The umpire sent him back to second base. He scored anyway. Sadie McMahon weakened, and the Spiders won.

The next afternoon a beer bottle just missed Kel's head. Cranks threw seat cushions and tin horns at McGraw as he caught a foul fly. The Spiders won again. Afterward, anyone wearing orange and black was whacked with clods of filth.

The Spiders won the next game as well, on the merits. The violence might have angered the Orioles. Instead it made them listless. Or maybe Cy Young did, for he stymied them all. Willie Keeler had had a wonderful season, having batted .377. He had always hit well against the rawboned right-hander. But today he went hitless.

A subdued crowd met the Orioles at Camden Station. The city authorities urged the cranks to exercise more restraint than the Clevelanders had, to show Baltimore as the genteel city it surely still was. The cranks were quick to reply. As the Spiders left their hotel they were pounded with eggs and rotten apples. At Union Park, potatoes and pieces of brick came flying from the stands. After the Orioles had won—their first victory in eight Temple Cup games—the Spiders piled into their open-sided omnibus. They had not left Huntingdon avenue when the rocks and bricks and clumps of dirt and a chunk of slag as big as a fist came raining down. The mob held the heads of the horses and tried to cut the harnesses, until the policemen and the squealing animals pushed their way through. The Spiders hid on the floor of the omnibus, their mitts and bat bags over their heads. "There is not a man in the party who has not more or less bruises and bumps, none serious, and the men are delighted that they are yet alive," wrote the scribe from the Cleveland *Plain Dealer*, who had lain buried under a half-dozen Spiders.

The Spiders seemed not to mind. The next afternoon, with two men out in the ninth inning, they were leading, 5 to 1, when McGraw and Keeler drew bases on balls and Hughey Jennings was hit by a pitch. The crowd stiffened with anticipation. Was Cy Young, twirling his third game of the five, tiring at last?

Kel hit a sharp one, which the shortstop fumbled, and McGraw crossed the plate. Steve Brodie came to the bat, as Willie edged away from third base. A double or a triple would tie the game. Young, the impassive giant, all 210 pounds of him, reared back. Wee Willie Keeler crept forward.

Brodie swung, and dribbled the pitch back to the twirler. The Orioles had been crushed in the Temple Cup Series once again.

*　　　*　　　*

O. P. Caylor waited for Willie Keeler and Joe Kelley to come back up to the baroquely decorated box, even as the curtain was rising on the final scene. The sharp-tongued *Sporting Life* columnist had invited them to share the velvet splendor of the American Theatre on a December evening to watch *A Runaway Colt* on the third night of its Broadway run. The two Orioles had ventured backstage to pay their respects to Cap Anson, who was playing himself as the star of Charles Hoyt's latest farce.

It had even a less plausible plot than the popular playwright's usual successes—something about how a bank cashier meant to win the hand of a secret heiress by bribing Anson to lose the game (and thus the pennant) to the Orioles. The fair-skinned slugger and his boys turned out to be everything good and the Orioles were otherwise. "Can Anson act?" Caylor had written after catching the debut up in Syracuse. "Can a cat swim? Can a duck catch mice?"

As the curtain went up, all nine Orioles were swarming around the umpire, kicking about a double play that had retired Keeler and Kelley. The chief kicker's face looked somehow familiar, and there was a wondrous realism in his stage work, so ably backed up by a little fellow with a peaked face and an oversized mouth.

A rooter up in the gallery shouted over the din on the stage, "Hi Swipsey, it's Joe Kelley and Keeler themselves, blowed if 'tain't." The cranks in the audience whooped it up. With two outs in the ninth, Anson came onstage and smashed a home run that decided the game.

A Runaway Colt would run for twenty-one more performances.

But the crafty newspaperman had already gotten his money's worth—some material for his Sunday column in Baltimore's *Morning Herald*. What about the prospects for a third straight pennant for the Orioles in 'ninety-six?

Both ballplayers said: A walkover.

And what about the recent deal for Dirty Jack Doyle, from the Giants, in exchange for Kid Gleason and $1,500?

Silence. Kelley crossed and uncrossed his legs, and stammered. Willie glanced over at Kel and managed at last, "Jack is quite a ballplayer."

Which he was. The baby-faced, Irish-born first baseman was one of the League's most scientific batters. "He is one of our kind of men—

active, ambitious and aggressive," Hanlon had declared. "Yes, we will have a Big Five next year."

Only the other four hated him. He still owed Willie $200 from the 'ninety-four Temple Cup Series. "Jack the welsher," the cranks had chanted whenever the Giants came to Union Park in 'ninety-five. "Settle up! Settle up!" Toward opponents he could be sullen and bad-tempered—and toward his teammates, too, came the word from New York.

Soon even Ned Hanlon started having his doubts. Doyle had begged to be rescued from the Giants, and Hanlon had never intended to match his $3,000 salary, much less reimburse Doyle for the $250 that Andrew Freedman had plucked from his paycheck to cover umpires' fines. When Doyle vowed to a New York newspaper that he would not come to Baltimore otherwise, Hanlon felt betrayed. He offered a choice: Doyle would play for the Orioles, or for no one.

Every returning Oriole had signed a contract for 'ninety-six. That left Doyle. When he arrived at Camden Station on a clear, cold February night, Hanlon was waiting. He had hired a gorgeous barouche and escorted the strong-minded ballplayer to Ganzhorn's Hotel, which was famous for its planked steaks and shad. Robbie and Joe Kelley and John McGraw had come, each sporting a dainty bouquet. Over oysters and sherry, Dirty Jack was made to feel at home.

"We start south this year with an entirely different state of feeling than we did last year," Hanlon announced to the newspapers. "All is peace and harmony this season, and the men will pull together from the start."

When he was asked about another pennant, Hanlon delivered a gaudy smile. With President Cleveland's prospects in mind, he said, "I am very much in favor of a third term."

John McGraw fell ill after an intrasquad game in Atlanta. The soaring fever suggested that the malaria had returned. He was rushed to an infirmary and found to have typhoid fever instead. The doctors did everything they could, from sponge baths to quinine sulfate and magnesia to a diet of milk and juice and broth, and still he got worse. The fever stayed dangerously high; the doctors feared the worst.

The Orioles went north without him. Before reaching Baltimore they learned how much they needed him. The rowdiness he had helped set in motion was getting out of hand.

They learned this in the hardscrabble Virginia town of Petersburg, where the minor league club was known for winning by fair means or foul. No umpire showed up, so each team supplied one. Petersburg's arbiter was the pitcher's brother, J. Quarles, who claimed the spot behind home plate to call the balls and strikes. After two innings the Orioles demanded a new umpire and got a Petersburg player. Petersburg was winning, 1 to 0, in the seventh inning when McGraw's replacement, Jim Donnelly, at bat with a count of three balls and no strikes, took a wild pitch.

"Strike!" the umpire rasped.

The Orioles said nothing.

The next two pitches were worse—both called strikes—and Donnelly shrieked at the umpire. Joe Kelley and Jack Doyle and even Willie Keeler joined in. Hughey Jennings was standing at the edge of the rhubarb when Petersburg's second baseman walked up to him and, without warning, socked him in the eye. Hughey toppled over.

Doyle leapt at the aggressor and sent him sprawling.

Suddenly hundreds of ruffians charged out of the grandstand, some wielding bats and fence pickets and stones. They threw Doyle to the ground, then Joe Kelley, and kicked both ballplayers and beat them with sticks. A six-footer seized Willie Keeler by the collar and shook him like a terrier roughing up a rat.

"Drop that little boy!" a policeman ordered. Willie crashed to the ground. The more respectable Petersburg cranks and the few policemen on hand saved the Orioles from the mob.

That evening Kelley and Doyle were standing in front of their hotel when J. Quarles and a friend came by. "Look here," Quarles said menacingly, "you've been talking about me, and I want to know what you mean by it."

A crowd gathered. The Orioles had started into the lobby when the locals caught up. In cramped quarters Kelley and Doyle wildly fought back. They were losing ground when Steve Brodie fearlessly forced his way in and lunged at one of the biggest bullies, shoved him to the wall, and punched him again and again. Furniture got wrecked. Someone threw Quarles through a glass door, before the police arrived.

The Petersburg authorities issued arrest warrants on assault charges—against the three Orioles. The ballplayers were spirited off to Old Point Comfort and put on a boat for Baltimore.

Had McGraw been around, he would have got his punches in, too. But even though the Orioles missed him, some of the players were secretly relieved not to have him around. He made them nervous—put them on edge. Maybe they no longer needed him to egg them on. Doyle had become one of the boys, having fought shoulder to shoulder in Petersburg, and had taken McGraw's place at the top of the lineup. At the opening game in Baltimore, when he trotted out to first base, he was greeted not with shouts of "Welsher" but with cheers; he doffed his cap so many times that he bent the peak. In the left field bleachers, the denizens of Kelleyville erupted as their hero trotted to his accustomed position. More than one pair of kid gloves was damaged when Wee Willie Keeler ran out to right field.

Against the Trolley Dodgers that day, they played with snap and ginger. In his first time at bat Willie smacked a pitch through to right field and streaked to second base. Later he got trapped in a rundown for what seemed like forever, before diving back into second base—safely. When Kel singled, Willie scored the first run of the season.

Hughey and Kel executed the first hit-and-run of 'ninety-six. Jack Doyle stole three bases. These were the Orioles.

But whenever they most needed a hit, they shut down. Robbie might have tied the game in the eighth inning with a single, but he rolled a pitch back to the twirler. Doyle stood impatiently on base in the ninth inning when Willie came to the bat. The first three pitches were balls, then a strike, and another. On the next pitch he astonished the cranks—he struck out.

Something was wrong. The Orioles hit safely only six times and made just as many errors. "Schoolboys in the field and old women at the bat," the *Morning Herald* scorned, tracing the vacuum on the Orioles to McGraw: "In tight games his presence or absence makes the difference between victory and defeat for Baltimore."

The Orioles lost the next day as well, because of Umpire Tim Keefe. Conceivably he had been standing in the wrong place when he declared Kelley out at second base—though no one had touched him—to squelch an eighth-inning rally. But calling the game on account of darkness when forty-five minutes of daylight remained, just as Brooklyn's pitcher was becoming the veriest of cherry pies—

for that, there could be no excuse. Only that he had it in for them. Maybe the umpires had been instructed that the League had no use for a three-time champion—though how could eleven strong-willed magnates agree on anything? More likely, it was Tim Keefe who had it in for them. Thanks to the now-absent McGraw.

Undeniably, McGraw had hurt them by antagonizing so many people, but they needed his bat and his quickness at third base. Yet it was more than that. Without him, they were not quite a team. How he had become their leader was hard to say—maybe it was that he cared the least about what anyone thought of him. Or that he was surest of what he wanted. When he wanted something, no one could outlast him. He could force his opponents—and his teammates, too—to his will.

Nobody could really replace McGraw. Robbie could jolly the men along but he could not move them by the force of his will. Partly it was Robbie's easygoing temperament, or the fact that he was a family man, and therefore knew that life held more important things than the outcome of a boy's game. He was the perfect captain for a volatile team, but not nearly a leader.

Nobody accused Jack Doyle of being easygoing. But he was disliked—at the least, distrusted—by too many of his teammates. Steve Brodie was a shade too eccentric. (How could you look up to a man who recited Shakespeare out in center field?) Joe Kelley was liked, even admired, not only by the ladies but by his teammates, too. He was strong and swift and jaunty—a manly man, everything a boy could wish to be. He had self-confidence and a competitive fire. It was hard to say for sure what was missing. That he lacked Mac's quick brilliance was not, in itself, disabling. It was more that there was something not quite responsible about him, at his core. It was not so much that he liked to drink but that he gave the impression he drank less out of the pursuit of pleasure than out of need. He played in every game, but somehow he could not be relied on. He was not quite a serious man.

That left only two players, really, who might commandeer Mac's hammock. Willie Keeler could be relied on, day in and day out, but he was a man with precious little cunning. He cared too much about what others wanted instead of what he wanted them to want—the bane of a small man content with the world. Maybe Willie was *too* nice to lead. He had no need to.

Hughey did, though it was not obvious. He was a different man without McGraw. He loved McGraw, and owed him more than he could say—his success at the bat, for one, and an introduction to the world of educated men. He had always let McGraw lead, and he would follow. McGraw would not be deterred and Hughey was sufficiently sure of himself not to mind. As an exuberant boy made to work in the mines, Hughey had learned to adapt—to reshape himself to the situation at hand. But surely he knew he was doing that, which left his integrity intact. Probably no Oriole was as popular among the cranks. Hughey was high-strung, but there was something stalwart about him—a good-natured fierceness, a cheerful willingness to get hit by pitches—that made men look up to him. He was without pretense. Unless his teammates were too full of themselves, they would do as he thought best.

That was how it fell to lovable Hughey to make sure that nobody loafed. He led by example, and soon he was batting over .400. He had help from Hanlon, of course, and from Jack Doyle, with their no-nonsense demeanors. Hughey started showing some hardness of his own. Once when he was on first base and Kelley was at bat, Kel missed the signal for the hit-and-run. After Hughey was thrown out at second base, he and Kel traded the most fervent left-handed compliments.

'Ninety-six unfolded much as 'ninety-five had. The Orioles sagged early (sinking as low as tenth place in the opening weeks of the season) and then found themselves. *How* they found themselves—that was the customary mystery. There was often a magic in the way a team suddenly started to play like a team, or suddenly stopped. It was as if the Orioles remembered who they were. Starting off on their first western trip, against Connie Mack's League-leading Pirates, Willie scored the first run and then saved one. As the ball soared toward the fence, Willie sprinted dangerously near, and snatched it just as everything collided. He tumbled into a pile of rubbish and came up smiling, the ball in his glove, then threw to first base to put out the runner, who had already reached third. Twice Hughey got hit by a pitch, and twice he raced from first base to third on singles to shallowest left field. With the game tied in the eleventh, Willie singled, stole second base, and scored on Hughey's base hit.

"That old conquer-all spirit is returning," a Baltimore scribe applauded.

The Orioles bobbed up into first place but slumped again after Robbie mashed the pinkie of his throwing hand. When the tip turned black it was amputated at the first joint. Robbie stood it like a man, without anesthesia. Hanlon pointed out that losing the tip of a finger would not harm Robbie's throwing, because the digit had been crooked already and only got in the way. But losing Robbie for five weeks, that was harder.

Robbie had been back for six days when the Orioles, close behind the Spiders, entered the ninth inning in Philadelphia trailing, 15 to 8. Kelley went to bat in a halfhearted way and poked around for a while until he drew a base on balls. Willie followed with a single past second base. Two more singles drove both of them home. No one thought much about it, especially when the next two men flied out.

After another single, Robbie came to bat. He had hit four singles already. He cracked a pitch to left field, for a three-bagger. It acted like an electric shock to the crowd. The Orioles were suddenly just two runs behind.

There was a great laying together of heads on the Baltimore bench. The light-hitting pitcher was due at the bat. The ballplayers parted. Out onto the diamond stepped John McGraw.

The Phillies twirler felt his knees go weak. The first time McGraw had shown up on the diamond in Baltimore, as a coacher, the applause went on for two long minutes; tears sprang to more than a few eyes, for a twenty-three-year-old who had faced death and won. Mac had pinch-hit four days earlier, to no effect. That would not happen again. He fouled off every good pitch and let the bad ones pass and took his base.

The Phillies were near to trembling as Joe Kelley swaggered to the plate. The outfielders moved back toward the fence and the infielders felt for the outfield grass. The powerful batter stepped in against a pitcher whose time had passed.

Kel dumped a bunt. The sprinting third baseman took a dying chance and flung the ball to first base—wildly. Robbie scored. McGraw got to third base, Kel to second.

Now it was Willie's turn at bat. He swung at the second pitch with all his might and blooped the ball into short center field. Three fielders converged. The shortstop got a hand on the ball but it was over his shoulder and it dropped to the ground.

For a moment the crowd was stupefied. Then the Philadelphians broke into shouts of admiration for what the visitors had done.

With McGraw back in the lineup, the Orioles won game after game after game. "His appearance put new life into the team, and his work was simply phenomenal," one of the Baltimore newspapers exulted. "There is only one McGraw, and he is a revelation."

But even with McGraw back, the Orioles had changed. They were kicking less, flaring up less, but they were still winning ballgames.

There was a calmness about them that was new. The Spiders had out-rowdied them and won. Now the Orioles had found slyer ways to win.

Maybe McGraw had changed, too. There was nothing like a brush with death to show a man that some things are more precious than a game. This season (what was left of it) McGraw had something to prove, that he was himself again. But what would happen if someday he had nothing he needed to prove? Even McGraw had to want something badly to excel at it.

The Orioles swept a tripleheader on Labor Day from the inept Louisville Colonels and a doubleheader from them the next afternoon. Four days later they clinched the pennant, their third in a row, the easiest yet.

"Three cheers for Hughey Jennings Bryan," came a shout through the disagreeable rain.

"Hurrah!" others in the crowd shot back. Twenty thousand Baltimoreans had mobbed the gaping space in front of the painfully plain-looking Music Hall, on Mount Royal avenue. They had come to see William Jennings Bryan, the young Nebraska orator who had burst on the political scene to seize the Democratic party's presidential nomination.

The crowd could be forgiven for confusing him with the Orioles' star shortstop, for both were young and handsome and had a way with words. The populist candidate had also played some baseball himself, as a hard-throwing amateur in his youth. And certainly the professional ballplayers felt treated like workingmen. Yet when it came to the issue of free silver, which dominated the presidential campaign, they were of mixed minds. These were young men who had started out with nothing and now had quite a lot—money, and the public's respect. They were men without woes. The Orioles had argued about free silver during their western trip in July, and at first the free-silver men prevailed—the sons of Ireland, after all, were sons of labor—but gradually the sound-money men showed them where their real interests lay. Were they the debtors whose interest lay in cheaper money? Not anymore. They already had their stake of capital, and wanted its value protected.

Many of the cranks, however, saw their interests differently, and they bristled with anticipation on this soggy September evening. An electricity raced through the crowd with the news that the candidate had arrived. The spectators strained for a glimpse as he alighted from his carriage. The thirty-six-year-old congressman was startlingly clean-shaven, with curly hair and a cheerful round face that was handsome like a spoiled son's. William McKinley, the stolid Republican candidate, sat tranquilly on his front porch in Ohio and let the crowds come to him. Bryan took to the hustings, beseeching the farmer who was in the grip of the railroads and the workingman under capital's thumb, denouncing the unfeeling trusts that had captured the nation's livelihood. He was the first candidate for the presidency ever to stump the country so intently.

The rain quickened as Bryan ascended the platform. Calcium lights and arc lamps illuminated his glistening face. He had turned up his collar and put on a hat. The onlookers kept their umbrellas closed so that everyone could see.

"Prosperity comes up from below—it does not come down from the upper crust of society," the Boy Orator of the Platte shouted. "Our opponents tell us that we are arraying class against class. I deny it."

"So do I," a voice cried out.

"We are simply telling people that they have a right to keep other men's hands out of their pockets."

He boomed his words into the slanting rain. Most of the crowd could not hear him. They cheered anyway.

The Orioles knew they would be the laughingstock of baseball if they lost the Temple Cup yet again. "Fake Champions," the critics had called them, and the words had stung. They would deserve the epithet, or so Hanlon and Robbie and Mac and Hughey convinced them, if they foundered for a third straight October.

They had hoped to play Cincinnati, knowing how few spectators the Spiders drew in Cleveland. The riotous ways of Patsy Tebeau and his boys—the entire team had once been arrested for attacking an umpire—had driven the self-respecting rooters away. But the Reds had collapsed and never recovered. So it would be the Spiders, whom the Orioles hated, being so much like them.

The Orioles started the series with perfect confidence. The Spiders did, too.

Fewer than four thousand rooters showed up at Union Park for the opening game, an even smaller crowd than the average during the season. There was no mystery about why. Ned Hanlon and Harry von der Horst had tacked twenty-five cents on to the price of every ticket, doubling the admission to the bleachers.

The ballplayers were annoyed at the chilly reception and at the dearth of ticket receipts they would share. Some of them were lucky to have made a little money on the side. They had lent their endorsement to a shoe store on Baltimore street in the souvenir scorebook.

KEELER: "NO FLIES ON THE HESS SHOE."

KELLEY: "THEY ARE THE STUFF."

JENNINGS: "THEY MAKE ME SMILE."

CLARKE: "GOT MARRIED IN A PAIR OF HESS SHOES."

None of this got in their way. Hughey struck three hits, Willie and Kel and Robbie got two apiece. Cy Young, twirling for Cleveland, was a little off. The Spiders played nervously, like beaten men. Patsy Tebeau wrenched his back and the Orioles won in a walk, 7 to 1.

The attendance dipped even further the next afternoon, but again the Orioles had no need for an audience. They were playing their most scientific ball of the 'ninety-six season. Hanlon used a pitcher he had barely tried all season—Joe Corbett, the younger brother and sparring partner of Gentleman Jim, the heavyweight champion, who had used scientific methods of boxing to lick John L. Sullivan and his brute strength. Joe, as cool and nervy as they come, pitched the Spiders to a standstill, taming them, 7 to 2. "[H]e pitched very good ball," Willie wrote in a diary he had just started to keep—"he will be a star pitcher in a short time look out for him."

After the game the ballclub announced that ticket prices would be restored the next afternoon—twenty-five cents for the bleachers, fifty cents for the grandstand, and seventy-five cents for a reserved seat. A good crowd showed up, and saw quite a game. It was close until the eighth inning, when Robbie opened with a two-bagger and scored on McGraw's single. After Mac and Willie put on the hit-and-run, McGraw scored on Hughey's faraway fly. Willie stole second and, when Kel scorched a pitch that the third baseman muffed, crossed the plate. The game, a third victory, was out of reach.

The Orioles boarded a train for Cleveland, where four games were scheduled. But, Willie confided to his diary, "we expect to win it the first day."

No more than two thousand cranks showed up, but they made their presence felt. In the fifth inning, with the game scoreless, the Spiders had runners on second and third. The crowd used drums and horns and human howls to try to rattle young Joe Corbett, but the smooth-featured right-hander kept a smile on his face. He faced ornery Jesse Burkett, whose average of .410 had made him the season's best batsman. Corbett, calm and in command, induced Burkett to ground out to Hughey. The next batter ended the inning.

That was as close as the Spiders got. Willie smacked three hits, and Corbett did too, and the Orioles scored two runs in the seventh inning and three in the eighth.

And so it ended. The Temple Cup, at last, was theirs.

The overwrought silver vessel was delivered to them at the Hollendon Hotel after the game. Harry von der Horst had it filled with champagne—fifteen bottles. William Chase Temple himself, who had watched the game from the grandstand, quaffed first from the foaming vessel. Harry was next, then Ned Hanlon and then Robbie and the rest of the team, until it was drained.

The nation's sportswriters hailed the three-time champions, now the postseason victors, as the greatest team the national game had ever seen. Cap Anson's old White Stockings, Frank Selee's three-time champion Beaneaters—Hanlon's Orioles were better. When the League published the official batting averages, Hughey Jennings ranked second, at .401. Willie Keeler, at .386, was fourth.

But it was the little right fielder the nation had taken a shine to. Blond, brawny Cap Anson had once been what red-blooded American boys aspired to be. Then it was daring and drunken King Kelly. Now Wee Willie Keeler had captured the public's imagination, as an underdog who used his heart and brains to make his way in the world.

The original idea had been for the Orioles to tour Europe as a team, playing exhibition games to pay their way. This past season they had conversed about little else. So they sent a scout to England—Ted Sullivan, the gruff old manager, who had taught Charley Comiskey to play off the bag and had once been ridiculed for suggesting that only eight players (all but the pitcher) should bat. If anyone could find a way for a tour to pay for itself, Ted Sullivan could. But he cabled back that weather would preclude too many games to make the tour financially practical.

The Big Four decided to tour Europe anyway. The newspapers gave them a hard time, picturing the boys on a cattleship—Hughey tugging on a steer, Kelley fending off bovine affections, Willie leaning out of necessity over the side. Willie and Hughey disembarked by steamship on the fifteenth of October. McGraw and Kelley chose a finer class of transport.

What gracious treatment Willie and Hughey received. A salute was fired in their honor. They played euchre with the captain and the chief engineer, and watched the whales frolic at sea. "Today was one of the finest days we have had on board the Ship," Willie wrote in his diary on their eighth day out—"it was something grand. Nothing of any importance occurred." They never got the least bit seasick. "It is a shame, after so many people had given us so much advice and so many different cures for seasickness," Willie wrote home once they docked. "It isn't right to fool the people that way. Goodness knows, we fool them enough in the summer."

But how pleased they were to sight land again—"you can't imagine how beautiful it looks until you are on the Sea for ten or eleven days," Willie confided to his diary. "We are close to the shores of Ireland the home of our parents it is very barren looking along the coast nothing but Light-houses and a few Cabins scattered here and there among the hills." How far his family's fortunes had come since Watergrass Hill.

They landed in Liverpool, and spent four days there, admiring the fog and the docks (with "a board walk just like the one in Atlantic City") and taking in the theater every night. Then to London, to find Mac and Kel.

They stayed ten days and had such a good time they overslept on Sunday and missed Mass for the first time in ages. Kelley sent letters home, to be published, whether for fame or fortune, using Willie as the butt of his jokes. At the Tower of London, Kel wrote, "Keeler alone was bored, declaring that the whole pile of rocks was not half as interesting as the jail in Brooklyn. Besides, he had never heard of Anne Boleyn or Mary Jane Gray. What had they done? Caught at shoplifting?

And were they let out after two days in a cell? Oh! If we had only left Willie in America."

The day they visited the Old Curiosity Shop, America went to the polls. When Kelley heard the results, he wrote home to Robbie: "Bryan got it good and hard, didn't he? It is pretty tough when the old Ninth Ward goes Republican," meaning the neighborhood that was home to Harry's brewery. Bryan had scared the industrial workers who feared his election would bring more layoffs—a word too many of them had come to learn. Of Baltimore's twenty-two wards, McKinley took twenty-one. He also carried the Electoral College, and with it, the keys to the White House.

The Big Four pressed on with their tour of Europe. "Amsterdam is a very pretty city," Willie noted. "The Streets and Houses here look so clean that it gets painful and you pray for something dirty." Then it was on to Brussels and Waterloo and Paris. "Your first glimpse of Paris is like looking at a beautiful painting that you can't fathom," he wrote with uncustomary poetry. They saw the seven-year-old Eiffel Tower and giggled at the Moulin Rouge and explored the Catacombs—to Willie, "one of the most gruesome places I ever was in."

Innocents abroad, indeed. They came home posing as sophisticates, wearing high silk hats and elegant topcoats.

=6=

Individual Glory

As the band played the opening strains of "The Star-Spangled Banner," the 'ninety-six pennant rose slowly up the flagpole just inside the center-field fence. At the same time the 'ninety-four and 'ninety-five pennants were hoisted to the tops of the twin poles newly built for them. In the stiff wind, the three pennants floated free. The thousands on the grounds burst into cheers. The ladies spun their parasols. The men's derbies nearly popped off their heads.

The National League had never known a ballclub to win four straight pennants, but even some of the skeptical New York scribes thought the Orioles looked like a cinch. As the 'ninety-seven season started, John McGraw was himself again. The pitching showed promise. The batting had improved—Hanlon's doing. Over the winter he had traded away Steve Brodie, whose stickwork and baserunning had slipped, for Jake Stenzel, Pittsburgh's unhappy center fielder. Stenzel lacked Brodie's grace and range in the field. But he was superior at the bat. (Stenzel had batted .361 in 'ninety-six, to Brodie's .297.) Brodie learned of the deal from a newspaperman.

What better way to take the Orioles' measure than to open the season against the Boston Beaneaters, presumed to be their strongest rivals for the pennant. And yet the Orioles looked unsteady at the start. The Beaneaters scored two quick runs when a sharp bounder hit rock-solid Henny Reitz in the face and Hughey—of all people—fumbled a ground ball.

Then the Big Four got down to work. It was like old times. McGraw and Keeler and Jennings and Kelley led the lineup. Willie stole the

113

Orioles' first base of the season, in the opening inning, and scored their first run—the first of ten that afternoon for the Orioles, to Boston's five. Willie hit a single and a double. Sure, he had played finer games than this one, but something important had started.

It continued the next afternoon. The Orioles showed their mastery of scientific hitting. Willie struck two singles. Both times he started to steal second base as Hughey punched the ball into right field. Once he got thrown out at third base, and later he scored the tying run (and Hughey the winning one).

Again the next day, Willie hit two singles, and the Orioles swept the Beaneaters.

At last they lost, to the Trolley Dodgers, though Willie got a hit. Then they copped the next five victories, as Willie hit safely two or three times in each. He beat out slow rollers that refused to go foul or poked a triple over the center fielder's head and often stole two or three bases in a game. He was an acrobat out in right field. When Jake Beckley of the Giants laced out a liner, Willie took a leap at the sloping right field fence and planted one foot on it while the other dangled in the air. When he landed, the ball was in his glove.

KEELER, THE WONDER, a headline read the next day.

Ten days later he made the catch that cranks would talk about for years. The Orioles were hopelessly trailing the lowly Senators at Washington's ballpark. It was late in the game when a Washington slugger put the end of his bat to a speedy pitch from Jerry Nops, Baltimore's new stoop-shouldered left-hander. Willie sprinted and got to the fence just as the ball did. Three rows of barbed wire ran across the top, six feet off the ground, to keep the cranks in the bleachers from storming onto the field. Willie leaped as high as he could and reached his bare left hand through the barbed wire netting. His sleeve caught on the barbs as he came down, gashing his arm. Blood splattered onto his cheek and down his neck. But the ball rested in his palm.

The Washington rooters were stunned. Then the applause started to build and swept through the bleachers and the grandstand. Willie had his arm bandaged and stayed in the game. When the inning was over, the Washington cranks made him doff his cap—three times—as he trotted back to the bench.

The season was almost a month old before Willie made an error. A few days later, the newspapers noticed he had hit safely in every game since the season began.

Into June, he was still getting a hit or two or three—occasionally, four—in every game. "Keeler is not a hard hitter, but rather a sure hitter," one of the newspapers explained. On the fifth of the month he managed only a bunt down the third base line and barely beat the throw to first. He was not the League's best batsman—Joe Kelley was, batting .419, and Willie stood seven points behind.

The Orioles won another seven in a row at Union Park. They edged past the Beaneaters into first place. Then the Pirates arrived and had Frank Killen twirl the opening game. He was a big left-hander who enjoyed frightening batters by throwing high hard pitches and then jeering at their manhood.

In the first inning he gave McGraw a base on balls, hit Willie with an inshoot, and tossed a wild pitch. He did not feel right and asked to be taken out. The crowd taunted him as he shuffled to the bench.

The Orioles won their eighth in a row. Willie hit a lone single—"but he kept up his record, of which he should be mighty proud," one of the Baltimore newspapers noticed. It went unmentioned that Willie had eclipsed the League record for hitting safely in consecutive games—forty-two, set by Bill Dahlen, Chicago's stubborn shortstop, in 'ninety-four.

The next game, Willie got three hits, including a double and a triple. Kelley and McGraw chopped down at the ball for base hits—Joe's a three-bagger—and the Orioles won.

The following afternoon Frank Killen insisted on pitching out of turn, to square his reputation. "And I'll beat them, too," he pledged.

Killen had usually pitched well against the Orioles but never quite like this. The weak-kneed pitcher of a recent afternoon showed the heart of a lion. He threw hard and his curves snapped like a kite in the wind. In nine innings he scattered five hits. In the third inning Willie tapped a slow grounder but Pittsburgh's third baseman made an astonishing pickup and nipped him at first.

That was the closest Willie got to reaching base safely.

He had gone hitless, for the first time in 'ninety-seven, after forty-four games. Or forty-five, counting his four hits in the last game of 'ninety-six.

When Willie next faced Killen, in September, he batted five times and collected five hits.

*   *   *

Mac and Robbie had gone into business for themselves. They opened a place they called The Diamond, on Howard street, above Franklin, across from the Academy of Music. There was nothing else like it in Baltimore. The entrepreneurial ballplayers turned the handsome brick building into a three-story palace of sports. The Diamond was an up-to-date, 'nineties version of a saloon, with oak finishings, elaborate mirrors on the wallpapered walls, and an electric scoreboard that showed the progress, play by play, of Orioles' ballgames. It was much more besides. The second story housed a billiard parlor and a reading room stocked with every sporting paper. A gymnasium with lockers filled the third floor. The bowling alleys, which shared the ground floor with the saloon, featured a patented appliance for returning the balls to the bowlers and were destined to leave their mark in sporting history. One day, The Diamond's manager had a set of battered old tenpins lathed down into smaller pins, to be matched with the palm-sized bowling balls on hand for cocked hat (using just the 1, 7, and 10 pins) and other beery variations. When the whittled pins flew into the air, they looked like a "flock of flying ducks"—McGraw said that, or maybe Robbie. A sportswriter for *The Sun* christened them "duckpins."

In the evening, after the day's ballgame was done, one or both of the proprietors would come around to The Diamond. *They* were part of what the place was selling. The famous ballplayers circulated as the customers crowded round. How unalike they were. Side by side, they looked like a vaudeville team, a country chicken next to a goose before Christmas. Robbie was only an inch and a half taller than McGraw but outweighed him by sixty pounds or more. The fat catcher was jovial, slow to anger, as resolute as the surface of the earth.

McGraw was anything but. He was judgmental, quick to anger, as mercurial as a volcano. He was no longer so scrawny, but his face was delicate, almost pixieish, yet also confident and strong. He dressed sharply and tried an arched moustache that lent him a devilish look. He was self-aware and meant to look his best. And mentally he was sharp as hell. Even as he was exploding, nothing got past him.

Yet Mac and Robbie liked each other—needed each other, almost. "Robbie was the sugar and I the vinegar of the club," McGraw explained. Each of them had what the other one lacked. The Diamond bore Mac's brash imagination and Robbie's methodical ways. Undoubtedly McGraw had conceived what The Diamond should be—the sporting headquarters for all of Baltimore. It would be up to Robbie to make sure it survived. They would make enough money to afford handsome and roomy row houses, side by side, out on St. Paul street.

The Diamond was not their only distraction. In February, so many people crowded into St. Vincent de Paul Church, with its whitewashed neoclassical elegance, that only the fortunate few at the very front could watch as McGraw took his vows. Mac's bride, Minnie Doyle, was the daughter of a clerk in the tax court, a minor notable in Democratic circles. Minnie had steady eyes and a sturdy jaw that seemed a match for Mac's.

The managers and the sporting pundits considered it an article of faith that getting married or starting a business—much less both at once—ruined a ballplayer for a year. They found further proof, after a fashion, in McGraw. His more-than-respectable batting average of .325 in 'ninety-seven was no higher than that of his typhoid-filled 'ninety-six and quite a bit lower than those in the two years before that or the four to follow.

His nuptials were not the last the Orioles would undergo. Joe Kelley had already announced his postseason plans to marry the daughter of John J. "Sonny" Mahon, a rising figure in Baltimore's Democratic machine. On the same day as Kel's wedding, which took place at Sonny Mahon's sprawling summer home in Pikesville, Hughey Jennings got married near Scranton, to Elizabeth Dixon, a local girl, sweet and beautiful. Both men saw their success at the bat droop the following season (by forty-one and twenty-seven points, respectively) and never recover.

Willie served as a groomsman at Mac's wedding and the best man at Kel's. Alone among the Big Four, Willie remained unmarried—and unencumbered. He had been sweet on a girl in Baltimore, but nothing came of it. Twenty-five now, and boyishly innocent, he had a sacrament of his own, in baseball.

Willie hit safely in each of the five games after Killen shut him down. In the next one, in Boston, he laid down a sacrifice bunt in the first inning and almost beat the throw. He tripped over first base and went sliding ten feet or more, wrenching his groin. He was helped from the ballgrounds to a nearby drugstore, where the injury was dressed. He was out of action for a week.

So he was sitting in the grandstand when Amos Rusie hurled one of his speediest incurves to Hughey Jennings. Rusie had held out for the entire 'ninety-six season, refusing to sign a contract that contained a reserve clause, so he was a little rusty. Hughey was crowding the plate and could not get out of the way of the pitch, and the thud was heard all over the ballpark. The ball hit Hughey a half-inch from his temple, over his left ear. His bat fell to the ground; he collapsed into the catcher's arms.

Hughey was laid on the dirt and his head was repeatedly bathed. At last he opened his eyes and sat up and insisted on taking first base. He came around to score and played an inning at shortstop. But his face was white when he returned to the bench. It took three men to stop him from going back onto the diamond. He was taken into the dressing room and broke down completely when he realized he was out of the game. He had fractured his skull.

The Orioles had ordinarily been lucky about injuries, but not in 'ninety-seven. The game in which Hughey was hurt also saw Jack Doyle hit in the eye with a bounding ball. Both ballplayers returned five days later, before Hughey broke the index finger on his glove hand. Kelley was taking electric treatments for his ceaseless stomach troubles. Robbie, spiked in a collision at home plate, missed more than a month.

Even when everyone was healthy it was hard to sustain the self-sacrifice and teamwork required for scientific baseball. In a way, excellence undermined itself. Joe Kelley was particularly susceptible to vanity, as he catered to the female tenants of Kelleyville, out in the left field bleachers. He would swagger out to his position and check if he had their attention. At least once he carried a looking-glass under his cap so that he could arrange his hair and keep his sun-drenched waves in place. In Cincinnati one July day, a mirror popped out of his pocket as he ran hard for a fly ball he was unable to catch. Kelley failed to notice, but not the cranks, who called it to the attention of the Reds' left fielder when the teams changed sides. As Kelley was climbing into the omnibus after the game, a Cincinnati ballplayer sidled up to him and said, "Here's something you lost, Joe." Blushing to the roots of his hair, Kelley grabbed the mirror and slipped it into his pocket, though when the crowd hooted, he took it good-naturedly.

And if it was not precisely vanity, then it was arrogance of a sort that caused Joe Corbett to fling down his glove, hurl the ball at the ground, and stalk off the rubber and over to the bench on a steamy August afternoon. The ball rolled to the grandstand. In the ensuing chaos, the seventh and eighth runs of the inning crossed the plate, putting Brooklyn ahead of Baltimore, 8 to 6. It was not the Trolley Dodgers but Corbett's own teammates who had provoked his temper. Jack Doyle had come to the mound to suggest that Corbett let another pitcher try his luck. Then Hughey had marched over. "Yes, get out," he said sarcastically. "You are no better than any of the other pitchers."

The Orioles' style of self-regulation was bound to cause these kinds of tensions. In a way, that was the point. Jake Stenzel learned fast. The first time his new teammates got on him for muffing a fly ball, "I got my Dutch up," the new center fielder said. "But when I cooled down I came to the conclusion that I was not the best outfielder in the world and should not object to taking a lesson occasionally. So, after that, instead of kicking when my mistakes were pointed out I held my tongue and waited until someone else blundered, when I turned in with the rest and helped roast him. The boys jolly just as often, and are never afraid of giving a man too much praise for a good play. It is either a roast or a jolly, and the constant talking keeps the team awake all the time. That is what makes it appear so peppery."

Nobody was immune. Kelley became the captain while Robbie was injured, but that hardly deterred McGraw and Doyle from going at him for failing to bunt and at Hughey for trying to steal second base with only one out.

The tensions pressed in from every direction. Jack Doyle and his teammates were often at one another's throats. He was cold-blooded; they were emotional. He showed no interest in being part of a team. He took a punch at McGraw—"in a cowardly manner," Mac told a scribe. "I got a bat and would have broken his jaw if Manager Hanlon had not stopped me." And there was still resentment directed at the Big Four, with their lordly salaries and influential airs.

Even among the Big Four, there were strains. McGraw, always needing a target, liked to pick on Willie Keeler, the only Oriole littler than he was. Both were pint-sized and Irish and smart as a hit-and-run. They had considerably less in common, however, than was apparent. Willie was a city boy and a happy one. Mac, raised an hour and a half by rail from Syracuse, had grown up hard. Mac had a talent for manipulation, even a need for it, and a knack for not letting it trouble him any. Willie cared nothing about things like that. He wanted to do his job as well as he could and to have fun, not necessarily in that order. Sharpening his spikes, he believed, was something a gentleman did not do.

When Willie returned to the diamond after tearing the nail from his middle finger, McGraw inquired—within the hearing of the cranks—if he had recovered yet from "the clap." Afterward, in the plain dressing room, Willie jumped on McGraw and they wrestled to the floor. Their teammates laughed until they realized that one of them might get hurt. So Robbie picked each of them up by the scruff of the neck and flung them into the bath.

Mac kept carping at Willie all season, one day for failing to throw home to catch a runner who started a rally.

"What did you mean by cursing me like that?" Willie said after the game, as they headed toward the tub.

"Play ball!" Mac replied with a sneer.

Willie jumped on McGraw. The two naked bantams wrestled on the dressing room floor. Doyle, naked as well, grabbed a bat and threatened to bust the skull of anyone who interfered. He laid 5–4 odds in Willie's favor.

Mac gave up first.

It was astonishing, really, that the Orioles stayed as close as they did—all summer, in second or third place, way ahead of the Phillies featuring Big Ed Delehanty and Napoleon Lajoie, their hard-hitting new infielder, or the Cleveland Spiders, with their graceful and gifted Indian rookie, Louis Sockalexis. Much of the Orioles' advantage was Willie Keeler. He had never known such a season. Hardly anyone had. It seemed he could place the ball wherever he liked. Trying to bunt, he would grasp his stubby bat near the center, his hands close together, and maneuver it like a supple shield, as if he were Robin Hood outwitting Little John.

"At least ninety percent of the batsmen have their weakness, but Keeler is flawless"—that, from Win Mercer, the hard-hitting twirler for Washington. "He can smash a slow curve and he can bat out speed. Nothing is impossible to him—curves, speed, height or anything else." His average at the bat was still at .397 in August; only Big Ed Delehanty, at .429, was ahead of him. Willie had cracked the most hits of anyone in the League, and was third in stolen bases. That was besides his prowess in the field. When Chick Stahl hit a long fly to right field at Union Park that was destined to win a game for the Beaneaters, Willie leapt up on the sloping fence and ran higher and higher and caught the ball just as it was going over. Holding the ball aloft, he plunged over the fence and fell outside the ballgrounds.

By early September, Willie's batting average had climbed to .412, the highest in the League, and it kept rising. Kel recovered his batting eye and Stenzel was showing more than his share. In a tie game against Chicago, Jack Doyle was on first base when Henny Reitz tapped the ball down to Cap Anson, who was standing nearby. The Old Chief leisurely gathered the ball in and trotted toward the bag, when he noticed Doyle dashing wildly for third. The impudence of the thing staggered Anson. He made a stab at first base and flung the ball across the diamond, wide of the bag. Doyle barreled on and with a headlong slide beat the ball to home plate.

The Orioles won nine in a row and ran neck-and-neck with the Beaneaters, who seemed to be fading. All of September the two teams kept trading places. They were evenly matched—practitioners of scientific baseball run by cerebral managers who sat on the bench in their street clothes.

The pennant was destined to be settled as September came to a close, when the Beaneaters arrived at Union Park for three games. Rarely had the National League pennant been decided as the season was ending. It had never been resolved by the two contenders' going head to head. Each team would have another series to play, but everyone knew that these three games would decide things.

The Orioles lost the first game but won the second, leaving them a percentage point ahead.

The crowd began to gather before daylight for the climactic game of the season. When the ticket-sellers showed up at eight o'clock, this Monday morning, they found a mob of impatient rooters. By noon any clerk who labored downtown, pleading a beloved uncle's burial, was lucky if he could find a spot to stand on a streetcar heading north. A half-hour after the gates were to open, at two, stabs at orderliness had succumbed to a surging mass of humanity. Half a hundred policemen at the center of the crowd stopped trying to control it and sought only to keep themselves from getting crushed. The ladies could not pass through, so Harry von der Horst ordered another gate opened for them and their escorts. That relieved the pressure only for a while. In front of the carriage gate, on Huntingdon avenue, the crowd grew dense. Cranks got pressed into the fence, which started to creak and groan. With a crash it gave way. Dust flew up and a mob of men and boys rushed into the ballpark.

Never before had so many people, anywhere, watched a game of baseball. The turnstiles admitted 25,390 people, besides the 700 who rushed through the carriage gate and the 3,500 who squeezed past the ticket-takers and another 5,000 on nearby rooftops. Men stood three or four deep—on stools, at the rear—around the rim of the outfield, even perched on the fence, and along both foul lines, from one side of the catcher round to the other. Outside, speculators were getting a dollar for a reserved seat and seventy-five cents for a fifty-cent admission, rising to five dollars and two dollars, respectively, once the gong was sounded.

The Orioles trotted out to the field, the late-season grass having been worn away in center field. Thousands of cranks had brought horns, rattles, drums, cow bells—a man of science could hardly hear himself think.

The ballplayers on both teams were visibly nervous, for none of them had ever played in such an important game before. Hanlon put Joe Corbett on the rubber again. The clean-cut right-hander had become the ace of the staff, with twenty-four victories so far this season. He had started the first game of the three, pitching keenly for three innings and lamely for four.

The great Billy Hamilton stood in as the first batter of the decisive game and smacked a single. Corbett hit the second batsman with a pitch. The next one laced a grounder that smashed Corbett's thumb. Joe, ordinarily known for his hardiness, asked to come out of the game. The cranks were relieved, but Hanlon was suspicious. He concluded that it was not Joe's hand that was causing the trouble, but his heart.

The Orioles kept bringing in pitchers, but the Beaneaters kept hitting, and the Orioles did too. Two-baggers—anything hit into the cranks surrounding the outfield—swarmed like mosquitoes in May.

Into the seventh inning the Orioles trailed, 8 to 5. Their rooters felt sure of a miracle. Three pennants were fine, and they expected a fourth. The Beaneaters were a team of the past, were they not?

Hugh Duffy led off for Boston with a single. After Jimmy Collins doubled, second baseman Germany Long came to the plate. He had saved the first game for Boston, in the ninth inning, when he leapt higher than a mortal could imagine to snag a liner off Willie Keeler's bat. This time he clobbered a pitch deep into center field. The crowd parted for Jake Stenzel's pursuit. Stenzel hesitated and only then went after the ball—and muffed it. And thus the Beaneaters went on to score nine runs. "If Stenzel made the catch, we would probably have won"—that was Murph's judgment, and he should know.

Hanlon agreed. It was a mistake he was not about to forgive. Early the next season, the center fielder who had proved timid under pressure would be gone.

Dusk was settling in before the game mercifully gathered to a close. Boston had won, 19 to 10. For Baltimore, preeminence was lost.

Surely his leverage would never be greater. Willie had batted a breathtaking .424 for the 'ninety-seven season, the best in the League and the second-best ever under the modern rules. He got more hits—239 in just 129 games—than anyone ever had in a season. No small accomplishment, the newspapers noted, for the smallest man in the big league. That, and helping the Orioles salvage a shred of dignity by thrashing the Beaneaters for the Temple Cup, though amid such public indifference that Mr. Temple was persuaded to withdraw his overdone decanter from future humiliation.

Willie was clear about his reasoning. "We can count on our fingers the number of years that we shall be able to play," he said to a scribe, explaining why he and Joe Kelley and Hughey Jennings had refrained from signing their 'ninety-eight contracts and mailing them back to Hanlon. McGraw had signed: 'ninety-seven had been disappointing and he had something to prove. The others had something else to prove. They had reached the official salary ceiling of $2,400 (Kel got an extra $200 as the assistant captain) and they wanted more.

Willie rebutted the argument that the ballplayers should be grateful for earning seven-and-a-half times as much as a coal miner, six times as much as a factory worker, four times as much as a street railwayman, twice as much as a federal clerk. Once a ballplayer's brief career is over, Willie asked, "how do we find ourselves? Why, we have spent the best years of our lives on the diamond, those years usually employed by young men in acquiring commercial or professional knowledge that will prove lucrative to them for many times the period usually allotted to a ballplayer. At the end of our baseball career we then find ourselves unfitted otherwise to earn any considerable money. This makes it plain that we must make all the money we can during the short period we may be said to be star players."

And something more: They deserved it. "We maintain that the people come to see us," Willie said, "that we are the attractions, that we do much to win pennants, and that we are worth what we ask."

Of course they were being selfish. But so were the ballclubs. There was no reason the ballclub should take advantage of *them*. And besides, Hughey pointed out, the 'ninety-eight schedule was set for 154 games, just about two dozen more than before. How could the ballplayers not deserve a raise?

The country had emerged at last from its economic depression. The four huge steel furnaces at Sparrow's Point had been fired up after three years of silence. A bumper crop of wheat in the Midwest (and Maryland too) sent more grain through the congested docks of Baltimore. Traveling salesmen started out earlier in the season than usual—a promising sign. The Orioles had drawn more spectators while finishing second in 'ninety-seven than in capturing the pennant in 'ninety-six. But the ballclub's profits had foundered as its payroll grew. Increasing it more would hardly do.

It was obvious to everyone that the recalcitrant trio had formed a union of sorts. They had company. Bill Clarke, the backup catcher, had refused to sign. Joe Corbett, home in California, was demanding $3,000 plus $300 for the round-trip railway fare.

Hanlon was indignant. "I would not care so much if I were not conscious that these men had been royally treated," he sputtered. "All of them have been the recipients of special favors and privileges, which the public know nothing of. They have been too well treated— that is the trouble."

He felt especially bitter toward Kel, presumed to be the master of the collaboration. Why should *he* complain? Was he not the highest-paid man on the team? Did he not make as much as any ballplayer in the League? And did he not drink too much and borrow money with abandon?

When Kelley showed up at Camden Station to see the team off to Macon, Hanlon blew up. He called his assertive left fielder aside and had a few short words. Any arrangements between them were off, he decreed, including the offer of $300 to step in as the captain whenever Robbie was on the mend. That job would go to somebody else.

The newspapers let it be known that Hanlon was thinking of trading Kelley to the Trolley Dodgers.

Kel only got more stubborn.

Willie stayed home in Brooklyn. Hughey accompanied the Orioles to Georgia but went on to Athens, to coach the University of Georgia nine. Hanlon begged him to come along to Macon for a few days, to help two new infielders settle in.

Hughey refused.

John McGraw was delighted that Jack Doyle was gone. Mac loathed Doyle. Everyone did. McGraw had said publicly he was unwilling to play on the same team again with Dirty Jack. In ways they were too much alike to share a bench. So Foxy Ned, mindful of the chemistry as well as the craft of a team, traded Doyle and Henny Reitz to the Senators in exchange for an untried first baseman named Big Dan McGann and a quick-as-electricity second baseman, Gene Demontreville—Demont, everyone called him—and twirler Jimmy McJames, a tall, slender medical student from South Carolina who threw an intricate curveball.

Macon was balmy this spring, but the ballgrounds seemed even scragglier than before. McGraw was his old self, full of vim. The practices went well, even as Hanlon heard nothing from the insurgents. Kelley and Clarke were practicing at Union Park. Hanlon waxed confident that the holdouts would give in. He told anyone who asked that he did not care if Corbett came back, and he was tickled when he read in the newspapers that Keeler and Kelley had made a $5,000 profit in a business deal. "I would like to have a photograph of that $5,000," he said. "I did not think that Willie would take any chances with his money. He must be getting reckless."

Then a telegram came, from Bill Clarke. He was coming to Macon. Hanlon had wired the catcher that his salary would be used to pay a replacement. When Clarke arrived the next day his teammates gave him an ovation. The spindly ballplayer said he had been foolish to stay away.

The Orioles played their way north to Baltimore, the azaleas giving way to mounds of snow. The boys got in two hours of good practice on the lumpy diamond at Union Park. Joe Kelley and Willie Keeler joined in. Both looked fit and ready. Everyone strained to catch what Hanlon would say to them and they to him. As it happened, Hanlon kept his distance.

That night the ballplayers reiterated they would never sign contracts until the ballclub met their demands.

A couple of days passed before Hanlon had a long chat with Willie, who refused to give in. The manager publicly swore he would make no concessions and warned he was looking for replacements.

Willie and Kel watched from the grandstand as the Orioles played an exhibition game against the Syracuse Stars from the Eastern League. When Kel's substitute nailed a runner at home, a crank in the bleachers hollered: "How do you like that throw, Kelley?"

The season was four days away, and Hughey was still in Georgia, when Hanlon invited his two reluctant outfielders in. For a long time they talked. None of them liked the impasse, and Willie wanted badly to play. So did Kel, though he was less inclined to say so. Hanlon was not a man with illusions. He knew he needed them, if he hoped for a pennant. His talk about replacements was only that.

And so a deal was struck.

Hughey arrived the next day. He and Willie would be paid $2,600 and Kel $2,700.

"I think we have the strongest team we ever began the season with," Hanlon said.

Mothers and wives and sisters and sweethearts stood in the drizzle and sobbed. They waved American flags as their men—boys, really—marched off in the vague direction of war. The guardsmen of the Fourth and Fifth Regiments marched to the rendezvous at Eutaw place and North avenue, then out along Reisterstown pike and to the Pimlico racetrack, which had been turned into a military camp. All over Baltimore, in countless windows and from thousands of housetops, Old Glory sparkled through the gloom. What a grand cause the nation was fighting for! The newspapers said so.

Just before six o'clock that evening, the twenty-fifth of April, a messenger from the U.S. Capitol arrived at the White House carrying a declaration of war. President McKinley, a Civil War veteran, had hoped to avert taking up arms against Spain. But the country had left him no choice. He examined the language in his office with the attorney-general. At eighteen minutes past the hour, the president signed his name.

Not a single League ballplayer felt immediately inspired to trade his salary and celebrity for $13 a month and the glories of war. The closest any of the Orioles came to the bloodshed in Cuba had occurred the previous spring, as the team barnstormed through Virginia on its way north from Macon. In Newport News, Hughey Jennings had hired a boatman to row him out to the warship at anchor on the James River.

"Who are you?" a naval officer had shouted down from the deck.

"Jennings of the Baltimore baseball club."

"Come right aboard, Mr. Jennings—we have heard of you before."

And so Hughey had boarded the USS *Maine*. The ship's baseball team was the crack club of the fleet. All of the players were white except for the pitcher, William Lambert, a fireman from Virginia and the son of one-time slaves. With his speed, curves, and control, he was a master.

The ship had left the peaceful waters of Virginia as the tensions with Spain over Cuban independence grew. The crew was asleep, before ten in the evening, the fifteenth of February in 'ninety-eight, when a mysterious explosion sent the *Maine* to the bottom of Havana Harbor.

The Orioles opened their 'ninety-eight season a few days before war was declared. The newspapers in Baltimore proclaimed that the advent of baseball would rival in excitement the onrush of war. They were wrong, of course. It *was* just a game. Maybe the war had been concocted, but real people would die. The parade to Union Park for the first game of the season was tame. The shoving and hustling of earlier years were gone. On a sunny afternoon only 6,518 cranks paid to watch the Orioles host the Senators. They exuded warmth instead of passion.

Harry von der Horst, in his private box, was looking as spruce as ever. He should have been worried: The crowd would be the largest of the season.

The ex-holdouts looked rusty. Willie Keeler, who had made seven errors in all of 'ninety-seven, committed two. Once, the ball slipped from his hand as he started to throw, and later he made a square muff of a fly ball. Hughey Jennings, the greatest shortshop in the land, let a ground ball pass between his legs.

But at the bat, everything felt familiar. John McGraw led off the first inning with a bunt and Willie poked a single to right field. Then they pulled off a double steal. Before the inning ended, five runs had scored—the margin of victory. Willie got four hits. Kelley and Demont did too.

Doc McJames pitched and quite nicely. The South Carolinian hurled sharp curves that left his former teammates slapping at the air. Hanlon had his other new twirler, Jimmy Hughes, pitch the next afternoon. Hughey Jennings had discovered him over the winter out in California, a tall, strong right-hander with speed and an especially deceptive slow ball. Against the Senators he was sharp, and the Orioles were, too. Willie Keeler made a long hard sprint for a circus catch, rolling over two or three times. The infield was a perfect stone wall. The rookie shut out the Senators on two hits.

The next time he pitched, against the Beaneaters, Jimmy Hughes did something twirlers had done just twice in the past five years, ever since the pitching distance had been lengthened: He pitched nine innings without giving up a hit.

It was in his rolling catch that Willie hurt his side and was out for three weeks. He was missed, and not only for his bat. He somehow kept the Big Four batting in concert. Without him the Orioles started to lose. "Keeler's presence makes a wonderful difference to the Orioles," the *Morning Herald* noted, "and when he gets back into the game the Birds will be flying high again."

But more was wrong with the Orioles than that. Hanlon had two good young pitchers, but only two. Corbett was still in California, insisting on $2,500 plus a railway ticket while Hanlon refused to pay a penny more than $2,400, even if it cost a pennant.

There was a listlessness about the Orioles, too. Hughey's arm was so lame—from too much use, no doubt—that he could barely throw to first. Almost everyone seemed distracted. Robbie was murmuring about retiring after the season to attend to his business interests, and he and McGraw were dickering to buy a stylish new saloon on Fayette street. Even Hanlon had his mind on other matters. Knowing he would never truly be in charge while subject to Harry von der Horst's whims, he had spent 'ninety-seven contriving to buy the lowly St. Louis Browns. (He had offered $75,000 but the owner insisted on $125,000.) To his ballplayers, Hanlon seemed more remote than ever. "I have yet to hear Mr. Hanlon compliment my work," Doc McJames confided in June. "Hanlon never says a word one way or the other—and that's the way a ball team should be run."

Whether it was because the Orioles were trying too hard or not hard enough, they failed to hit when they needed to most. They faltered even against the tailenders. DOPEY BALL PLAYING was the headline after the Orioles made four errors in losing to the Browns.

Certainly the public was distracted. All over the League, the war had shrunk the crowds by a fifth. If the depression had driven people in search of entertainment, the war against Spain *was* entertainment. The downfall of Manila (which turned Admiral Dewey into America's grandest celebrity), the Rough Riders on San Juan Hill, the capture of Santiago—the war blazed daily across every front page. How could a pastoral, stylized combat compete with the genuine article?

At Union Park the interest in baseball collapsed. By June the crowds sometimes numbered in the hundreds. The receipts just about paid for the lost baseballs.

At the Polo Grounds, in the doldrums of late July, the Orioles' new outfielder, Ducky Holmes, struck out in the fourth inning and waddled back to the bench. He was known here. He had played for the Giants in 'ninety-seven—and not especially well. Yet Hanlon had seen something in him. Holmes was short and squat but had surprising speed and a powerful arm. Hanlon was convinced he could hit .300 if properly coached.

He still needed work, and the New York cranks let him know it. "Oh! Ducky, you're a lobster," someone shouted from the grandstand. And from the box seats, a Tammany henchman of Andrew Freedman, the Giants' owner, called out, "You are rotten, Ducky—that is what we let you go for!"

"Well, I'm glad I don't have to work for no sheeny anymore," Holmes retorted.

Few people heard the slur on Freedman's Jewish blood. But as a Giant was coming to bat, a great commotion erupted around the ballclub's bench. Andrew Freedman, purple with rage, burst onto the diamond. The veins in his temple bulged against his tight curly hair. His jowls, already generous, looked ready to explode. He was prone to. Once, without warning, he had socked a newspaperman who was sixty-five pounds lighter. He had scrapped with an umpire who addressed him as "Freedman" instead of as "Mr. Freedman." Incensed by this latest insult to his dignity and his heritage, Freedman tore across to the umpire and shouted: "Lynch, I want that man Holmes thrown out of these grounds. He's insulted me."

Lynch said he had heard nothing and could not act. The umpire then asked Hanlon, who declined to remove his left fielder from the game. Freedman left for a moment and returned with two policemen and ordered them to arrest Holmes out in the field.

"Holmes, Freedman wants you to get off the grounds," he was informed.

"Who's Freedman?" The outfielder replied. "He's a dead one." And the cops laughed. Then Umpire Lynch ran out and told the officers of the law that *he* was the master of the diamond. The policemen, who understood authority, backed off.

Lynch ordered the game resumed, but the Giants manager, at Freedman's instruction, refused to to send a man to the bat. So a 1-to-1 tie was declared a forfeit to the Orioles.

The cranks stormed the ticket office, demanding their money back. It cost Freedman $1,750. And that was only the beginning.

Andrew Freedman was not a man who let things go. That was how he had reached his present station in life, as Richard Croker's right-hand man—the best man at the Tammany boss's wedding, his financial adviser, the fellow who could get things done. Freedman had served as the treasurer of the national Democratic party. In just three and a half seasons as the controlling owner of the Giants, he had hired six different managers—one of them twice—and fired seven. Freedman dressed fastidiously and was the only owner at League meetings to flash a bankroll. He never let up, and took pride in it.

He had already given Hanlon a check for $750, the Orioles' share of the ticket receipts. Freedman stopped payment on the check and declared Ducky Holmes barred from the Polo Grounds.

Hanlon was coldly furious. "This man Freedman needs to be taught a lesson," he said, promising to press for a $1,000 fine, permitted by the League constitution. "He thinks his connection with Tammany will allow him to do anything, and he believes he can ride roughshod over everybody. He will find his mistake."

Freedman was unintimidated. He leaned on the League's directors to suspend Holmes for the rest of the season. They were eager to punish vulgarity and, without bothering to ask Holmes for his defense, they complied.

This provoked a furor. Holmes hired a lawyer, who sought an injunction and threatened a lawsuit. Nervous as ever about venturing into court, the League's directors backed down.

Which was how Ducky Holmes became a drawing card—the ballplayer who had faced down the League. Suddenly he was a favorite at Union Park. Wherever the Orioles played, he was a celebrity who brought out a crowd. And with it all, his play improved. He started hitting the ball harder than he had since entering the League in 'ninety-five.

Maybe it was the spark that Holmes supplied or the onset of the summer's heat or the terror of a season going sour or, most plausibly, the revival of a rhythm the Orioles still felt in their bones. Or perhaps it was the glorious play by individual players. John McGraw was his old self again. He was even better at the bat than before, hitting over .340 and drawing more bases on balls and scoring more runs than anyone in the League. Willie was the League's top batsman again, within a slow roller of .400. He hit safely in twenty-five consecutive games. He almost never struck out. One afternoon in St. Louis, the Orioles had just tied the game in the ninth inning when Willie came to bat. Twice he tried to punch the ball over the third baseman's head but fouled it off. The Browns infield lined up along the left side of the diamond as the left fielder edged in. So Willie bunted toward first base and drove the winning run home.

In front of the Gibson House in Cincinnati one evening, a stranger approached Archie Ball, the Orioles' utility infielder, and asked him to point out Willie Keeler—"that great hitter. I'm from out West and have never had a chance to see him."

"There he is," Ball said, pointing to Willie nearby.

"Quit your kidding," the man from the West laughed. "I may be green, but you can't point out a kid to me and make me believe that it is Keeler, that great slugger."

Whatever the reasons, the Orioles seemed to be themselves again. In August the ginger returned to their fielding and the science to their stickwork. Even the pitching held up. They won twelve straight games, and pushed into third place, then into second, a few games behind the Beaneaters, not far from what they were certain they deserved.

Yet the Beaneaters kept winning as well and the Orioles had more weaknesses than they used to. They kept trying to hit the ball out of the lot when they ought to have been thinking. For scientific baseball to work, each player must put the interests of his teammates before his own. The Orioles were finding that harder and harder. Somehow they were not quite a team.

They still had a chance for the pennant when they arrived in Boston for two crucial games in October. Both teams were overanxious. The Boston management had prepared to put the overflow of spectators behind ropes in the outfield, but the stands held everyone who came. In the fourth inning, the Orioles led, 10 to 3. The Beaneaters had a man on base when Billy Hamilton lofted a fly ball into the cramped quarters of right field. Willie Keeler, back in the lineup after spraining his ankle a few days before, had not brought his smoked glasses along. So he was unable to gauge the ball in the sun and let it fall safely. Had he caught it the Beaneaters would have scored but one run that inning. Instead they scored six.

The Orioles kept making errors, while the Beaneaters played the sharpest kind of game—quick in the field and precise at the bat. They beat the Orioles at their own game, 13 to 10.

Willie, on the verge of his second batting title, donned his uniform the next afternoon but was hobbling too much to play. From the hard-bottomed bench he watched an uncustomary duel between twirlers. Doc McJames looked like a boy but pitched like a man, proving himself a match for the great Kid Nichols, who had already won thirty games this season, for the seventh time. The Orioles took a 2-to-1 lead in the eighth inning—obviously the last one, as the autumn afternoon turned to dusk. Despite the threat of rain, the crowd was larger than the day before, and louder. Two Beaneaters stood on base with two men out. Silence descended as a bounding ball wide of first base promised the end of the game. Big Dan McGann caught the ball and tossed it accurately to Doc McJames, who was in just the right place— and muffed it.

Hanlon was indignant. The Orioles had bungled away two games they should have won. Willie's lameness was no excuse. The manager railed at his ballplayers' indifference, at their sulking. Though perhaps he should have railed at himself. Was their attitude not his responsibility?

It was too late to matter anymore. All real hope for finishing on top again was gone.

Four weeks earlier, in a relentless rain, Maryland's Fifth Regiment dragged itself home. The grimy, unshaven veterans, the dust-caked heroes of a splendid little war, marched in precise formation from the railway station to the armory. Not since the Orioles had won the 'ninety-four pennant had so many Baltimoreans turned out to watch a parade. More than a hundred thousand people looked on. People were packed so tightly along Charles street that only their heads got wet. A welcome tore from every throat. Mothers burst into tears as their sons tottered past, for rare was the soldier who had not lost forty pounds or more. The spectators remembered the soldiers who would not be coming home. The newspapers had published a list. *Typhoid, Baltimore. Drowned, Chickamauga. Typhoid, Atlanta. Typhoid, Tampa.* From Baltimore they had gone first to Chickamauga, Tennessee, and then to Tampa, to be trained. In Tampa they had waited and waited for orders that never arrived.

They seemed more than five months older than when they had gone. The country did too. What a glorious victory it had won. It was a small war that promised big changes. A nation that had always looked inward was becoming an imperial power.

But the attendance at Union Park had never recovered from the war, having plunged by more than half for the longer season, the steepest drop in the League. Only 123,416 cranks saw the Orioles at home—barely 1,600 a game. All over the League, the war had squelched profits. Despite their second-place finish, the Orioles finished in the red.

Harry von der Horst was beside himself. This was the third year running that the ballclub had failed to turn a profit. It had been lucky to break even in the pennant-winning year of 'ninety-six, then offset the money it made on the road in 'ninety-seven with losses at home. Who could tell if the profits would ever return?

The problem was clearly more than the war. Maybe it was Baltimore. Twice as many people paid to watch the Orioles on the road. Perhaps it was possible even for cranks to get filled up with winning— bored with excellence. "When it was seen that we should lose the pennant in 1898 the attendance fell off considerably," McGraw recounted. "Baltimore was never a city to support a loser." No one could say why. Might it be a defect in the city's moral character, or nothing more than a clear-eyed understanding that baseball was only a game?

Or maybe the problem was the team. It was a ghost of what it had once been. The chemistry was wrong. The devotion to teamwork, the purity of effort—once that was lost, how might it be regained? How could a man who was sated be made hungry again? Everyone seemed so tired, so worn.

And how might the team be rebuilt? It would take money—but money from where? The ballclub was in the red and the brewery was caught in a competitive vise. Harry von der Horst saw no simple solution. A team past its prime was no easy thing to repair, and he had a scarcity of cash on hand for buying ballplayers. Worse, the other magnates were nervous about making trades with Foxy Ned. All the while, the players were grumbling about the extra ballgames and the clamps on salaries—sure to be tighter next season, after the financial losses.

This was no fun anymore. When Harry had started in baseball, back in 'eighty-two, it had been damn fun. He had been offered an American Association franchise just as Brooklyn was bowing out, and he had made money even as the Orioles finished last. He entertained the men of affairs (and their lovely wives) in the owner's box. He was more than a brewer, even more than a man-about-town. He mattered in Baltimore—never mind what his father had thought.

Plainly, baseball had changed. It was hardly more than a business anymore, and not an appealing one. The situation promised to get worse before it improved. The Orioles were not about to get better on their own. Who could tell if the attendance was coming back, given the popularity of bowling and boxing and racing and pool halls? Rowdiness on the diamond was driving away the crowds. Just about everyone was losing money, and figured to lose more. Things could not go on this way.

It was hard for Harry to know what to do. He should not have to bankrupt himself to bring baseball to the city of his birth. But he did have options. Proposals had come his way, unbidden. Andrew Freedman, on returning from Europe, had suggested swapping the best of the Orioles for a stake in the Giants. Harry said he had received "several flattering offers" to move the ballclub to some other city, but he declared that he had never given them serious thought. "I am a Baltimorean," he proclaimed, "and take enough pride in my native city to wish to see it at the top." But, he added ominously, "the only businesslike way in which we can make both ends meet is to transfer the team to a city where the attendance will warrant such an aggregation of players as we have under contract."

No one could tell for sure if Harry was bluffing. He denied that negotiations were under way. But it was obvious that something had to give.

PART TWO

Business

=7=

Syndicate Baseball

All day it had rained without remorse, but that did not daunt the fifty thousand New Yorkers who crowded around City Hall as 'ninety-seven elapsed, to celebrate something more than a new year. At the stroke of midnight, cannons boomed and fireworks exploded and people shouted into a sky as dark as the womb. A new city was born. No longer was it to be known as New York. Now it was Greater New York. No longer was it only Manhattan and a bit of the Bronx. They had consolidated with Queens, Staten Island, the rest of the Bronx, and the proud city of Brooklyn, the fourth-largest in the country. No longer did Chicago pose a danger of becoming the nation's most populous city. In the tick of a clock, a city of two million souls had become a grand municipality with not quite twice as many people, second in the world only to London.

Across the East River, the crowd was smaller and subdued. Brooklyn's City Hall was becoming Borough Hall. The "observance"—no celebration—was held indoors, in the Common Council Chamber, with its grand ceiling and oversized portraits in oil of Brooklyn notables past. The florists had made their profit from the longing for dignity. Members of the Society of Old Brooklynites were given seats in the front, and by nine o'clock the crowd filled every room in the sprawling building to watch a city pass away. A somber electricity was in the air. This was history.

St. Clair McKelway, the editor of the *Brooklyn Daily Eagle,* so long opposed to consolidation, was the orator for the evening. He had lush dark whiskers and wore pince-nez that made his muscular face even more forbidding. He used many more words than he needed, to put the best face on things. "There is no significance in the concurrence of clouds with consolidation," he began. It was his last note of levity. "No shroud shall be the marriage portion of Brooklyn," he intoned. "To a wedding and not to a funeral we are bidden."

The suitor had been the merchants of Manhattan. For decades they had lobbied for a consolidated government to administer the chaotic harbor and to make sure they had the rail lines and the utilities an up-to-date economy demanded. For Rockefeller and Carnegie and Vanderbilt—for oil, steel, railroads—bigger was better. Why not for New York?

Brooklyn had resisted. Its inhabitants loved what Brooklyn was. If Manhattan was a place of tenements and boardinghouses, Brooklyn was a city of houses and quiet streets. Neighbors knew their neighbors. A clerk or a workingman could afford a place of his own. He could pay a landlord $25 or $50 a month, a fifth of his earnings—and just half of what it would cost to live comfortably across the East River. Manhattan drew the rich and the poor and the single. The people in the middle, the families, lived in Brooklyn. From most places in Brooklyn a man could get to Manhattan in a half-hour's time, for merely five cents, on one of a dozen or more trolley lines. Brooklyn was home to more than a million inhabitants but had few of the amenities of a metropolis— not many banks, hardly any grand stores, scarcely a hotel, not even a morning newspaper. Yet it had no wish to be swallowed by its overbearing neighbor.

Still, by a margin of 277 votes (out of 129,211 cast), the people of Brooklyn had repudiated sentiment and acquiesced to consolidation. It was a matter of dollars and cents. Brooklyn was deeply in debt, by more than a tenth of the total valuation of its real estate. That left almost nothing to spend on sewers or water pipes or schools. The tax rate on homes was already too high, because the corporations that might share the burden of municipal costs were located in Manhattan. Every morning most of Brooklyn's menfolk crossed the bridge or rode a ferry to Manhattan, spent the day there creating wealth, and returned home at night. Indeed, under the terms of the charter King James II had promulgated three centuries earlier, Manhattan even controlled the ferries. Manhattan claimed most of the commerce, while Brooklyn was home to factories and warehouses and shops— everywhere, shops.

If Brooklyn hoped to thrive in the twentieth century, to see its future improve on its past, what choice did it have but to sell its soul?

*   *   *

Charley Ebbets, for one, had always favored consolidation. He had been elected to the new Greater New York city council in November (though so narrowly that his opponent was challenging the outcome in court) as a part of Boss McLaughlin's Brooklyn machine. He had already served a term in the state assembly up in Albany, and rumor had it that he was a candidate to lead the Democratic organization in the Twenty-second Ward. He was given a seat of honor at the ceremony in Brooklyn. Consolidation was the wave of the future, and Charley Ebbets was nothing if not a man of the future.

He was thirty-eight and a gentleman on the rise. If he hoped his dark handlebar moustache made his slender face look less boyish, it had done nothing of the kind. The curly-haired politician was affable and well-known around Brooklyn, in its sporting and social clubs. His father was the president of the Dime Savings Bank in Brooklyn, where Alexander Cartwright, the draftsman of baseball's first rules, had once worked as a teller. But Charley Ebbets was more than a fellow well-born. He was a doer. He had started as an architect but found the job confining. Then he published cheap editions of novels and sold them door to door. That was before he began working for the Brooklyn ballclub, back in 'eighty-three, as it was getting organized. (His brother was a friend of the owners.) At first he took tickets and hawked scorecards and cleaned the grandstands and kept the ledgers—anything that needed to be done. Soon enough he was the ballclub's secretary, an untiring aide-de-camp to Charley Byrne.

On New Year's Day of 'ninety-eight, as Charley Byrne lay on his deathbed—the doctors held out no hope—his able assistant hosted a small dinner party for the baseball scribes of Greater New York. Ebbets had invited them to the Clarendon Hotel, at the Brooklyn end of the bridge. He ushered them into the dining room off the rotunda, and they drank to the health of President Byrne. Then Ebbets stunned the hard-boiled newspapermen with an announcement: He had taken control of the ballclub.

He had signed the deal that day, to buy a third, more or less, of the stock in the club from George Chauncey and an associate. Chauncey had owned the Players' League franchise in Brooklyn, which had merged with the National League club after the 'ninety season. But Ebbets had more to say. Gus Abell, the sad-eyed millionaire who owned a majority of the stock, had given him an option until the first of February on enough shares to put 80 percent of the ballclub in the councilman's hands.

Ebbets was tight with a buck—the newspapermen knew that—but he was not a man of wealth. Where on earth had he come up with the money? There was talk it came from Gus Abell himself, but this was denied. "There is nobody backing me in this enterprise except Ebbets," Ebbets insisted. "I have put every dollar I own into the club, and I propose to run it in a way to popularize the sport in Brooklyn."

Baseball surely needed popularizing, for the ballclub was a mess. It had lost money every year since the Players' League collapsed. Abell alone claimed to have lost $100,000 since entering baseball. No wonder, given the team's persistent mediocrity. It played its games out in East New York, quite a ways from most of Brooklyn's cranks. That meant the ballclub could never sell enough tickets to buy itself a better team.

That would change now. In all probability, Ebbets said to the scribes, the Trolley Dodgers were not returning to Eastern Park. He had been looking for a site—where, he would not say. But he had taken options on two lots and planned to build a ballpark by spring.

And he had something else to offer the good people of Brooklyn. There had been talk that the consolidation of Greater New York might trigger the League's ban on locating two teams in a single city. To handle that would take the silky skills of a politician.

Was it distasteful to snatch control of the ballclub from a man in a coma? Maybe so, but Byrne's incapacitation meant that nobody was running the ballclub, and it showed. "The illness of Mr. Byrne has left the club in a chaotic state and we have realized that something must be done in the matter of selecting players and new grounds for next season," Ebbets explained. "I am sure that if he were here, he would endorse everything that has been said."

It was because Charley Byrne was dying that Gus Abell was willing to step aside. They had been partners in the ballclub for fifteen years now, despite striking differences in background and temperament. Charley Byrne was an excitable ex-sportswriter who ran a gambling hall and liked to hobnob with actors and playwrights. Ferdinand Augustus Abell came from what had become the finest of families, five generations removed from England. His uncle had founded *The Sun* in Baltimore, which Gus's first cousin now ran. Abell owned a gracious casino in Rhode Island, on Narragansett Pier, where the Vanderbilts were known to lunch on the piazza, at marble tables. Besides his cottage in Newport, he owned a mansion just off Fifth avenue in Manhattan.

The feisty Irish-American and the well-mannered aristocrat had worked perfectly together. Each had his job. Byrne ran the ballclub and Abell forked over the money. But now it was time for a break. For years Abell had wanted to sell his shares, and now the prospect of Charley Byrne's passing made baseball look bleak.

Three mornings later Charley Byrne succumbed. The short compact man known as the Napoleon of Baseball had been methodical and sharp in his practice of business—too sharp, perhaps, for many of his fellow magnates and his ballplayers as well. At his funeral, not even a third of the seats at St. Francis Xavier Church were filled, as just five ballplayers and a smattering of club owners bothered to attend the simple Mass.

The ballclub's directors had an easy decision when they met to elect a new president. Abell had already turned some of his stock over to Ebbets, enough to give him effective control, but held on to the rest. Prudence suggested keeping an eye on the youngest magnate in the League.

But surely Ebbets, too, had a knack for business. He worked hard and had a way with words—and with silences. He never revealed more than he had to. "The man who always tells the truth, the whole truth, and nothing but the truth is generally in hot water," he preached.

As the new president of the Brooklyn ballclub he moved with dispatch. His first order of business was to build a new ballpark. He personally selected the site, between First and Third streets and Third and Fourth avenues, nearer the densest parts of Brooklyn, within a nose's range of the greasy Gowanus Canal. It was on the spot that George Washington had raised his headquarters for the Battle of Long Island, a devastating defeat for the young nation's army, letting the British occupy New York. The site was catty-corner from the location of two earlier ballparks; like those, the new one would be called Washington Park.

Ebbets knew how to pay for it. He persuaded two trolley companies that stood to gain from the additional business to put up more than $15,000 to build the ballpark along their lines. Then he drafted the architectural plans himself. The roofed grandstand was pleasantly gabled, and he set aside two rooms over its main entrance as his handsomely fitted office. To funnel patrons into the stands, he designed something new: ramps to deposit the spectators partway up, so they would not all block the view of the people in front. Ebbets felt sure that the ballpark's location and its newness would bring in the crowds.

He was wrong. Maybe it was the distractions of the war or the rising popularity of other pastimes. Everyone seemed otherwise engaged.

The Trolley Dodgers too. Ebbets was not a man of patience. As the 'ninety-eight season started, he kept interfering with the manager, "Bald Billy" Barnie, who knew baseball like some men knew women. After thirty-five games, the team in sixth place, he let Barnie go, and named Mike Griffin, the popular center fielder, in his place. That lasted four games, three of them losses.

Then Charley Ebbets hired the only man he was sure he could trust: himself. In his top hat, such as all the club presidents wore, he sat on the players' bench and told them what to do. Soon rumors flew of a breach between the players and the management.

The Trolley Dodgers finished the season mired in tenth place, $20,000 in the red. The attendance in Brooklyn had slipped almost by half since the season before. Gus Abell was disgusted with having to put up money again.

The future looked worse than the past. Billy Barnie told the *Eagle* that unless the team got an infusion of talent, "there will not be a hundred people at the games here next season." Everyone understood that Greater New York would not stand for losers.

Nobody was surprised at Harry von der Horst's interest. If truth be told, he could not have imagined a more suitable arrangement. Other brewers in Baltimore had misgivings about shifting control of their businesses to a beer trust, but for Harry, it meant he could keep living in New York and not have to worry from two hundred miles away about keeping his brewery efficient in producing lager and selling it to local saloons. Now that he had finally gained full control over the Eagle Brewery, he had lost interest in it.

For the other brewers, too, a beer trust made sense. So in November of 'ninety-eight, seventeen of the twenty-one breweries around Baltimore filed papers of incorporation for the Maryland Brewing Company. By operating all of the breweries as one, the promoters explained, they could cut their costs for raw materials and brew a better beer without raising the price. Consolidation, they assured the public, would not necessarily mean fewer workers or diminished wages. Nor should the saloon keepers have reason to fret, for the beer trust would have no incentive to open more saloons and thus lower the price of beer.

The electric trolleys were next. The Baltimore Consolidated Railway Company sought to seize control of its main rival, offering eighty dollars a share for the Baltimore City Passenger Railway Company. It promised economies of scale, though the experience of other cities suggested that such mergers would mean shabbier streetcars that ran less often. Then suddenly a new suitor appeared. One of Baltimore's two minor railway companies, backed by a taciturn investment banker named Alex Brown and a syndicate of capitalists, bought City Passenger. People at the Consolidated were thunderstruck. Why had Alex Brown paid ninety dollars a share, unless he meant to buy the Consolidated as well?

The next day he did.

Sitting in his office at Baltimore and Calvert streets, besieged by hundreds of people desperate to know what was what, Alex Brown looked even more forbidding than usual. He had a round face and a vast forehead and piercing eyes and a pointed goatee that gave him a diabolical air. "We intend to improve the service wherever improvement can be made," he blandly told the man from the *Baltimore American*, the city's Republican newspaper. He acknowledged that much of the capital was coming from New York and Philadelphia—"but," he said emphatically, "you can state that the corporation will be controlled in Baltimore, and will not be a foreign company."

This was a sensitive point, and had been for two years at least, since local capitalists had lost control of the mighty Baltimore and Ohio Railroad. The nation's first commercial railroad had long been the most important company in Maryland. The state and the city had each owned a stake. But the depression had thrown the B&O into receivership, and J. P. Morgan & Company had given the railroad officials a choice. The New York financiers were not about to lend the B&O another dollar unless they were satisfied that it was in better financial shape than anyone figured—or unless Morgan was given absolute control. The railroad's board of directors, made up almost entirely of Baltimoreans, would soon be composed of seven New Yorkers, two Philadelphians, a Chicagoan, someone from Pittsburgh, and a lone member from Baltimore.

Monopoly was vaulting ahead. Maybe it was because of the war and the prosperity it had provoked. The commissions on war loans and the spiral in the money supply had put conglomerations of capital in the hands of financiers, who then created the industrial trusts. During the winter of 'ninety-eight, the consolidations that had been occurring in a trickle in Baltimore suddenly became a torrent. The Baltimore Brick Company absorbed all of the city's sizable brickmakers. The city's fourteen can factories became part of the American Can Company. The electric utilities were combined into one. Trusts prevailed among the gas companies and the cotton duck mills.

Baltimoreans kept control of the monopolies that carried national clout (such as canning and cotton duck) or that sold their wares exclusively to the local market (beer and electricity). But the city lost its dominion over anything produced locally for a larger market. The national fertilizer trust acquired the city's eight big fertilizer plants. The Baltimore Sugar Refining Company, two local tobacco companies, the city's type foundries, its shipping lines, its biggest bakery, a whiskey distillery, a piano company, a copper refinery—all had been wrested from Baltimore's control.

The local capitalists had always owned the engines of their city's wealth. Baltimoreans had controlled their own fate. And yet in the course of a year or two, everything changed. Baltimore was becoming a branch town.

Willie Keeler was looking prosperous, his smile still safely in place, as he wandered over from Brooklyn to Fifth avenue and Twenty-third street. His cheeks were flushed and his face was not as thin as before. He had been spending a quiet winter in Brooklyn, taking the occasional flyer in real estate. The Fifth Avenue Hotel, with its lushly formal spaces and elaborate chandeliers, was not his style. But Willie could get used to anything, even luxury.

Manhattan just before Christmas was a crystalline sight. Shoppers jammed Fifth avenue. The elevated trains were packed to the gates along Twenty-third street, and the fakirs worked their toys so that passersby stepped on them, not always with regret. Bloomingdale's advertised satin-bound smoking jackets for $3.97 and a swirl of timely items on sale—"Rough Riders" waterproof boots for $3.98, games called *Siege of Havana* and *War at Sea* for less than a dollar. Barbershops were selling Christmas trees, and so were department stores and even the occasional saloon. Patriotic New Yorkers were decorating their trees this year with American flags and pictures of Admiral Dewey.

Willie found it a nice diversion to see so many friends. The attendance at the National League meeting was the largest in years. The scribes crowded around the barstools of the marbled hotel like urchins at knotholes. Ballplayers and former players, managers and former managers, hangers-on of every description clogged the corridors—Joe Kelley and Johnny Ward and Connie Mack and Pat Powers and Billy Barnie and even Ban Johnson, the stout young president of the Western League. More was going on outside the gilded Parlor F than behind its closed doors.

Nobody was more sought after than Ned Hanlon. Mindful that the Orioles had been losing money, the other managers hoped he might be selling off some of his ballplayers. Foxy Ned broke bread with Johnny Ward, who had been out of baseball for nearly four years now and, despite a thriving legal practice, yearned to return.

Soon it was noticed that Hanlon was spending most of his time with somebody else—Gus Abell. Hanlon and Harry von der Horst spent most of Thursday conferring with the round-faced, slope-shouldered magnate, then dined with him that night. Everyone figured that the Brooklyn owner had pretty much retired, so his presence at the meeting was a surprise. "I could not stay away," he offered, suave and evasive at once.

Later it developed that Abell had taken the initiative—two years earlier, Hanlon divulged. Hanlon and Harry von der Horst had turned him down flat in 'ninety-six, but that was before they started losing money. Lately they had been making their interest known. Rumors swept the corridors of a deal between Baltimore and Brooklyn, of something more than an exchange of players—a wholesale swap, perhaps, or even a merger. Similar rumors had been whirling all winter, of a deal between Baltimore and New York or Baltimore and Philadelphia or Baltimore and Brooklyn. None of them had turned out to be true, at least not yet.

This time, the principals had little to say. Yet the more they stayed out of sight, the more plausible the rumors seemed.

Charley Ebbets was home with a bad case of the grippe, which had turned into pneumonia, but in his absence the other three magnates enjoyed one another's company. Abell, urbane and bewhiskered, was a perfect Chesterfield in his bearing, a courtly man who carried himself lightly. Like Hanlon he was a New Englander and could take on an air of seriousness when he needed to. Hanlon relished Abell's reputation as an owner who left the manager alone. And Harry also took to him right away. There was a rumpledness about Gus Abell that was easy to be near. Abell was as pleasant to a hotel porter as to a prince of Wall street. He made Harry feel as if he belonged.

When the three men got back from Delmonico's, the scribes cornered Hanlon. "No proposition whatever has been made to me, and all I know of the matter is the talk in the corridors," Foxy Ned replied. Then he immediately added: "I believe that if the plan could be carried out a great deal of money would be made."

For Hanlon the decision was simple. Of course he had loyalty to Baltimore: It was where he and Ellen had raised their five children. Baltimore, however, had shown no loyalty to the ballclub in 'ninety-seven and 'ninety-eight. So what rights did a city have to a team it refused to support? Hanlon was not in this business to lose money. This was not a toy to him, but his livelihood. It was business, not sentiment.

The idea made so much sense, from so many sides. The economics were unassailable. Brooklyn had twice as many inhabitants as Baltimore did, and Greater New York had many more. When the Orioles had started to win—it seemed so long ago now—they had drawn more than three hundred thousand cranks in a season to Union Park. If a first-rate team succeeded in attracting an equal percentage of cranks in New York, no ballgrounds could hold them. It might draw cranks not only from Brooklyn but also from southern Manhattan, just twenty minutes across the bridge from Washington Park, quicker to get to than the Polo Grounds so far uptown. "Something like $100,000 a year net profit," Hanlon figured—"easy money."

That would give Abell, at long last, a chance to recoup his losses. His casino was elegant but he meant it to turn a profit. The same went for his ballclub. More delicious still was the prospect of snatching business away from the Giants and Andrew Freedman. Abell had reason: The Tammany man had persuaded his cronies at City Hall to block construction of a subway station for Washington Park. It had been Abell's and Charley Ebbets's notion to drive Andrew Freedman and the Giants clear out of town, to make the Trolley Dodgers the only team in Greater New York.

Indeed, it was the Giants that offered the only precedent to what Abell had in mind. It dated back to the days of the Players' League, when the owners of five other National League teams had paid

$80,000 for stock in the Giants, rescuing them from bankruptcy, after the ballclub had drawn barely sixty thousand cranks all season long. Abell should know. He had been one of those owners.

The deal under discussion between Baltimore and Brooklyn envisioned something far grander. The Baltimore magnates would buy half of the Trolley Dodgers and move the pick of the Orioles to Brooklyn. What would happen with the Baltimore ballclub, they could not say for certain. Possibly the Brooklyn magnates might buy half of the Orioles, stranding the worst of both teams at Union Park. Or perhaps something more drastic was in the works. Off and on for months there had been talk of an eight-club league. That could not happen, to be sure, unless four clubs agreed to die. The Indianapolis agreement, which pledged a twelve-team league for a decade, made sure of that. But permission could be purchased, could it not? The owners could be induced to find it worthwhile.

The next morning Harry came down with the grippe. There was an epidemic. As he fought the chills in his hotel room, Hanlon and Abell closeted themselves for most of the day. They dined at six. By eight they had settled on Hanlon's title and salary. They had nothing more to discuss until Harry could join them.

This time, as they entered the hotel lobby, they had something to tell the newspapermen hungry for a story. Abell put the transaction on a businesslike basis: "We have something which the Baltimore people need, and they have something which we need. Therefore, why should we not make an exchange?" Hanlon alluded to the complications. "We have agreed on the deal in a general way, but details have not been specifically discussed, nor will they be until Mr. von der Horst can be taken into the conference," he said. "Personally, I should dislike to leave Baltimore, as my home is established there and I have many friends. But the fact is there exists conditions which make the new arrangements necessary."

Baltimore was aghast. While there had been months of fitful rumors, the city's cranks were unprepared for something like this. It was awful, impossible to grasp—*our* boys, playing in Brooklyn. BALTIMORE SOLD OUT, the *Morning Herald* gasped. The *Baltimore American* mourned on its front page, A BITTER PILL FOR OUR FANS. Only *The Sun*, in the Abells' grasp, left the news off the front page. GOOD-BYE, ORIOLES, was all the headline said. The stuffiest of the city's newspapers reported that the local cranks "had little to say and much of what they did utter was unfit to print."

They thanked God that Harry von der Horst was in his sickbed. Otherwise the Orioles might already be gone. Ordinarily, good old Harry was known to do whatever Hanlon wanted. Not always, though. It gave the cranks some hope.

Harry gave them more the following day, when he roused himself sufficiently to let a newspaperman in. "I shall do nothing hastily," Harry announced. "There are many details that must yet be looked into before a definite answer is given. The proposed deal is of such a magnitude that it cannot be made in a day, a week, or a month." Harry promised to take something else into account—"just how the public will feel about two clubs in one league being owned by one corporation."

Yet Harry had already joined one trust, the beer trust. Why not another?

As John McGraw described it years later, the deal was "the biggest sensation that baseball had yet known." Syndicate baseball, it came to be called. Even the people hurt by it, however, understood the reasons. The astringent logic of capitalism had left little choice. "It is a matter of business," the *Morning Herald,* the most populist of the Baltimore newspapers, explained to its readers, "and sentiment must go to the wall."

The arithmetic worked—anyone with a brain could understand that. The Baltimore magnates would come out ahead by pooling their interests with Brooklyn's—in effect, swapping half of the Orioles for half of the Trolley Dodgers. The accountants valued half of the stock in Brooklyn's ballclub at $125,000, and in Baltimore's at $20,000. The new Washington Park was worth $32,000, as against $15,000 for Union Park. This more than counterbalanced the difference in the value of the players. The eight Orioles figured to be Brooklyn-bound would bring $40,000, combined, on the open market, twice as much as the ten Trolley Dodgers presumed headed for Baltimore. For the Baltimore magnates, the numbers looked good.

But not for everyone on the team. As a matter of business, John McGraw was refusing to go, as was Robbie. "I will be right here, or nowhere," the catcher said. Business was booming at The Diamond, which had become the place for the sporting crowd in Baltimore to be seen. "If I should go on the new Brooklyn team, I would, in the minds of my friends, lose my identity as a Baltimorean," Mac patiently explained. "I have been in baseball for ten years and in business for two years. During the two business years I have accumulated more money than I was ever able to put together from ten years of ballplaying."

Hanlon, on returning to Baltimore, promised to persuade McGraw and Robbie to play in Brooklyn. But undoubtedly he understood their reasons, which were no different from his. Hanlon had explained to a friendly newspaperman that he would make no move that did not better him personally. This deal, it was clear to him, would.

For Hanlon, there was more to the deal than simple arithmetic. It would mean being out from under Harry von der Horst's thumb. It was hard to work for a man you did not respect. Gus Abell was different. He was a man of his word, who had already shown his trust. "Mr. Hanlon will have just the same authority over the team in Brooklyn that he had in Baltimore," Abell had said to a scribe. "He will be the 'Great I Am,' with none to say him nay."

Several days later, in Baltimore, Hanlon met with Harry to discuss the deal at length. Harry had recovered enough to attend to some brewery business. He said afterward he was inclined to go ahead with the deal but needed to think it over. The Brooklyn magnates, he said, would have to come to him.

Harry understandably had some pangs. He truly was a Baltimorean, even if he was living in New York now. He could not stand to have the good fellows of his native city detest him. He still had beer to sell, even through a trust. It was more than that, of course. A man's reputation mattered. If he sent the best of the Orioles away from Baltimore, what would his friends think of him? And yet he did prefer making money to losing it, especially to losing $20,600, the Orioles' shortfall in 'ninety-eight. After so many years in the black, Harry had grown used to turning a profit. In Brooklyn, he would again.

He needed to. His lawyers were still haggling with Emma's over a financial settlement for an amicable separation. Harry was putting half of the stock in his brewery (represented as shares in the beer syndicate) in trust for his wife and for the girls, who were women now, just into their twenties, with no husbands in sight. Harry needed to make money from baseball, not lose it, if he hoped to continue living in the style to which he had grown delightedly accustomed.

And nobody knew for sure where Charley Ebbets stood on the deal. A couple of months earlier, when the rumors burst forth, he was reportedly unwilling to give up half his holdings in the Trolley Dodgers. He had had advantages, to be sure, but nothing had come easily to him. He had torn how many tickets, added up how many columns of figures, swabbed how many benches, stayed how many late nights, bitten his tongue how many times, to reach his current position. He had waited fifteen years to run the Trolley Dodgers, and he had been the club's president for eleven months now. Except on the rare occasions that Gus Abell made his opinion known, Ebbets was in charge.

"I am in full control," he had boasted only a month earlier. So why would he want Ned Hanlon to step in as the Great I Am?

Yet he was in a box. The public in Brooklyn thought the deal was glorious—it would mean having the finest nine on the face of the earth. And Charley Ebbets was a public man. He was a politician with hopes for a future. He knew better than to stand in the way of the popular will.

Gus Abell, of course, still owned enough of the Trolley Dodgers to deliver half of the ballclub's stock to the Baltimore magnates by himself, but that would leave him with too little left to benefit, once the bolstered ballclub started making money, as it was bound to. That gave Ebbets some leverage, and he knew it, and had no hesitation about using it. From Abell he extracted a promise that he could stay on as the president if the deal went through. Still, Ebbets worried about having the title but no power, and Abell refused to give him assurances that he would not have to take orders from Hanlon.

On two occasions Ebbets made an appointment with Abell to talk about the deal. Both times Ebbets failed to show up.

One man found reason for pure joy in the prospect of syndicate baseball. Willie Keeler was going home. He had played for the Trolley Dodgers before, back in 'ninety-three, and had fallen short. But now that he had established himself in the big league, he had no reason to be nervous. "I can say frankly that I would rather play in Brooklyn, my home, than anywhere else," he exulted to the man from the *Eagle*.

The other ballplayers Hanlon had in mind taking with him to Brooklyn could not say the same. Joe Kelley had just bought a stately,

The 1896 Baltimore Orioles, winners of their third consecutive National League pennant, with manager Ned Hanlon in street clothes at center. *Back row (left to right)*: infielder Joe Quinn, pitcher Sadie McMahon, pitcher Duke Esper, pitcher George Hemming, catcher Frank Bowerman, catcher Bill Clarke, infielder Jim Donnelly. *Middle row*: center fielder Steve Brodie, pitcher Bill Hoffer, left fielder Joe Kelley, Hanlon, catcher Wilbert Robinson, shortstop Hughey Jennings, second baseman Henny Reitz. *Front row*: first baseman Jack Doyle, third baseman John McGraw, right fielder Willie Keeler, pitcher Arlington Pond. *Inset (upper left)*: pitcher Joe Corbett. (Babe Ruth Museum, Baltimore, Maryland)

Willie Keeler (*middle row, second from the left*) on the Allertons, a semipro club in Weehawken, New Jersey, for whom he played Sunday games in 1890 and 1891, while he was still a teenager. (Courtesy of the Keeler family)

The New-York Times, Saturday, October 1, 1892.

BEATEN BY A SINGLE RUN

THE NEW-YORKS FAILED TO BUNCH THEIR BASE HITS.

AS A RESULT THE PHILADELPHIAS
WON THE GAME YESTERDAY—
KEELER, THE NEW THIRD BASE
MAN, PLAYED, AND HIS WORK
GAVE GENERAL SATISFACTION.

On the Polo Grounds yesterday the contest between the New-York and Philadelphia Clubs was a very lively one. At one stage the New-Yorks looked like sure winners. Then the visitors went to the front, and secured enough runs to win the game by a single run. On both sides the fielding was of a most brilliant character, and the New-Yorks made over twice as many base hits as their opponents. Their batting, however, was scattered, while that of the Philadelphias was bunched.

The game was lost in the eighth inning. Rusie had run bases in his half of this inning, and when he went into the box it was apparent that he was tired. As a result, the visitors made three hits. These, with a base on balls, secured 3 runs and the game. Burke was not in condition to play and his position was filled by Boyle. The new third baseman, Keeler, played yesterday, and though he had little work to do als playing was admirable. He is a fast ball player, and the critics think that he will make his mark. In the game he was the only man who had a stolen base to his credit. Rusie pitched a good game, far better than Keefe, and if the New-Yorks had bunched their hits they would have won with ease. The score:

NEW-YORK.	R.	1B.	PO.	A.	E.	PHILADELPHIA.	R.	1B.	PO.	A.	E.
Keeler, 3b..	1	1	1	2	0	Hamilton, lf..	2	2	2	0	0
Lyons, cf....	0	2	1	0	1	Hallman, 2b.	0	0	2	2	0
Doyle, 2b...	0	1	3	0	0	Th'mpson, rf.	1	1	2	0	0
Tiernan, rf..1	2	2	0	0	Del'hanty, cf.	0	4	0	0	0
Ewing, c....0	0	5	1	0	Cross, 3b...	0	0	1	3	1
M'Mah'n, 1b.0	2	10	1	0	Connor, 1b..0	0	10	0	0
Boyle, lf....0	0	2	0	0	Clements, c..0	0	5	1	0
Rusie, p....0	1	1	3	0	Allen, ss....	1	1	1	2	0
Fuller, ss...1	2	1	3	0	Keefe, p.....1	0	0	4	0
Total....4	11	24	12	1	Total.......5	5	27	12	1

New-York............0 0 0 1 0 1 2 0 0—4
Philadelphia.........1 0 0 0 0 1 0 3—5

Earned runs—New-York, 2; Philadelphia, 2. First base by errors—New-York, 1. Left on bases—New-York, 6; Philadelphia, 3. First base on balls—Off Rusie, 3; off Keefe, 1. Struck out—By Rusie, 4; by Keefe, 2. Two-base hits—McMahon, Delehanty. Sacrifice hits—Doyle, Ewing, McMahon, Boyle, Keefe, Hallman, (2.) Thompson, (2.) Stolen bases—Keeler, 2. Wild pitches—Keefe, 1; Rusie, 1. Passed ball—Clements. Umpire—Mr. Emslie.

In his debut in the major league, on September 30, 1892, Willie Keeler smacked a single, stole two bases, and scored a run for the New York Giants. He was only the second left-handed third baseman in the National League's history. (UMI)

Harry von der Horst, a Baltimore brewer, enjoyed being the principal owner of the Orioles, for it lent him a certain panache. (From the Collections of the Maryland Historical Society, Baltimore, Maryland)

Ned Hanlon, the manager of the Baltimore Orioles and later of the Brooklyn Superbas, was a man of shrewdness and relentless logic who came to be considered the Father of Scientific Baseball. He was elected to the National Baseball Hall of Fame in 1996. (Babe Ruth Museum, Baltimore, Maryland)

Wilbert Robinson, known as Robbie, the Orioles' catcher and for many years their captain, served as the keel of a turbulent team. He jollied the boys along but was no good at forcing them. *(The Sporting News)*

John McGraw, a smart and savage third baseman, became the soul of the Orioles. He sharpened his spikes, held baserunners by the belt, terrified the umpires, and drove his teammates to a higher level of intensity. (National Baseball Hall of Fame Library & Archive, Cooperstown, New York)

Hughey Jennings, with a sunny temperament and a steely ambition, was a brilliant shortstop and also a fine batter—after McGraw taught him not to bail out from the plate. (National Baseball Hall of Fame Library & Archive, Cooperstown, New York)

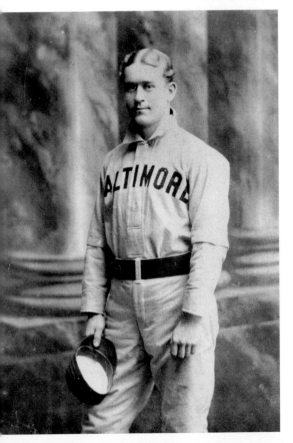

Joe Kelley, the Orioles' handsome left fielder, swaggered at the bat, tore up the basepaths, tangled with the umpires, and broke ladies' hearts. (Babe Ruth Museum, Baltimore, Maryland)

The Big Four of the Baltimore Orioles—*(from left)* Willie Keeler, Hughey Jennings, Joe Kelley, and John McGraw—flank Tom Murphy, the groundskeeper at Union Park. Murphy knew how to angle the baselines to help the Orioles' bunts and mixed slivers of soap into the dirt around the pitcher's box so that unsuspecting opposing twirlers would pick some up and lose their grip on the ball. (Babe Ruth Museum, Baltimore, Maryland)

Keeler, McGraw, Jennings, and Kelley (*clockwise, from upper left*) were friends as well as teammates, and were often seen on the town in the evenings. Though they all grew up in hardscrabble Irish families, they adapted easily to the rarefied world of celebrity. (Babe Ruth Museum, Baltimore, Maryland)

The Temple Cup, baseball's championship trophy from 1894 to 1897. William Temple, owner of the Pittsburgh club, conceived the idea of playing a post-season series between the first-place and second-place ballclubs in the twelve-team National League. The Orioles played in all four Temple Cup series, losing in 1894 and 1895 but winning the following two Octobers. (National Baseball Hall of Fame Library & Archive, Cooperstown, New York)

KILLEN WAS TOO SPEEDY.

Champions Were Unable to Connect With His Curves.

OUTPLAYED BY THE PIRATES.

Patsy Donovan's Crew Adopted a Few Oriole Tactics and Beat the Locals in the Last Game of the Series—Poor Work at the Bat and on the Bases—Hoffer Pitched.

Score:

BALTIMORE.	A.B.	R.	H.	O.	A.	E.
McGraw, 3b	4	0	0	1	3	0
Keeler, r. f	4	0	0	2	0	0
Jennings, s. s	3	0	1	1	6	2
Doyle, 1b	3	1	0	15	0	0
Reitz, 2b	4	0	2	0	3	0
O'Brien, l. f	4	0	1	3	0	0
Quinn, c. f	3	0	0	3	0	0
Bowerman, c	3	0	0	3	0	0
Hoffer, p	3	0	1	0	4	0
Totals	31	1	5	27	14	2
PITTSBURG.	A.B.	R.	H.	O.	A.	E.
Smith, l. f	2	2	1	7	0	0
Padden, 2b	4	1	0	4	1	0
Davis, 3b	5	0	1	0	3	0
Brodie, c. f	5	0	1	2	0	0
Donovan, r. f	4	2	1	1	0	0
Ely, s. s	3	0	0	2	7	0
Merritt, 1b	4	0	1	10	1	1
Sugden, c	3	1	1	1	1	1
Killen, p	4	1	1	0	4	0
Totals	34	7	7	27	16	2

SCORE BY INNINGS.
Baltimore ....0 1 0 0 0 0 0 0 0—1
Pittsburg ....0 1 0 0 0 0 1 5—7
Two-base hits—Jennings, Smith. Three-base hit—Davis. Stolen bases—Doyle 2, Quinn, Smith, Donovan. Bases on balls—By Hoffer, Smith 3, Sugden, total 4; by Killen, Doyle, Jennings, total 2. Struck out—By Hoffer, Davis and Killen; by Killen, Bowerman. Passed balls—Bowerman 2. Left on bases—Baltimore 5, Pittsburg 5. Innings pitched—Hoffer 9, Killen 9. Base hits—Off Hoffer 7, off Killen 5. First base on errors—Baltimore 1, Pittsburg 2. Time of game—Two hours. Umpire—Hurst. Weather—Clear and windy. Condition of field—Good.

Yesterday, for the first time this season, Willie Keeler failed to hit the ball safely at least once during the game. The nearest he came to making a hit yesterday was in the third inning, when he sent a slow one down toward third. He had it beat had not Davis made a remarkable stop and throw.

Willie Keeler began the 1897 season by hitting safely in forty-four consecutive games, a streak that was ended by Pittsburgh pitcher Frank Killen on June 19. The record stood for forty-four years, until Joe DiMaggio surpassed it with his fifty-six-game streak in 1941, but it was hardly noticed at the time. The *Morning Herald* in Baltimore mentioned the streak's end only in passing. (UMI)

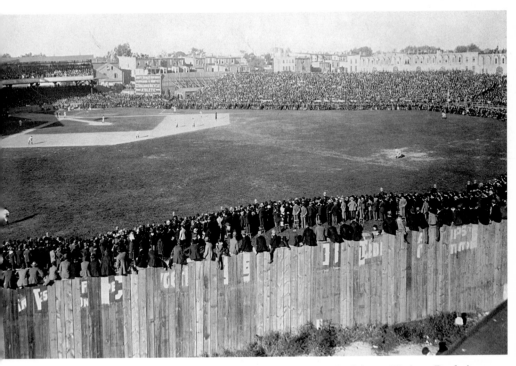

On September 27, 1897, nearly 30,000 cranks crowded into Union Park in Baltimore to watch the climactic game of the season—more people than had ever before witnessed a game of baseball. The Orioles lost to the Boston Beaneaters and missed their chance to snare an unprecedented fourth straight pennant. (Library of Congress)

MEN WHO CONTROL THE DESTINIES OF THE NATIONAL GAME.

The magnates of the National League, assembled for one of their regular business meetings in New York. Of his fellow magnates, Gus Abell once said, "Whenever I go to a baseball meeting, I never forget to check my money and valuables at the hotel office before entering the session chambers."

Standing (left to right): E. E. Becker (Boston), Chris von der Ahe (St. Louis), Ned Hanlon (Baltimore), Frank Robison (Cleveland), Harry von der Horst (Baltimore), Joseph A. Hart (Chicago), J. Walter Spalding (Chicago), Harry Pulliam (Louisville), T. Hunt Stucky (Louisville), John Rogers (Philadelphia). *Seated:* John T. Brush (Cincinnati), Alfred J. Reach (Philadelphia), Gus Abell (Brooklyn), League president Nick Young, J. Earl Wagner (Washington), Stanley Robison (Cleveland), Charley Byrne (Brooklyn). (UMI)

Charley Ebbets was a young man of ambition who took tickets, cleaned the grandstands, kept the books for the Brooklyn ballclub, and eventually came to own it. Later he built a ballpark named after himself. (National Baseball Hall of Fame Library & Archive, Cooperstown, New York)

Andrew Freedman, a Tammany Hall man who owned the New York Giants from 1895 through 1902, was the George Steinbrenner of his day. He fired managers fourteen times in eight years, and nearly turned the National League into a full-fledged cartel. (Transcendental Graphics)

The Fifth Avenue Hotel, on Madison square at Twenty-third street, was the headquarters of the Republican Party in New York and luxurious enough for the National League owners to use for their meetings. (Museum of the City of New York)

Ban Johnson went from being a sportswriter in Cincinnati to running the Western League. By force of will, he turned this shaky minor league into a full-fledged major league in 1901—having renamed it the American League—and forced the National League to treat the upstart circuit as an equal. (*The Sporting News*)

John McGraw jumped from the Baltimore Orioles to the New York Giants in 1902, raiding his old ballclub—and ruining it—as he left. In his thirty years as the Giants' manager, he became more and more imperious, for there was no one to rein him in. Under his iron rule, his teams would win ten pennants and three World's Series championships. (National Baseball Hall of Fame Library & Archive, Cooperstown, New York)

Willie Keeler jumped to the American League in 1903, joining the New York Highlanders for the highest salary a ballplayer had ever received—$10,000. He never lost the knack of inside baseball, though his throwing arm had lost its zip. (National Baseball Hall of Fame Library & Archive, Cooperstown, New York)

Hilltop Park, on a high bluff near the northern tip of Manhattan, gave the New York Highlanders their name, but the team soon became known by a different name—the Yankees. Columbia-Presbyterian Medical Center stands on the site today. (National Baseball Hall of Fame Library & Archive, Cooperstown, New York)

Jack Chesbro, the Highlanders' right-hander who brought the spitball to prominence, lost the pennant on the last day of the 1904 season with a wild pitch of a slippery baseball. He had won forty-one games that season, a twentieth-century record, but was never again the pitcher he had been. (National Baseball Hall of Fame Library & Archive, Cooperstown, New York)

After finishing his major league playing career with the Giants in 1910, Willie Keeler became a coach for his hometown club, the Brooklyn Dodgers. (National Baseball Hall of Fame Library & Archive, Cooperstown, New York)

A parade along Baltimore Street heralded the return of major-league baseball to Baltimore in 1954, after a hiatus of fifty-two years, when the St. Louis Browns became the modern Baltimore Orioles. (Babe Ruth Museum, Baltimore, Maryland)

deep-porched home in Baltimore, out Calvert street, near Union Park. Baltimore was Margaret's home, and now his too. He pleaded with Hanlon to trade him to Washington, then told the Senators' owner he wanted to come. Nothing came of it.

Hughey Jennings was horrified at the deal as well. "I think the Baltimore people have been treated shamefully," he said, "and if there was any way in which I could remain here I would do so." But even with the steel beneath his customary cheer, Hughey could hardly summon up the intensity he would need to resist, not after the double blow he had suffered back in November. First his father had died, still wearing the medal he had received on taking a pledge of temperance from a priest in Ireland at the age of fourteen. That was in the nature of things. But six days later, it was Hughey's wife. She had not been well since September, on giving birth to their daughter, Grace. She had gained sufficiently to join Hughey in Baltimore in hopes that the warmer climate might help, but instead she had grown rapidly worse, and passed away. Hughey said he would go to Brooklyn if he was forced to, though with regret.

Hanlon had given up on transferring McGraw and Robbie. Now that Baltimore was still to have a ballclub, it made sense to leave them as the core of the Orioles. Maybe the southern branch of the syndicate would not lose so many games—and even make a dollar or two.

The Big Four would dissolve, if the deal went through, though they would still be working for the same employer. That got them to thinking. The three who lived in Baltimore met and talked over the situation and agreed that if a pennant-winning team in Brooklyn was to be such a Klondike, they would like to have some of the nuggets for themselves. They wanted a cut of the profits, and had a figure in mind. McGraw allowed as how he might even be willing to play in Brooklyn if the money was right. "If we are to be the stars that are to bring through the turnstiles the crowds of people," he argued, "surely we should share in some degree in money made through our own efforts. We want ten percent, and expect to stick by this demand."

Kel, just back from New York, said Willie was with them. "We like Baltimore," Hughey explained, "but we are dependent upon the game for our livelihood, and should be given a share of prosperity when it comes. We will stand together in this matter, and the Big Four will again be a consideration."

If the magnates could combine, they argued, the players should have the same privilege.

Hanlon was adamant in his opposition. If the Big Four tried to block the deal, he warned, they would simply have to play in Baltimore next season at greatly reduced salaries or not play at all. He would not put up with the sulking and indifference that had lost the pennant in 'ninety-eight and ruined the interest among the Baltimore cranks.

Harry von der Horst's reaction was to laugh. "Baseball players will be baseball players, you know."

Despite the derision and the threats, there was talk that both Baltimore catchers, Robbie and Bill Clarke, had thrown in with the Big Four's demands. But it was not out of pique. Bill Clarke well understood how the world worked. Yes, he sighed, he was grieved that the old Orioles would be broken up. But he could find no fault with management, which was "out for money," just as the players were.

McGraw had another, more imaginative, idea. It was simple and, in its way, quite brilliant. To Harry it offered a way out of his predicament, once he had agreed to accept the deal with Brooklyn. He could keep his standing among his customers and friends and quiet the criticism about having two League teams under common ownership, while also providing him a cache of money that Emma need not share. So Harry named what he described as a very low price of $35,000, for Mac and Robbie to raise from backers and purchase the Orioles themselves.

Surely the two ballplayer-businessmen had the acumen and the contacts. They had been meeting with local capitalists to assemble a syndicate of their own to buy the team and keep it in Baltimore. Hanlon counseled them to employ cheaper ballplayers to reduce their salary list by $20,000 or $30,000. No matter what, he said, "whoever takes charge as manager the coming season will have a far better team to start with than I had in 'ninety-three."

There was every reason to think that the attendance in Baltimore would bounce back within two or three years. Had not every pennant-winning club suffered a subsequent slump in attendance? Even Hanlon acknowledged that it was bound to improve. "I consider Baltimore a good baseball city," he said. "In a year or so, under proper conditions, the old-time interest will come back in full force."

Maybe the logic was so compelling that Hanlon listened to his own advice. More likely it was Harry, overtaken by sentiment, who in the end refused to sell something he had loved for so long. Why should he have to sell the Orioles? Because a syndicate owned competing teams? Why, after all, should the cranks care who owned a ballclub? What business was it of theirs? And if there was money to be made from it, why should Harry give it to anyone else? It made no sense.

McGraw and Robinson were set to meet at the Hotel Rennert with potential investors when Hanlon sent word: The offer was withdrawn. Mac responded with equanimity. Maybe he had never believed otherwise. "Well, if they will not sell, they will not," he said, "and that is all there is about it."

Each week it was predicted the deal was about to be signed; the next week it was predicted again. This first week of February in 'ninety-nine, Charley Ebbets was presumed to be holding things up. What gave him away was his absence. Gus Abell and Ned Hanlon were at the Hoffman House, on Madison Square, plotting strategies and laying plans. From time to time Harry von der Horst joined them. Charley Ebbets did not.

Ebbets denied that he was blocking the deal, though Harry was sure he was. "He is only looking for prominence for political purposes," Harry confided to a newspaperman, "and knows that if the two clubs are merged he will be dropped." Harry had investigated how Ebbets could possibly have afforded his Trolley Dodgers stock and had learned that the money had indeed come from Abell. "He never paid a cent to the Brooklyn club," Harry said. After all of the handshakes, the announcements, the publicized offers of options, it was Abell, the man with the money, who still owned a majority of the ballclub. The newspapers claimed he held at least two-thirds, maybe three-fourths, of it, and was offering to buy the rest. But Charley Ebbets refused to sell his shares. It was said that he had written to one of his ballplayers vowing to stymie the syndicate deal.

He was looking for assurances, and he kept getting them, but he remained wary of the obvious camaraderie between Abell and Hanlon. He met with Abell, and yet again, to no avail. The pressure from the public was building. The *Eagle* filled its columns with letters blasting or defending him. "A swelled head." "Upon him alone rests the blame of last year's failure." "Shameful that a man can be so shortsighted. . . . He is fast losing friends right in his own neighborhood."

The Brooklyn stockholders—Abell, Ebbets, and Charley Byrne's surviving brother, William—scheduled a formal meeting for January twenty-fourth, then postponed it until February third.

On February second, Ebbets and Abell met at length in the Hoffman House. Then the Baltimore magnates joined them. It was agreed that Ebbets, as the Trolley Dodgers' president, would wield full control over the club's financial affairs and could travel with the team to that end. But on any matter touching on the ballplayers, Hanlon's word would be law.

With those understandings, Ebbets agreed to the deal.

"If selling beer were attended with the same difficulties as making this deal," Harry mused, "I think I should soon go out of business."

It cost three cents apiece for the ferry to Jersey City, where the Brooklyn Base Ball Club was legally incorporated, to take advantage of New Jersey's relaxed ways with corporations. As it happened, none of the stockholders made the trip. Not after William Byrne made his exorbitant demand.

He wanted $10,000, in cash, for the eighth of the ballclub he had inherited from his brother. On paper that was less than the stock was judged to be worth, but the accountants measured fiction and William Byrne insisted on hard money, backed by gold. Abell offered him $7,500 in cash and $2,500 in stock and was turned down flat.

It was easy to imagine why. The brother of the League's late, lamented politician was something of a politician himself. William Byrne lived in Manhattan and was a minor officeholder of Tammany Hall. "He is easily influenced by Andrew Freedman, who is afraid that Brooklyn will have a better team this season than New York," said Billy Barnie, the Trolley Dodgers' former manager. "It is all politics." Even before the consolidation, Tammany and the Brooklyn machine had never seen eye to eye. Besides, William Byrne had reasons of his own to take a hard line. After all, his brother, on his deathbed, had been shouldered aside by Ebbets.

This time Hanlon and Harry set a deadline. The Brooklyn magnates must make up their minds by two o'clock on Saturday afternoon, the fourth of February, or the deal was off. Hanlon had booked a train home to Baltimore that night.

The newspapermen gathered at the Hoffman House as the deadline came and went. They kept waiting. They were practiced at it. Night had fallen by the time the magnates returned. Hanlon's prim demeanor was out of place amid the hotel's marble balconies and voluptuous fixtures. Charley Ebbets had a smile on his face, so Abe Yager of the *Eagle* chose him as the likeliest respondent.

"Are there absolutely no new developments?"

"Really, there is nothing new," came the reply.

Gus Abell adjusted his coat and mumbled something about dinner. He and Hanlon slipped away. Ebbets conversed for a few minutes with Johnny Ward, who had dropped by to see how matters were progressing. Then Ebbets vanished, too, as the revolutionary-turned-lawyer stayed behind with the scribes. "Baseball is in as bad shape in Baltimore as it is in Brooklyn," Johnny Ward ventured, "and the deal is the one thing which will place the two clubs on a prosperous basis."

It was eight o'clock before the magnates reappeared. This time Hanlon was the one smiling.

The newspapermen's usual query brought a surprising response, from the most circumspect magnate. "I think you may say that the deal is now practically a certainty," Hanlon answered. Byrne would get his $10,000 in cash. Abell and von der Horst—the money men—would each own 40 percent of both ballclubs. Ebbets and Hanlon, who did the work, would get 10 percent apiece. Ebbets (it was learned later) would be paid $4,000 as the president in Brooklyn for 'ninety-nine and, if his performance warranted, longer. Hanlon, as the manager in Brooklyn and the president in Baltimore, would get $10,000.

At last the newspapermen left, except for Joe Vila of the *New York Sun,* who thus became the only scribe to discover the secret meeting at eleven-thirty that night. He followed the magnates to the Broadway Central Hotel and nabbed William Byrne as he crossed over the entrance. Was it true that he had agreed to give up his stock?

"I never made any such promise," Byrne replied, "and I'll bet that Hanlon didn't say so."

Joe Vila found Hanlon and brought the two men face-to-face. "Mr. Byrne," Hanlon snapped, "didn't you give me your word that you would sell your stock when you got $10,000 in cash on Tuesday?"

Byrne slowly shook his head and said coolly, "You probably misunderstood me."

"Have you changed your mind in regard to the price?"

"I don't know. I came down here by appointment to talk things over."

"Then come right in here," Hanlon heatedly replied, "and settle it one way or another."

Barely a minute later, Hanlon emerged with a smile on his face and rushed off for his train.

*   *   *

Four decades had passed since Baltimore had seen such a snowstorm. Blinding sheets of snow, fifteen inches in twenty-four hours, penetrated the window sashes in all but the sturdiest houses. The harbor iced over. Funerals were postponed. The downtown streets had a Sabbath appearance.

More than acts of God were battering Baltimore. Acts of man had their day. The city was losing control of its livelihood. As the dreaded baseball deal waited on the court to issue duplicates of William Byrne's stock certificates, Hanlon was deciding on his pick of the players. The disposition was not meant to be fair. Willie Keeler and Joe Kelley and Hughey Jennings and Big Dan McGann—two-thirds of the outfield and half the infield—were bound for Brooklyn. So were all three of the Baltimore twirlers who had won twenty games or more in 'ninety-eight. In exchange, the Orioles got four players who had batted below .300 and three pitchers who had won a total of four games in the major league.

The Orphans, the Leftovers, the Castoffs—those were the epithets the indignant scribes and cranks flung at what remained of the Orioles. Meanwhile, Hanlon had settled on a manager for the rump team. That he passed over steady, imperturbable Robbie said quite a lot about steady, imperturbable Hanlon. Robbie would stay on as the captain—the youngsters would need him as ballast. Yet they would also need to reach beyond themselves. Robbie would not inspire them or make them try their damndest. John McGraw would.

Steve Brodie had returned to Baltimore and Ducky Holmes was staying. That gave Mac a core. But McGraw liked what he saw in Jimmy Sheckard, Brooklyn's fleet young outfielder, and in an untested right-hander from the Peoria ballclub named Joe McGinnity. Then he went to work. He signed a hot-tempered second baseman from New Jersey and talked trade with the Senators and dickered with the Phillies for a pitcher and exchanged telegrams with the minor league clubs in Kansas City and Indianapolis. Everyone warned him that the new Orioles would have to dazzle if they hoped to lure Baltimoreans accustomed to rooting for champions back to the ballpark.

A sizable crowd of undemonstrative cranks gathered at the wharf to see the Orioles off to Savannah. "I am well satisfied with the boys," McGraw said before boarding the steamship. "They are all young, good willing workers. If the twirlers come up to expectations, and there is no reason why they should not, then Baltimoreans can look forward to an interesting time."

The same day, Hanlon and the Trolley Dodgers were to depart by steamship to Charleston, thence by rail to Augusta, Georgia. Willie Keeler was still insisting on an increase in pay, but the team's most delicate problem had been resolved. Joe Kelley had been grumbling that he might not play if he was not named captain. The problem was that Brooklyn's center fielder, Mike Griffin, had signed a contract with Ebbets months earlier naming *him* as the captain. Griffin was a loose disciplinarian and a popular choice with his teammates. And his eye was wonderfully quick and he had impressive range in the field. Hanlon faced a dilemma. Griffin, should he be demoted, would surely lose his edge.

The telegram from St. Louis, offering a salary $1,000 less than Brooklyn had promised to pay him, was the first Griffin knew he had been sold. He refused to report and filed a lawsuit against Charley Ebbets. Eventually the two sides settled, for $2,250, but Mike Griffin never played baseball again.

Kelley and McGraw had been promoted, and Hughey was grieving too much to care. Willie was the last of the Big Four to come to terms. He had wanted $2,800, but signed for $2,600—no raise, that is—just in time to go south.

He came down to the dock, along with Kelley and Hanlon and ten of the others. The steamship *Algonquin*, recently in an accident, needed two more days of repairs.

By then the seas were rougher by far. Everyone aboard got seasick, except for Ned Hanlon and Big Dan McGann and Wee Willie Keeler.

=8=

Business Beats
Sentiment

Every evening Willie Keeler put on his best duds and cut a figure on a street corner near the hotel in Augusta. In his bowler and rounded collar and carefully knotted cravat, he outshone the electric lights. It was said he had signed to pose for a swell tailoring establishment back in New York once the season was over.

The team that had finished in tenth place in 'ninety-eight faced terrifying expectations for 'ninety-nine. The *Brooklyn Daily Eagle* portrayed the new Trolley Dodgers as the strongest nine representing any city since the birth of the National League twenty-three years earlier—better than the old White Stockings or the strongest Beaneaters or even the Orioles that had just been shattered. They were the pick of the Orioles *and* of the Trolley Dodgers, even without McGraw. "Were it not for my connection with them," Hanlon said, "I would pronounce them the most likely candidates for the 'ninety-nine pennant."

Hanlon set about teaching the holdover Trolley Dodgers his system of strategies and signals. In their first game they took on the team from the Thirty-fifth Michigan Regiment, featuring President McKinley's nephew playing third base. Brooklyn won, 18 to 0.

The newspapers kept pointing to the harmony among the Brooklyn ballplayers, presumably because of its absence. Ten of them had been Trolley Dodgers last season and eight had been Orioles. Hanlon understood the dangers. "I can tell better how they will work together after I have seen them practice a few times," he said.

Everything had changed from before, including the team's nickname. One of the most popular vaudeville troupes in Brooklyn happened to be called Hanlon's Superbas. A wit in the press box dubbed the scrambled, strengthened team the Superbas. It stuck.

The syndicate's two teams made plans to play each other in Georgia. The also-rans from Brooklyn had become the mightiest of teams while the Orioles, so good for so long, were the underdogs now. What a rivalry it promised to be. Hanlon had ordered nearly identical uniforms, with a big "B" at the left breast, differing only in the color of the trimmings. For the Oriole uniforms, McGraw had the "B" moved to the center of the chest.

John McGraw set out to mold the Orioles who had never been Orioles before. They had come to Savannah expecting a cherry pie. The first morning Captain Robbie set the pace, as he ordered two hours of throwing and batting. The sweat poured off them; the boys wilted in the southern sun. Even Steve Brodie, a son of the South, once let the bat slip from his hands. They were ready to quit when Robbie cheerfully proposed running three times around the ballgrounds—four, for the laggards.

"Why, we have done more work today than the Brooklyn team did all last spring," one of the newcomers moaned. He and the other new Orioles woke up the next morning in unaccustomed pain.

The ballgrounds themselves were a mess. If they had been any good, Hanlon would not have turned them down for himself. The grounds had no drainage and a street had been cut through left field. McGraw arranged the use of the Catholic Club's showers, until the long cold walk from the dressing room and the malfunctioning hot water sent the boys to the meager bathrooms at the hotel.

McGraw waxed optimistic, though, about the Orioles' prospects on the diamond. The general opinion around the League held that they would settle into tenth place, perhaps as high as eighth. Mac disagreed. "We are liable to surprise some people in Brooklyn and Baltimore who have got an idea we will be tailenders," he said. "We will be strictly 'in it' this year."

On the third of April, Hanlon got a chance to judge for himself. The untried Orioles sidled into Augusta to face Hanlon's proven stars. Mac's youngsters were impatient at the plate, but they showed admirable ginger and were steady as the clay in the field. Robbie nailed the only Superba who tried to steal second. Steve Brodie and Jimmy Sheckard made theatrical catches. "My outfield will compare favorably with any in the major league," McGraw had said, taking a dig at Keeler and Kelley.

The game showed him up as Willie Keeler electrified the crowd. "But for his almost supernatural work in right field," one of the Baltimore scribes lamented, "Manager Hanlon's champions would have fallen with a dull, cold thud." After a long hard run Willie pulled down Jimmy Sheckard's fly against the right field fence and, in the next inning, leapt into the air and snatched Ducky Holmes's liner. The cranks in Augusta had never seen anything like it. Besides saving runs, Willie scored two of them, the difference in the 8-to-6 ballgame.

The Superbas had escaped, leaving Hanlon shocked at the Orioles' hustling ways. He saw them again in the next game as McGraw used a brainy young twirler named Dan McFarlan, who threw high fastballs with perfect control. Neither Keeler nor Kelley could touch him. This time the castoffs bettered their betters, 3 to 2.

The next day too the Orioles played like Orioles, having practiced the hit-and-run and the sacrifice bunt. Mac used another untried twirler, broad-shouldered Joe McGinnity. McGinnity had just turned twenty-eight—old for a rookie—having left baseball to open a saloon in Illinois because his wife was an invalid. His maturity was probably what accounted for his calm air of control. He was a big stocky man and a hard thrower, yet he was the easiest kind of pitcher to catch, the ball landing like a feather in the catcher's mitt. He was one of the quietest men on the team and maybe the hardiest. "Iron Man" was his nickname, because of the foundry he owned with his in-laws, out in the Indian Territory of Oklahoma. It described considerably more.

He puzzled the Brooklyn batsmen with his slow rising curve, the one he threw sidearm, almost underhand—Old Sal, he called it. He had invented it as a come-on to customers at his saloon. Against the Superbas he pitched with perfect control, using Robbie's shrewd guidance. Willie Keeler struck out and was held to one hit. In the seventh inning Robbie trotted out and asked the Iron Man if pitching too many curveballs might hurt his arm. "Why no," the strong twirler replied, "I could pitch these for three days." He was as effective in the ninth inning as he had been in the first. The Orioles won going away, 5 to 1.

"Why, this fellow must have been pitching all winter," Hanlon marveled. "He would have beaten any team in the League today."

Hanlon had promised not to treat the Orioles as a farm for Brooklyn—not like the St. Louis Browns treated the Cleveland Spiders. Those teams, too, had formed a syndicate. Frank Robison, the streetcar magnate who owned the Spiders, had recently acquired the Browns at a bankruptcy auction and was sending the best of the Clevelanders—Patsy Tebeau, Jesse Burkett, Cy Young—to St. Louis, where the revitalized team replaced the dreary brown trim on the uniforms with bright red piping and, at a newspaperman's suggestion, was just starting to be called the Cardinals. Robison planned to move the ballplayers back and forth as he liked, to maximize the attendance in St. Louis, now the nation's fourth most populous city, a promising market where the cranks would turn out for a winner.

But the terms of the Baltimore-Brooklyn syndicate agreement gave Hanlon the right to reshuffle players between the clubs only until April twelfth. "If I were a cartoonist," Robbie remarked, "I would represent Hanlon as a hawk, sailing around over the Oriole barnyard, ready to swoop down and carry off in his clutches any likely chick that showed itself."

First he snatched a catcher back from Baltimore in the fashion-plate figure of Broadway Aleck Smith. He needed a twirler, too. He had a choice, between Dan McFarlan and Joe McGinnity. Once Hanlon had decided, McGraw said publicly that he was grieved at what the Orioles had lost, but in truth, he could have only been relieved. Hanlon had taken the younger man, McFarlan, who went on to win a total of eight games in his major league career.

More was wrong with Brooklyn than its pitching. The night of the third game in Augusta, Hughey Jennings and John McGraw went out—as they had for years—to celebrate their birthdays, which were five days apart. Hughey had just turned thirty. He confided some awful news to his closest friend.

"It's no use, Mac," he said. "I can't throw."

"Nonsense," McGraw scoffed. "Everybody gets that in the spring."

"No, it's gone," Hughey whispered. "You saw me out there today."

For a couple of years he had felt his right arm growing weaker, from too many hours of practice, too many throws. "I could not get him off the field with a team of mules," Murph, the old grounds-keeper, remembered about Oriole practices. "He would keep throwing until his landlady called him for lunch." Now Hughey could hardly throw from shortstop to first base. All winter long he had taken treatments, to no effect.

But no matter what happened, he was determined not to return to the coal mines. Since boyhood he had wanted to be a lawyer; he began making plans to enroll in law school at Cornell the following fall.

Both teams meant to head back to Savannah, to continue their series. The Orioles had traveled to Augusta on round-trip railway tickets, and the Georgia Central had said that the Superbas could accompany them back to Savannah at the same reduced fare.

As they were to return, when it was too late to make other arrangements, the railway reneged, insisting on full fare. Hanlon refused. He would not be thrown down. Instead he blocked the railroad's sharp practice. Instead of traveling south to Savannah he discarded the schedule and went north to Virginia to play.

A baseball syndicate had taken on a local railroad monopoly. Neither backed down, so both lost.

It was Otto Wuest's idea, putting on a testimonial for the only Brooklyn native on the team. He was a family friend of the Keelers and an ardent admirer of Willie. Otto's plan was for a banquet on the fifteenth of April, the evening of the opening game. Two dollars would buy a seat at Washington Park and a place at the seven-course banquet (from the oysters on the half-shell to the fancy cake) as well as a vaudeville show and part of a gift for Willie.

The cranks around Brooklyn showed considerable interest. It was remarkable to have someone to gloat over. Manhattan often did, though rarely was it for a native. Brooklyn had no shortage of natives, many whose talents ranked with the best, but how often did they remain in Brooklyn once they had discovered success? Willie Keeler was a Brooklyn boy who had come home again. A better ballplayer had never grown up on the streets of Greater New York.

The only objection came from the prospective guest of honor. When the team got to Brooklyn, three days before the season was to start, Willie handed a letter to the man from the *Eagle*, for publication. "I have requested my friends to refrain from any public reception at the present time," he wrote. He gave no explanation; none was needed. He was happy to be home but he had no wish to be the center of attention. He knew from his previous stint with Brooklyn that around New York, too much success could arouse resentment as quickly as pride.

The Brooklyn ballclub had never sold so many tickets in advance for its opening game. All winter the cranks had been buzzing about the deal with Baltimore, and the syndicate had spared no expense in getting Washington Park ready for the crowds. Four hundred loads of loam and two hundred loads of ash had made the diamond as level as could be, other than the six-inch slope from the pitcher's rubber to the bases, to help the drainage. The club had built new bleacheries along the right field foul line in place of the ones beyond the center field fence—"half a mile from the diamond," a crank had complained to the *Eagle*. The fence was moved out eighty feet, making it likelier a ball would get loose, occasioning more inside-the-ballpark home runs.

Hanlon had pleaded for a clubhouse, but because of the expense it was left to Charley Ebbets to decide; the players were given the use of a stone shack under the grandstand. The money was spent instead on five thousand new seats, in every part of the ballpark, to bring the capacity to fifteen thousand. As many as twenty-five or even thirty thousand people were expected for the season's first game, against the Beaneaters.

No parade marked the arrival of baseball in Brooklyn, but the enthusiasm for the retooled team seemed genuine enough. At one o'clock sharp on a sparkling April afternoon, the ballpark's gates opened, setting off a scramble for the unreserved seats. Bunting was strung across the roof of the grandstand, flapping in the breeze. The cranks needed strong stomachs, which most of them had, to cope with the vortex of smells that competed for attention—the black fumes from the factory smokestacks nearby, the stench of sewage from the Gowanus Canal, the haunting odor of the hot dogs. Near third base a band played a medley from *Carmen,* which mingled with the babble of animated voices.

By half past three, the gong sounded for the game to begin. The turnstiles had admitted 20,167 spectators—nothing in the annals of baseball in Brooklyn could compare. The rooters stood in every aisle and at the back of the grandstand and around the rim of the outfield. Not every spectator had paid. Some had climbed telegraph poles, and patients watched from the windows of the hospital beyond the left field fence. The ballclub had erected huge screens so that no one could watch from the wide apartment house out past right field.

Harry von der Horst and a party of friends had arrived in a large tallyho. A cheer went up when he showed himself on the field. He looked around for the ballplayers and deduced with delight that the shouts were for him.

Hugh McLaughlin, the Democratic boss of Brooklyn, threw out the first pitch. A friend of the late governor, Sam Tilden, a friend of former president Grover Cleveland, McLaughlin was a man who was once weighed on a railroad scale. He betrayed not an ounce of resentment that Charley Ebbets had invited him only after Mayor Robert Van Wyck of New York, Tammany Hall's man, pleaded a previous engagement. His secret was patience, and a brusque honor. He had broken pledges made in public about policy but never, so far as was known, a personal promise. Boss McLaughlin smiled broadly as he hurled the ball and endangered Sheriff Creamer, who sat just in front.

At the gong the Superbas took the field. Their white uniforms were painfully clean against grass so green it might have come from a hothouse.

The two teams looked evenly matched. The Beaneaters, batting first, had won the past two pennants and had designs on a third. Sliding Billy Hamilton worked his way to third base and dashed for home plate when Germany Long smacked a fly ball out to left field. Joe Kelley hardly touched the ball before throwing it to the plate. In a cloud of dust, Sliding Billy was out.

Captain Kel drew quite an ovation when he led off the bottom of the inning, though he did nothing more to deserve it. Then Willie came to the bat. "Three cheers for Keeler," came the shouts. He tapped a slow roller to Boston's pitcher, gentlemanly Kid Nichols, and barely lost the race to first. Hughey, batting third, took a pitch in the stomach. Over Boston's protest he was given first base, and was stranded there.

Inning after inning, nobody scored. Nichols was pitching with his head as usual, and "Roaring Bill" Kennedy, the Brooklyn veteran, who stormed at his teammates for their mistakes with the glove, kept his careful control. The fielders did the rest. A wiry black dog, Boston's mascot, trotted out to watch when Germany Long came to bat, and the lithe shortstop offered a low sweeping bow. Then he smashed a pitch between shortstop and third, which Hughey dived for, and blocked, and threw sharply to first. What was this about a lame arm? Without an instant's hesitation the dog trotted over to the Brooklyn bench and stayed the afternoon.

In the sixth inning, Joe Kelley drove a grounder to Jimmy Collins at third base. Certain he was out, he paused on the way to first, so when Collins booted it he was short by a stride. Willie followed with a three-bagger into right field. Kelley would have scored. Willie never did.

Nobody did until the eleventh inning, when the Beaneaters worked their way to a run, created by Hughey's wild throw to first base. Brooklyn had one last chance. A pinch hitter grounded out, and Kelley did the same. Then Willie leaned in against Kid Nichols. In came a pitch that he bounced to Bobby Lowe at second base.

"As fine a game as I ever saw," Hanlon consoled himself. His team had shown itself the equal of the champions. Charley Ebbets had his own reason for a satisfied smile. "The crowd was a record breaker," he crowed. "It was the greatest day which the Brooklyn baseball club has yet known."

Andrew Freedman had no respect for standard courtesies. The Orioles wished to distribute fifteen hundred complimentary tickets for the opening game—as was the custom—and sought permission from the Giants for the loss of revenue the visiting ballclub would share.

"No arrangements will be made," the Giants wired back. Part of it was that Andrew Freedman and Harry von der Horst had loathed each other ever since the Ducky Holmes affair and an incident in the Waldorf-Astoria café the previous spring. When Freedman had remarked to Harry that he was allying himself in the League with crooks, bystanders had to restrain Harry from a forcible dissent. Now something more was at stake. A favor for Baltimore had become a favor for Brooklyn, the last thing Freedman wanted to grant.

As it happened, squabbling over the receipts at Union Park was not worth the bother. The diminished Orioles had had an encouraging spring, but the city had understandably turned a cold shoulder. There was no parade. Hanlon and von der Horst would not pay for a marching band. No hordes of cranks rushed the turnstiles. Four thousand came, most of them paying a quarter for a seat in the bleachers. The mayor showed up too late to throw out the first pitch.

He proved to be a master of timing. Both teams were nervous at the start, and the Orioles fell behind, 3 to 1. But McGraw would not let them give up. They kept at it, and the score was tied when they came to bat in the seventh inning. With a man on base, McGraw singled into right field. Trying to steal second, he got caught between the bases. But the Giants got rattled in the rundown, and the lead runner scored as McGraw slid into second. Mac scored, too, when Steve Brodie singled.

Which was how the game ended. The Leftovers led the Superbas in the standings, at least for a day.

That was no longer the case when the two affiliates went head-to-head at Washington Park eleven days later. Both teams were bunched near the middle of the League rankings. The Orioles had two men out in the fourth inning and a runner on every base when Robbie came to the plate. Under any conditions he was a dangerous man at the bat, but never more than when the bases were filled. Jack Dunn, a methodical right-hander twirling for Brooklyn, looked too small to be on the rubber. His thin face and high forehead suggested a self-contained bookkeeper. But he was aggressive and smart and commanded a perplexing assortment of curves. And he was obstinate, one of the few remaining ballplayers—all of them pitchers—who still refused to wear a glove.

He threw a shoulder-high pitch to the portly captain, who swung and missed. Then came another, and Robbie swung and missed again. Dunn's third pitch was at the shoulders. Robbie swung. He split the air.

Robbie felt nothing but disgust, and the Orioles deflated. When Willie Keeler led off in Brooklyn's half of the inning, everyone knew he would bunt. The infield crowded in. Willie knew to do the unexpected. He squared to bunt—and then bunted. The ball went ten feet, and Willie rushed down the baseline and arrived before the ball did. Then he stood on the base and laughed at the lobsters he had left behind.

He crossed the plate that inning along with four of his teammates, which was more than enough. Brooklyn won the next two games against the Orioles as well.

After thirteen games Willie was batting .500, but his club's record was barely that good. Hughey Jennings, nursing his arm, was to be out for a month. Fielder Jones, the fleet center fielder, was hurt. Hanlon was teaching the players who had never been Orioles about working as a team and being patient at the bat and thinking about the previous hitter and the one coming next. "It will be a month before the Brooklyn team is playing according to my liking," he said.

It took more like two or three weeks. The Superbas had climbed into a tie for third place with the Phillies, who invaded Washington Park in the middle of May. The bases were filled in the eighth inning when Keeler came to bat. By this time his average was slipping below .400. His slight swing drove a pitch on a line into deep left field. Big Ed Delehanty lumbered after it as Willie sprinted around the bases. The ball was skittish. Three teammates crossed the plate and then

Willie did, ahead of the throw. All over the ballpark, men tossed their hats into the air and women stood on their chairs to cheer.

The Superbas kept winning. Eight straight victories put them into second place, and making it twelve put them into first. Willie edged back over .400. They lost to the Orioles and then won eight more, putting them comfortably ahead of the Beaneaters.

"We landed at the top a little sooner than I expected," Hanlon said, "but it had to come."

That was when they started to lose. Maybe they needed to lose to find their full strength. Only Willie and Fielder Jones were batting well. Hanlon was accused—and hardly for the first time—of working his pitchers too hard. When Bill Kennedy collapsed on his way to the ballpark, the management accused him of drinking. He swore it was sunstroke and too little breakfast. A week later, still looking ill, he was given his release.

Hanlon made deals as he needed, to plug the holes. He had traded for Bill Dahlen of Chicago, a sulky but brilliant shortstop who might have been the finest infielder in the game had he bothered to try. Then he secured Duke Farrell, the solid catcher from the Giants, and acknowledged an earlier error by trading McFarlan for Doc Casey, a third baseman from the Senators.

It was almost July when Hughey Jennings returned to the diamond, but his woes went on. He was throwing wildly at shortstop—he made four errors in a single game—and batting .175. Any cheerfulness was strained. Brooklyn's lead over Boston dwindled and soon Hughey was back on the bench.

Foxy Ned knew what to do. He offered to trade Hughey to Louisville, along with $2,500, for a gawky but promising third baseman named Honus Wagner. The Colonels might have gone for it had Hughey not involved himself. He sent a wire to Harry Pulliam, the secretary of the Louisville club: "Don't consent to deal. Am in no condition. Will play no more this season. Bad arm." He explained to a newspaperman that he liked Louisville well enough but feared the franchise would vanish if the League scaled back to eight or ten teams once the season ended. "I am looking out for my own interests," he said matter-of-factly.

The Brooklyn magnates were incensed at Hughey's meddling. Charley Ebbets and Gus Abell insisted on suspending him. Hanlon suggested releasing him instead. Harry von der Horst, however, had something else in mind.

*   *   *

There was a dignity about John McGraw that no one had recognized before. He looked even younger than his twenty-six years. His cheeks were sleek, and an innocence burnished his slender face. His hair foppishly looped over his forehead on both sides of his center part. But otherwise, he projected certainty and self-assurance, an unstated promise that anyone who thwarted him would pay a price. A newspaperman in Cincinnati noticed that Mac no longer had a chip on his shoulder he was hoping someone would knock off so he could start a scrap. Running things suited him. It calmed him down. Not until August did he kick at an umpire's call.

He was playing the best baseball of his career. His batting average reached the .390s and stayed. One way or another, he got on base nearly half the time. He seldom got fooled by a curveball. He had stopped trying to knock the ball out of the lot and was one of the uncommon left-handed batters who could discipline himself not to swing at inshoots. He led the League in bases on balls and runs, and challenged for the lead in stolen bases.

And he was a student of the game. He knew that the Chicago nine had been torn into factions and that Brooklyn could be beaten if you went at their pitchers just so. He had learned a lot from Hanlon—and had taught his old manager some things. In McGraw's fertile mind, every soft spot suggested a tactic or two.

In the leavings of both teams he had been given to work with, he saw possibilities. Jimmy Sheckard had the speed and ginger to steal as many bases as McGraw. Candy LaChance, a big lumbering first baseman who had been careless in Brooklyn, could be taught not to be. Billy Keister, the Baltimore-born utility infielder, was built like a fire hydrant but knew how to hustle. Joe McGinnity was nervy and Robbie was solid and Steve Brodie lent experience and a usefully unrestrained spirit—Mac's kind of ballplayer.

McGraw kept the discipline loose, as Hanlon had. But he was quick to establish himself as the man in charge. Only Robbie was permitted to address him as an equal. They worked as complements. Robbie made sure the ballplayers felt content. McGraw made them mad. He goaded the young Orioles into doing their best.

In the field the Orioles betrayed a nervousness in their peppery play. Errors came in bursts. Their hitting was erratic and inefficiently timed. (Once they scored two runs on seventeen hits against Pittsburgh.) They won about as often as they lost. They sank into seventh place in May but reached third place in June—not bad for castoffs.

Then they started to surge. No single thing set them off. The Brooklyn cranks who remembered Candy LaChance as plodding toward payday were shocked to see him sweat. Jimmy Sheckard thrived on aggression. Keister started to hit. Steve Brodie's eccentricities kept everyone alert. Topsy Magoon, the light-hitting shortstop, was fast on his feet and soon a favorite.

And McGraw—always McGraw. His fielding was better than ever and he was stealing bases with abandon. Not until the fifty-second game of the season did he fail to reach base. He never let up, on himself or his men. He had only contempt for laggards. He kept up a steady run of comments that kept his men fighting to the last.

"The Baltimores are soaring," a Boston newspaper marveled before June was over. "Think of it! In third place!"

Around Baltimore, murmurings were heard about a pennant. People were joking at first. But they understood what a pennant race felt like. They knew that sentiment mattered.

"We will be up there somewhere in the bunch when the finish comes," McGraw pledged. "The Baltimore people are well pleased with the showing we have made. They are more enthusiastic about this team than they were about the Champions." Old-time cranks who had thrown up their hands after the team had been stripped of its stars had started to trip through the turnstiles at Union Park. This team they were coming to see, they *were* the Orioles.

McGraw saw one more piece to put into place. He missed Hughey Jennings. It was difficult for McGraw to make friends—or to keep them. He was an easy man to admire or envy but a hard man to like. He had probably never been as close to a friend as he had been to Hughey, not only from spring through fall but also over the winters at St. Bonaventure's. Being on a different team than Hughey, on opposite sides, just felt wrong.

Besides, having Hughey back would add ginger to the Orioles. Sentiment was their only shot at a pennant. Maybe Hanlon knew that, because he refused McGraw's request. Hanlon wanted Hughey, lame arm and all, as a utility infielder. Harry von der Horst, however, liked the idea of moving Hughey to the Orioles. Maybe he felt he owed at least that to Baltimore. Not that his opinion mattered very much. But after the Superbas started to lose and Hughey got in bad odor with the Brooklyn magnates, Harry's solution increased in allure.

"Imagine my surprise this morning," John McGraw remarked on a midsummer's night. The telegram Hanlon and Harry had sent him was decidedly different from the one he had received from Harry alone the night before. Harry had said that he would be arriving with Hughey, to trade him for Topsy Magoon. McGraw was delighted but for one thing: Earlier in the day he had made a sizzler of a trade with Chicago, dispatching Topsy Magoon for Gene Demont, the old Oriole second baseman. He had not asked permission from Hanlon, who was still the president of the Orioles and thus McGraw's boss.

Hanlon was coldly furious. Whether it was the defiance of his authority or his anger at being outmaneuvered—and perhaps over-taken—by a team of castoffs, nobody could tell. The answer was proba-bly both. Not that it mattered: Anyone who believed in a need for order could see this was no way for a self-respecting syndicate to act.

The wire the following morning wreaked Hanlon's revenge. Hughey would be traded to Baltimore, but for Demont *and* pitcher Jerry Nops.

McGraw exploded. Hanlon was cheating him. He had promised not to use Baltimore as a farm for Brooklyn, but now he was doing just that. What McGraw wanted did not count. Mac could not stand for it.

Harry showed up the same day with Hughey in hand. McGraw kicked and threatened to quit. Harry refused to give way.

It took a few hours for McGraw's temper to subside. He under-stood the rules. "They own the two clubs," he noted, "and of course can do as they please with them."

And so Hughey became an Oriole again.

He played that afternoon, at second base, so he could throw the ball to first. And he could. On the first play of the game he flung a sprinting Pirate out at first base. At the bat he smacked two triples that made the difference in the game.

All over Baltimore, McGraw was hailed for his defiance and his unexpected success. Still, as attendance in Brooklyn and St. Louis more than doubled, fewer cranks troubled the turnstiles at Union Park than in 'ninety-eight, and this time there was no war to explain it. Even the Republican newspaper blamed syndicate baseball. "Certainly the public would take very little interest in a yacht race in which all the vessels entered were owned by one man or one syndicate," the *Balti-more American* editorialized. "The same rule applies to the national game of baseball."

Baltimoreans loathed having a deal forced on them. Even in Brooklyn, trading away Hughey was viewed with suspicion. He was a favorite of the cranks, and Demont had no personal following. It looked like nothing but a ploy to help Baltimore. The wariness in Brooklyn and the outrage in Baltimore alarmed the magnates. *The Sun*, which rarely deigned to notice public discontent, detected "a torrent of indignant protest from Baltimore lovers of baseball, as well as enthusiasts all over the country, who want to see the national game on a higher level than that of mere dollars and cents."

Hanlon grew distressed at reading the vehemence in the New York newspapers. He 'phoned McGraw in Philadelphia and begged him—and Harry, too—to come and confer. They got to the Clarendon Hotel in Brooklyn before midnight. Gus Abell and Charley Ebbets also showed up. They met in a private room and emerged at one-thirty with a decision they had known before going in.

The Jennings deal was off.

Hanlon accepted none of the blame. "I opposed the deal from the start," he said, "because I knew it would cause trouble. But Mr. von der Horst had his heart set on getting Jennings and it would have meant a loss of friendship to oppose him."

Harry pleaded he had meant to strengthen the Orioles, not to harm them. "I only desire the good of the national game," he said.

Seized by the longings of the waning days of August, McGraw was prodding the Orioles to sweep the doubleheader in Louisville. Amazingly, the castoffs still occupied fourth place, a belt loop behind the Phillies and not much farther in the Beaneaters' wake. Brooklyn, not surprisingly, was out of reach.

Steve Brodie arrived just in time from Roanoke, where he had been nursing a carbuncle at the base of his spine. His return put some dash into his teammates. Before being waylaid, he had hit safely in fifteen consecutive games, and in twenty-two of twenty-three.

Joe McGinnity pitched the opening game. He was usually shaky in the first inning and this time was no exception: The Colonels scored two runs. After that he was invincible. The fielding was perfect behind him. Ducky Holmes and Billy Keister got three hits apiece and the game was soon drained of its tension.

Midway through the game a telegram arrived for McGraw, from home. It was about Minnie. Her appendix had burst. He must come quickly. McGraw stayed until the end of the game. Once the last Colonel was out he started for the hotel and then the railway station.

With Robbie in charge for the nightcap, the Orioles took a two-run lead, which sagged into a tie that lasted until dark.

McGraw was on the train as two surgeons from Johns Hopkins operated on his wife at home. When Mac arrived, he was relieved to learn of their success.

Which it was, until three nights later, when blood poisoning set in. All night long Mac sat at Minnie's bedside, and the next morning. Her family gathered around. Shortly after noon, without pain, she died. Like a fallen angel, so quickly taken. How lovely she had been, how fresh, at twenty-two.

Her husband was inconsolable. Hundreds of telegrams of condolence poured in. Hughey Jennings and Willie Keeler and Joe Kelley, groomsmen less than three years before, served as pallbearers.

Mac secluded himself in his high-ceilinged home on St. Paul street. He had known so much death in his life. He had seen his mother and four of his brothers and sisters die. He had turned to baseball as his salvation. This time baseball was the last thing he could endure.

The Orioles learned of Minnie's death when they got to Cincinnati. That afternoon their dopey playing defeated them. They won the next day, but then lost five in a row. Their patience was gone. They stopped working the pitcher. They forgot to cover bases. If they fell a couple of runs behind, they hung their heads and quit. Some of the players were openly rebellious. With Robbie they could act as they liked.

"The system of team play built up by McGraw is rapidly falling to pieces," the *Morning Herald* reported back from the West. "The wonder now is how McGraw ever got so much out of such material."

Inside of a week, sixth place loomed dangerously near. Robbie could not replace his business partner and neighbor, and he knew it. "If McGraw had not met with his bereavement," Robbie said after the Orioles had won a game at last, "I am sure we would have been right in the thick of the fight for first place."

After two weeks away, McGraw returned to the Orioles. He benched himself for another ten days. At last, he put himself into the first game of a doubleheader against the Spiders, who had become the most wretched victims of syndicate baseball. Their revolving cast of discards was producing the most pathetic season a major league ballclub had ever suffered through—20 victories and 134 defeats. None of their pitchers won more than four times. Hardly five hundred cranks had showed up for the opening game, and even fewer on the afternoons that followed. The ticket receipts averaged barely $25 a game, so that the visiting teams could hardly cover their hotel costs. By July, the Cleveland owner, Frank Robison, announced that the Spiders would play all of their remaining games on the road. The Exiles, they came to be called, or the Wanderers.

This was a team begging to be beaten. Twice, Mac hit safely, and he scored a run, as the Orioles won, 5 to 4.

The second game, which the Orioles won as well, he sat out.

Willie Keeler's batting average had been hovering around .400 all season long. He was second among the League batsmen, next to Big Ed Delehanty. But too many of his teammates, Kel included, slipped into slumps. Among the twirlers only Jack Dunn was reliable, and even he had been missing the mark of late. He said it was because of a strain in his side, though rumor had it he had lost too much at the track.

The Superbas were losing and the Beaneaters were drawing near. "The Brooklyn players want to win," Hanlon declared, as if that had been in doubt. "Mark what I say, that as soon as I can fix up the pitching corps the Brooklyns will make another great rush toward the flag. The team is strong and cannot tumble much longer."

But it seemed like a soulless strength, to some of the cranks. The fanatics at Washington Park hurled sarcasm at the Superbas whenever they fell behind and cheered on whichever team was winning. They did not feel as if the team belonged to Brooklyn. "They don't like to be picked up for 'suckers,'" a local scribe came to explain. "Without any question the merging of the Baltimore club with the Brooklyn club was never a satisfactory move to the patrons of the sport in this city. They looked upon it as a hold-up game to get their quarters and their half-dollars." Which of course it was. And to a profitable extent, it succeeded.

When Brooklyn's lead over Boston had shriveled to a single game, Andrew Freedman played his hand. He sold Jouett Meekin, the veteran right-hander, to the Beaneaters cheaply. Or lent him, the scuttlebutt had it, just to bring the Superbas low. The Brooklyn magnates were hardly in a position to complain that Art Soden, the Boston magnate, owned a piece of the Giants himself.

Hanlon was urged to snatch Joe McGinnity from Baltimore in self-defense. But he was not a man to make the same mistake twice. He kept tinkering and soon the Superbas started winning again. "Brooklyn will win the pennant," Harry von der Horst assured the borough's good citizens. "I say that with all sincerity, because we shall leave no legitimate effort go by in securing that end."

Hanlon signed a pitcher the Orioles had released and sent Big Dan McGann to Washington for Deacon McGuire, the steady veteran catcher, and tried again (without success) to buy Honus Wagner from Louisville. The pitching improved. Hughey was back in the lineup, now at first base—the Hughey of old, poking a double or a triple at the right moment, collaring sizzlers in the infield. Kelley was batting fiercely and well.

There was no gainsaying the Superbas' sheer quantity of quality. Facing Boston in a critical series in August, they walloped Kid Nichols and then Jouett Meekin.

Their lead had grown to eight games as September came to a close. They blew into Baltimore for four confrontations. The Orioles were going to finish in fourth place, no matter what. Nothing in the standings was at stake, but honor was. Hanlon told the Baltimore scribes that he would rather lose $1,000 than see the Orioles win.

Not that the cranks cared. Only 1,647 spectators came to Union Park to watch a contest for blood. The Superbas scrapped for every advantage. In the fifth inning Willie and Kel worked the hit-and-run—like old times, it was. No team was better at it. And yet every Oriole rose to the occasion. They took advantage of Jack Dunn's infrequent moments of unsteadiness. Twice Mac drew a base on balls and twice came around to score. Jimmy Sheckard stole second base and then stole home. They provoked errors and scored runs without getting a hit.

The Orioles led by two runs entering the final inning, then scored twice more. The Superbas replied with two runs of their own. They had two men out and a runner on third when Willie Keeler came to the bat. The Orioles knew to expect what was least expected. A swinging single made more sense than a bunt. So Willie bunted. Candy LaChance, the strongly made first baseman, tagged him out.

The Orioles won the next two games as well, before dropping the final game, 4 to 3. The attendance kept declining.

*   *   *

Brooklyn clinched the 'ninety-nine pennant in a romp, 13 to 2, over the Giants on October seventh. The club had been in first place since the twenty-second of May, the longest stretch since the League had grown to twelve teams.

The pennant was Brooklyn's first since 'ninety. But there was no parade, nor even talk of one. The club had drawn more patrons but not as many as the magnates had hoped or as the bookkeepers had assumed. Anticipated profits of $100,000 turned out to be half that, even as the low-budget Orioles, who had figured to lose money for the season, finished $15,000 in the black.

Not that Brooklyn's pennant would go uncelebrated. The Temple Cup was gone and nothing had replaced it. But there was talk of a testimonial for the new champions, all receipts going to the ballplayers. Instead of the traditional banquet, which would be tedious for the ballplayers and necessarily too small—and expensive—for many cranks to come, a vaudeville performance was arranged at the Academy of Music.

On the appointed Saturday evening, the understated brick building with the Gothic-arched windows on Montague street seemed besieged by hired carriages and people on foot. Men and women of prominence filled the boxes; bleacherites admired the florid decor as they crowded into the balconies. The decorations were dominated by the Stars and Stripes.

The vaudeville acts began at eight-thirty sharp, and after much singing, dancing, and animal acts, Charley Ebbets took the stage, his stylish moustache glistening in the lights. It was an evening for graciousness. Ebbets recalled Charley Byrne and praised Gus Abell's largess and lauded Captain Kelley for working wonders. Then he introduced the "the Dewey of managers"—the greatest, he said, the national game had ever known.

As the curtain went up, Ned Hanlon stepped to the front of the stage. He looked very somber in the lights. Brooklyn's pennant—the syndicate's pennant—was stretched wing to wing. Cheers rolled like thunder through the hall. Hanlon handed a check for $2,500 to Joe Kelley, for the players to divide among themselves. One by one, they were introduced to hurrahs.

Then Frank X. McCaffrey, the borough's assistant district attorney, walked out on the stage for one last presentation. "Brooklynites are essentially a home people. As a vigorous and health-loving community, we have long espoused the cause of the national outdoor game," he began. "So, when we have watched one of our own—a Brooklynite by birth and choice—rise to eminence in his chosen field, we point to him, with honest sincerity, as a typical Brooklynite."

Willie Keeler knew what was coming.

"His name is known, admired and respected wherever baseball has penetrated."

In the waves of applause, Willie was coaxed to the stage. He had finished the season fourth among the League's batsmen, with a .379 average, twelve points behind McGraw. Had Willie not hurt his leg in early September, he might have given Big Ed Delehanty's .410 a fright.

But it was not for his numbers alone that he was awarded a fine gold pocket watch. He understood that. He blushed and muttered a few words of thanks.

After a well-known local thespian recited "Casey at the Bat," everyone went home.

=9=

Survival of
the Fittest

John McGraw and Joe Kelley came up from Baltimore, but they soon
found the doings at the Fifth Avenue Hotel tiresome and went home.
Willie Keeler took the trolley across the bridge each day and kept coming back. Partly he was looking for diversion. He had little else he
needed to do other than finish his Christmas shopping and decide
whether to accept an offer to coach the Fordham nine.

As it happened, fewer ballplayers than usual showed up to prowl
the wide, well-lighted corridors for the National League meetings.
Maybe it was all the talk about establishing a new American Association, one that would charge popular prices, outlaw syndicate baseball,
and abandon the reserve rule. But still, Willie returned. Something
about the magnates was fascinating, like bugs under glass, or more like
an ant colony, busy with interaction. The newer magnates were different kinds of men. They were not the sporting men or the brewers or
the local merchants seeking a place for themselves in the community.
More and more, they were the streetcar magnates and the businessmen with a limited loyalty to a city or—increasingly, it seemed—the
machine politicians.

Pretty much all of the magnates had an impressive self-regard.
Only Charley Ebbets and John Rogers of the Phillies showed up at the
opulent hotel in silk hats, but the others had their own means of display. Harry von der Horst had a girth that suggested wealth. Barney
Dreyfuss, the jug-eared Louisville magnate twitted by the newspapers
as weighing barely ninety pounds in his patent leathers, showed a
beatific smile at the recent turn in his fortune: He had just managed
to send Honus Wagner and thirteen other players to Pittsburgh in

177

exchange for $25,000 and 50 percent of the Pirates. The Cincinnati owner, John T. Brush, in constant pain from his locomotor ataxia, preferred a puritanical harshness. Andrew Freedman of the Giants strutted his superiority by staying away. From the Democratic Club, on Fifth avenue twenty-six blocks to the north, he held court like a governor and dined with friendly magnates every evening.

Whatever game they were playing, Willie knew it was a different one than his.

Every so often the door to the parlor would open and a platoon of newspapermen rushed over to surround the magnate who had emerged. Then they retreated with looks of disgust when he had nothing to say.

But nobody inside could keep a secret for long. Soon everyone knew that they were talking about turning themselves into an eight-team league. They had thought about doing so from time to time, since 'ninety-four at least, not very long after they had so solemnly promised to stay at twelve teams for a decade. The perennial tailenders suffered a perennial lack of excitement among their cranks and thus never got the money to improve. It seemed inevitable that two or four teams would be lopped off. But to break the Indianapolis agreement would take a unanimous vote, with the attendant expense of purchasing the acquiescence of the ballclubs chosen to fade away.

The mutterings had grown louder of late. Eight of the twelve ballclubs had finished in the red for 'ninety-nine, no longer with a foreign war to blame. By season's end, after the grandstand in Louisville had burned to the ground, the Colonels as well as the Spiders had taken to playing all their games away from home.

And something else had changed. John T. Brush and Andrew Freedman had buried the hatchet. They had been enemies for years, since they fought for control of the Giants after the 'ninety-four season. Brush had been one of the Giants' rescuers back when the Players' League collapsed, and he had tried to buy enough of the ballclub to run it. But Freedman, with his Tammany skills, used a front man and cornered all the available shares to freeze his rival out. Later he physically attacked the wobbly Cincinnati magnate in the barroom of the Fifth Avenue Hotel, until a friend of Brush's stepped in and beat him up.

They deserved each other, these two bitter men. In appearance they were opposites. Brush was a lean, angular man with a hard-bristled moustache and an aquiline nose jutting from his bony face. Freedman was plump in all the wrong places; his face lacked muscle tone. His eyes, set low in his face, seemed to rest with disdain on whatever they watched. On either side of a thick brush of a moustache, the sag of his jowls suggested a touch of cruelty.

Both men had an indomitable will. Brush had spent many a night writhing in bed, with the shooting pains from his degenerating spinal cord, rather than yield to opiates. Friends said that when he was engaged in a business deal, his face bore no more expression than a cast-iron safe. Maybe it was because everything came hard to him that he demanded so much from everyone else. When he was thirty he had opened a clothing store in Indianapolis and made it one of the largest in the West, with branch houses in numerous cities. He became the controlling owner of the League franchise in Indianapolis and then the Reds in Cincinnati. He knew little about judging ballplayers but quite a lot about bending magnates to his will. Since Charley Byrne's death he had become the League's preeminent politician. The magnates admired him, and were scared of him, too. He was fifty-four now, and using a cane, and was not afraid of a soul.

That enabled him to take the initiative. He was tired of losing money. He was certain that an eight-team league—no longer top-heavy, without perpetual losers, without teams consigned to the road— was better as a business proposition. He had thought so for years. But after two years of losses by most of the ballclubs, now was his chance. He needed allies, and knew where to look.

He had Art Soden make the approach. The ballplayers detested the Boston magnate, who had originated the reserve clause and had once blacklisted a Beaneater for refusing to tip his hat. But his fellow magnates thought him a man among men. He, too, owned a piece of the Giants and thus was a natural to carry the message to Freedman.

The Tammany magnate had been flaunting the power of weakness. Outmaneuvered for the moment by his enemies in Brooklyn, he had refused to spend any money on the Giants, with the intention not of hurting himself but of hurting the League. It was common knowledge that no major league could prosper without a strong team in New York to draw the crowds and bring in the receipts that the visiting teams shared. The Giants had sunk to tenth place in 'ninety-nine and could well go lower, through Freedman's strategic passivity.

When the two antagonists finally met, neither Brush nor Freedman would divulge what they had discussed, but they clearly emerged of a single mind about the enticements of an eight-club National

League. It was even said (and just as heatedly denied) that the climax of the conversation had been an agreement to include Brooklyn's ball-club among the four to be undone. That would have been Freedman's price, of course, so he could have Greater New York to himself.

He could point to the language in the League charter that limited a city to a single franchise. Better still, he could make it a matter of right and wrong—no, good and evil. They would attack Brooklyn by declaring war against syndicate baseball. Never mind that a syndicate of owners from other teams had owned a minority of the Giants for nearly a decade. "Syndicate ball and methods have done more to injure the game than anything else," Freedman announced to the newspapermen, "and the first fight will be against that bane." Only if syndicate baseball was abolished would he invest money in the Giants. He and Brush had allies in Boston, Philadelphia, and Pittsburgh. In an eight-club league, they would rule.

In Cleveland and in Louisville, so little was left of the ballclubs that the League could cheaply buy their consent. In Washington the Wagner brothers were willing as well: Their public expressions of concern were known to be nothing but bargaining ploys.

But in Brooklyn, Charley Ebbets and his political clout stood in the way. Mayor Van Wyck had named him to the Greater New York committee to welcome a warship home from Manila during the war against Spain. He had recently been made the second vice-chairman of the Kings County Democratic Committee. Boss McLaughlin could hold his own with Boss Croker, for Brooklyn was too big to be pushed around. Charley Ebbets would see to it.

Something else was in Brooklyn's favor. Its team was the strongest in the League. Buying it off would therefore cost the League's magnates more money than they were willing to pay, whether to do Andrew Freedman's bidding or anyone's.

A nine-team league would never do, and immediately the solution looked obvious. In the corridors and the lobby, by the shiny cuspidors in the darkened bar, most of all in the chandelier-lit parlors where the magnates conferred, all the talk was of Baltimore.

So what if the Orioles had turned a profit in 'ninety-nine? It only showed that a syndicate offered unfair advantage. Abolishing the Baltimore franchise would not let Freedman have New York to himself, but surely it would bring pain to the magnates he wanted to hurt.

Harry von der Horst was blunt. "The Baltimore club is not for sale," he told the scribes even before the meeting opened. Who could say if it was his loathing for Freedman or his affection for Baltimore or merely his fears for the sale of his beer? Quite likely all of that. Harry let it be known that any violation of the Indianapolis agreement would wind up in court. He warned of an injunction that might prevent every club in the League from taking the field the next spring.

Ned Hanlon likewise made his objections known. "Why should we sell out in Baltimore?" he demanded to know. "We have a valuable franchise." This carried a hint of bargaining more than heartfelt refusal. After all, Hanlon and Ebbets were already on record as favoring the concept of an eight-club league. Hanlon considered it the only logical solution to the problem the magnates faced. There was talk that he had mentioned a price for the Orioles, one he knew was higher than the magnates could afford.

The magnates met for five minutes on Tuesday and six hours on Wednesday. They argued mainly over a minor league infielder the Giants and the Superbas had both claimed. The squabble became a test of strength between the ballclubs and a reflection of their grander contest, over survival itself.

The larger question was debated on Thursday. The magnates convened at the unusually early hour of eleven o'clock and met until seven in the evening. Three of the to-be-eviscerated ballclubs had agreed to terms. Only Baltimore refused.

Harry von der Horst stayed away, at his private club. He came once but, he claimed later, lost $1,500 by being away from the stock market while he waited for business to start. On Friday, though, he was in the hotel when John T. Brush came looking for him. In a corridor they met face-to-face. The severe, gray Brush had already conferred with Gus Abell, Charley Ebbets, and Ned Hanlon on Freedman's behalf.

"Where have you been, Harry?" Brush began. He was not a man of social graces. "I want to talk some baseball matters to you."

He grabbed the lapels of Harry's coat.

"You can't talk any baseball matters to me here," Harry said, raising his voice. "Brush, you were once a leader in baseball matters, and men were accustomed to rely upon you for counsel. Today you are taking orders from those who control your actions. If you want to talk to me socially, all right. But when I have any reason to communicate with you on baseball matters I shall do so before a full meeting."

"But—"

"But nothing," Harry shot back. "Who constituted you a committee to seek a conference with me, I should like to know?"

181

Another long session had been planned for Saturday, the last day of the League meeting. It lasted little more than an hour. The magnates were unable to force Baltimore and Brooklyn to the wall, but they made sure of a procedural momentum. They left the question to a four-member Circuit Reduction Committee, which included Brush and his allies in Boston and Philadelphia. The committee's stated objective was to find a means of reducing the League to eight teams. Its real mission was to negotiate a price with the four fated ballclubs. That came down to persuading the Brooklyn magnates to sell the Baltimore franchise to the League.

It seemed as if they might. "I have no hesitation in saying that the existence of an eight-club league next season is virtually settled," Charley Ebbets said, after meeting with the magnates of the clubs to be abandoned. Foxy Ned's studied silence had spooked the magnates. But he made clear that he would bargain. Asked about newspaper reports he had named a price for the Baltimore franchise, he retorted: "No, no! Not for $50,000." McGraw alone, he said, was worth $30,000.

"Of course, if we get our price we will sell out," Hanlon hastened to add. "Everything I have, except my family, is for sale at a price."

A light snow blanketed Baltimore on New Year's Eve in 'ninety-nine. Many of the Catholic churches conducted midnight Mass, not the custom at the close of a year. The ascetic, wise Pope Leo XIII had given his permission.

It was no ordinary turn of a year, by the calendar at least. The sophisticated opinion understood that the nineteenth century had still another year to last. The editorial pages patiently explained that because there had been no Year Zero, the twentieth century would not begin until 1901.

Nobody cared.

Whenever it ended, the nineteenth century had surely been the most wonderful the world had ever known. Everyone agreed on that. The century had seen more progress "than all the previous history of the race," *The New York Times* marveled. Friction matches had not existed before the century began, nor steamboats, railroads, cast-iron plows, the telegraph, electric lighting, telephones, or Roentgen rays.

Just in July, crowds had gathered along the streets of Baltimore to watch the test of a newfangled machine called an automobile.

Prosperity ruled the land. The panic was over, the depression was gone. "The United States the Envy of the World," the headline in the *Times* financial supplement affirmed.

Around Baltimore, whistles blew and guns fired into the air as midnight arrived. All over the city, church bells chimed.

City patriots could be excused for hearing something solemn in the echoes. In this best of all possible times, why did Baltimoreans feel so unprotected? The city was somehow losing its stature in the world. The prospect of losing the Orioles, the city's place in the major league, was only a reflection. What Baltimoreans wanted seemed not to count. No one had even bothered to ask them. Their destiny was no longer their own.

No one was to blame, really. The rules of the economy were ruthless, everyone knew that. Maybe more troubling than any private anguish was the mildness of the public reaction, the air of resignation. It was as if Baltimoreans had come to understand their reduced place in the world.

John McGraw's lawyer rapped at the front gate of Union Park, carrying a writ of ejectment. It was three o'clock on a sunny Saturday in February 1900. He demanded to be let in.

McGraw himself was in Philadelphia, pursuing backers for an American Association franchise. Mac had taken charge of Baltimore's entry in such a league, though there was still talk he might try a franchise in New York instead. But he was not about to leave The Diamond. Nor was Robbie. Only by staying in Baltimore could they protect their investment. So they had lined up financing for an American Association franchise in the fallen city from, among others, the manager of the Eutaw House, the vice-president of the German Ginger Ale Company, and an executive at one of Baltimore's biggest banks. The main money man was none of these. It was Sonny Mahon, Joe Kelley's father-in-law, the scion of the city's Democratic machine. That made it practically a civic venture—and why not? If the National League discarded Baltimore, only a new American Association could prevent the proud city by the Chesapeake from becoming a minor league town.

Ned Hanlon had allowed the lease on Union Park to expire in January, and quite sensibly. Why pay $3,500 in rent on a ballpark for a franchise about to disappear? Hanlon was not a man to spend a dollar he could save. The Players' League had failed. The new one would, too.

When the owners of Union Park offered a lease to John McGraw, he snapped it up (for all but the corner out in right field that Harry von der Horst owned). Hanlon, however, still held the keys and thus controlled the ballpark. He posted armed guards inside and made sure *No Trespassing* signs were nailed on the fencing.

On the Huntingdon avenue side of Union Park, the high board fence had been planed so smooth that no one could shinny up. So as McGraw's lawyer knocked at the front, a half-dozen of his confederates stole around to the Barclay street side, beyond the left field corner. Phil Peterson, the ginger ale executive who was slated as the president of the new ballclub, scaled the fence and jumped down to the roof of the umpires' shack.

Only then did the defenders inside notice the trap. They rushed over with ladders.

On the roof, half the size of a pitcher's box, Hanlon's groundskeeper confronted McGraw's man Peterson and grabbed him by the waist. The two men struggled. Peterson got the groundskeeper in a hammerlock, but Hanlon's man broke free and forced Peterson toward the edge.

Suddenly the police leapt down onto the roof and a deputy marshal flung himself between the competing envoys of the national game. In the confusion the rest of McGraw's phalanx clambered over the fence. It was all the bluecoats could do to keep them from Hanlon's defenders.

The duelling armies of angry men, too excited to be cold, clustered down on the ballgrounds. Each group demanded that the other be arrested. Nobody was. The deputy marshal explained that the job of the police was not to dispense justice but to keep the peace.

Which, to McGraw's men, was enough. They were inside. They carried guns and clubs but found no need to use them. They raced across the hard bare ground to third base, McGraw's home.

They lodged there for the night. Hanlon's forces made a camp of their own around first base. A single policeman, embodying the majesty of the law, positioned himself in front of the ticket office.

McGraw's lawyer rushed to court to secure an injunction, to prevent the Orioles management from removing or destroying any of

Union Park's fixtures. McGraw's men—the Boers, as they came to be called, after the Dutch settlers fighting the imperial British in South Africa—liked to sit along the Huntingdon avenue fence, smoking their pipes and delivering surly replies. Both camps stayed on for much of the month, provisioned by friends on the outside.

McGraw was regarded as the brains of the proposed new league. So he rushed back to Philadelphia when the financing fell through, to line up a new capitalist, a theater owner said to be interested in hiring Joe Kelley as the manager. If Kel jumped, maybe Willie Keeler and Hughey Jennings would, too. A league could get off the ground with such a foursome. McGraw said he had letters from Ducky Holmes and Joe McGinnity and a couple of other Oriole pitchers promising to follow.

On the fourteenth of February, at a hotel in Chicago, the new American Association was born. It allotted franchises to Baltimore, Philadelphia, Boston, and Providence in the East, and St. Louis, Milwaukee, Detroit, and Chicago in the West.

The next day the League collapsed. The theater owner in Philadelphia wired McGraw it would take him another three weeks before he knew for sure about available ballgrounds, making it too late to start the season on time. Having seven clubs in a league meant having none.

"Yes, the jig is up," Mac said sadly.

Even so, Harry von der Horst said he felt betrayed by the men— McGraw, he meant—whose salaries he had paid for so many years. "The local sentiment which has ruled me has been killed by those I have called my friends," Harry lamented, "and I can see Baltimore baseball now only from a purely business standpoint."

For two days a dozen newspapermen had been hunting all over Cleveland for the members of the Circuit Reduction Committee. The four magnates had registered at the Hollenden Hotel under false names. They ate together on the second floor and made sure they were never seen together in the lobby or on the street.

On the upper floors they conferred with the magnates from the four targeted ballclubs. With the Cleveland and Louisville owners they talked about selling the franchises to an ambitious minor league that had recently upgraded its name, from the Western League to the American League. The Eastern League was to buy the Washington and Baltimore franchises. The New York Giants were promised the pick of any players left behind.

Dollars were discussed with every club but Baltimore's. Ned Hanlon and Charley Ebbets and Gus Abell had come to Cleveland, but they refused to name a price until Harry von der Horst arrived.

He showed up only as the committee members had started to leave. They had settled nothing. Rumors put Baltimore's price as high as $75,000, but surely that was excessive. Hanlon maintained that was how much the Orioles would earn in the next two seasons, before the Indianapolis pact expired, not even counting the value of the ballplayers. Harry, still loath to sell, might have intended the price to be prohibitive.

No agreement was struck.

Hanlon insisted in public that the Orioles planned to stay put. "For the fourteen hundredth time," he snapped at a Baltimore newspaperman as February slid into March, "I will say that in my opinion the circuit for 1900 will consist of ten cities, including both Baltimore and Washington." The Orioles kept preparing to go south.

John McGraw knew better. As the Orioles manager he had been given no authority to strengthen the team.

Gus Abell was too wealthy to feel the need to mince his words. "I have been in the baseball business for eighteen years," he said to a scribe for the *Evening World* on his way into the League's March meeting at the Fifth Avenue Hotel, "and in all that time have never known the magnates to do anything honestly or fairly. Whenever I go to a baseball meeting, I never forget to check my money and valuables at the hotel office before entering the session chambers."

The other magnates were furious when they read his remarks. The genial millionaire kept his hands in his pockets and stood his ground. In the lobby, Barney Dreyfuss, the bantam magnate in Louisville, loudly accused him of being part of the cabal that had given the Colonels such an awful schedule in 'ninety-nine. "I am against you now," he cried out, "and shall vote with the League. I don't care what share I shall have to pay."

Survival of the Fittest

A more important League gathering had never drawn less interest. It had been twenty years since so few ballplayers and managers and minor leaguers and even scribes had bothered to attend. In only six of the League's twelve cities did a newspaper even send a man. This was taken as a measure of how far the magnates—and the national game—had fallen in the public's estimation.

Most of the decisions on the agenda were easy. The magnates changed the shape of home plate from a diamond to a pentagon, to give the pitchers a flat edge to aim at instead of a point. They cut back from two umpires to one because of the expense. They approved a resolution lauding Andrew Freedman and reimbursing him the $1,000 he had been fined in the Ducky Holmes affair, plus 6 percent interest. The vote, it turned out, had been taken by mail; the check was already in Freedman's pocket.

The real work went on elsewhere. At the Sturtevant House, John T. Brush conferred with Harry von der Horst and Ned Hanlon and Charley Ebbets late into the night.

When the magnates reconvened the next afternoon, the Circuit Reduction Committee made its report. Cleveland and Louisville were willing to give up the ghost but Baltimore and Washington continued to balk. The Giants and the Beaneaters—Freedman and Soden—refused to pay more than $10,000 per franchise. That satisfied Louisville alone. Cleveland demanded $25,000 and Washington's price was $46,500 for the franchise plus its players. Baltimore was still holding out for $75,000 but seemed willing to take less if it could sell the ballplayers on its own.

As the shadows of a late winter's day turned into darkness, inside the palatial hotel the wrangling went on. The Wagner brothers agreed to lower their price by the $7,500 that Boston had paid for two of the Senators' stars and a utility man, but by no more than that. The magnates broke for dinner, then resumed.

All evening, Harry von der Horst kept saying no. The best bargaining, after all, comes from true reluctance. He had a feeling for Baltimore, even if he no longer lived there.

Shortly before midnight the magnates emerged, in smiles. The solution had been there all along. Louisville was to get $10,000 for its franchise; Cleveland, $10,000 and another $15,000 for its ballpark. Washington had agreed to $39,000 for its franchise and players. And Baltimore, too, had come to terms, for $30,000 plus whatever its ballplayers fetched.

187

"We got our price," Hanlon announced. "The deal goes through." The eight surviving ballclubs would raise the $104,000 by putting aside 5 percent of the gross receipts of every ballgame.

Only Harry von der Horst sounded wistful. "When I put my signature to that agreement," he sighed, "I said, 'Good-bye, old Baltimore.' I can tell you sincerely that I felt bad."

Still, he had signed.

Harry von der Horst sat in Ned Hanlon's well-appointed living room, in the commodious home at the corner of Mount Royal and Lafayette, in a genteel neighborhood. Three years earlier Hanlon had paid for the house in cash, an impressive $7,000. It was money well spent, for it allowed him to live a short walk from the Music Hall and the music he loved.

Hanlon had another visitor—Frank Robison, now of the St. Louis Cardinals. They had already struck a deal before leaving New York.

Two others were summoned that evening. John McGraw and Wilbert Robinson must have trembled to see Robison seated there. They were dumbfounded when they were told the news.

St. Louis! No city in the League was farther away. They had been peddled for $16,000.

"The idea of going away to St. Louis, where we would be seven months away from home and our business, is very repulsive to me," Wilbert Robinson blurted to a newspaperman that night. Robbie was such a homebody, so devoted to his wife and children. "For my part," he said, "I will get out of the game rather than submit to any such deal."

Mac felt the same. He faced the added horror of having to defer to Patsy Tebeau, the St. Louis manager, who was so much like McGraw— only less gifted—that Mac despised him.

He and Robbie understood that playing for Brooklyn would ruin the competitive balance of the League. McGraw even saw that he and Hanlon could no longer fit on one bench. He had been counting on playing for New York—he knew that Andrew Freedman wanted both of them—and it would put them only four or five hours from The Diamond. Or why not Philadelphia? They could come home once a week.

The problem was not the money. Robison promised a generous salary and even a cut of what he had paid for them. The problem was everything else—the distance, the separation, the insult. McGraw had been the manager of the Orioles, Robbie had been the captain. They were being treated like chattel, in a cold-blooded sale, without being told, much less asked. Hanlon claimed the transaction was a matter of business—"a last resort," he said. But he could have sold them to any team in the League. It was hard not to think it was personal. St. Louis was a good thirty hours away by rail. This was not about business—or it was, but not in the way Hanlon meant. It was about the battle over Union Park, the wrangling over Hughey, Mac's efforts to start a rival league. He had embarrassed Hanlon, infuriated Harry. This was about betrayal and revenge.

But if they were to be treated as property, at least they were valuable property, and they knew it. This gave them leverage. It was the middle of March and the teams were traveling south. McGraw and Robbie refused to go. How could they risk the $10,000 income each of them could expect from The Diamond to assure the $5,000 in salary the Cardinals had in mind, of which $1,000 would go toward making a second home in St. Louis? How long would the crowds patronize The Diamond if they lived halfway across the continent? One of them had to be on hand from time to time, if only to sign the paychecks.

Hanlon and Harry came to The Diamond and talked to them for hours. They offered financial inducements. Mac and Robbie said no.

A few days later McGraw saw Gus Abell in New York.

"Hello, Mac," Abell saluted. "I have just offered to bet 100-to-1 that you will play in St. Louis."

"You lose your money," McGraw replied. "I shall not leave Baltimore this season."

"Then you won't play ball," Abell answered.

McGraw and Robbie talked about forming a City League of semi-pro teams. They met with a theatrical manager about playing out on Belvedere avenue, at Electric Park, with its cafés and roller coasters and whimsical towers, its modern young crowds with quarters to spare, and a ballgrounds with 10,000 seats. On Saturdays and holidays a semi-pro league at popular prices might draw quite a few cranks.

Robison wired McGraw to meet him in Cleveland and accompany him to St. Louis to join the Cardinals. Mac wired back that he had given his final word.

*   *   *

There was talk of a union again. Nearly a decade had passed since the Players' League failed and the Brotherhood died. Now the number of jobs in the major league had shrunk by a third, and the balance of strength between labor and capital, between supply and demand, had shifted accordingly.

The American Federation of Labor stood ready to assist. Samuel Gompers, an ardent admirer of the national game, was eager to help the ballplayers organize. "We were told it would be impossible to organize the seamen," the labor leader said, "but we did it." In baseball he blamed the players' timidity.

That was changing. Something ugly was coursing through baseball, and the cranks knew it. The players fought the magnates, and the magnates fought themselves. "The game is not benefited by all these squabbles between the magnates," Charley Ebbets said. "The public wants to see baseball, not all this strife."

Hughey Jennings made it known that he was thinking of quitting, not only because of his arm. He blamed the magnates as well—Hanlon in particular. Hughey had wanted to try his hand as a manager and had hoped that the Phillies or some other club would sign him, but Hanlon insisted on an exorbitant price. "I am capable of being a success as a leader, just as much as the man I have been under for the past seven years," Hughey complained to a friend in Wilkes-Barre in a letter that managed to find its way into print. "When the chance is open to me to show my worth in the managerial line, and he blocks it, to my way of thinking it is almost—if not quite—time to call a halt."

Hughey had learned from his days in the coal mines, watching his father and his uncles and his brothers, what a misfortune it was to labor under another man's thumb. At the least he needed a more dependable profession. "The grab-all policy of the present magnates," he said, "is not going to do the game any good."

When the Superbas went south, to Augusta again, Willie Keeler stayed back in Brooklyn. He went down to the ferry to see his teammates off, then returned to the wood-shingled shack on Pulaski street he shared with his parents and his brother Tom, now a stationery salesman. His mother was ill and Willie had refused to sign the contract Hanlon had sent him. He objected principally to the clause that reserved him to Brooklyn for three seasons.

"Not that I don't like Brooklyn and that I don't like the Brooklyn management," he explained, "but I am averse to being held to a three years' agreement that seems to be all in favor of the other people. I think that a year's claim on a man should be enough for any baseball concern."

The next week, with his mother still sick and his contract unsigned, Willie packed his valise and met up with Joe Kelley in Baltimore and left for Augusta.

Shock, disgust, grief—such were the descriptions of Baltimoreans' reactions to the Orioles' demise. Hanlon and his Superbas swept into Baltimore on their way north and saw the bitterness firsthand. They laid claim to Union Park on Good Friday, for an intrasquad game. The National League controlled the lease again, since the rival circuit's stillbirth. But there was a complication: Several weeks earlier, the University of Maryland had applied to rent the ballpark on Good Friday to play Yale. No contract had been signed, but assurances had been received.

Hanlon went to the Maryland team's manager and pointed out that he could exclude the college nines entirely but he would be gracious and consent to play Maryland on Thursday and Yale on Friday. When the kind offer was declined, he proposed letting the college nines play on Friday if they finished early enough for Brooklyn's intrasquad game. Mindful of the crowd such a doubleheader would draw, Hanlon felt sufficiently generous to allot the college teams two-thirds of the ticket receipts, though he declined to allow the university men inside the box office.

Union Park's blemishes deepened in the shadow of the clouds. The bleachers looked gray and impossibly old. Even under the grandstand roof the seatbacks were worn. The field appeared uncared for. Maybe six hundred rooters had passed through the turnstiles; others turned back once they learned that Hanlon would receive a third of the gate.

At four-thirty, after the varsities had played five innings, Hanlon asked them to surrender the field. He and the Maryland manager argued. After a while Hanlon agreed to let the spectators decide.

One of the college players went over to the ladies' stand and asked if the Brooklyn club should be given the field. The answer was a perfect shriek of feminine "No's." At the men's stand the reply was deeper and louder. In the bleachers the "No's" got buried by an avalanche of expletives. Brooklyn was urged to find its way to a place hotter than Baltimore on an August afternoon.

Within minutes Hanlon escorted his ballplayers back to the hotel. The Maryland nine's share of the receipts came to $23. The college boys puzzled over the arithmetic.

Six days later, when the National League season opened, Union Park sat uncustomarily silent. And it remained silent a week later, when the Eastern League got under way. The minor league had voted to put teams in Baltimore and Washington (in place of Springfield and Hartford) and had only to agree to terms with the National League over Union Park. The big league understood its bargaining strength and demanded $4,400 in rent, which was more than a new minor league franchise could afford.

Especially when the cranks seemed not to care. Who could say if their fickleness had driven the Orioles under? Whatever their guilt, they had been betrayed. That was a fact, or the closest to one that the ambiguities in any mortal's behavior would ordinarily permit. Even Hanlon had admitted that the business of baseball in Baltimore would snap back. Like any business it had cycles. But the Orioles had vanished and a new American Association had died before it was born and the sixth most populous city in America (with seventy-four thousand more people than a decade before) had no willingness to welcome minor league ball. "Baltimore is not a minor city in sport or in anything else," an editorial writer squawked. A baseball writer grieved at Baltimore being "made to join company with Buffalo, Syracuse, Wilkes-Barre, Skowhegan and other way stations."

So there was no minor league baseball and not even a semipro league. Baseball in Baltimore was nothing more than talk—and more of it at The Diamond than anyplace else. It was a warm rambunctious place, especially with McGraw and Robbie around so often now. They talked endlessly about baseball, though the sport had gone on without them.

McGraw had missed the start of a season before, but from illness, not by choice. It was inconceivable. Spring was in the air, and Mac and Robbie were working indoors.

Frank Robison kept after them. He had a mild face but a determined nature. A corrupt broker had once cost him more than a million dollars and control over Cleveland's street railways (to Mark Hanna, now the financial angel to the man in the White House), but he had clawed and litigated his way back into a fortune. Adding John McGraw and Wilbert Robinson to a team already featuring Cy Young and Jesse Burkett augured a pennant for a club that had finished a disappointing fifth the season before. April turned into May, and Robison dispatched another pair of telegrams to the adjoining houses on St. Paul street. They described a new offer. Besides the previously offered salaries of $5,000 and $3,300, respectively, and $3,500 apiece from the purchase price, he would pay them another $1,000 each as a bonus to sign. For McGraw, that meant $9,500 all told. It would be the largest sum a ballplayer had ever been paid.

They had come to believe that they had to sign with St. Louis or quit playing baseball. Robbie was thirty-six, but Mac had just turned twenty-seven, too young to retire. Besides, not playing would hardly help business at The Diamond. It might not hurt in the first year, but how about the second or the third or the eighth? The Diamond was lucrative and fun—McGraw never tired of the attention—but it was not enough for him. Business took strategy and outsmarting the competition. But it was not baseball. It lacked the direct aggression, the combat, of the national game. Mac needed something like war, almost to live.

Robison begged the two ballplayers to meet him in Cleveland, just to talk. They left by railway the following day, even as McGraw insisted that he was still opposed to playing in the West.

In Cleveland they extracted two concessions, only one of which was announced at the time. Mac and Robbie were to be granted a short vacation whenever the team traveled East, to take care of business in Baltimore.

The other would not be commonly known for a while. They demanded that the clause be stricken from their contracts binding them for the following season, so they might become free agents in the fall. Robison complied, figuring no harm in it, so long as none of his other ballplayers knew.

Mac and Robbie signed their names and boarded a train for St. Louis.

Willie Keeler had no quibble with the money; it was what the money meant. Was he treated with respect, as a full-grown man? Was he getting his due?

He had refused to sign a contract for the 1900 season even after he got down to Augusta. Only when Hanlon agreed to reserve Willie's services for one year instead of for three did he sign. Hughey Jennings did, too, once he was offered what he wanted in a salary.

Willie was eager to face the new five-sided plate. He was not as sure as everyone else that the twirlers would benefit. "It may be a benefit and it may not," he said. "It's just likely that it will get the pitcher too regular in his habits, and he will be feeding the ball so closely over the plate that every man who comes up will knock it a mile. There are some pitchers in the League who surely would lose by becoming too regular in their work. It is the fact that they are a little wild that helps them along, for the batters are afraid of them and don't want to come up where they think they are going to have their heads knocked off."

Willie showed no signs of any benefit himself, not at first. The Superbas started well, but not Willie. His practice was never to talk about a slump until it had lifted, and even then he would say little. "I had no luck at all in the beginning of the year," he confided during the summer. "It didn't make any difference whether I bunted, or whether I hit them out, I couldn't place them away from the fielders. They nipped me on what I thought would be safe ones just because they happened to be playing right for the best that I had."

How he snapped out of his slump he was hard-pressed to say. He liked to think it happened on an afternoon when the most he could do was send up weak flies. "When there was a chance to bring in a couple of runs, I sent a pop fly to the second baseman, and as I walked out to my position a kid up in the topmost row of the bleacheries shouted as I passed: 'Say, Willie, wot limit do you play? If you don't stop staying up all night four flushings, the pitcher'll knock the bat out of your hands.'"

Willie had laughed. He was the last man on the team to play poker until dawn. But somehow he found his batting eye. "You can fool a manager once in a while," he said, "but the kids on the bleacheries—never!"

Ned Hanlon had been careful not to predict a second straight pennant for Brooklyn. But everyone else did. Who could beat them? St. Louis might give chase, with Mac and Robbie now, but how could the Cardinals match Brooklyn, batsman for batsman? Or the Pirates? They had Honus Wagner from Louisville but hardly anyone else. Brooklyn had Willie and Kel and Hughey, along with Fielder Jones in center and Bill Dahlen at second base. Nor was their pitching Hanlon's usual sore spot, now that he had plucked the Iron Man, Joe McGinnity, from Baltimore.

Tactically, Hanlon's mind had never been sharper. He had never seemed so scientific. Even Frank Selee said so, somewhat sulkily, for he had failed to prod his Beaneaters to play the sort of inside baseball he had pioneered. Ballplayers nowadays, the old-timers complained, wanted credit for whatever they did. Sacrificing was considered too much of a sacrifice.

But Hanlon's boys knew baseball's hard-nosed ways. Early in the season they tried more hit-and-runs than even the old Orioles had. Once the other managers started to mimic him, even the ones with sluggish runners, he turned to the sacrifice bunt. By the time his rivals caught on, he had shifted tactics again and had the Superbas chop down at the ball or hit away. They led the League in stolen bases, by ducking back to the base instead of foolishly bolting. They scored more runs per hit than any team in the League. Hanlon stayed three or four weeks ahead of his seven rivals. Whenever they began to expect something, he did something else.

But the more the Superbas won, the smaller the crowds at Washington Park. All over the League the attendance had dropped, whether because of competing amusements or merely because of what baseball had become. The games went on for too long, often for two-and-a-half hours or, on occasion, almost three. Too many cranks were going home to cold suppers.

In Brooklyn, the crowds should have fought their way in. Willie started out slow but soon his hard hits began dropping in. Joe Kelley had been losing track of pitches but started hitting for keeps. When he was batting well—he struck a home run that never stopped going and he had a passing acquaintance with .400—Kel was the happiest man on the team.

By June they passed into first place and were never headed. And still the crowds stayed away. Only when Pittsburgh briefly made a race of it in September, and Joe McGinnity offered to pitch the rest of the games, did the attendance in Brooklyn revive.

But even then, not by enough. Everyone had expected Brooklyn to win the pennant, so fulfilling that expectation brought no excitement. And there was something about the team that left Brooklyn's cranks cold. The management, for one thing, would open just one window for the twenty-five-cent tickets, creating a line a half-block long. A lot of people either bought fifty-cent tickets or walked away, and the ones who got in took it out on the Superbas whenever they lost. The taunts would start in the bleachers—"the swell heads got done up again, did they?" Or, "the smart guys aren't as smart as they think they are."

But it was more than the long line for tickets that grated. This was not Brooklyn's team, and the cranks knew it. Too many of them felt taken, manipulated by the syndicate. "The transfer of the Baltimore team to this city with no other object than one purely mercenary sat heavily on the Brooklyn baseball stomach," a resident scribe understood. Local pride was gone. The players were hirelings, strangers to Brooklyn.

Kel complained he would never be popular if he played in Brooklyn for forty years. "I don't like Brooklyn at all," Hughey said.

Only Willie Keeler was no stranger. He had become accustomed to sitting each summer evening in front of the Girard Brothers cigar store, beneath the el on Broadway, enjoying a good Havana cigar and chewing the fat with his chums. Early in the season he had been batting .237, but he finished at .362, behind only Honus Wagner, Elmer Flick, and Jesse Burkett. By the end he could hit any pitch that came near the plate. Or else he would draw a base on balls and come around to score. Umpires trusted his judgment and would call it a ball if he chose not to swing. He was loved in Brooklyn. It was simple as that. The borough that had once been a city was developing a taste for the underdog.

=10=

A Competing League

Willie Keeler was fresh back from Cuba, telling the story of the unfortunate baseball tour. "We were expecting two or three brass bands or something of that kind welcoming us." Instead, a single Cuban had met the Superbas and the Giants at the dock in Havana. "It didn't take long for us to find out that we had been hung up," Willie said, "that none of the arrangements had been made that had been promised and that we did not even have a ballground upon which to play." When at last a game was organized, Cubans stood outside and laid into the Americans as a cheap lot of dubs—that made the ballplayers laugh—who knew nothing about baseball and had only come to make a little money. Half the crowd melted away.

Willie sailed home to Brooklyn as soon as he could. "The next time that I go to Cuba," he said, "I am going with a party of excursionists."

He had an even better reason than spinning yarns about a liberated Cuba to venture across the bridge for the League meeting at the Fifth Avenue Hotel. *He* was on the agenda—not the formal one, but the one that mattered. The Giants wanted him, and they had asked Hanlon to put a price on his head. Willie had no interest. He liked playing in Brooklyn—loved it, really. Nor was Hanlon about to let him go. Especially not to Andrew Freedman, if Harry von der Horst had anything to say about it.

There was still another reason for Willie to brave the bustle of Fifth avenue, lined with spires and grand edifices, on the coldest day of the winter so far. The Players' Protective Association had asked for—and been reluctantly granted—an audience with the magnates.

(It was about the least that they could do, given the murmurings yet again about a rival league.) Hughey Jennings was the union's secretary, and Willie and Kel served as Brooklyn's representatives.

Uncharacteristically, the magnates threw the session open to the public and the press—a sure sign that nothing would happen. Harry Taylor, the skinny first baseman who had been traded with Hughey from the Colonels to the Orioles back in 'ninety-three, presented the ballplayers' demands as the lawyer for the Association. "The public, under the present system of contracts, looks upon the player as a slave," he said. Ballplayers, he posited, should no longer be reserved for more than three to five years, nor traded or sold or farmed without their consent.

Several times the magnates asked him: Nothing more? Each time he replied: No, nothing more. He was asked to submit a memorandum to a three-man committee of John T. Brush and the magnates from Boston and Philadelphia.

By nightfall the document was finished, and any hope for a settlement was gone. Harry Taylor had added a few things to his rendering of the ideal contract: Ballclubs should pay physicians' fees for injuries suffered in the course of a game; players must not be suspended more than three times in a season or for more than two weeks at a time; a committee of arbitration should pass on all differences between owners and players.

The magnates howled about the embellishments, calling them a breathtaking breach of faith. Any prospect of favorable consideration, they announced, was dead.

"From the very start," Hughey retorted, "I have felt that the League did not intend to consider our demands, and the way they have wriggled out of it today shows that I was right."

The ballplayers' threats of holding out for the season brought derision from the magnates. "They're only bluffing," Charley Ebbets scoffed, "and when the time comes around for advance money they will all weaken. The demands of these fellows are simply preposterous. Ballplayers have been well paid. They have endured no hardships, and have an easy life."

He was right, of course. What better life could a young man know? The players were the best at what they did, skilled workingmen and entertainers both. They expected to be treated with proper regard, and also understood that it would require fear, on the magnates' part, to bring that to pass.

A Competing League

* * *

John McGraw and Wilbert Robinson were impressed with their visitor. Ban Johnson was a true giant. His head was huge, almost comically cylindrical. His neck sagged, almost out to his jawline. His sheer bulk gave him an air of command, yet under all that flesh, beneath his sleek shock of dark hair, he looked startlingly young. He was not even forty, though he had already ruled an upstart league for a half-dozen years. (That was after a decade as a baseball writer in Cincinnati, where he had feuded with John T. Brush.) He had turned the Western League, a minor league that had once collapsed, into the best-run circuit in organized baseball. He clamped down on rowdyism and made sure that umpires got their due, then he placed a club in Chicago over wails from the National League. Ban Johnson had ambitions.

Mac and Robbie had become a part of these ambitions. Johnson had renamed his minor circuit the American League and aimed to turn it into a second major league. To do so, he needed cities in the East, and Baltimore and Washington stood abandoned—and inviting. Johnson saw that he could take over the cities the National League had given up, with ballparks already in place and known populations of cranks, to throw the established circuit on the defensive. This only hinted at Johnson's aggressiveness. He meant to strike the National League at its heart, by putting franchises in Philadelphia and Boston as well as Chicago. He would go into Cleveland, too—surely an absence of rowdyism would bring back the cranks there—and also Detroit and Milwaukee, tried-and-true Western League cities. The National League barons would know they were in for a fight.

The corpulent president wanted magnates he could trust. He found a Cleveland industrialist who put up money for four of the ballclubs. An old friend, Charley Comiskey, had taken the helm in Chicago. Connie Mack, the former Pittsburgh catcher and manager who had been running the Milwaukee club, was awarded the Philadelphia franchise. He looked gaunt but was known for his endurance, having caught a record 112 games back in 'ninety. The gentlemanly New Englander did not drink or smoke or swear and was a man of business sense who would listen to reason—made to order for a man of authority like Ban Johnson. Mack looked around Philadelphia and found a financial backer in Ben Shibe, a sporting goods magnate.

199

As for Baltimore, it was obvious which pair of men had the public standing to run a new league's ballclub, though Ban Johnson could be forgiven if he felt a little reluctant, given the well-mannered sort of league he had in mind.

As it happened, they came to him first. The two old Orioles had hated St. Louis and cared nothing for the Cardinals. They could not summon up the fire and spirit they had unleashed in Baltimore. "The sentiment was missing," McGraw explained. They would get themselves ejected from games and steal across the street to the racetrack. The Cardinals were a team of factions, and despite the abundance of stars, they slipped to sixth place in the slimmed-down eight-team League. In August, when Patsy Tebeau was chased out as the manager, McGraw refused to take his place.

He and Robbie approached Ban Johnson at Harry Goldman's urging. Judge Goldman, who dispensed justice in the northwestern district of Baltimore, had long been a friend of Ned Hanlon's, to the extent the remote manager had friends. With his dark pompadour and his handlebar moustache and his ordered, businesslike face, he even looked like Hanlon. But Judge Goldman was a Baltimorean first. At base he was a crank. He had been the left fielder for the Pastimes, the city's old amateur club before the National League began, and for years he had been one of the "Eighteenth Degree Rooters" who never missed a game at Union Park. He wanted nothing more audacious than the restoration of big league baseball to Baltimore. The Orioles were gone because no one would stand up for Baltimore. Judge Goldman would. So he was about to become a part-owner and the secretary-treasurer of an American League ballclub.

When Ban Johnson visited Baltimore, he and Harry Goldman bowled at The Diamond—tenpins, not ordinarily the choice of revolutionaries. "The American League was formed to protect the national game and to take it out of the hands of a set of men who have very nearly wrecked it," Ban Johnson regaled a scribe who had happened by. "I have just arrived from Washington, and things are all straightened out there—the grounds have been secured." Frank Robison had tried to stop Mac and Robbie from escaping St. Louis. He told them he had struck the option clause from their contracts but not the reserve rule, which was an agreement among the magnates and thus could not be waived. McGraw swore he would sue. He had something more useful than right on his side. Robison still owed him $1,000 in salary (and $900 to Robbie), a breach of contract that gave the two old Orioles the right to sign wherever they liked.

For Johnson, the idea behind the American League was clean baseball, with all the rules enforced. It was a brilliant marketing ploy, resting on a nostalgia for ordered times. The new major league would allow no kicking at umpires. The ladies would feel welcome at the ballpark. Authority was to be given the proper respect.

This hardly described John McGraw, but there was no denying that his presence could bring attention and success to the new franchise and to the new major league. Johnson had no doubt that McGraw could be controlled. From the start, the American League understood the worst about human nature and responded. Johnson insisted on holding an option to claim 51 percent of every ballclub's capital stock, including the ground lease for each ballpark, to guard against desertions in the baseball war sure to come.

Mac promised everything he needed to promise. He even seemed to mean it.

"Today marks the beginning of an effort to repair the great wrong done Baltimore." Thus did Sheriff John B. Schwatka, a respected physician in East Baltimore who had attained his high office as a stalwart of the Democratic organization, open the ceremony. Nearly a thousand cranks had braved the February winds to cheer the return of baseball to Baltimore. The gilded spade had been exhibited at The Diamond the night before, decorated in Oriole colors and bearing the legend: "Today I break ground for the American League and begin to bury the old National League."

Ned Hanlon controlled Union Park again and had refused to let the upstarts take a lease on it. So they found a place to build their own ballpark, three blocks to the north, along the York road. The structure went up quickly. Nothing was fancy; its only flourish was a cupola atop the plain roof of the grandstand, with boxes for the newspapermen, the telegraph operators, and the club's directors. Almost before he signed up any ballplayers, McGraw hired Tom Murphy, the Orioles' old groundskeeper, who had gone to St. Louis and then briefly to Brooklyn, to knead the new ballgrounds to the new management's liking.

The team, Mac announced, would be called the Orioles. "Should any other club dispute the title," he said, "why, we would be willing to play a contest for it."

Soon the Orioles began to look familiar. Besides Murph and Robbie and McGraw himself, Steve Brodie and Henny Reitz were signed out of the minors. Then came McGraw's coup.

Joe McGinnity's twenty-nine victories for Brooklyn had led the National League in 1900. But the Iron Man was talking about quitting baseball for his iron foundry. He was disgusted. "The National Baseball League is a baseball trust and does pretty much as it pleases with the players, you know," he said to a scribe who was watching him prepare the molds for a run of office stoves. "But there is one thing the managers can't do, and that is they can't make one play against his will. The player owns the right not to play at all, but that is about all the rope he has."

A few weeks later the Iron Man arranged to cross paths with McGraw at the railway station in St. Louis. They huddled on a corner bench in the waiting room. Balancing a contract for $2,800 on his knee, the right-hander scribbled his name and jumped leagues.

McGinnity was not the first to jump. Napoleon Lajoie, the graceful second baseman who had been a smashing batter for five years with the Phillies, had caused a sensation when he and four of his teammates were reported to have signed with Connie Mack's new Philadelphia Athletics, planning to play two dozen blocks away. The floodgates between the leagues opened. By the time the 1901 season started, more than a hundred National Leaguers had signed with the American League—among them, Cy Young and Kid Gleason and Fielder Jones and Clark Griffith, the leathery pitcher who switched teams in Chicago. Ban Johnson and the American League magnates had been cunning in making peace with the ballplayers. They recognized the Players' Protective Association and agreed not to reserve any ballplayer for more than five years or to sell or trade a man without his consent. Few National Leaguers could resist.

Some players jumped twice, even more. Jimmy Sheckard, Brooklyn's gutsy center fielder, was naive and unassuming but knew how to add. He signed with the Orioles and drew $100 in advance money—twice. That was before Charley Ebbets and Ned Hanlon and a lawyer came to visit and convinced him that they held an option on his labors. They handed him a contract, which he signed. When Mac and Robbie came a-visiting, Sheck said he had been bulldozed and signed with them. Then he followed McGraw to Hot Springs, Arkansas, where Mac liked to spend the winter, and kept out of sight in the Indian Territory, at Joe McGinnity's side. But when he got home to the hills of Pennsylvania, Ebbets was waiting. They visited a lawyer in Philadelphia. Yet again, Sheckard signed his name.

"A quarter century ago this sport was simple, clean, easily enjoyed, free of selfishness and guile," the *Morning Herald* remembered. "Today, alas! it has fallen into evil ways, become the tool of greed, the victim of hucksters."

McGraw signed two of the old Oriole twirlers, Jerry Nops and "Handsome Harry" Howell, and also Roger Bresnahan, a promising pitcher and outfielder with Chicago. Even from Hot Springs, Mac kept piecing together a team. He wired Robbie that he would be bringing to Baltimore a couple of National Leaguers—Jimmy Williams, Pittsburgh's hard-hitting third baseman, and "Turkey Mike" Donlin, the emotional and powerful St. Louis outfielder.

"Doesn't that make a crackerjack of a team?" Robbie bubbled to the man from the *Herald*. "What do you think Eddie Hanlon will say when he hears we have signed these men? He will have a fit."

Soon word came from Hot Springs that McGraw had found another ballplayer on the big lawn of his hotel, a natural, a full-blooded Cherokee named Tokohama. He had looked like a black man at first, McGraw explained to a newspaperman down from Baltimore, but then Mac noticed that his black hair was straight. McGraw tested him, hitting all kinds of hard ones. The Indian stopped them all. Then he showed himself deft with a bat and fleet of foot.

"He is a real Indian," Mac insisted, "and not the negro Grant as so alleged."

John McGraw was no social pioneer. He wanted only to put the best ballclub he could on the diamond.

But not after Charley Comiskey objected. The skinflint owner of the American League team in Chicago threatened to "get a Chinaman of my acquaintance and put him on third" if McGraw persisted. And so the color bar stood.

Willie Keeler was a quarry from the start for the new league, and so prized was he that two managers, John McGraw and Connie Mack, rode out to Brooklyn and took him to lunch. A skyscraper and two brownstones, all wrapped in overcoats on this bleak February day, ducked into the marble-floored rotunda of the Clarendon Hotel, at Washington and Johnson streets.

As they crossed to the dining room, there before them were Charley Ebbets and Ned Hanlon sharing a table. Mack, who had been the sort of catcher to immobilize the opposing batsmen with compliments, knew how to make men his friends. But he and McGraw stalked by without bowing, even as Willie stopped to shake hands with the men who paid him.

Certainly Willie had nothing to hide. How could it hurt him to be seen consorting with men who wanted to pay him more for his services? Since the season's end, the Brooklyn ballplayers had been peeved that the management had treated them with such disdain. For winning a second straight pennant in 1900 they had received nothing resembling a thanks, much less a bonus. All they got was notification that their services had been reserved for 1901.

The club's magnates were in no mood to be generous. They had won the pennant but had finished in the red. The whole point of the syndicate baseball deal had been to make sure the turnstiles at Washington Park never stopped spinning, and yet attendance had fallen by a third. Maybe there was nothing interesting in a second straight pennant. The Superbas had somehow lost their allure.

Everyone felt ornery. Charley Ebbets, for one. He had refused to give shortstop Bill Dahlen the gold bat-and-ball sleeve buttons that a committee of rooters had awarded his teammates because Dahlen had not bothered to patronize the testimonial at the Academy of Music. "You insulted the committee by not attending," Ebbets told his obstreperous infielder face-to-face, "and you can't have the buttons."

At the Clarendon, Ebbets could not have been happy watching his right fielder being tempted. Keeler looked pleased as his lunch partners left, though nobody would say whether he had agreed to jump leagues. "I do not know whether Keeler signed or not," Ebbets said to a scribe, "but I wish to say that if any of the Brooklyn players sign with the American League they will be proceeded against in the courts." And then he said: "We are not looking for trouble, but if the American League wants it we will contribute our share in making the fight go to a finish."

Ebbets was feeling squeezed from all sides. Rumors were rampant that he was in his last year as the ballclub's president. There was talk, which he denied, that he might try to succeed mild-mannered Nick

Young as the National League president, though there was no sign that the sixty-year-old veteran of the government bureaucracy in Washington wanted a successor. Ebbets was also fighting off reports that the Superbas might be moved to Washington—or even Baltimore—especially if the American League were to enter New York. He could guess the source of these rumors—the man with whom he was eating. Ned Hanlon had been saying publicly he would not mind managing a team in Baltimore, which he called "one of the best cities of the country for a residence."

And now the club was losing ballplayers to the American League. What the Superbas had gained by syndicate baseball they were now losing in fierce competition, to an invisible hand that bore a passing resemblance to justice. Joe McGinnity and Fielder Jones had already jumped, the thin-faced center fielder contemptuously telling the press, "These magnates need a little throwing down. They are getting to run things too much their own way." Then another Brooklyn outfielder and two of the club's pitchers and both third basemen jumped leagues—almost half the team, all told. Other clubs experienced their losses, but none was hit harder than Brooklyn.

"If ballplayers would have a little more gratitude, it would be far better for the game," Hanlon said. "The players have been every bit as grasping as the owners."

Would Willie jump? Like the other players, he wanted more money and felt no sympathy for the magnates' losses. After all, they had never given him a bonus when times were flush. Everyone presumed that Willie would jump to Baltimore, for he liked the city and had plenty of friends there—Mac, Robbie, Murph, now McGinnity. It was almost like home.

And yet it was not home. Brooklyn was home. And his mother was ill. Indeed, she was dying. Her kidneys were failing and there was nothing Dr. Wuest could do. Willie was not about to leave Pulaski street, not now. In his twenty-nine years he had lived nowhere else for longer than a season of baseball. The newspapers called him "a home man," close to his parents. And so he was.

Willie mailed his contract back to Hanlon, signed.

Three weeks later, on the twenty-fifth of March, his mother died. She had spent forty of her sixty-four years in America. Three of her children had lived and two had died. Life had been good to her a little more often than not. She was buried at Calvary Cemetery, beside her babies, as her husband and her living sons mourned.

*　　*　　*

The opening game was rained out, and again the next day. At last, on the final Friday in April in 1901, the sky cleared and baseball returned to Baltimore.

The procession left the Eutaw House at one o'clock sharp. It was the liveliest parade the city had seen since the soldiers had limped home from Tampa. Thousands of people lined the sidewalks downtown and cheered lustily at the Fourth Regiment Band and at the carriages, fifty or more of them, that pranced behind. John McGraw and Wilbert Robinson had to keep doffing their caps. There were hurrahs for everyone, for the owners and the managers and the ballplayers—the Orioles and the Boston Somersets both—and the newspapermen. Then came the delegates from the Baltimore Federation of Labor and the South Baltimore Rooters Organization and the Cigarmakers' Union and the Bricklayers' Union and the Lafayette Baseball Club and so on. The Baltimore Shooting Association carried twin mottoes on the sides of its four-in-hand: "Farewell, National League, Syndicate Ball, and Mercenary Methods." And: "Welcome, American League, Honest Ball, and Sportsmanlike Methods."

The parade took a shorter route than usual along the principal avenues downtown, to give the teams a chance for some extra practice, but the enthusiasm did not suffer. Flags swathed business after business along Baltimore street, and where Fayette and Liberty streets crossed, the residents of Chinatown turned out en masse. The young ladies of the Woman's College lined the dormitory windows along Charles street and flourished their handkerchiefs. As the procession passed Union Park, which bore the worn look of a relic, having lain idle for more than a year now, the old-timers turned to remembering the huge crowds and grandstand plays they had seen inside.

Then the parade turned onto the York road. The new ballpark, Oriole Park, came into sight. The flags waved briskly from the top. A cheer went up.

The ballplayers practiced for a while. They needed it. Daunted by the expense, the Orioles had refrained from going south, but had trained at the cage of Johns Hopkins University downtown, around Eutaw and Monument streets.

Not since the climactic game against the Beaneaters back in 'ninety-seven had baseball in Baltimore drawn such a crowd—more than ten thousand cranks, including the two thousand who crowded the foul lines, behind ropes. Every seat in the grandstand and in both bleachers was taken, in an unbroken sea of cravats and bobbing derbies.

Ban Johnson himself was on hand to throw out the first ball, to mark a new major league's entry into a humbled old city. Joe McGinnity, recovering from malaria, rubbed the ball in Murph's refined dirt and shot it to Robbie.

John McGraw led off the bottom half of the first inning, looking resplendent in his fresh uniform and black cap. As he strode to the plate he was given a three-minute ovation. He also received a basket of roses that almost concealed him. With a polished graciousness—he had learned quite a lot at college—he bowed his thanks.

Then he stepped in and smacked a pitch against the right field fence—a two-bagger. Mike Donlin's three-bagger and Jimmy Williams's base on balls and a double by Billy Keister, the chunky shortstop, brought three runs home.

Each of the Orioles received a bouquet as he came to the plate. They responded with a hard-hitting game—as the new league intended. The National League had changed its rules, so that a batter's first two foul balls were now counted as strikes, to speed up its games. The American League kept the old rule, letting fouls go free. That encouraged batting, which drew the crowds. The formula seemed to be working, at least on opening day: Everywhere, the new league was outdrawing the old one.

The Orioles had more going for them than their bats. Jim Jackson, the rookie center fielder, ran down five fly balls, snatching one of them just before it hit the ground. The cranks gave him a nickname— Stonewall Jackson. Joe McGinnity's speed was off, yet the great curve-baller kept the Somersets guessing. He tired in the last two innings but held on to win, 10 to 6.

Enough streetcars showed up to speed the happy Baltimoreans home.

Some days the Orioles played like champions, with quickness and inside work. Joe McGinnity, pitching almost every second game, was practically invincible. He was rock-solid reliable and never one to boast. In a game against the Cleveland Blues, his admirers presented him with a diamond pin. He sold his foundry and moved his family to Baltimore.

And there were the other days. The Orioles kept swinging at bad pitches; when they most needed a hit, the ball went straight at a fielder. Some of it was plain bad luck. Steve Brodie put his knee into a plaster cast. Henny Reitz, baffled at the bat, was issued his release. Robbie got malaria, recovered, then broke a finger. (Roger Bresnahan took his place and proved to be a better catcher than a pitcher.) In July, Billy Keister's only child died along with his father and his mother-in-law; the shortstop made ninety-seven errors in 115 games, more than anyone in the American League. The Orioles were lucky to win almost as often as they lost.

Their saving grace was McGraw. "The tighter the situation the better Mac plays," a newspaperman discerned. "He never quits."

His relentlessness defined him. But it did not always work to his favor. Over time, the only way to get along with Mac was to let him have his way.

It was only a matter of days before he and Ban Johnson collided. Nobody was surprised. Both men believed in authority—their own. John McGraw was a small man with sharp needs who felt humiliated by defeat. Ban Johnson was a large man who believed deeply in the quality of his own excellent judgment. A newspaper in Baltimore supposed he was intent on "exercising an authority very similar to the Czar in the broad domain of Russia." He had been reared in a Presbyterian household that demanded obedience and adherence to strict rules. He was willing to submit to the rules as he wrote them, and figured everyone else should as well.

The Orioles were in Philadelphia, playing Connie Mack's Athletics, when the umpire kept calling balls on pitches that sliced across the plate. Mac shouted and squawked and trod on the man of authority's corns and was ejected from the ballgame. When the bad calls persisted, the Oriole pitcher, Crazy Schmit, lay down on the grass in disgust and was sent in his manager's wake.

Mac got thrown out again eight days later and then twelve days after that. Ban Johnson dealt him a five-day suspension.

"It would not be so bad if I thought I deserved it," McGraw huffed. "It is perfectly absurd to expect that men will not stand for their rights, and we have got to have better umpiring if we are to have better discipline."

The antipathy between Mac and Ban Johnson broke into the open over the unoffending figure of Hughey Jennings. This most diligent of ballplayers was winding up his first year of law school at Cornell and was also coaching the university's nine. When he was finished in June, he had promised McGraw, he would forsake Brooklyn and the National League and play once again for Baltimore.

Ban Johnson had his own plan. He meant for each American League team to be allotted three or four National Leaguers, none to be signed without his say-so. Johnson may have been a sworn enemy of syndicate baseball but he understood its advantages. He made up his mind that Hughey Jennings should play for the Athletics. Putting Hughey at first base and Nap Lajoie at second was bound to steal spectators from the Phillies.

The czar caught a train to Ithaca late in April. The two men talked. What a pair they were—a knockwurst of a man and a carrot-topped scallion. Ban Johnson led Hughey to believe that McGraw had waived his services, and so secured his consent. As a native Pennsylvanian, Hughey had longed to play in Philadelphia for years.

When McGraw learned of the deception, he exploded. He wired Hughey to come to Baltimore as soon as he could.

No, Ban Johnson decreed: If Hughey jumped to the American League he must play in Philadelphia.

No one was about to back down. Hughey arrived in Baltimore on the nineteenth of June to play for McGraw. "Of course, I know nothing about the rules and agreements of the American League," the would-be lawyer said, "but I do know that I gave Mac an option on my services last spring."

The man in blue was under orders not to umpire the Orioles' game with the Milwaukee Brewers if Hughey took the field. The Orioles suggested using ballplayers as umpires, but Hughey declined to play. Fleeing the National League while defying the American League could make him an outlaw in both leagues at once. "Then, if, as I believe, the two leagues consolidate next year," he said, "I will be or may be blacklisted."

Hughey gave the American League forty-eight hours to let him play in Baltimore or "I will go to Hanlon and tell him my services are at his disposal."

Judge Harry Goldman took an early train to Philadelphia to negotiate a deal with Connie Mack and Ben Shibe. The stolid Baltimorean offered $3,000 if the Athletics would waive their rights to Hughey.

No.

Or $5,000.

No.

Then the Athletics offered a decent first baseman and a weak-hitting infielder, if the Orioles would let Hughey go.

Harry Goldman's answer: No.

All this, for a lame-armed ballplayer whose days of batting .300 were gone for good. Clearly, more than an infielder was at stake.

Harry Goldman took a train home.

Hughey Jennings had practiced with the Orioles that morning in Baltimore. That afternoon he watched the game from the grandstand.

The next day he was gone. He caused a sensation when he showed up in Philadelphia. And not with the American League's Athletics. He ran onto the field of the Baker Bowl, in the uniform of the National League's Phillies.

The Athletics were enraged. Not even silent Connie Mack could hold his tongue. "He never intended to play with us," the gangly manager snapped, "and only kept from signing to help McGraw."

Hughey saw nothing sinister in what he had done. He had taken the obvious course, without guile. "One would think that the American League had the disposal of my services and I had nothing whatever to say in the matter," he argued with a matter-of-fact dignity. "Naturally I refused to be dictated to in this way, and as I could not play with McGraw I accepted the most satisfactory berth that was offered me."

The war of words between the new league's oddly matched titans grew more vehement. Johnson accused McGraw of treason, of meeting secretly with John T. Brush about jumping back to the National League. "Now we have information he is trying to double-cross us," the big man rumbled. "We want no Benedict Arnolds in our midst."

"So the Julius Caesar of the American League calls me a Benedict Arnold, does he?" McGraw snarled. "I think I have the interests of the league quite as much at heart as he."

Which was not the same as saying that Ban Johnson's information was wrong.

By midsummer, the Orioles had managed to climb into third place in the American League, close behind Boston and not beyond reach of Chicago. Cranks in Baltimore talked, not always sheepishly, of a pennant.

The injuries had healed. McGraw's batting average was rising toward .350. Devilishly handsome Mike Donlin was slashing home runs. Steve Brodie shone in the field and at the bat. Joe McGinnity was showing his nerve—"Old Sal" was giving the batsmen fits. To try to lure him back to Brooklyn, Hanlon offered a $1,000 raise and a summer's stay for his family at Coney Island. The Iron Man laughed and said he would stay where he was.

On the twentieth of August, playing at home against the Detroit Tigers, McGraw was rounding first base when the cartilage popped out of his knee, the one he had dislocated a month before. He could barely walk the next day and had to be driven to Oriole Park. It was a good thing he came.

The afternoon before, a cordon of police had escorted Umpire Tommy Connolly from the field at the end of the game because his judgments had so inflamed the crowd. Harry Goldman met with Connolly and warned him about the public's feeling and suggested he be reassigned to another city. The man in blue refused. McGraw wired Ban Johnson and pleaded for a new umpire. There was no reply.

Fifty police officers patrolled the ballpark. In the third inning a Detroit batsman's long drive fell a foot foul but Connolly called it fair, putting Detroit three runs ahead. Jack Dunn led off the next inning with a grounder. The play was close but clear—he beat the throw to the bag. Connolly called him out.

The Orioles leapt from their bench and surrounded the umpire. Joe McGinnity rushed over and stamped on Connolly's toes and squirted a thick brown stream of tobacco juice in his face, and then another. The crowd swarmed out of the seats and onto the diamond. McGraw, on the bench, limped as fast as he could to Connolly's side and protected him from the irate cranks. Seconds later the police rushed in and formed a cordon around the besieged umpire. Harry Howell, the Oriole twirler, tried to deck him but was pulled away. As the umpire was hustled through the crowd, a clerk punched him in the jaw.

Connolly did not forget to shout as he was taken off the field, "Game forfeited to Detroits!"

The clerk was arrested along with three of the ballplayers, the Iron Man among them. The judge fined the combative clerk twenty dollars and court costs. Billy Keister was out a dollar and court costs for the crime of profanity; the other ballplayers were simply released.

In Joe McGinnity's case, Ban Johnson was considerably less sympathetic. Spitting in an umpire's face—the man of authority was apoplectic. The telegram arrived the next day: McGinnity was suspended, indefinitely.

Once Connolly had filed his sworn statement, Johnson settled on a punishment. He banished Joe McGinnity from baseball, for life. He had just done the same to Frank Shugart, Chicago's journeyman shortstop, for slugging an umpire. Not for twenty-four years, since three Louisville Colonels had colluded with gamblers to throw a ballgame, had a player been expelled for life from the national game.

McGraw kept uncharacteristically quiet for a few days, until the Orioles traveled to Chicago, the American League headquarters. The doctors had told him to stay in bed for two to three weeks, for his knee to recover. He ignored them.

He and Joe McGinnity paid a call on Ban Johnson. They played to his vanity, which was easy, there being so much of it. The Iron Man, with his air of honor and his clean-shaven face, was contrite. He acknowledged that he had hurt baseball. But surely the ultimate penalty was unwarranted.

McGraw and Johnson met in private. Mac did what he had to. He was learning the uses of diplomacy at last. They retracted many of the ugly things they had said about each other, and emerged in peace.

Four days later Joe McGinnity was reinstated. Frank Shugart was not.

In Brooklyn, Ned Hanlon appealed for someone to fill in at third base. The season had seen nothing so far but injury and illness. His catcher was already playing first base.

At last Willie Keeler stepped forward and said, "I'll make a stab at it, Ned, if you won't increase my salary."

Other than a single game in 'ninety-eight, he had not played third base for eight years. In his first game, against Pittsburgh, he fielded eight hard grounders, with perfect throws. He turned two double plays, one by himself, pulling down a liner and doubling up the fleet Honus Wagner. Mainly because of Willie's fielding, the Superbas defeated the Pirates, 4 to 1. It was barely June but the ballplayers whooped as if they had won the pennant. When somebody tried to congratulate him, Willie said: "Don't do it. I may explode tomorrow." He remembered how his fielding had betrayed him the first time he played for Brooklyn.

It had been left to Willie Keeler and Jimmy Sheckard to carry the team, and both were having wonderful seasons. Even with the new rule counting the first two fouls as strikes, Willie did not strike out until the thirtieth of May. The magnates had meant it to speed up the games, but Willie objected. Except for McGraw, nobody in baseball was better than he was at fouling off pitches. The public, he argued, wanted heavy hitting. "The cranks want to see a team have a chance to win," he said, "even if the opponent is four or five runs ahead." He hit safely forty-two times in the first twenty-five games, his average hovering near .400, top in the league. Sheckard was not too far behind.

But they were only two of nine. Hughey was gone and Joe Kelley, playing first base, might as well have been. He was the captain but would fail to run out a ground ball. Others followed his lead, and the twirlers, for their part, were *too* relaxed. For half the season, the team struggled to escape the second division. Following every spurt came a letdown. The Superbas slipped to sixth place.

And where was Hanlon? Nobody knew. He was there, of course, in the dressing room or on the bench, but to no apparent effect. Maybe no one was listening to him. Or possibly he was distracted—but by what? The cranks in Brooklyn began to wonder if their confidence in Hanlon was misplaced.

In the middle of July, in the ghastly heat, Hanlon read his pitchers the riot act. Usually a manager got down on his knees and begged his young charges to behave correctly. Hanlon raged that men who were paid $300 a month should damn well earn it. The next time Doc McJames got in trouble on the rubber, Hanlon made it clear he would finish the game. The young doctor took strength from having no choice. And then when he won, he was not alone in having his hopes restored.

In time the batting revived, and the teamwork. The Superbas, playing with something like their old-time form, edged back into the first division.

Soon the pennant race involved four teams, and then three. Brooklyn was in second place, behind the Pirates, who had lost just one ballplayer to the American League—Ban Johnson's scheme to leave them strong to ruin the National League's pennant race. Honus

Wagner had moved from third base to right field and recently to short-stop, and though he looked bowlegged and clumsy, he somehow got to every ball and was punishing the opposing pitchers at the plate.

Pittsburgh was a victory away from clinching its first pennant when the Brooklyn club arrived at the Pirates' ballpark on September twenty-sixth, fresh from scoring forty-nine runs in three games to sweep the tailenders in Cincinnati. The Superbas, the champions still, understood pressure.

So they played their stupidest game of the season. It was not so much their two errors that hurt them as their mental lapses. In the sixth inning, as the Pirates rallied to within one run, Pittsburgh's compact second baseman, Claude "Little All Right" Ritchey, bunted to Brooklyn's pitcher, who turned to throw and found nobody covering first base. Joe Kelley stood dawdling in the infield, for no evident reason.

Three batters later the bases had filled when Pittsburgh twirler Jack Chesbro lofted a foul near the grandstand. Kelley and the catcher gave chase. Kel made the catch and turned to throw to the plate. No one was there. The runner on third raced home with the tying run. A single then sent Ritchey across the plate, with the pennant.

Hanlon seethed. He chewed his players out. He might as well have scolded himself.

They were probably destined not to get along. They were so different from each other. Charley Ebbets was a politician and a man about town, Ned Hanlon a man of logic, aloof and self-contained. They were only two years apart in age but it seemed like more. Ned Hanlon, forty-four now, had always been old beyond his years. His hair was slowly turning white. Ordinarily he chewed his moustache to shreds in the course of a game and never laughed much. If there was anything he hated it was having someone who knew nothing about baseball tell him what to do.

Even if Ebbets was not always aware of what he did not know, like Hanlon he had a knack for detail. He was a master at scheduling; almost every season he prepared the entire league's calendar of games. (So why should anyone grouse if Brooklyn got to play all of its holiday games at home?) And both of them were—as the latest lingo had it—cheapskates. In all his years in baseball Ebbets had handed out only three personal passes, "three times as many as there is any reason for giving," he reckoned later. One was for a deformed boy, so hunched over at the hips he could not reach the ticket window, who had entrusted his only coin to a man who then spent it on himself—Ebbets had deemed no one else worthy of his sentiment. He could risk thousands of dollars without batting an eye and an hour later withhold $2 from a workman for a job sloppily done—a little man in little things, it was said, and a big man in big things.

Almost forty-two, he looked young still. His face was trim and his features were firm and his hair was dark and tamed, his lush handlebar moustache lending weight to his thin face. He was almost puppyish in his enthusiasms. He throbbed with ideas—not only the entry ramps but also ladies' days and rain checks and all sorts of things, some of them sagacious and some not. He had been a fervent bicyclist for years and an officer in the Good Roads Association. Lately he was crazy over bowling and was even thinking of running for president of the American Bowling Congress. He enjoyed the feel of authority. Once, he had protected a besieged umpire from a mob of angry cranks; because Ebbets was a councilman the police had assisted him to a man.

Ebbets had learned to trust his own instincts, which had brought him such success. He was careful in his bookkeeping and allotted Hanlon only so much money to strengthen the club. And as a former team manager himself, he was not shy about conveying his suggestions about which ballplayers to hire or let go.

This was more than Hanlon could bear. Yes, Ebbets had been a manager—a terrible one, seated on the bench in his silk hat, guiding the 'ninety-eight Trolley Dodgers to thirty-eight victories and sixty-eight defeats. Ebbets was not a practical baseball man. Only he did not know it.

For more than a year there had been talk that Hanlon was interested in going to some other city, for he had never seemed all that happy in Brooklyn. Now the story spread that Andrew Freedman had invited him to manage the Giants, for $25,000 for two years' work. It was true—Hanlon said so. Only he had promised Harry von der Horst he would never part ways without Harry's say-so. "He has done a great many good turns for me," he said, "and I told him that so long as I was in baseball I would stick by him."

Harry must have said no, for Hanlon turned the offer down. In return, Brooklyn raised his salary from $10,000 to $12,500.

Yet Hanlon was hardly content. He had a brainstorm: Why not shift the ballclub from Brooklyn to Baltimore? The attendance in Brooklyn was awful, even less than it had been before 'ninety-eight. Purely from a business standpoint, keeping the franchise in Brooklyn instead of in Baltimore had been a mistake.

Not to Charley Ebbets, though. He was a businessman only to a point. He believed in Brooklyn. The borough was the biggest thing he put his faith in. He loved the public and the public loved him. His loyalty was to Brooklyn and, by extension, to himself.

=11=

Betrayals

In the summer of 1901, Andrew Freedman quietly invited the three National League magnates he counted as allies to his estate at Red Bank, along the New Jersey shore. John T. Brush of Cincinnati now found walking an exercise in unceasing pain. Art Soden of Boston and Frank Robison of St. Louis, those right-thinking, dull-looking businessmen, would do as Freedman prescribed. The man from Tammany Hall had figured out how to take on the American League, which was drawing more cranks in the cities the rival leagues shared and nearly as many league-wide—quite an accomplishment, given the National League's more populous cities. Ban Johnson was known to have his eye on New York. How could a league be a major league without a team in the nation's preeminent city?

Weeks would pass before word slipped out (in the pages of the New York *Evening World*) about the nature of their solution, and months before anyone believed it. Not much more than a year before, these magnates had mounted a crusade against syndicate baseball, as practiced in Brooklyn and Baltimore. Now they proposed a grander syndicate, encompassing all of the National League. "Give me time," Brush had written Robison, "and I will put together a scheme that will revolutionize baseball."

A Tammany-connected law firm drew up the articles of incorporation for the National League Base Ball Trust. It was to be run by a board of no more than five men, who would hire all the managers and assign the players to teams in whatever combination yielded the highest return. The teams would no longer be individually owned. The trust would own them all. The teams' ex-owners would hold shares in

217

the trust—of uneven size. New York's magnates would merit a 30 percent stake in the trust and each of the other three clubs represented at Red Bank were down for 12 percent. The clubs kept away would get less; the smallest share (6 percent) was reserved for the Brooklyn club, which had captured the past two pennants.

Rumor had it that Brush had conceived the scheme and planned to become the treasurer of the trust, with Freedman to become president. Freedman had bolstered Brush's plan with an idea from horseracing. The ballplayers would no longer sign contracts. Instead, like jockeys, they would have to be licensed. Anyone who misbehaved would be denied a license, making discipline a cinch.

It was brilliant—gloriously modern. Without a doubt, a league of scientific efficiency would vanquish all comers.

All the magnates at Red Bank needed was a fifth vote.

Finding one in Brooklyn was out of the question. So too for Chicago and Philadelphia, whose magnates had fought Freedman for years. That left young Barney Dreyfuss, the former Louisville owner who had bought himself a controlling share of the Pirates.

Brush took his persuasive powers to Pittsburgh and he pressed every argument he could. A trust would add to the bottom line. It would augment the magnates' control of the game. Dreyfuss, though, had reasons to be wary. He was more a rooter than a businessman. Since coming to Pittsburgh he had never missed a game at Exposition Park and never failed to keep a detailed scorecard. He was also a small man with a German accent who knew what it was to get the short end of the stick. Not many years had passed since he had seen all his holiday games disappear from the schedule because he had displeased the men in control of the league. Like Andrew Freedman, he was a Jew among Christians, but unlike the wily New Yorker he often found himself at others' mercy.

Not anymore, however. The Pirates were in first place, earning a profit, flying high, barely touched by the American League's raids. This stymied Brush. Before leaving, he warned that several big clubs would quit the league and start a new one, leaving Pittsburgh out. Dreyfuss refused to be bullied.

The plans for a syndicate aroused fears about the future of the national game. "An impracticable and wicked scheme," *Sporting Life* was quick to judge—"wicked, because its consummation would mean the murder of professional baseball. This sport can only thrive on sentiment, which in turn lives on local interest and ownership, and would surely be strangled by a 'community of interest' manipulated from New York or any other central point of power."

The magnates gathered yet again at the Fifth Avenue Hotel. In the plush parlors with the decorous furnishings, the arguing went on and on. "All I want to see is the good of the game," Andrew Freedman, who this time had deigned to attend, protested to his fellow magnates on the fourth and final day.

The more Barney Dreyfuss was pushed, the more he resisted. He was ordinarily a peaceable man but now he became aggressive. On the matter of a baseball trust, he had made up his mind.

"I am against it," the littlest magnate declared, "because it would kill baseball."

On a vote of 4 to 4, the national game survived.

Willie Keeler came down from Brooklyn, carrying a set of silver oyster forks. He joined Robbie and Kel and Steve Brodie and their wives. Long before six o'clock, when the ceremony was to start, hundreds of friends and kinfolk and cranks and even con men gathered in front of St. Ann's Church. The dark gray stone edifice out on the York road, a half-dozen blocks short of Oriole Park, had an air of tragedy about it, nothing like St. Vincent's, so white and welcoming, where John McGraw had been married the first time.

It was cold on this January evening in 1902. The moment the Crusader-arched doors swung open, the bearers of the precious invitations pressed inside. Soon there was no room even to stand.

Precisely at the appointed hour, John McGraw took his place by the altar. After all he had been through, it was hard to believe he was only twenty-eight. He was a young man full of confidence, utterly alert. Every feature on his face was unapologetic.

A few minutes passed. The crowd started to fidget.

Then the strains of the opera *Lohengrin* filled the church. Blanche Sindall appeared at the back. She had a fashionably plump face with a swirl of black hair and a sweet, intelligent manner. She was almost pretty, in a settled sort of way. Her gown of embroidered chiffon had a magnificent diamond ornament, the gift of the groom. She leaned on her father's arm as she strolled down the aisle. Her family was everything that McGraw's was not. Her father was a wealthy man, a self-made man, who built houses and had moved his family into the one he liked best. His wedding present was a house on Charles street.

Only the wedding party could hear what the priest had to say. People in the pews were puzzled as to why the groomsmen and the maid of honor seemed desperate to laugh. "Lead her around the hard 'bases' of life," the man of God was urging Mac, "until she reaches the 'home plate' of happiness." And: "The church 'signs' her over to you. You will not have trouble to 'manage' her."

The organist played Mendelssohn as the couple retreated up the aisle. Blanche's face was wreathed in smiles. Her husband's looked stern.

Despite their midseason optimism, the Orioles had faded to a fifth-place finish in 1901. The second division—no one in Baltimore had imagined such a thing since 'ninety-three. "The Season has been one of many adversities," Harry Goldman reported to the ballclub's directors, because the attendance of just 141,952 brought losses of $7,926.40. But the adversities continued even as the team prepared to leave for training camp in Savannah the following March.

Mike Donlin did his waiting in a Howard street saloon. Sometime between noon and half past eleven one night he switched from beer to absinthe. Across the street, at the Academy of Music, the cast of *Ben-Hur* was going home. Two of the chorus girls crossed Howard street toward their boardinghouse, then crossed back to use the telephone in the Academy lobby.

Donlin had been thrown out of the saloon and had urinated on the artificial palms in the lobby of the grandly gothic Academy of Music, a cathedral of art. He called out to the chorus girls. Women loved him—that he knew. Mamie Fields, one of the showgirls, asked her friend what he had said.

When he seized Miss Fields by the arm, a gentleman who shared the boardinghouse stepped in. "Pass on fellow, these girls do not know you."

The strapping young slugger had been (except for McGraw) the Orioles' finest batsman in 1901, nursing an average of .340. He socked the interloper in the face.

"Please don't hit him," Miss Fields gasped.

So he turned and punched her, too. As she lay quivering on the pavement, blood gushing from her mouth and nose, Donlin ran across the street into The Diamond. When the other showgirl gave chase, a wall of men blocked her entry. The ballplayer was hustled out the back and to the depot and fled the city.

Judge Goldman happened to preside at his hearing. Yet the offense was too egregious to dismiss. The ballplayer was bound over to a grand jury and stood trial within a week. The victim showed off her two black eyes. The slugger got six months in jail.

John McGraw knew what to do. "We are catering to the public of Baltimore and must meet their demands," Mac wired from Hot Springs. "Would advise indefinite suspension."

The other owners, in Baltimore, spurned his advice. They released Mike Donlin outright. It was not until August, with good behavior, that he would be released from jail.

But there was good news, too—Joe Kelley was back. He had not belonged in Brooklyn. His life was in Baltimore, and his father-in-law, Sonny Mahon, was rising through the city's Democratic ranks. Mahon had started as a precinct runner, became a finder in the State Tobacco Warehouse, then sergeant-at-arms for the City Council. Soon he was a councilman himself, the youngest the city had ever seen. Yet his talents were greater than that. He knew little about books but a lot about men. ("It isn't justice any of us want in this life—it's mercy," he understood.) In his younger days he had been quite a boxer. He was fat now, but he still liked a good fight. He was the chief lieutenant to the city's boss, and his ascent was not done.

Even back in 'ninety-nine there had been been talk that Mahon would buy the old Orioles, the National League ones. Then he was Baltimore's money man in the stillborn American Association. Early in 1902, he bought a big block of stock in the American League Orioles and was immediately elected the ballclub's president.

With Mahon's help, Joe Kelley secured an interest in the ballclub and was to play left field and probably captain the team and serve as the manager on the road when Mac was attending to his business interests at home. What Robbie thought of this, he never said in public.

Before Christmas, Mac had promised that he was arranging a big surprise for the baseball world. Soon it became known that Willie Keeler was conversing with officials of the Baltimore ballclub, and Hughey Jennings, too. The Big Four, reunited in Baltimore! A Golden Age restored!

But for his part, Willie was noncommittal about his plans for 1902. He had no lack of offers from the American League. He could return to Baltimore as Joe Kelley had. (Willie had even been offered some stock.) In Philadelphia, Connie Mack, as calmly shrewd as ever, was after him. Another story had Willie signing a two-year contract with Chicago at a salary of $4,200 and a $1,000 bonus. Detroit's offer, though, was the richest. Willie confirmed the figure himself—$5,000 a year. "You know that is a big lot of money for playing ball," Willie sighed.

Hanlon took the first train of the day up to Brooklyn from Baltimore. He had been more than willing to let Joe Kelley go. Kel kept asking for loans and had a soft spot for liquor, and Hanlon had counseled him to take the best offer he could find. But Willie, that was different. He managed himself. He never drank and he tried his hardest without being asked. Ebbets liked him too. Willie was a homeboy and thus a draw, if anyone was. It had been a long time since Brooklyn had been so stirred up over a ballplayer.

Willie and Hanlon talked, just the two of them. Foxy Ned was too canny not to use his every advantage. The truth was obvious: Willie had no desire to play in Detroit or Chicago or Philadelphia or even Baltimore. He *was* a homeboy. His mother had died and his father was an invalid. Pulaski street was the only home he had known. Hanlon warned him that if peace came between the leagues Willie might find himself stuck out in Detroit, forever reserved. In Brooklyn, he would captain the team.

"I was tempted to make a move," Willie said during a visit to Baltimore the following month, January 1902, "but I have cooled down now somewhat, and shall look the situation over carefully and try to do what is best for me. I would like to play in Baltimore, where I have so many friends, but, of course, as you will readily see, it is a question of money. It is natural that I should try to get all I can out of the present situation. It won't last forever."

Willie had told Hanlon he would remain in Brooklyn for $1,000 less than Detroit had offered. Yet even that was more than Hanlon or Ebbets would pay, for they would have to pay more to the other players as well.

But Willie was adamant. He had gone as far as he would go. He would not be taken for granted, by anyone. "I am told by the newspapers that I have decided to stay in Brooklyn for next season," he said, "and that President Ban Johnson, of the American League, says that I will not be taken from Brooklyn. Well, all I can say in regard to that is that I am not being managed by President Johnson, and am not wedded to Brooklyn, and will play where I can get the most money."

It was John Montgomery Ward, the ballplayer-turned-lawyer, who saw a way out of Brooklyn's predicament. He proposed to the public a way to keep Willie in Brooklyn: He would arrange to be one of fifty cranks willing to contribute enough to match Detroit's offer. The people of Brooklyn cheered Johnny Ward. "He almost equals Carnegie of Pittsburgh," one wrote to the *Eagle*. "I certainly pity Mr. Abell, as I hear he is only worth $1,000,000. Why not place poor boxes in all the principal stores to help the poor man out."

The money was raised, and Willie stayed where he belonged. "I expect to play ball for six or seven years longer," he explained, "and, while it is not absolutely necessary for me to continue on the diamond, as I have been unusually lucky in my investments, still the question was whether I should take a chance on a couple of years elsewhere or a longer period here, where I am known and where my future is the brightest. If I ever get out of baseball it is here that I shall be and it is here that I expect to make friends. Consequently I decided to stick to Brooklyn."

Hanlon let it be known that he was delighted to see that sentiment had returned to baseball.

Eleven months had passed since the judge at the Court of Common Pleas in Philadelphia had ruled in Nap Lajoie's favor. The Phillies' lawsuit had been dismissed on the grounds that Lajoie's contract—and every ballplayer's—lacked mutuality, because a ballclub could let a player go on ten days' notice or use the reserve clause to keep him forever while the ballplayer had no such choice. So Lajoie had spent 1901 with the Athletics, batting an astonishing .422.

The Phillies appealed (Willie Keeler and Ned Hanlon received subpoenas) and the Pennsylvania Supreme Court had its say just before the 1902 season started. The ruling stunned the American League. The justices determined that the lower court had ignored something important about the mutuality of the contract: Lajoie's salary. He had been paid $2,400 for the loss of his freedom—a bargain freely agreed to.

The state court's decision applied only in Pennsylvania, a circumstance that suggested a solution for the American League: Send Lajoie to another state. To Cleveland, Ban Johnson decreed. So whenever the Cleveland Blues played in Philadelphia, Lajoie would spend the day taking his pleasure in Atlantic City, New Jersey.

Hanlon wired Kelley and McGinnity, the players he had lost to Baltimore, and ordered them back to Brooklyn. They shrugged it off as a bluff. A Maryland court, they were advised, would take a year or more to decide any lawsuit Hanlon might file, and there was no reason to assume that it would rule as Pennsylvania's had.

"At the present rate," a scribe mused, "it will not be long before every star player in the country will carry a lawyer around with him, when the contract signing season is on."

The Superbas trained for the 1902 season in the pretty little capital of Columbia, on the lovingly groomed campus of the University of South Carolina. Hanlon was stuck back in New York, at the National League meeting, where his fellow magnates told him it was a compliment that the American League was after more of his players. He would have preferred an insult.

Willie Keeler went south with the team not only as the captain but also as the acting manager. He had never wanted to be anything more than a ballplayer. He had no ambition to run things. McGraw wanted to, and was doing so. Hughey and Kel had been trying. Not Willie. He was the last of the Big Four to become a captain. He was not big on talking. He had no desire to tell others what to do. Certainly he did not like it when anyone tried to tell him.

As the captain, surely he could lead by example, especially since he and Cy Young had just spent three weeks coaching the Harvard nine. If he could teach those smart fellows something, why not a bunch of ballplayers? In South Carolina he kept the men on edge, doing their damndest. There was no need for him to talk. The ballplayers did not want to disappoint him.

Hanlon had been busy scrounging up players—youngsters, mainly—to take the place of the men he had lost. Hanlon faced rebuilding most of a team he had assembled with such care and—far beyond dollars—at such cost. Along with Joe Kelley, Jimmy Sheckard had jumped to Baltimore, this time for real. Tom Daly, the determined second baseman with remarkable range, had signed with Charley Comiskey's team in Chicago. Deacon McGuire, the catcher, had signed two contracts, one with Brooklyn and another with Detroit.

This was war, and the American League was winning.

Willie was relieved when Hanlon finally showed up. Hanlon was too, to see his refashioned ballclub at work. "I do not say that it is a perfect team," the high-priced manager said, "but it is quite good enough to begin with."

But in truth, there was no reason for any team to expect to overtake Pittsburgh. Once again, the American League had left the Pirates alone, to squelch the pennant race, and once again Ban Johnson had succeeded. With robust batting and sharp fielding and the league's most powerful pitching, the Pirates took first place the second week of the season and never weakened. They won 103 out of 139 games, more than a team ever had.

Only literally was Brooklyn in the same league. The true competition was for second place, but it soon became apparent that Brooklyn would play no part in that race either. The young infield easily got rattled. Jimmy Sheckard was back—yes, again—after four games in Baltimore, but he had slipped in his prowess at the bat.

"Jump, jump!" a crank in Chicago hollered down, needling Sheckard about leaping back and forth between leagues. And when Willie caught a high fly, someone shouted that he should have let Sheckard catch it, for "he can jump!"

"You'd never get a prize for that one," Willie called at the bleacheries.

"Ah, g'wan," the crank yelled back, "you're getting awful chesty since you were made captain."

But though he still enjoyed jousting with the cranks, Willie was not playing with his customary vigor. He did not bunt enough, and too often he hit the ball straight at a man in the field. He started slow at the bat, hitting .275. And it was his inclination, when not playing his best, to talk even less than usual. So he had nothing to say. "Willie is studying up some new angles," a scribe noted, "to make good his formula, 'Hit 'em where they ain't.'"

The Superbas lost five in a row and sank into sixth place. Their pitching was wild and they scattered their hits and committed errors when it mattered the most. After they dropped three out of four to the lowly Cardinals in the middle of May, they found themselves in the cellar.

Yet they were not tailenders, and they knew it. Without warning or reason, things turned around. The June weather got hot and the batting did, too. Willie started hitting as of old. His average rose almost to .350, the best on the team by far. Sheckard revived. One of the youngsters poked a home run over the fence, the club's first of the season. Bunts and line drives started coming in bunches. The Superbas won five straight, which became eight, then ten of eleven. With the speed of an automobile they chugged into third place, and then into second—Hanlon's doing, or so it was assumed.

The season settled into a three-team race for second place among the Superbas and the Beaneaters and the Chicago club, a rebuilding team that now called itself the Cubs. Not until the final two days of the season did Brooklyn, with its superior pitching and batting, edge Boston for second place, though the club still trailed Pittsburgh by a record twenty-seven-and-a-half games.

At Washington Park, the cranks had taken the Superbas to heart at last. The unpopular players, the ones too lazy to leg out every grounder, were gone. Back when the team was driving for consecutive pennants, the bleacherites taunted the players whenever they lost. The rookies and journeymen Hanlon had mustered (and who Willie inspired) could be relied upon to lose ball games they should have won. But now the sadder outcomes were treated as Brooklyn's hard luck.

Hard luck also prevailed in Baltimore, as the Orioles stumbled into the 1902 season. In their first game at home, they did not bunt until the eighth inning and barely bothered to rattle the Athletics' pitcher.

McGraw's knee had left him too gimpy to play. Most of the team's batsmen were tame, even Joe Kelley. Robbie's average sank to .185. The baserunning was stupid and the twirling had slipped; only fitfully was Joe McGinnity what he had once been. Patience was gone. From the top down, everyone seemed distracted. A headline explained an Orioles loss: LEFT BRAINS IN THEIR BAT BAGS. It was a high-salaried team—the payroll totaled $41,000—that occasionally climbed from sixth place into fifth, or sank into seventh.

In mid-May, back in the lineup, Mac got savagely spiked. Detroit's left fielder slid high—on purpose, by all appearances—and opened a three-inch gash just below Mac's left knee. McGraw tagged him and fell to the grass. When he saw the severity of his wound, he was stung to fury. He leapt at the Tiger and smashed him in the jaw. Then Mac was carried off the diamond.

He was out for five weeks. No sooner was he back, on the twenty-eighth of June, than he was thrown out of a game for protesting a decision against an Oriole runner who had failed to step on third base. Mac's refusal to leave the field brought a forfeit. "The usual ragtime argument," one of the Baltimore newspapers said. Except for one thing. Even the Oriole runner who had been called out hinted that the umpire had been correct.

Soon Ban Johnson sent word of a suspension, Mac's second of the season, this time of indefinite duration. Joe Kelley had already been suspended, for squabbling with an umpire.

McGraw had counted on being suspended—planned on it, in fact. Ten days earlier he had slipped away to New York at Andrew Freedman's invitation. They had met in the Tammany man's private office. When McGraw brought his lawyer in, Freedman objected to discussing private business before a stranger. Mac insisted that if Freedman's clerks could sit in the next room and listen, his lawyer could sit in, too.

Freedman had a scheme in mind—to snatch John McGraw and Joe Kelley for the National League. Even Freedman's enemies among the National League magnates had seen the genius in the plan. It would cripple the American League. McGraw, more than anyone, had turned the Western League into the American League by giving it a strong eastern presence. Luring him back to the National League was something Freedman's colleagues would help him pay for. As a war measure, so to speak.

It was an offer that no man could resist. To manage the Giants, for $10,000 a year—and in New York, the biggest stage in America. McGraw would also be rid of Ban Johnson, and in such a satisfying fashion. This was justice. The rumors were rampant that the czar of the American League meant to sell Baltimore out and move the franchise to New York. So McGraw struck first. Any true Oriole would.

Nor was Ban Johnson, if truth be told, displeased.

McGraw saw a means of escape from his Baltimore contract. He had advanced nearly $7,000 to the ballplayers out of his own pocket. He went to the ballclub's directors and demanded to be reimbursed or released. The discussion went on longer than anyone wanted, and at last the directors let him go.

When the newspapers learned the news, Mac remained coy. "I am in love with this city as a place of residence," he said, "and I would not lightly leave here. Of course, circumstances might arise that would compel my departure, but I assure you that I should go with regret."

Still, it caused an uproar when he signed a contract with Freedman on the ninth of July. He had been promised full control of the Giants and had agreed to manage them for two years, with an option in Andrew Freedman's hands of two more. Freedman shelled out another $10,000 to the Orioles to secure McGraw's release.

The recriminations came swiftly. McGraw claimed to have been driven from the league. "I can't stand for Ban Johnson having his umpires make a monkey of me and treat me like a dog," McGraw growled. The American League, he charged, was deeply in debt—"a loser."

"The muttering of an insignificant and vindictive wasp," Ban Johnson stung back.

Yet for all the vituperation, the air of mutual betrayal, McGraw was coldly calculating. "I am not in baseball for my health," he said, "but for what I can make out of it." The *Baltimore American* understood: "Looked at in a cold business light, this is the opportunity of McGraw's life. If he can deliver the goods in New York, there is no reasonable limit to his powers in the baseball world, and he will attain that for which he has worked for years with remarkable intelligence—to become the Napoleon of the national game."

Mac vowed to shake the Giants up. Only the kid pitcher Christy Mathewson and one or two others measured up to what he thought a ballplayer should be. He made no secret of how he meant to fill the gaps. "Well, you know, they are all out for the money," he said with a laugh, "and if I see a good man in the American League I am going to get him, if I can."

Baltimore cringed. The city had taken in John J. McGraw a decade earlier as a raw, skinny boy and helped to make him a man of affairs. He promised the newspapers and the Orioles' directors that he would leave his former ballclub alone.

The next day it was reported that he had offered Orioles curveballer Joe McGinnity a $2,000 raise to jump to the Giants but that the Iron Man had refused.

In the immediate aftermath of McGraw's departure, resentment and fury and the need to prove something to themselves—and to everyone watching—turned an aggregation of individuals into a team.

The Orioles had faced the worst and survived, which meant that nothing could hurt them. Overnight the sluggishness vanished. They were brainy and scientific in sweeping three games from the Washington Senators. With Robbie and Kelley named as joint managers, peace descended. The two old teammates were close; Kel had named his third son Wilbert just the summer before.

But on the sixteenth of July, the unthinkable happened.

It was widely believed that McGraw was somewhere in Baltimore, though none of the newspapermen could find him. Rumors thrived about Joe Kelley as well, that he was dickering to manage Brush's club in Cincinnati, where Bid McPhee had just quit. Kel met secretly at the quiet but stylish Stafford Hotel with Brush, who had registered under an assumed name. On the fifteenth, Kel had wired a Baltimore newspaper that he would be willing to manage the Reds once his father-in-law had disposed of his stock in the Orioles.

The next day the plot was unveiled. It played out at the Stafford, along Charles street near the Washington Monument, in the presence of a distinguished local lawyer, Joseph C. France. Sonny Mahon had been summoned from his summer home in Rehoboth Beach, Delaware. John McGraw had been hiding at his father-in-law's house, in steady touch with Joe Kelley. Mac came to the Stafford not as a stockholder in the Orioles but as a representative of Andrew Freedman.

The business went quickly. Mahon had collected 201 of the 400 shares in the Baltimore Baseball Club—his own and Joe Kelley's and the shares McGraw had ostensibly sold to him on departing for New York and the ones Robbie had swapped for McGraw's half of The Diamond. Mahon signed all of them over to France, who was acting as a trustee—for Andrew Freedman.

The instant the club's president finished scrawling *John J. Mahon,* Andrew Freedman and the National League magnates—for all of the clubs except Brooklyn had been willing to kick in—owned a majority of the Orioles in the American League. The reported price of $50,000 was the grandest sum a baseball transaction had ever known. But the money involved was nothing beside the audacity—a ballclub secretly buying another, in the opposite league. Nothing like it had happened before, or would again.

Immediately a half-dozen of the Orioles were given their release. The Giants signed the four of them McGraw liked best. One was Joe McGinnity, who was as tough as McGraw and more in control of himself, and thus (in Mac's view) even more to be admired. And Roger

Bresnahan, just as tough, a detective in Toledo when he was not playing ball—for whom there was no position on the diamond he was unable to master. Along with Big Dan McGann and a journeyman pitcher named John Cronin, they boarded the 7:36 train that night for New York. They were Giants.

Then John T. Brush claimed his share, in the persons of Cy Seymour, the underachieving center fielder, and Joe Kelley, Cincinnati's new player-manager.

The Orioles had blown apart, for the third time in less than four years. The onset of syndicate baseball, the death of the National League franchise, and now the conspiracy that left the Orioles naked before the baseball world. Baltimore had been betrayed yet again—"betrayers in high places," the editorialist raged—by men the city had taken to its heart.

Ban Johnson was in Washington and came to Baltimore the next morning. He conferred at length with Judge Goldman but took no steps to try to undo what had been done. He could have exerted his right to seize control over 51 percent of the stock and over the ballgrounds. He might have tried to reverse the sellout by challenging it in court. Yet he did nothing of the kind, for reasons he was not quite ready to admit.

That July afternoon, in the hot heavy air, the new St. Louis Browns (who had replaced the Milwaukee Brewers) took the field at Oriole Park. But no Orioles showed up. Only six players were available—seven, counting Robbie, just back from his mother's funeral in Massachusetts. He had known nothing of the plot and pledged not to abandon Baltimore. "This is my home," he said, "and I expect to live and die here, and it is here that I want to play."

What remained of the Baltimore Orioles had no choice but to forfeit the ballgame. Now Johnson wasted no time in seizing control of the franchise. A seven-team league meant no league at all.

He prevailed on the other teams to rush ballplayers to Baltimore to field a team, but made sure it would not be a good one, to make it all the easier to uproot.

Tom Murphy got down on his hands and knees in the midsummer dust near the Oriole bench. The white posies in the flower bed spelled out a name—*McGraw.* One by one, Murph plucked the posies out.

*   *   *

By December, when the shift in franchises was announced, the news came as an anticlimax. There had been rumors for months. Even before the 1902 season started, Ban Johnson had moved the league's headquarters from Chicago to lower Manhattan, on Broadway. The western magnates objected, but the timing was right. Tammany Hall had been voted out of power, for the moment, so Andrew Freedman could not put a street through any site Ban Johnson might pick for a ballpark.

From the first the talk had centered on moving the Baltimore franchise, especially after the patchwork of Orioles limped to a last-place finish. With Robbie at the helm, they lost twice as many games as they won. For the record, Ban Johnson had denied that any move was afoot. "Baltimore might be a good club to put into New York," he had allowed, "but that will be left entirely to them."

"Them," though, was now Ban Johnson and the American League. Harry Goldman and the other minority stockholders still owned 49 percent of the Orioles, which counted for nothing. Johnson had made up his mind. Putting a club in New York would assure the American League's stature as a major league, and Johnson turned his attention to securing a site for a ballpark.

With the attention swirling around the arrival of American League ball in New York, Andrew Freedman made a dramatic announcement: He was finished with baseball.

He never said why he was selling the Giants. He did not need to. It was clear that he had lost.

And he had the perfect buyer—the hardest man in baseball, its wiliest politician, John T. Brush. Brush, in turn, was selling his holdings in the Cincinnati ballclub to the city's Republican boss, George Cox, and to the Fleischmann brothers, who had made their fortunes in liquor and yeast. Max Fleischmann had managed semipro teams before, and Julius was currently Cincinnati's mayor.

For their part, Baltimoreans were sad but unsurprised—numb, really. Yet again they had lost to New York. Again big-time baseball was gone. Only three of the old Orioles would live to see it return.

"One thing I would like to say is that I did not sneak into Philadelphia, nor did I try to conceal the fact that I was there." Charley Ebbets was describing his late-season foray to snatch back a few American

Leaguers. "I went to the hotel, registered in my own name, as I always do, and sent for the players with whom I wished to talk business for the coming year. I wouldn't have cared if Connie Mack had come along with them. I would have made them as good offers in his presence as I did when he wasn't around."

Mack's understated presence proved unnecessary, for Ebbets returned to Brooklyn empty-handed. And not for the first time. He had already tried to lure Deacon McGuire back from Detroit and Fielder Jones and Tom Daly from Chicago and four of the others from Cleveland. He had succeeded only in fattening the costs to the American League clubs of keeping their prey. But that was fine by him. Ebbets had made it clear that he wanted a war of extermination.

As if he could win one. This was not a marketplace for a miser. The owner in Detroit was willing to carry a $50,000 payroll to win a pennant, though he could never hope to recoup such a sum unless the club succeeded. Even so, the Tigers renewed their year-old offer to Willie and enriched it, to $11,000 over two seasons.

Willie was torn. He loved playing in Brooklyn, before his family and his friends. He was used to Ned Hanlon. "We know each other's ideas pretty well," Willie said. "He knows what to expect of me and I know what he wants."

But he also wanted the money. Willie had been buying real estate and was thinking of putting up five-story brownstones. His father respected money, and now Willie meant to make some.

He was considered the ballplayer that Brooklyn could not afford to lose, and he knew it. "Brooklyn suits me pretty well," he had said before the 1902 season ended. "If some other club puts up good money I presume Brooklyn will go as far as the next one to meet it. Anyhow, I shall not leave Brooklyn until Ned Hanlon understands exactly what I intend to do. He will have a good, and perhaps better, chance than anyone else to do business with me."

Hanlon, wary of seeming too eager, did nothing.

Jimmy Sheckard and four of the youngsters signed their contracts and returned them to Hanlon. Willie did not. He stayed away from the ballclub and out of the newspapers.

When Ban Johnson published a list of American Leaguers for 1903, Willie Keeler was on it, assigned either to Detroit or to the anticipated new franchise in New York. Then the Superbas issued a list of ballplayers who had signed for 1903. Willie was on that, too.

Still, he kept mum.

*   *   *

The night the season concluded, Willie boarded a train to Indianapolis. He met up with the All-Nationals, who were traveling to California—and possibly Hawaii—with the All-Americans on a barnstorming tour. To the ballplayers this was a business trip. They had kicked in $175 apiece for expenses, and expected a return.

They stopped off in Chicago on the way west. The boisterous, big-shouldered city carried the heavy odors of commerce. Willie Keeler had some business of his own to conduct. He got word to Ban Johnson. In private, they met.

At least twice before, American League magnates had tried to entice him to jump. This time he dealt with Ban Johnson directly. Willie had a question to pose: Was it certain the American League would have a team in New York?

Yes, he was assured.

Then Willie was interested.

Ban Johnson promptly suggested a salary of $10,000. No ballplayer who was not also a manager had ever been paid so much. John McGraw had recently offered such a sum to Nap Lajoie to jump back to the National League but the Cleveland star had declined. The American League president knew that Willie, besides being a wonderful ballplayer, would be every bit as strong a drawing card as the great Lajoie. He offered a two-year contract along whatever lines Willie wanted.

In less than fifteen minutes a document was drawn. Willie would be absolved of all fines and suspensions—as if he would incur any—and he would be paid even if he was unable to play.

William H. Keeler—he signed his name. But until he finished his barnstorming for the league he was leaving, no one must know.

The teams played twice in Sacramento on Thanksgiving Day. Both times they were worth the price of admission. Five hundred people paid in the morning to watch the All-Americans, clad in red, white, and blue, beat the All-Nationals, in black and yellow, by a single run. In the afternoon, before a crowd of twelve hundred, the result was reversed. The major leaguers' speed and clean hitting thrilled the Californians, who had seen only minor leaguers.

They watched Willie Keeler of the All-Nationals the most, not only because of his reputation but also because he was a pal of Sacramento's own Jay Hughes, the Superbas' tall young curveballer with the deceptive slow pitch. "According to Jay," a Sacramento newspaper reported, "there was never such a sticker since the game was originated as little Keeler." Willie played second base, with admirable range, and batted his customary second. He hit safely in each game and scored twice in the afternoon.

The All-Americans won on Saturday and again on Sunday.

On Sunday night, Hughes led a party of his ballplaying comrades out to a sportsman's reserve for a week of duck-shooting. Six of them, including Willie and Jack Chesbro and Jake Beckley and Joe Cantillon, the All-Americans' square-faced manager, squeezed into a two-seated surrey.

The night was utterly black, and the road beyond Sacramento was rough. After they had gone five miles or so, the horse approached a fork in the road and started to turn. Without warning, the wheels of the rig started to slide down a two-foot embankment. For what seemed like an unrelentingly long moment, the buggy no longer felt earthbound and overturned, throwing the ballplayers from the surrey—out and for a moment upward. Then they landed.

Joe Cantillon, the middle-aged manager, wrenched his left knee. Jake Beckley, two hundred pounds of him, came down hard on Willie Keeler. Willie's leg was in pain but his left shoulder hurt more, which scared him. That was his throwing arm, his salary-making arm. He had dislocated that shoulder two seasons earlier. Now he had dislocated it again, or sprained it, or worse.

The uninjured ballplayers righted the rig. They all continued to the shooting reserve, and stayed there. Two days later Jack Chesbro went into Sacramento for provisions, carrying twenty plump ducks and the unfortunate news: Joe Cantillon was on crutches and Willie Keeler would be out of the game for a while.

When the teams made their way to San Francisco, Willie visited the chief of surgeons at the Southern Pacific Railway. The doctor snapped the collarbone back into place, then bandaged it up.

Rumors flew back East that Willie would be unable to play for three months—or for good—but he swore he would be ready by opening day. Joe Cantillon accompanied Willie back on the train as far as Chicago. Willie went on to Brooklyn, his throwing arm in a sling. Charley Ebbets had his scouts out, from Jersey City to Pulaski street, in hopes of intercepting Willie before the newspapers did, before Willie publicly announced what everyone suspected, that he was jumping leagues.

Abe Yager found him first. The pint-sized sporting editor of the *Eagle* cornered him in his living room on Pulaski street. The neighborhood felt crowded now, pressed on all sides by the city. Willie had gained quite a bit of weight. Gold eagles filled his pockets from the most prosperous of all baseball tours. His left arm was in a sling.

The newspaperman asked him point-blank if he had signed a contract to play in New York for the American League.

"Sure," Willie replied. "The people here can't give me the money the American League has promised me. I signed with them, when I was in Chicago a couple of months ago. I've only a few years longer to play ball and the money they offered me was enough to induce me to leave Brooklyn. I signed only a one-year contract with Hanlon and I believed myself free to sign wherever I liked."

"What about the sentiment of the Brooklyn people?" he was asked. "Did you consider that?"

"Sentiment don't go when the coin is to be considered," Willie shot back, "and I tell you that I'm getting a salary for two years that nobody can touch. Sentiment? Who remembers a ballplayer after he gets through with the game? Charley Ox, maybe, or somebody with long whiskers. I'm a philosopher, I am, and believe in the good old coin, as doled out by my Uncle Sam."

Charley Ebbets professed to be surprised when Abe Yager told him what Willie had said. "We have a two years' contract with him," the magnate protested, "and I hardly see how he could have taken the step he did and be fair to us."

If the ballclub could prove he had signed for two years, Willie replied, of course he would have no choice but to play in Brooklyn again. "I still believe I signed with Brooklyn for 1902 only," he said. "If they try to do me, they cannot have me for a million. I will play in Detroit or anywhere else rather than be forced to play here."

All over Brooklyn, cranks were sore as hell. They felt wronged—yet again. First they were given a team that, with a single exception, was not really theirs. Then they lost the team, player by player, and now even their hometown hero was gone. He had found his price, even with his arm in a sling—a staggering $71.50 for each game, whether he played or not.

"No one blames Keeler for getting all he can out of the baseball business," a local scribe wrote, "but as he belonged to Brooklyn not only as a player on the Brooklyn team but as a resident of the city, he was doubly secure in the affection of Brooklyn patrons, and his desertion is resented all the more. While no one wishes him bad luck there isn't a small boy nor a large one, either, on Prospect slope that doesn't wish all kinds of bad luck to the man who took him away. After all, it would be a good thing if there were more of that kind of sentiment in baseball. It makes the game."

Two afternoons later Willie had his shoulder examined with Roentgen rays at St. Mary's Hospital, not far from his home. His shoulder was bared of bandages and he sat in front of the noisy, formidable machine. The German scientist Wilhelm Roentgen had been awarded the first Nobel Prize in physics, in 1901, for his discovery six years earlier of what he had referred to from the first, in homage to the mysteries of science, as X rays. Imagine, a set of tubes and wires that could see through your body and diagnose its ills—Edison meant to put one in every home.

As the magical machine began to buzz and whirr, Willie ducked, and then he remarked with a grin, "I'd rather be on the slab, facing the wild chucks of 'Rube' Waddell, than be facing this."

Once his shoulder had been bandaged again, he placed his throwing hand under the X ray, which showed an aggregation of crooked joints. "That is one of the queerest bunches of digits I ever saw," the radiographer said.

The photographs of Willie's shoulder offered up a surprise. They showed no evidence of a fracture. "There will be absolutely no interference with the free motion of the shoulder," Dr. Wuest stated, "and Mr. Keeler can play as well as ever when the season opens in April."

That evening Willie had the bandages removed. As he left for Pulaski street, free of restraint, he felt vastly relieved. "This is the greatest load ever lifted off my mind, even greater than that which weighed on me during my first year as a captain," he confided to Abe Yager. "I got the impression it was all up with Willie as a ballplayer, and I haven't had enough experience yet to pose as a bench manager. Now that I'm okay, I'll start right in practicing for the work of annexing my signature to fat checks on the first and fifteenth of the month. Incidentally, too, I'll play considerable baseball."

Though never again as well as he had.

=12=

Playing 'Til Dark

No one had expected the National League magnates to sue for peace. But clearly they were ready for radical departures. For the first time in memory they passed up the Fifth Avenue Hotel for their winter meeting and moved four blocks away to the Victoria Hotel, with its steam elevator and eighteen luxurious suites paneled in black walnut. It was fancy enough for magnates trying to forget that their best days had passed.

Nearly every club in the National League had seen its payroll grow like the outfield grass in April; some of their salary lists had nearly doubled. The war was far too expensive and, worse, the National League was losing. Its clubs had been badly outdrawn in 1902. (The American League had seen a real pennant race, which the Athletics had won.) Half of the National League ballclubs were still losing money and saw no end in sight.

And now the upstarts had laid claim to New York. The magnates of the old league knew they were licked.

Business, they decided, came before pride.

That evening three men entered the dining room of the Hotel Criterion, fifteen blocks north of the Victoria along Broadway. In the lead was a man with a pudgy, frowning face and a drooping moustache. Garry Herrmann was the president of the Cincinnati ballclub and a man of affairs back home, as the city's water commissioner and Boss Cox's right-hand man. As the chairman of the Peace Committee, which the National League's magnates had appointed, he brandished yet another qualification: He had been a friend of Ban Johnson's since boyhood.

Herrmann trudged into the hotel with the other two members of the Peace Committee, the magnates from St. Louis and Chicago. Inside, the American League president was breaking bread with John Kilfoyl, the upstart league's owner in Cleveland. Johnson courteously received the National League delegation and promised an official reply within twenty-four hours. Then he ordered champagne.

It took weeks—a judicial injunction and the use of back channels and a gathering of magnates in Cincinnati—before peace was officially declared. When it came it was almost entirely on the American League's terms. And yet among the National League magnates only John T. Brush and Charley Ebbets voted against letting the American League keep Keeler and Lajoie and Delehanty and the like and against moving a team into New York. Precisely what they received for their sudden willingness to make the vote unanimous and withdraw their lawsuits was never made known. "We have been liberally treated by our associates," was all Ebbets would say.

Peace brought a new equilibrium to the national game. A decade of turbulence was over. The game was to be run by a three-man national commission, with the deciding vote in the hands of Garry Herrmann, a National League man who deferred to the American League president. New understandings were reached. Jumping from league to league would be a thing of the past. Wherever a player was, he would stay, unless his ballclub decided otherwise. The American League accepted the reserve rule, which was now in its interest as well, meaning that the players had lost all leverage. Baseball was a business, and both leagues agreed to the terms. Within a year, Ebbets predicted, there would be interleague play.

Order had been restored. A half-century would pass before another franchise was moved.

Scrambling back across right field, chasing the hard drive from the opening batsman at the unfinished ballpark, Willie Keeler stopped short at the rope. This was to be a place of heroic dimensions—542 feet to the center field fence. But the ground was still rough, of sun-baked dirt. Beyond the rope was a hollow where a pond had been. Under the ground rules, the Senators' slightly built shortstop was granted a two-bagger.

Only six weeks had passed since Ban Johnson had found a site for Hilltop Park. It was in Washington Heights, the loftiest and farthest reach of Manhattan, which few New Yorkers had ever seen. He had secretly leased land belonging to the New York Institute for the Blind, between 165th and 168th streets, just west of Broadway, nine blocks farther from civilization than the Polo Grounds. The would-be infield had been a wild waste of brushwood and boulders. The blasting had gone on day and night; horsecarts hauled the debris away. Soon the infield was sodded and flat as a billiard table and the wooden stands rested on stone foundations. The contractor had done everything he could.

That would be Thomas F. McAvoy, a former police inspector and the local district leader for Tammany Hall. For all of Ban Johnson's talk about the new league's moral standards, he knew what it took to get something done. He meant to overcome any lingering influence the Giants still had with the Manhattan Democratic machine. The American League had donated $2,500 to Tammany's election fund the previous fall. On the day that Johnson announced the ballpark's location, he also named the new club's president. Joseph Gordon was a mild-mannered coal merchant with an elegant waistcoat and a white-fringed pate who had been president of the New York Metropolitans back in the 'seventies and, maybe more to the point, had long been a Tammany stalwart. He lent the new team a nickname—the Highlanders, as in Gordon's Highlanders, the famed Scottish regiment, also alluding to the altitude of Hilltop Park.

Soon it became clear that the estimable Mr. Gordon was a figurehead. The real power belonged to Frank Farrell, one of the ballclub's seven stockholders, who had a bland fleshy face that concealed everything he knew. He was a big man in Tammany Hall—the pool-room king of Manhattan and the head of New York's gambling syndicate. He was also a friend of Big Bill Devery, the flamboyantly corrupt ex–police chief, who was likewise made an owner, as the public would soon learn. Devery and Farrell sat side by side near the Highlanders' bench to watch the opening game.

On that day the sun was strong and a breeze from the Hudson blew the humidity away. The sandwich and lemonade men shouted through the horns and the whistles and the cow bells. The grandstand was still without a roof, but more than sixteen thousand spectators had squeezed into the ballpark; each had been given a little American flag at the entrance. After Bayne's Sixty-ninth Regiment Band played "The

Star-Spangled Banner," the cheers echoed across the river to the New Jersey Palisades and back.

Ban Johnson, celebrating his conquest, threw out the first ball.

He had made sensational raids to put a first-rate team in New York. Willie Keeler, the captain, received the most raucous applause of the day. Other than Honus Wagner and Nap Lajoie, there was probably no better player in baseball. The starting twirler, Jack Chesbro, nervy and stockily built, had won twenty-eight games the previous season, more than any other National Leaguer. With the Pirates no longer off-limits, the new franchise had grabbed Chesbro and twenty-game winner Jesse Tannehill and Wid Conroy, a scrawny shortstop about to play second base. Jimmy Williams came from the dead Baltimore franchise; venerable Germany Long jumped leagues from Boston. Clark Griffith, the man in charge, the brainy and nervous pitcher-manager, had been lured from the American League club in Chicago. He commanded the costliest team the national game had ever known.

Willie, batting second, choked up on his squat bat and drove a pitch into left field for two bases. Jimmy Williams smacked another one and Willie scored the first run at Hilltop Park. Chesbro was masterful, and Willie scored twice more—all the runs the Highlanders needed.

They won four of their first six games at home, then went west while their ballgrounds were finished. Upon their return, the Highlanders were well in control of seventh place. Willie was hurting, though he gamely continued to play. "I can make about two throws in every game," he said. His injured leg was slowing him down. All season long he would feel the effects of the surrey accident.

Yet it was more than that. Willie truly regretted leaving the National League; he never crossed paths on the diamond with the rest of the Big Four anymore. And Manhattan was nothing like Brooklyn. The buildings were too tall—a man always had to look up—and the hubbub never ceased. It might take an hour or more by carriage (twice as long by trolley) from Pulaski street all the way to Washington Heights. It was Greater New York, but it was not home.

Willie was not the only one who had wilted. Germany Long got sick, and Chesbro and Tannehill could not find a rhythm. Most of the batsmen slipped into slumps. After a game Willie took inconspicuous roads home. "Why, I am even ashamed to look my father in the face after the showing we have been making since the season opened," he said to a friend. "With such an aggregation of stars as we have, we ought to do much better." Or maybe, some of the cranks started to think, the problem was *too* many stars.

Even when Willie started to hit the ball hard, and the Highlanders edged up out of the second division, the cranks stayed away. When the *Evening World* deigned to mention them in the sports columns at all they were called the Invaders, so close was Hilltop Park to the Polo Grounds. Rumors persisted of friction on the high-salaried club. Besides, Hilltop Park was so inconvenient—fifty-five minutes from downtown on the Third avenue el, changing cars at 125th street to the Amsterdam avenue line. Why continue past the Polo Grounds if you wanted to see good baseball? John McGraw's team used the old Baltimore style and featured not only Iron Man McGinnity but also that blond college boy, Christy Mathewson, with his baffling "fadeaway."

The Highlanders ended 1903 in fourth place, as the most disappointing team in the American League. Only Keeler had batted over .300—at .313, his lowest average in a decade. The new club had spent quite a bit more on its ballplayers than it had received.

Frank Farrell pushed Joseph Gordon aside. He was known to be unhappy with Clark Griffith as well, who had not shown the proper deference. It was widely believed that Farrell had another manager in mind. One afternoon in November, the Tammany man was seen driving his newfangled automobile to the racetrack. Beside him in the front seat sat a dark-haired man who cut a familiar figure in Greater New York. Was Ned Hanlon merely along for the ride, or for something more?

Just once before, back in 'eighty-nine, had a pennant been decided on the final day of the season. This time, the Boston ballclub led the American League by a game and a half. So if the Highlanders swept the doubleheader at Hilltop Park on the second Monday in October of 1904, the pennant was theirs.

All morning the skies had threatened, but just before one o'clock, when the first game started, the sun broke through. The crowd was the largest ever to watch baseball on a workday in Greater New York—28,584, by official count. Thousands of them stood behind ropes across the cavernous outfield. Hundreds of cranks who had come down from Boston congregated in the grandstand down by third base and screamed, as annoyingly as they could, the lyrics of "Tessie," the popular love song they had made their own. The electricity in the air was more than the memory of lightning.

Since the middle of the summer, the Highlanders and the Pilgrims—for such were the Somersets called now—had taken turns in first place. John T. Brush had already announced that the Giants, the pennant winners in the National League, would refuse to play the victor in the World's Series. That was McGraw's doing, or so it was assumed—his retaliation against Ban Johnson. But there was more to it than revenge. The Giants were scared. Not so much of the Boston club, though that team had bested the Pirates in the best of nine in the first World's Series the previous October. It was the Highlanders, or so everyone said. Imagine losing to the Invaders for the primacy of Manhattan and Greater New York. For McGraw the memory of the Orioles' Temple Cup humiliations were still too strong.

"Muggsy is afraid to play," came the dare from Clark Griffith, who had stayed on as the Highlanders' manager. He must have been right, because even his calculated insult provoked no response.

A mighty cheer went up as the Highlanders took the field. They aroused more excitement than ever before. The huge two-dimensional bull rising out of the Bull Durham advertisement on the outfield fence almost seemed to join in. "Happy Jack" Chesbro trotted to the pitcher's box, a bulldog of a man, of medium height but burly, with a stubborn face and thick hair parted down the center. He had promised to pitch as often as he was needed to win the pennant. He had won forty-one games this season and had lost just eleven. His secret was a spitball, the erratically darting pitch he had been developing all season. No one had ever learned to control it before, but Chesbro had. Recently he had even been able to signal his catcher whether the pitch would drop by three inches or by a foot. The spitball, the old-timers said, was bound to revolutionize baseball as much as the curveball had decades before. "The spitball has come to stay," Chesbro declared.

He was not the only Highlander having an enviable season. Willie Keeler was himself again. It had been several years since he had felt so fit in the spring. He was making his customary hair-raising catches and was batting better than .340, just about thirty points higher than the season before, second only to Lajoie. He had been spiked in Washington two weeks earlier but remained at his post.

When Chesbro came to bat in the third inning, the game without a score, a delegation from his Massachusetts hometown presented him with a fur overcoat and cap. Instead of the customary two foul balls and a strikeout, Chesbro slashed a pitch to the right field corner, for three bases. Hilltop Park had never heard so much noise.

The batsman ahead of Willie struck out and then Willie stepped in. Chesbro stretched off third base. Boston's big right-hander threw three rather wayward pitches. Willie swung at all of them, and missed.

When the ninth inning came the score stood 2 to 2. The Highlanders had to win—or lose the pennant. With Boston's catcher Lou Criger fidgeting on third base, Freddy Parent stepped in to face Chesbro. The scrappy shortstop had struck out twice already. Chesbro threw three pitches past him, two of them for strikes. Then he threw a spitball. He said later he had thrown it a little too hard. He explained that Boston's pitcher had also been wetting the ball, so that it was slippery. For all of these reasons, and none, the ball soared over the catcher's head and banged against the backstop.

In came Criger with the pennant for Boston.

The Highlanders' loss was nothing, though, next to the latest misfortune visited on their erstwhile rooters in Baltimore. On a wintry Sunday morning eight months earlier, a fire had started in the basement of John E. Hurst & Company, a dry-goods firm near the edge of downtown. The authorities eventually concluded that the stump of a lighted cigar or perhaps a cigarette or a match had blown through a crevice in the sidewalk and ignited the blankets and cotton goods stored in open cases.

At first it was an exhilarating sight. The fire horses galloped and the engines clanged, drawing crowds that were ten or twenty deep. A fireman was inside when he heard doors slamming in the upper floors of the six-story brick building. Suddenly everything shook—a smoke explosion. The roof blew off and flames shot out with a loud whistling noise.

Then the fire burned briskly to the east, toward the heart of the city. Flames leaped intersections, spreading mercilessly from building to building, taking wrathful turns in shifts of wind.

Women sobbed as they watched fire devour their jobs. Businessmen trying to salvage the contents of their safes dodged the falling embers and the officers of the law.

Within an hour, the blaze was out of control. Entire blocks were afire. Firemen squirted trickles of water at vast walls of flame; the spray became steam and only fed the inferno.

The asphalt in the streets burst into flame. The Baltimore and Ohio Railroad Building, the Maryland Trust Company Building, the sixteen-story Continental Trust Company Building—the city's tallest— all burned like paper. The roar of the fire sounded like a mountain-top gale.

"We are in the hands of God," the acting fire chief said.

Nobody knew how to stop the flames. They crossed Charles street in the middle of the night and moved pitilessly east toward Jones Falls and south toward the wharves. Firemen and equipment and horses arrived from Washington. Then came other contingents from Philadelphia, Wilmington, York, and Altoona.

The power that men could wield was reduced to child's play. *The Sun* and the *Morning Herald* and the *American* were all driven from their buildings. The *Herald*'s twenty-three-year-old city editor, Henry L. Mencken, led a staff of more than two dozen to Washington to borrow the presses of *The Washington Post*. From the railroad station in the capital, the unsentimental journalist could see a red gleam over Baltimore.

At Jones Falls, the broad stream that sliced south through the city, the firemen made a last line of defense. They parked thirty-seven fire engines on the bridges that spanned Jones Falls and along the roadway beside it, and they kept the hoses in full spray. Every time a brand flew across, the men rushed to extinguish it. And thus East Baltimore was saved.

Thirty hours after the Great Fire broke out, the center of Baltimore had burned to embers. There was nothing left to consume. More than seventy square blocks, 140 acres, 1,526 buildings, and four lumber yards had turned to rubble. Lonely spars of buildings, in the ghostly shapes of driftwood, guarded the cinders.

The city would rebuild—new wharves, wider streets, a new century's efficient downtown. But something was gone. A grace, a sentiment, an attitude toward life—a golden age was in ashes.

The best years were past for Harry von der Horst as well. Too many years of high living had ruined his heart. The newspapers said he was dying, but Harry was sure they were wrong.

He also knew that life was not what it had been. The beer trust was a bust. The seventeen breweries, sloppily managed, had started a price war against outside competitors and found themselves awash in losses. The Maryland Brewing Company had gone bankrupt and was reorganized under a new name. So in 1903, in pursuit of efficiency, the syndicate shut down the Eagle Brewery. It was silent now, thirty-seven years after it had been an oil cloth mill.

Harry must have been thankful that his father was not alive to see it.

Then Harry's luck in the stock market changed, and he lost much of the fortune he had not yet had a chance to spend. "The man with money to burn may live to rake the ashes," Harry said when it was too late.

He was still the secretary of the Superbas and a major owner. But he seldom went to ballgames anymore and he had less to do with running the club—not that he had ever had very much. After more than twenty years in baseball, Harry was ready to get out.

Ned Hanlon had been waiting for this moment for years: It was the way out of his predicament. The ballclub's constitution gave the president the power to overrule the manager, and Charley Ebbets had used it, time and again. Hanlon had never been given the rein he had had in Baltimore, which is what he needed to build the team he could see in his mind. Gus Abell had promised it to him, but he was in Cape Cod, raising fancy vegetables and watching the Superbas play when they visited Boston. So Ebbets was in charge, and liked it.

Foxy Ned saw a way out. If only he could buy Harry's stock, he would own half the club, and maybe even move it to Baltimore, out of Ebbets's reach.

Only there was an obstacle: Harry was unwilling to sell to him. Indeed in the middle of March he asked to redeem the stock that Hanlon was holding in exchange for a loan. He let Hanlon understand he was putting the stock in Emma's name. Clearly he *was* dying and thinking of his daughters.

The following week, Hanlon learned from the newspapers that Ebbets had arranged the sale of Harry's shares into friendly hands. The Brooklyn politician, unable to afford them himself, had scoured the borough for backers. He found one among his bowling buddies— Henry Medicus, the owner of Brooklyn's biggest furniture store, who wanted a toy. Harry von der Horst kept a few shares for himself, so he could stay on as club secretary.

Even in public Hanlon could not keep silent. He was chilled to the bone by Harry's deception. Three years earlier he had spurned

Andrew Freedman's offer out of loyalty to Harry. How could a man be so careless with his word? That was not merely a matter of sentiment. In business your word was your bond.

Evidently not in baseball. Harry had thrown him down. There was no other explanation. "It looks now as though he had made some arrangement with Ebbets," Hanlon said, "so as to either oust me or cut me down."

He was soon to learn which. Ebbets was conversing with Hanlon over lunch about the impending practice trip south, back to South Carolina, when he mentioned that the manager's salary had been almost halved, from $12,500 to $6,500. "Economy is the watchword of the new stockholders," Ebbets high-mindedly explained to a reporter. Everyone else's salary was being cut too, including his own.

Hanlon was indignant. Just last fall he had turned down three jobs at his elevated salary. When he got home to Baltimore he made up his mind and issued a statement: He would no longer manage in Brooklyn.

Ebbets came down from New York with the ballplayers. On the train from Baltimore to Washington he and Hanlon talked. It was clear who held the upper hand. The season was about to begin; no jobs were open. The two 10 percenters—the rivals—came to terms. After laboring on a handshake since his second season in Baltimore, Hanlon signed his first contract in thirteen years, to manage at a salary of $7,500 for one more season. In Brooklyn it was understood that this would be his last.

The summons came as Emma von der Horst and the two girls were summering in Maine. Though they were hardly girls anymore—Lulu was turning thirty, Lottie twenty-eight. Neither had married, or ever would.

Emma was too ill to leave for New York. Lottie stayed at her bedside as Lulu hurried off, to the Rutland Apartment House at Fifty-seventh street and Broadway in Manhattan.

Charley Ebbets was already there. But on this hot summer's night, Lulu arrived too late.

Harry had known for three months that death could come at any instant, from an aneurysm of his aorta. He had accepted the news without a murmur. With his companions he had been nothing but cheerful.

They were all he had. He had lost his family and he had lost his brewery and he had lost both of his ballclubs. In his fifty-four years, he had gained more than his measure and then squandered it.

Willie Keeler strolled into the Flatiron Building, the headquarters for the Highlanders and, of late, for the American League. The thin wedge of a skyscraper where Broadway angled across Fifth avenue, at Twenty-third street, caused gusts to collide and send skirts flying up over ladies' shoetops. This drew the men gawking and, by and by, it was said, the cops started issuing an order: "Twenty-three skiddoo."

Willie sought out the Highlanders' president. "I'm ready to sign for next year, Mr. Farrell," he said.

"How much salary do you want?" The Tammany man was not subtle when the subject was money.

"Whatever amount you put in the contract will be all right."

The war between the leagues was over. For the players, peace was hell. "Since they've settled up this baseball war there isn't any other place for me to go," Willie complained to a scribe, "and as I haven't heard that anybody is negotiating for my release, I suppose New York will have to be good enough for me."

Most ballplayers' salaries were eroding. Not Willie's. But it was not growing either. Nearly thirty-three, Willie was slowing down. "He's got a bad leg and he doesn't throw so powerful as he once did," a fair-minded ballplayer whispered to a newspaperman he had learned to trust. "However, he'll stick in the game so long as he can hit the ball."

Hitting the ball, though, had become harder for everyone. The batting averages had tumbled, from .275 to .255 to .244, since the American League had adopted the foul strike rule in 1903. Pitchers were throwing more and more spitballs. Even for Willie, connecting with one that broke right was simply a matter of luck.

Willie believed in luck, maybe because he had had so much of it. He also believed in making adjustments. He started using a thirty-two-inch bat, two inches longer than the one he had known. If he was conceding he needed an extra advantage, the bat gave him one. Willie was batting close to .400 early in 1905, but week after week his average dwindled, to .327 by August and .302 at season's end—still, the second-highest in the league. Not for a dozen years, since the pitchers had been shoved back five feet, had the ball seemed so dead and the pitchers in such control.

The next year his average improved by two percentage points (while the league's improved by eight). Willie was called the youngest-looking old player in the national game. He hit little but singles anymore, but plenty of them, and beautifully placed. He did not strike out until the 106th game of the season. He was playing on instinct and smarts.

But in 1907 everything seemed to go wrong. His body had thickened; so had his face. During spring practice a Southern League pitcher struck him out. On opening day he struck out again. He denied he was about to retire. "I surely expect to play ball for several years yet," he said. "I don't know what I'd do if I had to go to work."

But nothing improved. In his fifteen years as a professional ballplayer, he had never batted under .300. This season he never came close. He was barely above .250 when an injured finger laid him up for weeks. He finished the season batting .234, with only seven extra-base hits. Nobody knew why for sure. In public he said almost nothing. The newspapers said he was worried about his father, whose arteries were clogging and causing such pain. Willie had tried to get him to quit working on the DeKalb avenue line. "G'wan with you, you little spalpeen," his father had kicked. "What harm is there in a man sticking to an honest job, especially when he is happy with his lot?" Even after Willie arranged for his father to be fired, the old man kept going around to the switchyard to fill in for the man who replaced him, for free.

But now Pat Keeler was in pain and none too firm on his feet, and Willie and Tom, both living at home, tried to persuade him to move out of Pulaski street, away from the cloying smell of the Scharmann brewery and the press of houses where fields had been.

Pop would hear none of it. Pulaski street was home.

Over the winter Willie thought about retiring. He had been saying he was playing his last season, though he had said that before. He considered moving to Baltimore and buying a tiling business. There was talk that he might play in Cincinnati for Kel. Talk, though, was all it was. He knew he was going nowhere, not with his father so frail. Besides, nothing was as lucrative as baseball, hour for hour—nothing Willie could do, anyway. Frank Farrell persuaded him to sign for another season. Willie was the financially fluctuating ballclub's biggest draw, an institution really, the little man embodying the nation's mightiest city.

He offered more than a draw at the gate. He lent some steadiness to the Yankees—for that was what the newspapers had started to call the Highlanders, so as to fit snugly into headlines, inspired (or so it was said) by the red, white, and blue flags flying atop Hilltop Park. They had been very erratic. After finishing second by a wild pitch in 1904, they had sunk to sixth place in 1905, then reascended to second and, in 1907, slipped back into the second division. They showed the unstable chemistry that money can buy.

Clark Griffith hung on as manager, subsisting on nerves and gumption. For the last month of the 1906 season, the bantam with the tightly drawn face survived on a high-tension diet of olive oil and raw eggs. Farrell had evidently come to respect Griff's blunt honesty. It was a rare enough quality—in politics or in baseball—that even a Tammany man might feel moved to admiration.

The Yankees started off the 1908 season with some flair. Willie saved the opening game in the tenth inning by nailing an Athletics runner at the plate with a startlingly accurate throw from deep in the outfield, making way for the Yankees to win, 1 to 0, in the twelfth. Anyone who thought Willie was washed up had reason to think again.

They were pennant contenders. Griff had said so. He assured Farrell that Chesbro's arm was as strong as in 1904. The manager had made a few moves, trading for a second baseman, two promising outfielders, and a pair of pitchers.

The Yankees emerged in first place in May, to build a lead that promised a pennant at last.

Yet most of the new men were disappointments. Kid Elberfeld, the combative shortstop—the Tabasco Kid, he was called—got spiked in early May and was finished for the season. Willie injured his throwing hand again. He was batting .255 and showing the strain in all aspects of his game. The team soon slipped into a slump that fed on itself. In June, the Yankees won just four games in a stretch of sixteen. Attendance fell off. "If it gets any smaller," the *New York Globe* man remarked, "they'll have to put fractions on the turnstiles."

That was enough to put the management and the manager at each other's throats. Rumor had it that Griff's tenure was shaky. It was a declining twirler named Bill Hogg who brought matters to a head. When the manager kept him off the mound, Hogg went to Farrell and complained that he had not pitched enough and was ordered to face

St. Louis. He got slaughtered. Farrell ordered him suspended. But Griff was opposed on principle to docking a ballplayer's earnings and refused to enforce the suspension.

Suddenly, while the team was in Philadelphia in late June, Griff quit. Or was fired, one of the newspapers soon had it. In either event, Farrell needed a manager in a hurry.

He made overtures to now-idle Ned Hanlon, who expressed interest in starting the following spring. That was too long to wait.

Farrell's beady eyes fell on Willie Keeler. There had been talk about Willie as a manager back in 1905, after the Yankees had fallen into sixth. But the pundits had wondered if he would accept. Might he be too modest, too reluctant to intrude in the limelight? A ballplayer needed only to hit and catch and throw. But for a manager, style mattered as much as skill—more, really, for it determined how successfully he inspired the players and charmed the newspapermen and the politicians and all the others whose opinions shaped a ballclub's fate.

Farrell had stayed with Griff in '05. This time he fancied Willie. Maybe he wanted someone who would always try his damndest or—just as important—who would not challenge him for control of the ballclub.

Farrell went looking for Willie at the hotel in Philadelphia, but the little right fielder was gone.

He had decided not to be found. He had no wish to be a leader of men. Why would he want to tell others what to do, what not to do? He knew Farrell was coming and had made himself scarce. It was rumored he had fled the city by train. He did not want to say yes and he did not want to have to say no.

Kid Elberfeld was named the manager instead.

The majority stockholders of the Brooklyn Baseball Club were so intent on the business at hand that none of them noticed the flitting shadow in the hallway. Outside the counsel's offices in Jersey City, a deputy sheriff lurked.

An earlier attempt to serve papers on Charley Ebbets on his way to Philadelphia had failed because he had not accompanied the team for its last series against the Phillies in 1906. This time, to allay any suspicion, the lawyers for Ned Hanlon and Gus Abell had asked if they might file their lawsuit in Manhattan instead. Permission, as expected, was refused.

The stockholders retreated into the inner sanctum for their annual meeting and cast their votes for the directors strictly along factional lines. Charley Ebbets and Henry Medicus and three of their compatriots won 51 percent of the ballots; the minority stockholders, Ned Hanlon and Gus Abell, amassed 49 percent. When Harry von der Horst had sold his stock to Medicus, Abell had thrown in with Hanlon, though he had evidently sold a few, decisive shares to Brooklyn's baseball politician.

The moment the balloting was finished, the door burst open and the deputy sheriff stalked in. The papers he served charged Ebbets with having drawn $10,000 in pay, even though the ballclub's constitution limited the president's salary to $4,000, and charged Medicus with receiving $4,000 as the secretary and treasurer, instead of $2,000. A lot of money was at stake—$16,000 over two years.

Hanlon had another surprise. He stood up and laid down a copy of the New Jersey Corporation Act and pointed to Section 43. The ballclub had failed to notify the secretary of state of its annual meeting, meaning that anyone in office when the error was committed was ineligible to serve as a director. That would remove Ebbets, his son Charles Jr., and Medicus from the board and put the runners-up— Hanlon, Abell, and Abell's lawyer—in their places. In other words, the minority stockholders would control the ballclub, possibly under a new name: the Baltimore Orioles.

That was how Charley Ebbets became sainted in Brooklyn. "We intend to keep the team in Brooklyn, whereas the minority interests want to take it to Baltimore, according to their own statements in the press," he announced. "Their policy is to pull the club apart, ours to hold it together in Brooklyn." It was a politician's—and a ballclub owner's—dream.

Hanlon had been gone as the manager in Brooklyn for more than a year now. They were still the Superbas, but no longer superb, having landed in the cellar in 1905, losing 104 games with a bunch of nobodies. "The worst season in twenty-three years," Ebbets said. He had made no money available for trades and Hanlon was going through the motions. All the while Hanlon had been dickering with Cincinnati, where Joe Kelley seemed to have aged in his four hard years as the manager of a team near the middle of the pack. Kel's face had spread and his hair had retreated and animosities with his ballplayers had upset their playing (and kept his stomach in turmoil). He resigned even before Hanlon was hired, but he remained on the ballclub. With Hanlon in charge, he batted a spectral .228.

For years the old Orioles had debated how much of their success had been Hanlon's doing and how much theirs. Joe Kelley was on record as crediting Hanlon, but now that Hanlon had full authority over the Reds, Kel could have only been pleased to see their performance droop. Ebbets was delighted when the Brooklyn ballclub overtook Cincinnati for fifth place as the 1906 season came to a close.

Hanlon filed his two lawsuits the following month, and a third one the next February. This last one had the most money at stake. It was over the $30,000 the National League had paid to abolish the Baltimore franchise. Hanlon had received the money and lent it to the Brooklyn club, which was financially hurting from the war between the leagues. Not a cent had ever been repaid.

"This is a case of sour grapes on the part of Mr. Hanlon," Ebbets proclaimed. "It looks as if some people were jealous because the Brooklyn club made a little money last year."

Ten days passed and still the Brooklyn club's lawyers made no reply in court. The real answer was arranged in a hotel room in Boston, where Ebbets and Abell met through the night. At five in the morning they shook hands. Ebbets could summon up only $500 in cash. So he paid Abell $20,000 in promissory notes for 40 percent of the ballclub and bought Hanlon's stake for $10,000.

The lawsuits were withdrawn and Ebbets pocketed the $6,000 held aside from his 1907 salary.

Sporty, genial Charley Ebbets called reporters into his office at Washington Park to announce the grand news: For the first time since the Brooklyn ballclub was founded, all of it belonged to Brooklyn.

His ballplayers would spend the next seven years in the second division.

Soon after Kid Elberfeld took charge, the Yankees slid into the cellar and never left. His hot temper was just the wrong thing to bring out a ballplayer's best. Factions erupted. Willie went home to Brooklyn for the last six weeks of the 1908 season, out of disgust for the new manager's ways.

Nor was Willie any too pleased with himself. He was batting .263 and his arm was so weak that he made just nine assists from the outfield all season, instead of the thirty-nine he had made in his first season in Baltimore. He admitted he was not the Keeler of old. It was not only that he was thirty-six. He also blamed having to play in the worst sun field in the league, at Hilltop Park. "After I came out of that field on a real sunny day it would be some time before I could see things clearly," he explained. "It injured my batting."

After the season was over he announced that the rumors were true—he was retiring. Financially, Willie could stay at home for good if he liked, living off the rental income from the dozen or more apartment houses he owned in Brooklyn. He went to Frank Farrell and said he could no longer do the club any good.

That lasted four weeks. Farrell wanted him. Willie was just about the only drawing card the Yankees had. And everyone knew that Willie would never be content to sit around on Pulaski street with nothing to do. Playing baseball was better than that—in truth, better than anything. He was still a crank at heart.

"Yes, I am going to quit baseball," Willie said, "but it won't be until the wrinkles choke me to death." In a letter to *Sporting Life* he said he was feeling all right and would be hitting them "where they ain't" as usual.

In the spring practice—in Macon, to come full circle—Willie found he could not outrun his bunts.

In the opening game of 1909 at Hilltop Park, he received a glorious ovation. He met up again with Joe Cantillon, who was managing the Senators. Willie hit two singles in a 17-to-0 victory over a mediocre third-year pitcher—maybe Cantillon regretted discovering him—named Walter Johnson. The Yankees finished the week in first place.

Then came weeks when Willie wondered why he had stayed. He was batting .228 when he suffered a charley horse that put him out for most of a month. Soon after he returned, he was running for the clubhouse at the end of a game when he crossed paths with Bill Hinchman. The stocky Cleveland outfielder spiked Willie's right foot, freakishly severing a tendon.

Three weeks later Willie was back again. The Yankees had fallen to fifth place but seemed determined to stay out of the cellar. He became the Yankees' hottest batsman and they finished the year in fifth place, three and a half games out of fourth. Willie wound up with a respectable batting average of .264, in ninety-nine games. But this time it was clear he was not coming back.

The following February, Farrell announced that he had spurned offers by two American League clubs for Willie's services and, as a tribute, granted the faithful right fielder his unconditional release. That way Willie could come to his own best terms with any team he liked.

That very night, a banquet was held for Willie at the grand old Iroquois Hotel in Plainfield, New Jersey. Almost eighteen years had passed since he had last played ball there, with the Crescents of 'ninety-two. Willie was touched that seventy-five citizens of Plainfield remembered him. A banquet had never been thrown in his honor before, not counting the one he had rebuffed on his return to Brooklyn.

When they presented him with a silver loving cup, he had no choice but to deliver a short speech. He recalled how he had signed his first contract in Plainfield and how the management had helped him when the Binghamton club gave him a chance to advance.

The management had done nothing of the kind, of course. But that was how Willie chose to remember it.

Even before he retired he was known as the Brooklyn Millionaire. It was not meant to be arithmetically accurate, but he was reputed to be worth $100,000, even $200,000. Besides the apartment buildings in Brooklyn, he owned vacant lots in up-and-coming towns out on Long Island. Along with Griff and Frank Farrell, he owned a piece of the Eastern League club in Montreal. That was besides what the American Tobacco Company paid for the tiny cards with color lithographs of his likeness (and those of other stars) that started appearing in five-cent cigarette packages in 1909.

And then John McGraw came calling. For all of his belligerence on the ballfield and in business, Mac was oddly sentimental. He was easy with loans and sinecures for old pals. He hired Willie Keeler as a pinch hitter and batting coach, largely for the sake of old times.

That put Willie back on the team he had started with, though it was no longer a team of sluggers—or of giants. They were skilled in the hit-and-run, aggressive baserunning, and inside baseball. McGraw directed every play, every movement, from the bench, turning the Giants into an arrogant, domineering team that did as he ordered or else. They had been at or near the top of the National League ever since McGraw had shown up and made the Polo Grounds his.

Willie could help. He taught Fred Snodgrass, the new center fielder, how to smash the ball by swinging from the wrists, but Willie was simply not good enough to play as a regular. Twice he appeared in the outfield, neither time in right, and otherwise was a pinch hitter or runner. It took Willie until late June before he managed to hit a pitch where a fielder was not.

He batted ten times in nineteen games and delivered three hits. For one last time he reached .300.

On the fifth of September he was a pinch hitter in the ninth inning for Hooks Wiltse, the Giants left-hander, and put the ball into play but failed to get on base. Willie had appeared in his 2,123rd—and last—major league game. He finished with 2,932 hits and a career batting average of .341, higher than anyone before him other than Big Ed Delehanty and Sliding Billy Hamilton. He held the season records for hits (239 in 'ninety-seven) and singles (206 in 'ninety-eight). More important than the records was how he had shaped baseball. He had modified the prevailing notion of the correct way to bat: Instead of swinging from the very end, ballplayers now commonly gripped the bat farther up. Instead of swinging with all their might, they might take a short quick chop at the ball and occasionally a fore-arm swing. The evidence was easily at hand. The past three American League pennants had belonged to the Detroit Tigers, led by their good-natured manager, Willie's old friend Hughey Jennings, and their twenty-three-year-old right fielder Ty Cobb, who brought a vicious intensity to everything Willie Keeler had taught. Quick as a cobra, pitiless with a bat, slashing on the basepaths, Cobb was the epitome of everything the old Orioles had been, and the best hitter Willie had ever seen. Not by himself, to be sure, but probably more than anyone else, Willie Keeler had changed the nature of the national game.

He was thirty-eight but he believed he had some good baseball still in him. McGraw released him, to Toronto in the Eastern League, where Joe Kelley was the manager. Willie seemed rejuvenated playing for his friend. He went south to Macon without a contract and returned north with the Maple Leafs, batting second and playing right field. In the opening game of the 1911 season, he poked two timely hits and scored three runs. The next day he got a hit, and almost every day after that—often two or three hits, once even four.

After his four-hit game a severe cold kept him out of the lineup for two weeks. When Willie returned, playing Jersey City, a batsman drove

a ground ball out to right field that spurted past him, for a three-bagger that decided the game.

Willie knew what to do. He told his teammates that if he could no
longer smother an ordinary grounder, his time had come.

And yet the next spring found him in uniform again, as a batting
coach for Brooklyn.

One of the newspapers dubbed it "New York's private world's
series." Willie had played for both the Giants and the Yankees. "I
want to see Mac win, of course," he said in early October 1921,
before the nine-game series between the Manhattan rivals began.
"But don't forget that I'm a charter member of the Yankees. I'd love
to see one of the games, but my doctor is against me leaving the
house on account of the condition of my heart. But I'm going to
plead with him to let me go."

The vague chest pains and rapid breathing had started even while
he was playing, but had been just petty annoyances then. By the end of
1917 his ankles and feet had swelled and he found breathing a contin-
ual source of discomfort. He knew how it would end. His father had
died of bad arteries in the summer of 1912, the day before the cornerstone was laid in Flatbush for a palace of sport with a marble rotunda
to be known as Ebbets Field.

Willie's friend, Dr. John Breen, took him to the Polo Grounds,
which both teams currently called home, for the sixth game of the
World's Series. The afternoon was mild and clear, but they should have
gone the day before.

The bettors had favored McGraw's Giants, competing in their
sixth World's Series. The Yankees had never played in one before,
but in their second season with their grand new star, they had cata-
pulted to the top of the standings. With the series tied at two games
apiece, a great roar had gone up when Babe Ruth unexpectedly hob-
bled to bat in the opening inning. Worse than the muscle tear in his
leg was the infected scrape on his left elbow—still bandaged, with a
tube to drain the pus—that he had suffered in the second game
while stealing third base.

Larger than life, Ruth was the new American hero. He had stroked
an astonishing fifty-nine home runs during the season, surpassing the

previous record of fifty-four, which he had set the previous season, which in turn had broken his record of twenty-nine set the season before that. Maybe it was the thinner bat he used or his perfect coordination. A physicist explained that the Bambino had somehow learned to strike the ball at the "center of percussion" more often than anyone before him. Whether it was science or magic or a sacred grace, the young slugger who hailed from Baltimore had hit the only home run in the series so far.

So when he had limped to bat in the fourth inning of the fifth game, he laid down a perfect bunt along the third base line. He sprinted to first, safely. When the next batter's wicked liner trickled through the left fielder's hands, the oversized man on bandaged legs scored what turned out to be the winning run.

That night Ruth's doctors were adamant. The wound must drain for two or three days or he would risk permanent injury. So Ruth watched the next game in street clothes, his arm in a sling, in a box he shared with his wife near the Giants' third base dugout. But even in his absence, his presence loomed large on the field. Willie watched a game that Babe Ruth had remade. Another Baltimorean, Chick Fewster, took Ruth's place in left field and hit a home run that broke a 3-to-3 tie the Giants had managed earlier in the inning on two home runs of their own. It was not Willie's game anymore. Power and size had taken it back.

Any thought of innocence was gone. The nation had only recently learned how the Chicago White Sox had thrown the 1919 World's Series to the Cincinnati Reds. The "Black Sox" scandal caused the magnates to hire a commissioner to restore moral order to the national game. Judge Kenesaw Mountain Landis, a white-maned scourge of corruption, used his dictatorial powers to clean up the sport, banishing the eight Black Sox from baseball—guilty or not—and forcing John McGraw to sell his interests in a racetrack and casino.

After the game, Willie visited the Giants' clubhouse to congratulate McGraw on the come-from-behind 8-to-5 victory. Joyous at tying the series again, the Giants laughed and wrestled like schoolboys on a day's outing. With the Babe injured, the Yankees were lost.

After ten minutes in the clubhouse, Willie emerged. A mob of fans surged at the steps, screaming for McGraw and Frankie Frisch and Highpockets Kelly. Willie, unrecognized, fought his way through the crowd.

He never saw another ballgame.

*   *   *

One day a gray-faced man with eager eyes watched the boys playing baseball on a lot in Brooklyn. A slashing liner landed close to the foul line, near where he stood. The boys argued and argued and then came his way.

"What was it, mister?" they shouted.

"Foul, that far," Willie Keeler showed with his hands.

"Aw, what's that guy know about a hit?" snorted one of the boys whose team claimed it was fair.

Willie shuffled away. What *did* he know anymore?

He had kept his hand in, or tried to. In 1915 he had been a coach for the Brooklyn Tip-Tops (named for the white bread its owners made in their bakeries) in the short-lived Federal League, then he had finished the season as a scout for the Boston Braves. He bought a gas station near Ebbets Field and sat around and gabbed with the ballplayers who stopped by.

"Any man can be a good fellow as long as his money holds out," Willie once said.

Maybe his problem was the quality of the investment advice he had received from his friends. Or the collapse in real estate prices that followed the Great War. Or the gas station that went belly up. Or his continuing allergy to work, intensified by pain. Or the cost of the medicines he needed. He contracted tuberculosis, and was cured.

Sooner than anyone might have imagined, the Brooklyn Millionaire was something closer to a pauper. Shortly after he watched Babe Ruth's refashioned game, Willie and his brothers sold their father's house. Tom and Joe were living a few blocks away, and Willie had already moved the ten blocks to Gates avenue, into a boarder's room in a rented house.

His brothers were in no position to help him out. His apartment houses were gone. The empty lots he owned in Nassau County were worth little enough, even assuming they could be sold. That gave Abe Yager and Charley Ebbets an idea. The sportswriter and the magnate knew that Willie was not about to accept charity, so they circulated a letter to various baseball bigwigs on behalf of the William H. Keeler Fund, structured as an interest-bearing investment in the mortgages on the twenty-one lots Willie owned on Long Island. (Charley Ebbets had taken a mortgage on them.) What better way to help a proud man who would not accept a handout? "If we could collect four or five thousand dollars more, the money (which is always under our control) would be a big help to Willie, more so than medicine, as he is constantly worrying over his condition," his benefactors wrote.

They hoped to raise $7,500 but stalled at $1,765.

Shortly before Christmas in 1921, Charley Ebbets presented Willie's plight to the magnates of both major leagues, who voted to lend the beloved old ballplayer $5,500—$2,750 per league—which he would repay once his lots found buyers. "The league owners, hardhearted though they may appear to some fans, have shown a trace of sympathy which must be appreciated," a New York scribe wrote.

Willie sat in his Morris chair, in the second-story bow window, and watched the world pass by. His hair was gray and his features had grown gaunt. He had given up the only home he had ever known, on Pulaski street. Gates avenue was not a quiet place. The el along Broadway, a half-block away, rumbled into the night. But the residents were decent and clean—draftsmen and electricians and printers and such, making their way. He had only a short walk to anything he needed. He could look across at the windowless brick wall of the Gates Avenue Theatre or down toward the man-made shadows of Broadway or west toward the car barn at the corner, housing the red-and-yellow trolleys. Quiet was not something Willie relished anymore, if he had before.

Gates avenue held another charm for him, too. The newspapers said he was living with his sister, but Willie Keeler had no sister. Clara Roberta Moss was unmarried and in her mid-forties, five years younger than Willie. Born in Washington, she had left and never gone back. On Gates avenue Clara was the renter and Willie was the boarder. To each other, they were more than that. How much more, no outsider could tell. Soon enough Willie would make his feelings known.

His friends visited. He had been unable to travel to Baltimore for the parade and banquet to honor the twenty-fifth anniversary of the old Orioles' reign. So Hughey Jennings and Joe Kelley and Wilbert Robinson had come to him, laughing about old times. John McGraw stopped in from time to time. Later he said Willie had wasted to a skeleton. At Christmas, Charley Ebbets and Abe Yager came by. Ebbets was in poor health himself. "Charley, I'd like to get a little money as my time is short," Willie said, "and even a guy when he cashes in wants to be clean."

Four days before Christmas in 1922, Willie Keeler signed his last will and testament. He had been born poor and he would die poor, but he seemed not to mind.

Not until several weeks after his death, when his will was made public, did he make his intentions known. Everything he owned was worth just $3,500. He left none of it to his brothers or to his intimates from the diamond. All that he had, he left to Clara. In the end, Willie Keeler found love.

EPILOGUE

Camden Station was mobbed. Fifteen hundred Baltimoreans crowded inside. Some of them sat on boxcars. The train came in at 9:35 A.M., precisely on time. The new Orioles emerged in uniform, with a lifelike Baltimore oriole on the cap.

They pushed through the station and boarded charter buses for the ride through the darkly modern downtown, up narrow and elegant Charles Street, to Thirty-fourth Street, at Hopkins Circle. The entrance to the university, which had moved out to Homewood in 1916, had become the traditional starting place for Baltimore parades. Teenagers clambered up the monument to the severe-looking bust of Johns Hopkins, the Baltimore merchant prince, for a better view.

Fifty-one years, six months, and sixteen days had passed since the Orioles had last played a big league game in Baltimore, losing to the Boston Somersets, 9 to 5. Now there was a new team of Orioles, known for the past fifty-two seasons as the St. Louis Browns. The previous September, after twice saying no, the American League owners had finally approved the sale of the Browns to a group of Baltimore businessmen—mainly brewers. So on this fifteenth of April in 1954, the Orioles at last were coming home.

Rain had threatened all morning. But the schools were closed and the children came early and plunked themselves down on the curb. A dignified woman holding a Pekingese on a pink satin pillow sat beside them. Men in homburgs and ladies in overcoats packed the sidewalks. The police estimated that 350,000 people, all told, lined the route of the parade. The crowds were densest along Charles Street, where hawkers peddled pennants and balloons and canes in orange and black. Along Madison and Howard and Baltimore Streets, to Holliday Street, to City Hall Plaza, people cheered the return of major league baseball.

It meant the world to Baltimore. To be sure, the minor league Orioles had achieved more than their share of distinction during the past half-century. They had delivered Babe Ruth and later Lefty Grove to a grateful world. Jack Dunn's fabled team won seven straight International League pennants, from 1919 to 1925—still a record for organized baseball.

Yet even a worthy minor league team would hardly do. Not for a city as up-to-date as Baltimore was. It had risen from the ashes, with a shiny steel skyline. After the Great War it had annexed enough sparsely settled land to triple its size. Enough branch factories went up to make Baltimore an integral part of the national economy. Increasingly it was a city like any city, with skycrapers modeled after New York's. By now it was bursting at the seams—the nation's sixth-most-populous city, within sight of a million people.

"We've long looked forward to the day when Baltimore would regain its rightful place in the big leagues," burbled an advertisement for the Gunther Brewing Company, which was donating to Memorial Stadium the largest all-electric scoreboard in America. "Now we're together and we'll stick together . . . even on days when you can't buy a hit."

"A wonderful, wonderful parade," Blanche McGraw called it—and she was right. Mac's widow, seventy-one now, shared a convertible with Mrs. Clark Griffith, whose husband, the owner of the Washington ballclub, occupied another car with a robust-looking Connie Mack, now ninety-one. Bill Clarke, eighty-five now, after thirty-six years coaching baseball at Princeton, was an honorary marshal. The only Oriole who had batted below .300 back in 'ninety-four was gaunt but spry—not surprising for someone who had always looked like an old man in the making. (Dirty Jack Doyle had been invited at the last minute but was waiting at the hotel for someone to come with instructions, and Bill Hoffer, one of the old Orioles pitchers, stayed home in Iowa, uninvited.) The fresh-faced vice-president of the United States and his lovely wife, Pat, waved from the back of a Cadillac.

The parade took almost an hour and a half to pass by. Twenty-two bands played. Eleven pastel convertibles carried a pair of ballplayers apiece, perched atop the back seat, flinging thousands of plastic baseballs into the crowd. Whenever the cars slowed, boys besieged them in pursuit of the souvenirs. Then came the thirty-two jeep-drawn floats. No expense had been spared. One featured a larger-than-life Babe Ruth with a mighty bat in his hand; another one bore busts on Greek pedestals of the eleven old Orioles enshrined in Cooperstown (counted generously, to include Babe Ruth and Lefty Grove and Rogers Hornsby of the minor league club). A 'nineties float featured a barbershop quartet. The Retail Merchants Association's showed the Baltimore skyline. The clowns and the grotesque heads and the high-wheeled bicycles delighted the children. The men watched the Baltimore Colts and the Baltimore Bullets and the former Miss America.

The very last place in the long, long parade, the place of symbolic dishonor, was empty save for a sign: "Reserved for the New York Yankees." It gave everyone an opportunity to jeer the descendants of an earlier Orioles, who had become the New York Highlanders and then the Yankees, and had lately won five consecutive World Series, earning the enmity of anyone who refused to worship temporal power. Yet who might be able to deprive the arrogant young men in pinstripes of a sixth championship?

Not the new Orioles. The consensus among the Baltimore sports-writers put them in sixth or seventh place, and even that seemed a trifle optimistic. The Browns had finished dead last in 1953. This season, everyone figured on a three-way race for the cellar, with the Philadelphia Athletics and the Detroit Tigers challenging the Orioles for ineptitude.

A light rain started before noon, but by a quarter past two, fifteen minutes to game time, the grounds crew had rolled up the spun-glass tarpaulin. The field looked good. The outfield had bare spots, but the infield had none. Nor did the seats. Two fifteen-year-old girls from Milford Mill High School had been the first to get in line—at a quarter to five that morning—for bleacher tickets. The second deck at Memorial Stadium had just been completed, bringing the capacity in the concrete bowl to 48,399. The Orioles had already sold twice as many tickets for this season's games as the Browns had peddled in all of 1953.

There was genuine joy in the crowd. Old men reminisced. "I have seen those immortals in the flesh and in action," James A. Newell had penned in that morning's *News-Post*—"McGraw and Robinson and Jennings, the diminutive Willie Keeler, Joe Kelley and the rest of the great assemblage shepherded by Ned Hanlon." He remembered them "creating a new concept of the game, shedding luster upon the home town and, when dispersed, forming the nucleus from which other great teams were developed." It was true. The old Orioles had given rise— life, really—to all three of the ballclubs in Greater New York. They had made the Dodgers, they had nourished the Giants, and they *were* the Yankees.

The new Orioles had already opened the season in Detroit. Don Larsen pitched sturdily though imperfectly, giving up three home runs for a 3-to-0 loss. Then they won the next day, 3 to 2. Today's pitcher, against the White Sox, was Bob Turley. He was a husky young fire- baller, touted as a modern Walter Johnson, whose major league career so far amounted to two victories and seven defeats.

The afternoon was blustery—it was still drizzling—as the U.S. Army Field Band marched out to center field and the Orioles emerged from their dugout to take their places along the first base line. Suddenly the sun broke through, though only for a moment. The clouds had resumed their reign by the time the vice-president threw out the first pitch, from behind the Orioles' dugout. This was new for him. He had been slated to get the season started at Griffith Stadium the previous spring, but a heavy rain had washed out the game and President Eisenhower returned from golfing in Georgia in time to do the honors.

"This is a great day for baseball and a great day for Baltimore," the vice-president announced. "May the new Orioles be as good and strong as the old Orioles." He frowned in concentration as he wound up and got the franchise under way.

The electricians still labored on the new scoreboard, so the Ori- oles used the minor league appliance instead. Turley, though, did not disappoint. The baby-faced right-hander struck out nine White Sox, including cleanup man Minnie Minoso—twice. "When he stopped Minoso," Chicago's general manager, Frank Lane, said afterward, "he cut off our power."

The Orioles showed some power of their own. Clint Courtney, the bespectacled catcher called Scrap Iron, slammed a 350-foot home run to start the third inning. To lead off the fourth, Baltimore's broad- shouldered third baseman, Vern Stephens, drove one farther still. That was enough. The game ended, 3 to 1.

"There's no science left in this modern game," columnist Red Smith had lamented just the day before—"no double squeeze plays, no triple steals." Except that the Orioles had scored their third run on a bloop double and a bunt and a slashing single to right field. New Ori- oles indeed.

*   *   *

No one had bid for Ned Hanlon's services when his contract with Cincinnati expired after the 1907 season. Both seasons he managed the Reds, they finished sixth. Had Foxy Ned lost his knack? His heart? His precision of judgment? Had he failed as a manager once he redis-covered sentiment?

He was no less logical than before, but now he exuded a loyalty toward the city he had left and to which he returned, knowing it was home. Maybe the sentiment had been present before; if so, nobody had noticed it. Not that he had changed what he was—careful, cun-ning, unassailably businesslike. That was *him*. He had made himself the wealthiest man ever to leave the national game—worth a half-million dollars, it was said, counting his real estate in Pittsburgh, Brooklyn, and Baltimore. In Pittsburgh he had accepted the second mortgage on a livery stable to satisfy a $2,000 loan and replaced it with a poolroom and bachelors' apartments worth $40,000.

In baseball he was every bit as shrewd. He had regained control of Union Park and purchased Oriole Park as well, in a quick $3,000 deal (for a property that had cost at least $15,000) as Baltimore was losing its American League franchise to New York. That became the home of his new Orioles, in the Eastern League. He had bought the Montreal ballclub and moved it to Maryland. First he put Wilbert Robinson in charge, then Hughey Jennings. For a city with a certain level of expec-tations, these minor league Orioles were shockingly mediocre.

He found neither pleasure nor wealth in his new ballclub. In 1909, he unloaded the Orioles to Jack Dunn, his old Brooklyn pitcher, who was as wily and methodical as Hanlon himself.

Hanlon had just about given up hope of moving a major league team to Baltimore when the outlaw Federal League sprang up in 1914. He had first made a mark in the baseball business back in 'ninety, as a protagonist in the Players' League, in its failed rebellion against the two major circuits. The Federal League, too, denounced the reserve clause and persuaded National Leaguers and American Leaguers to jump. So Hanlon came full circle as the largest investor in the Balti-more Terrapins.

The scavenged Terrapins, or Terps, spent most of May in first place, to the delight of pennant-starved Baltimoreans. They played well enough to ensure that fewer than two hundred spectators were on hand at the Orioles' ballpark across the street to watch the minor league debut of a local southpaw named George Herman Ruth—Jack

Dunn's "babe," the wags had it, after the owner-manager had accepted custody of the nineteen-year-old from St. Mary's Industrial School. Soon Dunn would sell him, along with nine other Orioles, to make up his losses.

Yet the Terps tumbled into third place and never emerged. The next year the league was a flop, the Terps even worse. They finished in the cellar, twenty-four games out of seventh place.

When the two established leagues bought out the upstart Federals, Baltimore's franchise and players went unclaimed. Hanlon and the other owners wanted to buy the St. Louis Cardinals and move them to Baltimore, but the National League owners refused. Baltimore, Charley Ebbets complained, was inhabited by "too many colored population to start with."

So Hanlon and his associates sued organized baseball for violating the antitrust laws. Five years passed before Oliver Wendell Holmes, Jr., whose father had offered early evidence of baseball at Harvard, delivered his opinion for a unanimous Supreme Court. Baseball, he decreed, was not commerce in the usual sense and thus could act, if the owners wished, like an industrial trust, exempt from the nation's antitrust laws. Once again, Hanlon had lost.

By this time he already understood what he had missed. He was a Baltimore patriot now. The mayor had named him to the Park Board in 1916 and unanimously the City Council approved. He served for the next twenty-one years, the last six as its president. His second son, killed at the Marne, lent his name to a park.

"There are many different kinds of success," Hanlon had once said, "but few of us are able to take our pick."

A dozen of the men he had managed went on to manage others. And so his direct influence over the national game extended almost to the end of his long life. "The father of modern baseball," *The Sun* described him in 1937, when he died at the age of seventy-nine.

Hughey Jennings was starting his final semester in law school, about to fulfill one of his two childhood dreams. (He would satisfy the other one—twice—in seeing the pope.) On a wintry day in February 1904, Cornell's indoor swimming pool was invitingly steamy. Hughey dove in. He did not know that the water had been drained.

He was knocked unconscious and broke both his wrists. He was alive. But his days on the diamond were done.

He remained as the manager of the minor league Orioles through 1906, and as a part-owner, having invested $3,600 but never drawing a dividend. These were frustrating years for him. The Orioles played well but not well enough. Occasionally fewer than a hundred fans showed up. Baltimore then was "about the worst baseball town on the map," Hughey said later.

He was a lawyer in the winter, for the Baltimore law firm of Willis, Homer, France & Smith, which in 1902 had served as the agent for the conspiracy that put the Orioles into Andrew Freedman's hands. Surely he would make a mark in his chosen profession.

That was before the call came from Detroit. The Tigers needed a manager with the right personality to hold together a fractious but talented team.

Detroit's best player, right fielder Ty Cobb, was in his third season, showing himself as the ballplayer he would become. But he was already despised by his teammates, the Tigers' poisonous animosities proving an antidote to their explosive brilliance on the field. They needed Hughey's cheerfulness. He had useful experience with ballplayers like Cobb. Who could be harder to get along with, after all, than John McGraw?

And it worked. Hughey infused a wonderful degree of harmony, enthusiasm, and grit into the Detroit team. (He had telephoned Hanlon for advice.) His first season he blew a whistle to fire up his players from the coaching box along third base until Ban Johnson threatened a ten-day suspension if he kept on. So he started shouting, "That's the way," adding "ah!" for some snap and go. That became "The way—ah!" then "Ee-yah!" Soon he was known for the piercing cry—"Ee-yah!"—dozens of times in a game, as he hopped around the coaching box.

Hughey was the biggest reason the Tigers won the American League pennant in 1907, his first year as their manager, then again in 1908 and 1909. Everyone but Ty Cobb said so.

All three years, though, the Tigers lost the World's Series. Hughey managed them for eleven more years and was never in another. In the winters, he practiced law in Scranton with his brother.

Hughey's gift was a peppery, unrestful temperament that, by its nature, was something other than steadfast. He was drinking too much. In 1911, not far from his home, he drove a touring car off a bridge into the Lehigh River, breaking both legs and an arm and fracturing his skull. He was not expected to live. Yet he did.

"Life is full of trials," he had said, "which is a good thing for the lawyers."

After the Tigers finished seventh in 1918 and again in 1920, Hughey was fired. His old friend came to his rescue. Hughey joined the Giants as John McGraw's assistant for a generous $25,000 salary—"just to manage me," Mac explained.

Evidently Hughey was worth it, for the Giants won four straight pennants and were competing for a fifth. But late in the 1925 season, as the Giants were falling short, Hughey seemed moody and distracted. He escaped back to Scranton and suffered a nervous breakdown. All these years, how much had his cheerfulness kept concealed?

During his year in a sanitarium he caught tuberculosis. He recovered, physically and mentally, and went home. But he was finished with baseball—and soon with everything else. He contracted spinal meningitis in early 1928.

"I owe baseball more than the game owes me," he said to a kinsman in his sickroom hours before he died at the age of fifty-eight. "Keep it clean and honest."

His season's record for getting hit by a pitch, forty-nine times in 'ninety-six, stood until Ron Hunt of the Montreal Expos got plunked fifty times in 1971.

Maybe Joe Kelley had wanted too badly to be one of the boys to have excelled as a major league manager. For a ballplayer's respect must be earned. Certainly Kel's successor in Cincinnati had his doubts about him. "Confidentially, I would suggest to you not to give Kelley any more advance," Hanlon wrote in a postscript to Garry Herrmann, the ballclub's president and part-owner. "Should he get more, I am afraid he will not give his best efforts to the club."

But managing in Toronto seemed to suit him. Maybe it was that he carried authority more naturally with the younger players. He took a team of tailenders and, in his first season, led them to an Eastern League pennant, not only as the manager but also as a first baseman hitting .322. So the Beaneaters drafted the thirty-five-year-old minor leaguer for 1908. Boston was home. That was where he had started his major league career. Now he would finish there.

He served as the manager and batted .259 as Boston sagged into sixth place. He assailed the quality of the modern ballplayers, compared with the old-timers. The owner wanted him gone, so at season's end he returned to Toronto and stayed six more years. When he left at last, he was given a silver loving cup stuffed with a thousand dollar bills.

He had talked before about taking a political job back in Baltimore. His father-in-law made mayors and governors fall in line. First Kel took a job at the state's Registry of Motor Vehicles and then, for many years, at the city's Register of Wills.

Joe Kelley succeeded in not working too hard. His wife would know he had stopped at a bar on the way from work if he covered his mouth as he turned the corner of North Calvert Street, toward home. Once he went to retrieve Babe Ruth, who was presumed to be drinking; the Babe returned sober, but Kelley was drunk. He was portly and ruddy-faced but still walked with a swagger. Before dinner he would sit in a rocking chair on the porch of his handsome row house and rock.

Kel began to seem lonely, as if time had passed him by. Which it had. Nothing much had changed in baseball, but everything had. Asked what was different than in his day, he replied, "The first and the fifteenth of the month."

In 1943, at age seventy-one, he was laid to rest at New Cathedral Cemetery, where Hanlon and two of Kel's beloved old teammates lay, near the edge of a city they had made their own.

He was nothing like Hanlon as a manager. Foxy Ned was all brains and strategy. John McGraw had both, and more. He brought the force of an unbending personality. He was hard on his players—that understated things—but he made them play their best. They *wanted* to play for him. For he cared about little but winning.

No manager had ever been so successful. He took the last-place Giants into second place in 1903 and won the pennant the following two years. Once he won three in a row and later four straight—ten, all told, in his thirty-one years with the Giants.

He was larger than life, and gloried in it. He was one of the most famous men in America. A cigar had been named for him. He and Blanche were seen all over New York, the only city that could hold the Little Napoleon. He was paid the most of anyone in baseball (besides what he earned during the winters on the vaudeville stage). In 1925 he was profiled in the sixth issue of a sophisticated new weekly magazine called *The New Yorker:* "He is the incarnation of the American national sport. . . . There is no man in baseball more coldly, cruelly commercial than John J. McGraw, manager and magnate, and no man more self-lessly engrossed in the game for the game's sake than Muggsy McGraw, baseball artist."

He understood baseball not only as a struggle on the diamond but also as a business. Nobody had a better feel for the national game as entertainment. He understood, for instance, that a ballclub in New York could profit from having a Jewish player, and in late 1923, in hopes of competing for fans against Babe Ruth's Yankees, Mac acquired Mose Solomon from a Class C team in Kansas and intro-duced him to the public as the Rabbi of Swat. In two games Solomon went 3 for 8 at the bat but was a klutz in the outfield. That, though, was not his sin. McGraw wanted him to stay for the World's Series, though he would not play or get paid, just to have him sit on the opposite bench from the Sultan of Swat. Instead Mose Solomon went home to play football for money. *That* was his sin—disobeying. McGraw never asked him back, though starting in 1926 he kept another Jewish player, Andy Cohen, a hard-hitting infielder, around for three seasons.

Mac was no longer the scrawny kid starved for every morsel. He had filled out. That was being kind. He looked stuffed, bloated, rotund; two hundred pounds now filled his five-foot-seven frame. Something had changed in John McGraw when he was truly in charge. Or more likely nothing had changed except the removal of all con-straints. As a ballplayer he had never let up; he had pushed his oppo-nents, his teammates, the umpires, until they relented. But always, someone else—Ned Hanlon or Patsy Tebeau or Ban Johnson or Andrew Freedman—had held the upper hand. Now nobody did. John T. Brush admired McGraw, who was everything a businessman-ballplayer should be, and even loved him, as much as he was capable of sentiment. So Mac could do as he liked, and he did. He called every play from the bench. Legend had it that he fined a player who punched a decisive home run because Mac had ordered him to bunt. In the 1923 World's Series, he refused to let the Yankees replace their ailing first baseman, Wally Pipp, with a native New Yorker just up from the Eastern League named Lou Gehrig.

Mac could be kind—exceedingly so—to old friends. At various times he put Willie Keeler and Hughey Jennings and Dan Brouthers and Sadie McMahon and Wilbert Robinson on the Giants payroll. Just as quickly he could turn against them. In the final game of the 1913 World's Series, Robbie had been coaching at third base and thought McGraw had given a steal sign, so he sent a lame Fred Snodgrass to second base, for an easy out. That night Mac and Robbie—old friends, former neighbors, one-time business partners—shared too many beers. Mac, who had given up abstinence, blamed Robbie for the loss and fired him on the spot.

"Get the hell out of here," Mac roared.

Robbie could not bear to have his dignity violated. He doused McGraw with a glass of beer and stalked out. The two men, whose wives were the closest of friends, did not speak to each other again for seventeen years.

All the while the Giants kept winning. McGraw scorned the cork-centered ball and thought that the ballooning batting averages and increasingly common home runs made for a less interesting game. But if the dead-ball era was dying, Mac was supple enough to find himself some sluggers. Whatever was required to win, he would do.

Winning was getting harder, however, for he hated being on the road. As early as 1907 he had talked about retiring. "The very sight of a railroad train appalls me," he had said. Every spring and summer his health gave way; his sinuses brought infection and swelling. He denied rumors he would hand his job to Hughey Jennings. "I wouldn't know what to do with myself if I quit the game," Mac rasped. "The game is my life."

The weight of celebrity had also begun to wear on McGraw. Everyone wanted a piece of him and too often he was willing to oblige. He and Blanche had no children, no reason to stay home. Speculative investments found him, too. He became the president of a real estate venture near Sarasota, Florida—Pennant Park, it was called—and persuaded his friends and admirers to invest. Orders had already started to drop off when two 1926 hurricanes punctured the Florida land boom and brought foreclosure. Settling the lawsuits cost Mac $100,000.

He was in his fifties and already seemed terribly old. Maybe it was because he had done everything so young. Having lived so intensely for so many years, he was bound to wear out. By the late 1920s his judgment in trades had soured and his sure touch in handling pitchers was gone. He was nearer the end than the beginning and was not alone in that. When he and the Giants visited St. Bonaventure's in 1927 to dedicate a new athletic field in his honor, he insisted it be named the McGraw-Jennings Field, for his dying friend as well.

The unrelenting pain and pressure took their toll. In the late spring of 1932, with the Giants in the cellar and a hard road trip ahead, John McGraw bowed to what every mortal must face. He was the most successful manager the game had ever seen. But now he was done. His announcement drove Lou Gehrig's four home runs in a game (the first since Ed Delehanty's in 'ninety-six) off the top of the sports pages.

Two years later, at the age of sixty, he was dead.

Wilbert Robinson caught his final game with a broken finger. It was on a hot summer's day in 1904 and he was backstopping for the minor league Orioles. At a testimonial at The Diamond a few nights later, he was given a silver cup that held eight quarts. Hughey Jennings, his successor as the team's manager, presented on behalf of the players a three-foot bronze figure wielding a hammer, designated "Labor." Robbie was a man with a trade, besides behind the plate. He had opened a meat market in Baltimore and worked as a butcher, in addition to running The Diamond. Robbie had always known how to work.

He had never wanted to be a manager. Back in 'ninety-nine he had been content to let McGraw, ten years his junior, serve as the manager of the National League Orioles while he continued as the captain. He had not minded stepping aside for Hughey, either. Robbie was good at jollying his teammates but not at pushing them. He had never been fined by an umpire or a manager; only twice had he ever been ejected from a game.

He had no intention, after retiring, of being anything but a businessman and raising a family. But he could not stay away from baseball. In 1908 he sold the meat market and let go of The Diamond and signed on as a coach with the Orioles. The following season McGraw hired him as a coach for the Giants.

Five years later, when McGraw chased him from a saddened tavern, it so happened that Charley Ebbets was looking for a manager. He wanted to snatch Hughey Jennings from Detroit but he was not available. Robbie was his next choice. The Dodgers needed pitching (and everything else), and Robbie was someone a domineering owner could live with.

They made quite a pair. Robbie was rounder—more than 250 pounds, eventually—though Ebbets was catching up. Their temperaments, however, were blessedly different. Mild-mannered Robbie tended to see the good in people. Ebbets, with his self-important airs, seemed to anticipate betrayal. They became fast friends.

The Dodgers—called the Robins now, after their new manager—were a perennially floundering ballclub whose owner tried to make money by not spending much. Uncle Robbie (as he was universally known) noticeably helped. His jovial, nurturing presence kept everyone relaxed. The club rose to fifth place his first season, then up to third. In 1916 and again in 1920 they took the pennant. Brooklyn fans had come to love them; unlike Hanlon's Superbas, this team felt like it was truly theirs. The club outplayed the Giants, which infuriated McGraw. The bad blood between Mac and Robbie only intensified the rivalry.

For eighteen years Robbie did an honorable job, too often (as the 1920s went on) with dismal teams. The Daffiness Boys, they were dubbed, after their antics on the field. And then Robbie was gone, caught between factions in the management.

He and Ma moved to Georgia, where they had long spent their winters. Robbie became the president of the minor league Atlanta Crackers. He was at his home in Atlanta on an August day in 1934 when he fainted in the bathroom, breaking his arm. "This broken arm doesn't hurt me," he told the doctor who came to tend him. "I'm an old Oriole. Wrap it up and let me stay here."

In the ambulance he lapsed into unconsciousness: He had had a stroke, and did not last the evening.

His record of seven hits in a nine-inning game, back in 'ninety-two, would be matched only once. And nobody played so many years as an Oriole until Brooks Robinson—no relation—surpassed him seven decades later.

*   *   *

In terms of continuous service with a single ballclub, Charley Ebbets had become the senior magnate in the national game. For all of his self-conscious shrewdness, he had acquired a certain wisdom. "Baseball is in its infancy," he had declared at a Waldorf-Astoria banquet in 1909. People had snickered. He turned out to be right.

Charley Ebbets was a man of ideas. He introduced enunciators to Washington Park, using megaphones mounted on the grandstand, connected by telephone wire to the press box. But he was still dissatisfied with the Dodgers' home. Washington Park seated only 18,000 and the lease was soon to expire. For three or four years now Ebbets had been searching all over Brooklyn for a place to build a ballpark. He wanted a monument—to baseball, to Brooklyn, to himself. He had settled on a foul-smelling shantytown in Flatbush known as Pigtown. It was centrally located, and land was cheap. Secretly, patiently, lot by lot, he had bought up all four-and-a-half acres. Now he was ready to build.

He left it for Len Wooster of the *Brooklyn Times,* chewing on the butt of a dead cigar, to ask him what the new steel ballpark would be named.

"I don't know," the magnate replied. "I hadn't thought about it."

"Why don't you call it Ebbets Field?"

Charley Ebbets consented.

On a hot afternoon in July 1912, a priest, a minister, and a rabbi offered their blessings as the cornerstone was swung into place. It was filled with mementos—a baseball, a letter from President Taft, a photograph of Ebbets. True democracy might be found in the bleachers, where all classes and nationalities mingle, the Reverend James Farrar preached. "At Ebbets Field, we all will be of one creed. Our creed is the credit of the team and Charles H. Ebbets is our patron saint."

Maybe it was being worshiped that made him so careless. He and Minnie had already separated, living not far from each other in Flatbush. Charley, sixty-two now, had taken up quarters with the lovely young woman who had been a neighbor. Grace Slade Nott was just a year older than Charley's son, who called her Aunty. Grace's husband, the manager of the Colonial Hotel, had named the elder Ebbets as co-respondent in his 1908 divorce and said he would file a $50,000 lawsuit for alienation of affections. Either he backed down or the rivals settled out of court—any politician would have to make sure of it—and stability of a sort had been achieved. That was before Minnie glimpsed Grace sporting in a fancy automobile, reveling in luxury, after Minnie's own allowance had recently been cut. She filed for divorce.

This was in 1919. The judge, suspecting collusion, refused to grant the decree. Had Minnie not acquiesced in her husband's unfaithfulness for nine years, as long as the money sufficed?

Two years later she tried again, accusing Charley of misconduct with an unnamed woman in Albany. This time the divorce was granted. Minnie was to receive a comfortable home on Ocean Avenue and a monthly income of $625 for life. To guarantee that the payments would be made, the Squire of Flatbush agreed to deposit collateral with the Mechanics Bank of Brooklyn—half of his stock in the ballclub, free of debt.

Then he married Grace.

By now he owned just 50 percent of the ballclub. The problem had been Ebbets Field itself, which had proved far more costly to build than he had foreseen. He could afford to finish it only by turning half the stock over to the contractors, the McKeever brothers. To build a ballgrounds in his name, Charley Ebbets had lost control of his beloved team.

Fighting with the McKeevers soon became a habit. One point of contention was Charley Jr., an amiable alcoholic with a spare and frightened face, who was the secretary of the ballclub, as his father had been. That was until he went off to Bill Brown's Physical Culture Farm out in the countryside of New York—"to recuperate," the newspapers said. By opening day of the 1923 season, the club had no secretary.

Young Charley twice tried to return to the field that bore his family's name. Both times Steve McKeever threw him out. So the boy—he seemed like a boy, though he was well over forty by now—filed a $20,000 lawsuit for assault and another for $4,270 in back pay.

"I doubt if you fully realize the unpleasant and embarrassing position I am in," the senior Ebbets explained in his lucid handwriting to his son's attorney. "I do not want a step taken which may tend to injure professional base ball or the Brooklyn Base Ball Club; nor can I do anything which would injure my Son."

Charley Sr. had been ill. His face was puffy and deeply lined. But there was still a set to it, a tenacity, a wide strutting chin that had turned a ticket-taker into a magnate. Before setting sail on a European vacation, he had been unable to walk twenty-five feet without losing his breath. When he returned he felt rested and relaxed. But by summer his heart was giving out again.

He was in his suite at the Waldorf-Astoria on the eighteenth of April in 1925 when he awoke early and knew he was dying. Grace, young Charley, two of his daughters, and his sister Ada gathered at his bedside.

As his funeral cortege passed Ebbets Field, the Robins and the Giants crowded around home plate for a silent tribute. The mourners waited in the rain at Greenwood Cemetery, as the narrow grave was redug for the oversized coffin. The ballclub's new president, Ed McKeever, caught a cold, which turned into pneumonia. Eleven days later he, too, was dead.

Charley Ebbets's divorce, as it happened, was the source of the ballclub's undoing. The Brooklyn Trust Company, which had swallowed the Mechanics Bank, still held half his stock. The rest of his stock, in the family's hands, was useless to a buyer without the bank's half of the ballclub. "No reasonable offer will be refused," his son-in-law had written to the National League president. Young Charley tried to buy it. So did Mayor Jimmy Walker. A Boston merchant tried. The American Legion earmarked $1.5 million to buy the ballclub. A Brooklyn jeweler foolishly paid $1,000 for an option on the stock held by Ed McKeever's heirs before looking into Charley Ebbets's.

Whoever made a visit or two to the Brooklyn Trust fled in terror. In the years since Ebbets's death, the ballclub had fallen a million dollars in debt, encumbering the stock. Half was the mortgage on Ebbets Field, the rest had been piled on a little at a time. Charley Ebbets would not have allowed it, but he was no longer around to protest.

Yet the way he had written his will had made everything worse. It had set the members of his already fractious family at one another's throats, fighting over an estate worth more than a million dollars, most of it consisting of stock in the ballclub. On the one side were Grace and Genevieve, Charley's eldest daughter—the favored heirs. They inherited larger shares of the estate than the other two daughters or, certainly, than young Charley did. He was left nothing except some old clothes and a sum of $2,000 a year, doled out monthly.

Young Charley was fortunate, as things turned out. He got his payments until 1933, when the Great Depression squelched them. The other heirs, in the meantime, had seen little of their inheritance. Because young Charley and his disparaged sisters had challenged the terms of the will, everything was tied up in court.

For twenty-four years the probate battle went on, a tale worthy of Dickens. The filings mounted, the lawyers profited, the estate dwindled. There was nothing to invest in the Dodgers, who floundered. The battle was still going on in 1944 when young Charley died, at sixty-five, on the fourth floor of a tenement in Manhattan. He left two-thirds of his estate to his housekeeper and none to his three children.

Around this time Walter O'Malley entered the picture. If young Charley had been given the world and lost it, Walter O'Malley worked hard for everything he stole away. He was forty-one then, an engineer and a lawyer, who had been doing legal work for the Brooklyn Trust Company. He had become a protégé of the bank's president, George McLaughlin, who was the authority in the ballclub's operations. McLaughlin had him named the club's attorney, replacing Wendell Willkie, who had been nominated for president in 1940 and had recently died.

Walter O'Malley was stout and thick-faced, as Charley Ebbets had become when he grew old. O'Malley had been born in the Bronx, a son of the city's commissioner of public markets. Even as an undergraduate at the University of Pennsylvania he had been a political operator. He had gone to Fordham Law School at night, then worked for a Children's Court judge in Brooklyn and, a year later, married the judge's daughter. Walter O'Malley had always been a man to recognize opportunity.

One presented itself in 1944. He negotiated a deal for the 25 percent of the Brooklyn ballclub's stock held by Edward McKeever's heirs. The price was $240,000. The stock would come to be held by three men. The central figure, as the newspapers understood, was the Dodgers' brainy new president, their pillar of rectitude, Branch Rickey. John L. Smith, the president of Chas. Pfizer & Company Inc., the wartime manufacturer of penicillin and a major customer of the Brooklyn Trust Company, was presumed to be the man with the money. The third man, Walter O'Malley, presumably was not. How he financed it, nobody knew.

But the lawyer understood something no one else did. All the offers to buy the Ebbets stock that was still in the thrall of the bank had foundered on the ballclub's encumbering debt. Most of that had been paid off, though, after the successful seasons that continued into World War II, and O'Malley saw a way to free the stock. The divorce agreement between Charley and Minnie Ebbets was unavailable to the public but not to a lawyer involved with the ballclub. The court papers made clear that establishing a $250,000 trust paying 3 percent interest would yield enough income to satisfy the obligations of alimony, thus emancipating the stock.

O'Malley surely understood something else: the desperation of the Ebbets heirs. There were eleven of them, and some were destitute. One had been forced to declare bankruptcy during the Depression. They had waited decades and were still empty-handed. Now young Charley was dead. And still they waited.

In August 1945, as the world awaited an announcement of surrender from the palace in Tokyo, their waiting ended in Brooklyn. "Rickey and Two Associates"—as a headline writer had it—purchased the Ebbets estate's half of the Brooklyn ballclub's stock, paying a strapping $750,000. Brooklyn Trust backed Walter O'Malley with a $200,000 loan.

Rickey, Smith, and O'Malley now held 75 percent of the ballclub. The Dodgers were theirs. "Thus the name of Charley Ebbets passes out of baseball," the *Eagle* mourned, "except for Ebbets Field."

It was obvious to everyone that Branch Rickey was in Brooklyn to stay. He had arrived not quite three years before from the St. Louis Cardinals, where he had invented a farm system and had become known as the shrewdest mind in the national pastime. Yet he was also a morally serious man who had vision and the courage to pursue it. (Soon he would break the color line, some sixty years after Cap Anson had imposed it.) He knew how to take what little a ballclub had and to make it more than that.

He and Walter O'Malley were destined not to get along. O'Malley thought of baseball as a business, nothing more. He was not prone to sentiment, or even to thinking long-term. When Rickey wanted to spend money on a farm system, O'Malley stood in his way. When Rickey proposed converting an old naval air base in Vero Beach, Florida, into a baseball training facility, O'Malley resisted. The quiet war went on.

John Smith died in 1950, just as Branch Rickey's contract was about to expire. O'Malley persuaded Smith's widow to let Brooklyn Trust administer her stock. Now it was in his control.

Rickey saw what was happening and realized that his future in Brooklyn was gone. He had an offer to run the Pirates, though he would have to give up his Dodgers stock to take the job. O'Malley had him in a bind. He offered to buy Rickey out, for no more than the stock had cost. But Rickey found his revenge. Their agreement required O'Malley to match any third party's bid. Rickey lined one up, from a friend of a friend. Instead of the $346,667 that O'Malley had offered, he had to pay $1 million, plus $50,000 to the disappointed bidder, who handed it over to Rickey.

O'Malley never forgave Rickey for outsmarting him. But the ballclub was his.

Then he turned his attention to Ebbets Field. Its 32,000 seats no longer sufficed. It was already doubled-decked all around. Its odd dimensions used to be charming; now they felt cramped.

Yet the ballpark was no longer surrounded by fields. There was no room to expand, no place for fans to park their cars. Walter O'Malley wanted a new stadium, demanded it: He would pay for it himself. But he needed the land. He wanted a site at Atlantic and Flatbush Avenues, in the center of things, but Robert Moses, the city's parks commissioner, who controlled the land in New York City the way Tammany Hall once had, proposed an idea of his own. He insisted on building a stadium in Flushing Meadow—in Queens.

The impasse was a given from the start.

So O'Malley went looking for another home, inviting the attention of the city of Los Angeles. He understood balance sheets. So what if the Dodgers had made more money in recent years than any other National League ballclub? The Boston Braves had moved to Milwaukee and became the first club in the league to draw more than two million fans, twice as many as the Dodgers drew. And that was in Milwaukee! In Los Angeles, there was no telling what the limit might be.

Surely the Dodgers were O'Malley's to do with as he liked. Yet it was hard to imagine a ballclub that belonged more to its fans. Brooklyn, after all, had precious little left to call its own. The middle class had been moving out to Long Island or New Jersey, leaving swaths of Brooklyn to the poor. Elegance had turned into slums. Over the past fifty years, Brooklyn had grown accustomed to being a borough, to letting Manhattan take the lead.

Maybe that was why Brooklyn loved the Dodgers so much. For years they had been the laughingstock of the league. Even the fans called them the Bums. They *were* Brooklyn, the embodiment of a borough with too little left to lose.

Which made their successes, when eventually they came, all the sweeter. Jackie Robinson, Pee Wee Reese, the Duke. In the wake of the war, they won six pennants in ten years. In 1955, after years and years and years, they captured a world championship—and over the Yankees! How much more joy could there be?

Any fatalist would know.

Once before, Brooklyn had paid dearly for its success. Its ballclub had combined the best of two teams and won back-to-back pennants, then lost the most when competition took over. More than a half-century had passed before the ballclub ranked again as the finest in the land. Now Brooklyn would pay.

O'Malley had persuaded the New York Giants to follow the Dodgers to California. How could a single team play nearly two thousand miles or more from all the others? Airplanes now flew coast-to-coast, but it would take two teams, at the least, to justify the travel costs.

Horace Stoneham had already been thinking of leaving. His father had acquired the Giants from the heirs of John T. Brush. For years the ballclub ran itself—that is, John McGraw ran it. Then for many years nobody ran it, and it showed. At last Leo Durocher, a former Dodger, kicked some life into the team. But Durocher was gone, and lately the Giants had been lagging in the standings and suffering at the gate. Stoneham had been thinking of moving the Giants to Minneapolis, where he owned a minor league team. It would be no more difficult (and surely more lucrative) to move to San Francisco.

In public, O'Malley kept silent. The last home game of the season came around and still no announcement was made. None was needed. O'Malley was waiting for approval of a ballgrounds in Los Angeles, in the extravagant acreage at Chavez Ravine.

Only 6,702 fans paid their way through the turnstiles for the last game at Ebbets Field. It was a somber mood for a Tuesday night. After Junior Gilliam scored a run for the Dodgers in the opening inning, the organist played "Am I Blue?" Then "Que Sera Sera"—it was 2 to 0 now—and "Thanks for the Memories," and, at last, "Auld Lang Syne." Fans stood in the stands and wept.

The announcement came on the eighth of October. Publicity men from the Dodgers and the National League loitered in the World Series press room at the Waldorf-Astoria and delivered the news: The Dodgers would play in Los Angeles in 1958.

Walter O'Malley was nowhere to be seen.

Brooklyn felt betrayed. "Other teams were forced to move by apathy, or incompetence," Arthur Daley wrote in *The New York Times* (the *Eagle* had folded two years earlier). "The only word that fits the Dodgers is greed."

Greed was nothing new, to be sure, in the national game. But Brooklyn had left itself especially vulnerable. It had allowed itself to love the Dodgers. They had played in Brooklyn, under one name or another, for seventy-five years. That was how long a lucky man might live. The line stretched back, from Jackie Robinson to Babe Herman to Zack Wheat to Willie Keeler and deeper into the past—even, in a way, to the Brooklyn Atlantics, the first team to defeat baseball's original professional nine. It was a connection to timelessness that could bring tears to men's eyes, with the sort of sentiment that makes life worth living.

None of that mattered anymore, not in the end. Efficiency and the logic of business were having their day. It stood to reason: There was no better way to measure things than the bottom line. Walter O'Malley and the other magnates before him had done nothing wrong. They had merely added things up and acted sensibly. The people of Brooklyn were losing something they loved, and there was nothing they could do about it. They had no case.

The people of Baltimore had learned the same thing once—three times, really—and the lesson had stuck. They had never felt quite in control of their lives again. Surely this was rational, if unfortunate. The people of Boston and St. Louis and Philadelphia had perhaps not minded so much losing the Braves and the Browns and the Athletics, for each city had a ballclub remaining. A place like Los Angeles or Manhattan protected itself by not caring, even if it meant a life that lacked a certain passion. Brooklyn's mistake, and Baltimore's, was in caring too much. That was their undoing, and their splendor.

Appendix I

Major League Standings
1893–1904

1893 NATIONAL LEAGUE	WINS	LOSSES	PERCENTAGE	GAMES BEHIND
Boston Beaneaters	86	43	.667	—
Pittsburgh Pirates	81	48	.628	5
Cleveland Spiders	73	55	.570	12½
Philadelphia Phillies	72	57	.558	14
New York Giants	68	64	.515	19½
Brooklyn Trolley Dodgers	65	63	.508	20½
Cincinnati Reds	65	63	.508	20½
Baltimore Orioles	60	70	.462	26½
Chicago Colts	56	71	.441	29
St. Louis Browns	57	75	.432	30½
Louisville Colonels	50	75	.400	34
Washington Senators	40	89	.310	46

1894 NATIONAL LEAGUE	WINS	LOSSES	PERCENTAGE	GAMES BEHIND
Baltimore Orioles	89	39	.695	—
New York Giants	88	44	.667	3
Boston Beaneaters	83	49	.629	8
Philadelphia Phillies	71	57	.555	18
Brooklyn Trolley Dodgers	70	61	.534	20½
Cleveland Spiders	68	61	.527	21½
Pittsburgh Pirates	65	65	.500	25
Chicago Colts	57	75	.432	34
St. Louis Browns	56	76	.424	35
Cincinnati Reds	55	75	.423	35
Washington Senators	45	87	.341	46
Louisville Colonels	36	94	.277	54

Appendix I

1895 NATIONAL LEAGUE	WINS	LOSSES	PERCENTAGE	GAMES BEHIND
Baltimore Orioles	87	43	.669	—
Cleveland Spiders	84	46	.646	3
Philadelphia Phillies	78	53	.595	9½
Chicago Colts	72	58	.554	15
Boston Beaneaters	71	60	.542	16½
Brooklyn Trolley Dodgers	71	60	.542	16½
Pittsburgh Pirates	71	61	.538	17
Cincinnati Reds	66	64	.508	21
New York Giants	66	65	.504	21½
Washington Senators	43	85	.336	43
St. Louis Browns	39	92	.298	48½
Louisville Colonels	35	96	.267	52½

1896 NATIONAL LEAGUE	WINS	LOSSES	PERCENTAGE	GAMES BEHIND
Baltimore Orioles	90	39	.698	—
Cleveland Spiders	80	48	.625	9½
Cincinnati Reds	77	50	.606	12
Boston Beaneaters	74	57	.565	17
Chicago Colts	71	57	.555	18½
Pittsburgh Pirates	66	63	.512	24
New York Giants	64	67	.489	27
Philadelphia Phillies	62	68	.477	28½
Brooklyn Trolley Dodgers	58	73	.443	33
Washington Senators	58	73	.443	33
St. Louis Browns	40	90	.308	50½
Louisville Colonels	38	93	.290	53

1897 NATIONAL LEAGUE	WINS	LOSSES	PERCENTAGE	GAMES BEHIND
Boston Beaneaters	93	39	.705	—
Baltimore Orioles	90	40	.692	2
New York Giants	83	48	.634	9½
Cincinnati Reds	76	56	.576	17
Cleveland Spiders	69	62	.527	23½
Brooklyn Trolley Dodgers	61	71	.462	32
Washington Senators	61	71	.462	32
Pittsburgh Pirates	60	71	.458	32½
Chicago Colts	59	73	.447	34
Philadelphia Phillies	55	77	.417	38
Louisville Colonels	52	78	.400	40
St. Louis Browns	29	102	.221	63½

Appendix I

1898 NATIONAL LEAGUE	WINS	LOSSES	PERCENTAGE	GAMES BEHIND
Boston Beaneaters	102	47	.685	—
Baltimore Orioles	96	53	.644	6
Cincinnati Reds	92	60	.605	11½
Chicago Orphans	85	65	.567	17½
Cleveland Spiders	81	68	.544	21
Philadelphia Phillies	78	71	.523	24
New York Giants	77	73	.513	25½
Pittsburgh Pirates	72	76	.486	29½
Louisville Colonels	70	81	.464	33
Brooklyn Trolley Dodgers	54	91	.372	46
Washington Senators	51	101	.336	52½
St. Louis Browns	39	111	.260	63½

1899 NATIONAL LEAGUE	WINS	LOSSES	PERCENTAGE	GAMES BEHIND
Brooklyn Superbas	101	47	.682	—
Boston Beaneaters	95	57	.625	8
Philadelphia Phillies	94	58	.618	9
Baltimore Orioles	86	62	.581	15
St. Louis Cardinals	84	67	.556	18½
Cincinnati Reds	83	67	.553	19
Pittsburgh Pirates	76	73	.510	25½
Chicago Orphans	75	73	.507	26
Louisville Colonels	75	77	.493	28
New York Giants	60	90	.400	42
Washington Senators	54	98	.355	49
Cleveland Spiders	20	134	.130	84

1900 NATIONAL LEAGUE	WINS	LOSSES	PERCENTAGE	GAMES BEHIND
Brooklyn Superbas	82	54	.603	—
Pittsburgh Pirates	79	60	.568	4½
Philadelphia Phillies	75	63	.543	8
Boston Beaneaters	66	72	.478	17
Chicago Orphans	65	75	.464	19
St. Louis Cardinals	65	75	.464	19
Cincinnati Reds	62	77	.446	21½
New York Giants	60	78	.435	23

Appendix I

1901 NATIONAL LEAGUE	WINS	LOSSES	PERCENTAGE	GAMES BEHIND
Pittsburgh Pirates	90	49	.647	—
Philadelphia Phillies	83	57	.593	7½
Brooklyn Superbas	79	57	.581	9½
St. Louis Cardinals	76	64	.543	14½
Boston Beaneaters	69	69	.500	20½
Chicago Orphans	53	86	.381	37
New York Giants	52	85	.380	37
Cincinnati Reds	52	87	.374	38

1901 AMERICAN LEAGUE	WINS	LOSSES	PERCENTAGE	GAMES BEHIND
Chicago White Stockings	83	53	.610	—
Boston Somersets	79	57	.581	4
Detroit Tigers	74	61	.548	8½
Philadelphia Athletics	74	62	.544	9
Baltimore Orioles	68	65	.511	13½
Washington Senators	61	72	.459	20½
Cleveland Blues	54	82	.397	29
Milwaukee Brewers	48	89	.350	35½

1902 NATIONAL LEAGUE	WINS	LOSSES	PERCENTAGE	GAMES BEHIND
Pittsburgh Pirates	103	36	.741	—
Brooklyn Superbas	75	63	.543	27½
Boston Beaneaters	73	64	.533	29
Cincinnati Reds	70	70	.500	33½
Chicago Cubs	68	69	.496	34
St. Louis Cardinals	56	78	.418	44½
Philadelphia Phillies	56	81	.409	46
New York Giants	48	88	.353	53½

1902 AMERICAN LEAGUE	WINS	LOSSES	PERCENTAGE	GAMES BEHIND
Philadelphia Athletics	83	53	.610	—
St. Louis Browns	78	58	.574	5
Boston Somersets	77	60	.562	6½
Chicago White Stockings	74	60	.552	8
Cleveland Blues	69	67	.507	14
Washington Senators	61	75	.449	22
Detroit Tigers	52	83	.385	30½
Baltimore Orioles	50	88	.362	34

Appendix I

1903 NATIONAL LEAGUE	WINS	LOSSES	PERCENTAGE	GAMES BEHIND
Pittsburgh Pirates	91	49	.650	—
New York Giants	84	55	.604	6½
Chicago Cubs	82	56	.594	8
Cincinnati Reds	74	65	.532	16½
Brooklyn Superbas	70	66	.515	19
Boston Beaneaters	58	80	.420	32
Philadelphia Phillies	49	86	.363	39½
St. Louis Cardinals	43	94	.314	46½

1903 AMERICAN LEAGUE	WINS	LOSSES	PERCENTAGE	GAMES BEHIND
Boston Pilgrims	91	47	.659	—
Philadelphia Athletics	75	60	.556	14½
Cleveland Blues	77	63	.550	15
New York Highlanders	72	62	.537	17
Detroit Tigers	65	71	.478	25
St. Louis Browns	65	74	.468	26½
Chicago White Stockings	60	77	.438	30½
Washington Senators	43	94	.314	47½

1904 NATIONAL LEAGUE	WINS	LOSSES	PERCENTAGE	GAMES BEHIND
New York Giants	106	47	.693	—
Chicago Cubs	93	60	.608	13
Cincinnati Reds	88	65	.575	18
Pittsburgh Pirates	87	66	.569	19
St. Louis Cardinals	75	79	.487	31½
Brooklyn Superbas	56	97	.366	50
Boston Beaneaters	55	98	.359	51
Philadelphia Phillies	52	100	.342	53½

1904 AMERICAN LEAGUE	WINS	LOSSES	PERCENTAGE	GAMES BEHIND
Boston Pilgrims	95	59	.617	—
New York Highlanders	92	59	.609	1½
Chicago White Sox	89	65	.578	6
Cleveland Blues	86	65	.570	7½
Philadelphia Athletics	81	70	.536	12½
St. Louis Browns	65	87	.428	29
Detroit Tigers	62	90	.408	32
Washington Senators	38	113	.252	55½

APPENDIX II

Career Records of "The Big Four"

WILLIAM HENRY KEELER
Born: March 3, 1872, Brooklyn, N.Y.
Died: January 1, 1923, Brooklyn, N.Y.
Height: 5'4½"; Weight: 140
Batted Left, Threw Left
Inducted into the Baseball Hall of Fame, 1939

YEAR	TEAM	G	AB	R	H	2B	3B	HR	RBI	SB	AVG
1892	New York (NL)	14	53	7	17	3	0	0	6	5	.321
1893	New York (NL)	7	24	5	8	2	1	1	7	3	.333
	Brooklyn (NL)	20	80	14	25	1	1	1	9	2	.313
	Total	27	104	19	33	3	2	2	16	5	.317
1894	Baltimore (NL)	129	590	165	219	27	22	5	94	32	.371
1895	Baltimore (NL)	131	565	162	213	24	15	4	78	47	.377
1896	Baltimore (NL)	126	544	153	210	22	13	4	82	67	.386
1897	Baltimore (NL)	129	564	145	**239**	27	19	0	74	64	**.424**
1898	Baltimore (NL)	129	561	126	**216**	7	2	1	44	28	**.385**
1899	Brooklyn (NL)	141	570	**140**	216	12	13	1	61	45	.379
1900	Brooklyn (NL)	136	563	106	**204**	13	12	4	68	41	.362
1901	Brooklyn (NL)	136	595	123	202	18	12	2	43	23	.339
1902	Brooklyn (NL)	133	559	86	186	20	5	0	38	19	.333
1903	New York (AL)	132	512	95	160	14	7	0	32	24	.313
1904	New York (AL)	143	543	78	186	14	8	2	40	21	.343
1905	New York (AL)	149	560	81	169	14	4	4	38	19	.302
1906	New York (AL)	152	592	96	180	8	3	2	33	23	.304
1907	New York (AL)	107	423	50	99	5	2	0	17	7	.234
1908	New York (AL)	91	323	38	85	3	1	1	14	14	.263
1909	New York (AL)	99	360	44	95	7	5	1	32	10	.264
1910	New York (NL)	19	10	5	3	0	0	0	0	1	.300
Total (19 Years)		**2,123**	**8,591**	**1,719**	**2,932**	**241**	**145**	**33**	**810**	**495**	**.341**

Appendix II

JOHN JOSEPH McGRAW
Born: April 7, 1873, Truxton, N.Y.
Died: February 25, 1934, New Rochelle, N.Y.
Height: 5'7"; Weight: 155
Batted Left, Threw Right
Manager: Baltimore (NL), 1899; Baltimore (AL), 1901–02; New York (NL), 1902–32
Inducted into the Baseball Hall of Fame, 1937

YEAR	TEAM	G	AB	R	H	2B	3B	HR	RBI	SB	AVG
1891	Baltimore (AA)	33	115	17	31	3	5	0	14	4	.270
1892	Baltimore (NL)	79	286	41	77	13	2	1	26	15	.269
1893	Baltimore (NL)	127	480	123	154	9	10	5	64	38	.321
1894	Baltimore (NL)	124	512	156	174	18	14	1	92	78	.340
1895	Baltimore (NL)	96	388	110	143	13	6	2	48	61	.369
1896	Baltimore (NL)	23	77	20	25	2	2	0	14	13	.325
1897	Baltimore (NL)	106	391	90	127	15	3	0	48	44	.325
1898	Baltimore (NL)	143	515	143	176	8	10	0	53	43	.342
1899	Baltimore (NL)	117	399	140	156	13	3	1	33	73	.391
1900	St. Louis (NL)	99	334	84	115	10	4	2	33	29	.344
1901	Baltimore (AL)	73	232	71	81	14	9	0	28	24	.349
1902	Baltimore (AL)	20	63	14	18	3	2	1	3	5	.286
	New York (NL)	35	107	13	25	0	0	0	5	7	.234
	Total	55	170	27	43	3	2	1	8	12	.247
1903	New York (NL)	12	11	2	3	0	0	0	1	1	.273
1904	New York (NL)	5	12	0	4	0	0	0	0	0	.333
1905	New York (NL)	3	0	0	0	0	0	0	0	1	—
1906	New York (NL)	4	2	0	0	0	0	0	0	0	.000
Total (16 Years)		**1,099**	**3,924**	**1,024**	**1,309**	**121**	**70**	**13**	**462**	**436**	**.334**

HUGH AMBROSE JENNINGS
Born: April 2, 1869, Pittston, Pa.
Died: February 1, 1928, Scranton, Pa.
Height: 5'8½"; Weight: 165
Batted Right, Threw Right
Manager: Detroit (AL), 1907–20; New York (NL), 1924–25
Inducted into the Baseball Hall of Fame, 1945

YEAR	TEAM	G	AB	R	H	2B	3B	HR	RBI	SB	AVG
1891	Louisville (AA)	90	360	53	105	10	8	1	58	12	.292
1892	Louisville (NL)	152	594	65	132	16	4	2	61	28	.222
1893	Louisville (NL)	23	88	6	12	3	0	0	9	0	.136
	Baltimore (NL)	16	55	6	14	0	0	1	6	0	.255
	Total	39	143	12	26	3	0	1	15	0	.182
1894	Baltimore (NL)	128	501	134	168	28	16	4	109	37	.335
1895	Baltimore (NL)	131	529	159	204	41	7	4	125	53	.386
1896	Baltimore (NL)	130	521	125	209	27	9	0	121	70	.401
1897	Baltimore (NL)	117	439	133	156	26	9	2	79	60	.355
1898	Baltimore (NL)	143	534	135	175	25	11	1	87	28	.328

YEAR	TEAM	G	AB	R	H	2B	3B	HR	RBI	SB	AVG
1899	Brooklyn (NL)	16	41	7	7	0	2	0	6	4	.171
	Baltimore (NL)	2	8	2	3	0	2	0	2	0	.375
	Brooklyn (NL)	51	175	35	57	3	8	0	34	14	.326
	Total	69	224	44	67	3	12	0	42	18	.299
1900	Brooklyn (NL)	115	441	61	120	18	6	1	69	31	.272
1901	Philadelphia (NL)	82	302	38	79	21	2	1	39	13	.262
1902	Philadelphia (NL)	78	290	32	79	13	4	1	32	8	.272
1903	Brooklyn (NL)	6	17	2	4	0	0	0	1	1	.235
1907	Detroit (AL)	1	4	0	1	1	0	0	0	0	.250
1909	Detroit (AL)	2	4	1	2	0	0	0	2	0	.500
1912	Detroit (AL)	1	1	0	0	0	0	0	0	0	.000
1918	Detroit (AL)	1	0	0	0	0	0	0	0	0	—
Total (17 Years)		**1,285**	**4,904**	**994**	**1,527**	**232**	**88**	**18**	**840**	**359**	**.311**

JOSEPH JAMES KELLEY

Born: December 9, 1871, Cambridge, Mass.
Died: August 14, 1943, Baltimore, Md.
Height: 5'11"; Weight: 190
Batted Right, Threw Right
Manager: Cincinnati (NL), 1902–05; Boston (NL), 1908
Inducted into the Baseball Hall of Fame, 1971

YEAR	TEAM	G	AB	R	H	2B	3B	HR	RBI	SB	AVG
1891	Boston (NL)	12	45	7	11	1	1	0	3	0	.244
1892	Pittsburgh (NL)	56	205	26	49	7	7	0	28	8	.239
	Baltimore (NL)	10	33	3	7	0	0	0	4	2	.212
	Total	66	238	29	56	7	7	0	32	10	.235
1893	Baltimore (NL)	125	502	120	153	27	16	9	76	33	.305
1894	Baltimore (NL)	129	507	165	199	48	20	6	111	46	.393
1895	Baltimore (NL)	131	518	148	189	26	19	10	134	54	.365
1896	Baltimore (NL)	131	519	148	189	31	19	8	100	**87**	.364
1897	Baltimore (NL)	131	505	113	183	31	9	5	118	44	.362
1898	Baltimore (NL)	124	464	71	149	18	15	2	110	24	.321
1899	Brooklyn (NL)	143	538	108	175	21	14	6	93	31	.325
1900	Brooklyn (NL)	121	454	90	145	23	17	6	91	26	.319
1901	Brooklyn (NL)	120	492	77	151	22	12	4	65	18	.307
1902	Baltimore (AL)	60	222	50	69	17	7	1	34	12	.311
	Cincinnati (NL)	40	156	24	50	9	2	1	12	3	.321
	Total	100	378	74	119	26	9	2	46	15	.315
1903	Cincinnati (NL)	105	383	85	121	22	4	3	45	18	.316
1904	Cincinnati (NL)	123	449	75	126	21	13	0	63	15	.281
1905	Cincinnati (NL)	90	321	43	89	7	6	1	37	8	.277
1906	Cincinnati (NL)	129	465	43	106	19	11	1	53	9	.228
1908	Boston (NL)	73	228	25	59	8	2	2	17	5	.259
Total (17 Years)		**1,853**	**7,006**	**1,421**	**2,220**	**358**	**194**	**65**	**1,194**	**443**	**.317**

SOURCE: *Total Baseball,* 5th edition (New York: Viking Penguin, 1997).
Note: Statistics in boldface led the league.

Acknowledgments

One of the delights of writing this book has been the people who have helped me. I daresay that baseball people are easier to know, by and large, than the ordinary run of politically minded Washingtonians I encounter in my day job. I leave it to readers to determine whether it's baseball or politics that truly counts as the national game.

I'm grateful to the descendants of the old Orioles who have been free with their time and materials. Charles Keeler, Willie's grand-nephew, generously lent me the family scrapbook and photographs, and John Clegg gave me a copy of the ballplayer's 1896 diary. Thanks also to Joe Kelley's daughter-in-law, Mary G. Kelley; to Hughey Jennings's granddaughter and great-grandson, Grace and Tom Doherty; and to Steve Brodie's grandson, Bob Chapman.

Baseball historians are a breed apart, with a pleasure in sharing what they know that seems as anachronistic as the game they love. Jim Bready, the reigning expert on the old Orioles, could not do enough to help. He and John Thorn and David Q. Voigt saved me from many a mistake by reading the manuscript, as did Al Kermisch, who spent years reading newspapers at the Library of Congress and apparently has remembered every scrap of it.

At the Library of Congress, one of the rare government agencies that really works, Dave Kelly was perennially thoughtful and smart. Librarians are good eggs, especially my sister-in-law Lynn Sawyer, who always makes everything easier. Thanks also to Jim Gates, Tim Wiles, Scot Mondore, Eric Enders, and W. C. Burdick at the National Baseball Hall of Fame library, and to Greg Schwalenberg at the Babe Ruth Museum. Gil Klein came through with a set of *Harper's Weekly*.

Acknowledgments

Trying to write a book while holding down a job is no mean feat. I've appreciated the support I've received from my many friends at *National Journal,* especially from former editor Dick Frank for his quiet encouragement. Jim Dillon guided me through the maze of the Brooklyn courthouse. My good friend Bill O'Brian helped editorially and in all kinds of other ways.

When it comes to an editor's touch, Paul Golob has been the sort of editor that supposedly doesn't exist anymore—thoroughly hands-on, discerning in judgment, astonishingly knowledgeable, and awfully fun. This book wouldn't have happened without him, or without my agent, Gail Ross, who kept faith.

It surely wouldn't have been possible, or bearable, without my wife, Nancy Tuholski. How she has put up with this, I'm not quite sure. (Sometimes it's best not to ask.) She made life go on while everything was swirling.

Burt Solomon
Arlington, Virginia
July 1998

NOTES

Chapter 1: The Fields of Brooklyn

p. 3 **was propped up on pillows:** Some of this description is verbatim from *The Sporting News*, on Jan. 11, 1923.

p. 3 **The pain:** "He had become wasted to a skeleton and had been suffering intense pain," John McGraw said to the *New York Herald*, Jan. 5, 1923.

p. 3 **He had already told Tom:** This was reported in the *Brooklyn Citizen*, Jan. 2, 1923.

p. 4 **"really medicine for him":** Dr. Wuest was quoted in the *New York World*, Jan. 2, 1923.

p. 4 **without striking out:** *The Sporting News* asserted on Jan. 11, 1923, that this had happened in 1898. Keeler himself claimed to have gone through 700 times at bat— from late 1895 through the spring of 1897—without a strikeout, according to an interview he gave shortly before his death to umpire Billy Evans. "While I prize all my records, going through 700 times without striking out is easily the best in my opinion," he said. But baseball historians nowadays are skeptical. Al Kermisch, who writes "From a Researcher's Notebook" for *The Baseball Research Journal,* said in an interview in March 1995 that the story is "absolutely not true." Keeler, he said, never went through a season without a strikeout. *Total Baseball* reports that Keeler struck out 12 times in 1895 and 9 in 1896. Starting in 1897, however, information on which batters struck out disappeared from the box scores, but Bob Davids of the Society for American Baseball Research reports he has counted at least two strikeouts by Keeler every season from 1894 to 1909.

p. 5 **"Keep your eye clear":** Keeler said this to Abe Yager of the *Brooklyn Daily Eagle,* according to several secondary accounts, such as one by Wendell Plumlee of *The Philadelphia Inquirer* in an article, "Keeler as a baseball innovator," in *Baseball Digest,* March 1979, vol. XXXVIII, p. 77–79. *The Sporting News,* in Keeler's obituary, said that a reporter was to get a signed article from Keeler on how to hit and received a manuscript that, in its entirety, said "Hit 'em where they ain't." In an article in *Esquire,* August 1942, former umpire Billy Evans traced the saying to a visit by Mark Roth of the *New York Globe* to the bench in 1906. But the epigram appears in print as early as May 1902. All of these stories may be true.

p. 6 **"I like playing ball so much"**: This is quoted in an unidentified obituary in the Keeler file at the library of the National Baseball Hall of Fame and Museum, in Cooperstown, N.Y.

p. 6 **"In baseball, as in any profession"**: Keeler was quoted in *Sporting Life* on Jan. 10, 1903, p. 2.

p. 10 **carrying the family name of O'Kelleher**: This is according to an article in the *Baltimore American,* Oct. 15, 1906, p. 12. Keeler is apparently the source for the article but he isn't quoted directly.

p. 10 **the twenty miles over Watergrass Hill**: This anecdote was told to me by Charles Keeler, Willie's grandnephew.

p. 10 **They saved every cent, and**: The deed to 376 Pulaski street was recorded at the city register in Brooklyn on Oct. 14, 1869, in the name of William Kaler, apparently because a city clerk had misunderstood. The 1921 deed by which his sons sold the house described the deceased owner as "sometimes known as William Kaler."

p. 11 **"You never put out any garbage"**: This back and forth was recounted by Charles Keeler, who was also the source of the information about Pat Keeler's outside pursuits.

p. 11 **the boys could steal past**: This is according to a letter to the "Old Timers" column in the *Brooklyn Daily Eagle,* July 23, 1944, p. 8.

p. 11 **street games galore**: This list of games, and the conclusion that the greatest number of games involved a bat and a ball, is from "Street Games of Boys in Brooklyn, N.Y.," an article by Stewart Culin published in *The Journal of American Folk-Lore* in July–Sept. 1891, pp. 221–37.

p. 12 **He was clever with his dukes**: This sentence and the next two are almost verbatim from *Sporting Life,* Jan. 26, 1907, p. 3.

p. 12 **A matronly teacher**: This anecdote is from an unidentified clipping, apparently from the *Brooklyn Daily Eagle* in 1906, entitled "'Wee Willie' Keeler in Schoolboy Days," in the Keeler file at the Hall of Fame. The story is also told in *Sporting Life,* Jan. 26, 1907, p. 3, shortly after the teacher, named Emma Keeler, died.

p. 12 **"For four years we had a team"**: This is from an interview with Keeler in the *New York World* in 1903, republished in *The Sun* (Baltimore) on Feb. 25, 1903, p. 9.

p. 12 **Willie's father had put a bat**: This comes from an unidentified clipping, apparently in about 1908, from the Keeler file at the Hall of Fame.

p. 12 **"People say that a man or boy"**: Keeler was quoted in the 1903 interview with the *New York World.*

p. 13 **"We were only sandlot kids"**: Keeler was quoted in his obituary in the *Brooklyn Standard-Union,* Jan. 2, 1923.

p. 13 **The Rivals were playing**: The story of Willie's victory over the Star-Athletics comes from an unidentified clipping, apparently from 1906, carrying the headline "'Wee Willie' Keeler in Schoolboy Days," in the Keeler file in Cooperstown.

p. 13 **"I got lots of practice with the Rivals"**: Keeler was quoted in an interview with the *Brooklyn Daily Eagle* after the 1897 season, in an undated clipping in the Keeler scrapbook.

p. 13 **"After I left school":** This is from the 1903 *New York World* interview.

p. 13 **He was offered a decent wage:** This is from a May 1994 interview with Charles Keeler.

p. 13 **his father got a summer job for him:** This anecdote is drawn, some of it nearly verbatim, from an unidentified clipping in the Keeler file in Cooperstown.

p. 14 **"My father said I didn't want to work":** This is from the 1903 *New York World* interview.

p. 14 **Willie was first paid:** Keeler said explicitly that he started playing with the Acmes at the age of sixteen in the 1903 *New York World* interview. The biography given in a pennant souvenir book published in 1894 (and found at the Babe Ruth Museum in Baltimore) suggests the same. But in an 1898 interview with the *Brooklyn Daily Eagle*, which was reprinted in *The Sporting News* on Jan. 29, 1898, Keeler gave a timetable suggesting he first played for the Acmes in 1890, when he was eighteen. A list of the teams he played for, printed in the *Plainfield* (N.J.) *Courier* on Oct. 5, 1891, also puts him on the Acmes the year before.

p. 14 **"About the first time a boy":** This is from an article under Keeler's byline, entitled "Willie Keeler Tells How He Hits with a Short Bat," published in *The Commercial Tribune* of Cincinnati on June 9, 1901.

p. 15 **His employers had no fondness:** This somewhat implausible story was reported by the *Baltimore American,* Oct. 15, 1906, p. 12. James Bready, the leading expert on the Orioles of the 1890s, brought this to my attention.

p. 15 **"My father was convinced that professional":** Keeler was quoted in his 1903 *New York World* interview.

p. 15 **"Let them sneer at Keeler no more":** This was from the *Plainfield Press,* Aug. 24, 1891.

p. 15 **"Of all the records I ever made":** Keeler was quoted in his obituary in *The Sporting News,* Jan. 11, 1923.

p. 16 **"The Gorhams were not a nine":** This is from the *Plainfield Daily Press,* Sept. 28, 1891.

p. 16 **"But he picked up the ball so easy":** These quotations and those in the next two paragraphs are from an unidentified clipping of an interview with Doescher in the Keeler scrapbook. Keeler remembered that Frank Leonard had still been the manager in Binghamton and that he had sent a player down to scout a catcher named Brush and found Keeler instead. But a June 2, 1892, clipping from the *Evening Telegram* in New York indicates that Doescher had already taken over. Keeler's resignation letter to the Plainfield manager was dated June 5, 1892.

p. 17 **"I know you will not feel hard":** Willie's letter to the manager, T. H. Keller, was printed in the *Plainfield Courier,* June 9, 1892.

p. 17 **"The public is awake to the fact":** This is from the *Binghamton Republican,* June 6, 1892, p. 8.

p. 17 **batted him all over the lot:** This is verbatim from the *Binghamton Republican,* June 8, 1892, p. 8.

p. 18 **"In the Eastern, I had been called":** Keeler was quoted in the 1903 *New York World* interview.

p. 18   **a salary of $1,600 to Willie:** This is according to the obituary for Keeler in the *New York Tribune,* Jan. 2, 1923. The *Brooklyn Daily Times* obituary put the salary offer at $1,800. An article by Bill Hicks in 1914 or 1915 in an unidentified clipping in the Keeler file in Cooperstown put the figure at $1,000.

p. 18   **his persuasive manner and his oily tongue:** These phrases were used to explain Pat Powers's success in signing Keeler in *The New York Times,* Sept. 28, 1892, p. 9.

p. 18   **"brought me into fast company":** Keeler was quoted in the 1903 *New York World* interview.

Chapter 2: The National Game

p. 19   **Oliver Wendell Holmes played:** This is according to *Base-Ball: How to Become a Player,* by John Montgomery Ward, 1888, p. 13.

p. 19   **Lincoln was out playing baseball:** This tale is told by Albert G. Spalding in *America's National Game,* reprinted by the University of Nebraska Press in 1992 from the original 1911 edition, p. 361.

p. 19   **Andrew Johnson:** Johnson did so at a meeting of supporters in the White House, according to *Baseball: The Presidents' Game,* by William B. Mead and Paul Dickson (Washington, D.C.: Farragut Publishing Co., 1993), p. 11. Johnson, the book says, had also been given an honorary membership in Tweed's Mutual Club of New York.

p. 19   **Sixteen years later, Benjamin Harrison:** President Harrison watched Cincinnati defeat Washington, 7 to 4, in eleven innings on June 6, 1892, according to *Baseball: The Presidents' Game,* p. 13.

p. 20   **"a fruit of the inventive genius":** This is from Ward, p. 21.

p. 20   **There had recently been talk:** Harold Seymour wrote in *Baseball: The Early Years* (New York: Oxford University Press, 1960), p. 280: "The argument given in 1892 was that batting in the latter part of the game tired the pitcher and made him an easy out. On the other hand, if he did happen to hit for extra bases, he was 'fit for the ambulance' from running out his hits."

p. 21   **The rules on pitching put a premium:** This is nearly verbatim from Ward, p. 47.

p. 22   **"A veritable team of Samsons":** This is from *My 66 Years in the Big Leagues,* by Connie Mack (Philadelphia: John C. Winston Co., 1950), p. 72. Mack reached the major leagues in 1886 at the age of 23.

p. 22   **No Helen:** Helen Dauvray's failure to show up in San Francisco or in New York was reported in *Sporting Life* on April 19, 1890. The Wards divorced in 1893.

p. 23   **Even as his boat docked:** This is according to *American Baseball: From the Gentleman's Sport to the Commissioner System,* by David Quentin Voigt (University Park: Pennsylvania State University Press, 1983), p. 159.

p. 24   **Ballplayers with pregnant wives:** This is drawn from *100 Years of Baseball,* by Lee Allen (New York: Bartholomew House Inc., 1950), p. 95.

p. 24   **"What was formerly a pastime":** This is from an article by Ward in *Lippincott's Magazine,* August 1886, quoted in the 1951 House Judiciary Committee hearings on the study of monopoly power in organized baseball, p. 1435.

p. 24   **"in the eye of the baseball 'magnate'":** The article, entitled "Is the Base-Ball Player a Chattel?" appeared in the August 1887 issue of *Lippincott's Magazine.*

p. 24 **more than a hundred players:** Charles Alexander put the number at 107 for the National League and the American Association, in *Our Game* (New York: Henry Holt and Co., 1991), p. 53, and Harold Seymour put it at 90, possibly for the League alone, in *Baseball: The Early Years,* p. 223.

p. 25 **"There is nothing to discuss":** Spalding is quoted in Allen's *100 Years of Baseball,* p. 101.

p. 25 **he sought out Al Johnson:** I've relied mainly on Allen's and Seymour's accounts.

p. 25 **"There was a time when the League":** The manifesto was reprinted in *Early Innings: A Documentary History of Baseball, 1825–1908,* compiled and edited by Dean A. Sullivan (Lincoln: University of Nebraska Press, 1995), p. 188.

p. 26 **by quick-pitching him or letting him fidget:** This is almost verbatim from the article on Spalding by William E. McMahon in *Baseball's First Stars,* edited by Frederick Ivor-Campbell, Robert L. Tiemann, and Mark Rucker, published in 1996 by the Society for American Baseball Research, p. 154.

p. 26 **Soon Al Spalding became the Barnum:** This is drawn from Benjamin G. Rader's introduction to the University of Nebraska 1992 reprinting of Spalding's *America's National Game,* p. xii.

p. 26 **"How are things going":** Spalding recounts this conversation in *America's National Game,* pp. 295–96. I've guessed at the epithets, which Spalding left as blanks, and left out two lines of dialogue after the first two. Spalding: "You don't mean to say that the managers are getting discouraged." Kelly: "Aw, [damn] the managers!"

p. 27 **"If either party to this controversy":** Spalding was speaking specifically of the National League and the rebellious players, on p. 285 of *America's National Game.*

p. 27 **implacable enemy:** "With the sole exception of Comiskey, however, the managers' posts and the captaincies of the PL teams rested in the hands of [National] League players, and it was the League that the Brotherhood regarded as its implacable enemy," David Nemec wrote in *The Beer and Whisky League: The Illustrated History of the American Association—Baseball's Renegade Major League* (New York: Lyons & Burford, 1994), p. 211.

p. 28 **"Spalding says he wants war":** Billy Barnie, the manager of the Baltimore Orioles and the Association's vice president, was quoted in Seymour, p. 253.

p. 28 **"My big fellows!":** This is the version of the story told by Frank Graham in *New York Giants—An Informal History* (New York: G. P. Putnam's Sons, 1952), p. 9. There are others. In *The Giants: Memories and Memorabilia from a Century of Baseball* (New York: Abbeville Press, 1993), on p. 17, Bruce Chadwick has Mutrie exulting over a victory against Philadelphia: "'Look at them,' he spluttered, 'they're . . . they're . . . Giants!'"

p. 30 **That Pat Powers was intent on replacing:** The *Brooklyn Daily Eagle* reported this on Oct. 1, 1892, p. 2.

p. 30 **Delehanty:** This is the spelling that was used in newspapers at the time. Later, a birth certificate turned up that had the spelling as Delahanty, which is how reference books now have it.

p. 30 **took two vicious swipes at the ball:** This is nearly verbatim from O. P. Caylor's account in the *New York Herald,* Oct. 1, 1892, p. 9.

p. 30 **"He is a clever fielder":** This is from the *New York Tribune,* Oct. 1, 1892, p. 4.

Notes

p. 30 **"jumped at once into popular favor":** This is from the *New York Press*, Oct. 1, 1892, last page.

p. 31 **Surely third basemen must be:** A large third baseman "will have a longer reach for both thrown and batted balls, he will be a better mark to throw at, and, by reason of his superior weight, he will have more confidence in the face of reckless base-running," Ward wrote in *Base-Ball: How to Become a Player,* pp. 92–93.

p. 31 **"materially weakened":** This was from the *New York Sun*, May 9, 1893, p. 4.

p. 31 **"Here is the record of Keeler":** This is from *The New York Times*, May 9, 1893, p. 3.

p. 31 **He came to Johnny Ward with tears:** Ward told this story in an interview with the *Brooklyn Daily Eagle,* June 17, 1900, p. 9.

p. 32 **"It was painful to watch little Keeler":** This is from *The New York Times*, May 11, 1893, p. 3.

p. 32 **"My field work was still ragged":** This is from an interview with Keeler in the *New York World,* reprinted in *The Sun* (Baltimore) on Feb. 25, 1903, p. 9.

p. 32 **"Some folks tell a young player":** J. C. Kofoed quoted Keeler in *The Sporting News* on Jan. 11, 1923.

p. 32 **"I took excellent care":** This is from Keeler's 1903 interview with the *New York World*.

p. 32 **two unfamiliar faces emerged:** This account is drawn from the *New York World* on July 28, 1893, p. 14.

p. 32 **the team already known as the Trolley Dodgers:** *The Baseball Encyclopedia* names the "Trolley-Dodgers" as Brooklyn's American Association team from 1884 to 1888. Standard histories of the Dodgers trace the name to the profusion of trolley lines around Eastern Park. But Tom Knight, considered the baseball historian of Brooklyn, maintains that the ballclub never used the name.

p. 33 **"I got orders to come over here":** Keeler was quoted about his July 27, 1893, debut in an unidentified clipping in the Keeler scrapbook.

p. 33 **"There will be a shaking up":** Byrne was quoted in the *Brooklyn Daily Eagle,* July 21, 1893, p. 2.

p. 33 **"I am glad to be able to play":** Keeler was quoted in the *New York Sun,* July 28, 1893, p. 4.

p. 34 **"gilt-edged":** This is from the *Brooklyn Daily Eagle,* July 30, 1893.

p. 34 **threw up his hands in horror:** This is verbatim from the *New York World*, Aug. 4, 1893, p. 6.

p. 34 **"no, not in the big league":** Keeler was quoted in an interview with the *Brooklyn Daily Eagle* sometime in 1898, from the Keeler scrapbook.

p. 34 **"The worst thing that could happen":** Ibid.

p. 35 **Shredded Wheat:** This list is from *Victorian America: Transformations in Everyday Life 1876–1915,* by Thomas J. Schlereth (New York: HarperCollins, 1991), p. 174.

p. 36 **When the market for cigars slumped:** This account of Binghamton's labor troubles is drawn from *Parlor City Cigar Makers in the Gilded Age: Binghamton, N.Y., 1877–1894,* a 1988 honors thesis by Scott North at the New York State School of Industrial and Labor Relations, Cornell University, on file at the Broome County Public Library.

p. 36 **Ordinary people did not understand:** This is according to H. W. Brands, the author of *The Reckless Decade: America in the 1890s* (New York: St. Martin's Press, 1995), in an interview.

Chapter 3: Foxy Ned

p. 38 *"Nein":* This dialogue comes from a deposition that Harry von der Horst gave on Aug. 3, 1895, in a lawsuit filed in Baltimore City Circuit Court by his brother's three children. Harry recounted the dialogue back and forth in detailed paraphrases that I've turned into quotations. These papers are located in the Maryland State Archives in Annapolis.

p. 39 **it had cut him off from his source of cash:** This is according to the obituary of Harry von der Horst in *The Sun* (Baltimore), July 29, 1905, p. 12.

p. 40 **A golden eagle:** This description of the von der Horst brewery is drawn from *Brewing in Maryland,* by William J. Kelley, privately published in 1965, p. 372.

p. 40 **Every year at bock-beer time:** This is drawn from a 1951 article in *The Sun* (Baltimore), in the vertical files in the Maryland Room at the Enoch Pratt Free Library in Baltimore.

p. 40 **"Well, we don't win many":** Von der Horst is quoted with a thick German accent in *The Baltimore Orioles,* by Frederick G. Lieb (New York: G. P. Putnam's Sons, 1955), p. 13.

p. 41 **"My connection with the baseball club":** This quote is from a deposition that Harry von der Horst gave on June 27, 1895, in the case of *Henry R. von der Horst v. Lottie von der Horst, infant,* filed in 1894 in Baltimore City Circuit Court. The records are kept in the Maryland State Archives in Annapolis.

p. 41 **a quarter of the city's cigarmakers:** These figures are from *Baltimore: The Building of an American City,* by Sherry H. Olson (Baltimore: Johns Hopkins University Press, 1980), p. 228.

p. 41 **Open sewers ran along the curbs:** This is according to *Baltimore on the Chesapeake,* by Hamilton Owens (Garden City, N.Y.: Doubleday, Doran & Co. Inc., 1941), p. 301.

p. 41 **the most western of the eastern ports:** This was cited in an article, "A Maryland Pilgrimage," by Gilbert Grosvenor, in *The National Geographic Magazine,* Feb. 1927, p. 174.

p. 42 **The dirt and grime of an industrial age:** This phrase is from *Baltimore—A Not Too Serious History,* by Letitia Stockett (Baltimore: Norman, Remington Co., 1928), p. 136.

p. 42 **a crucible of colliding forces:** Thanks to Paul Starobin, a colleague at *National Journal,* for this phrase.

p. 43 **"That would seem to cover the whole business":** This is from the *Morning Herald,* May 3, 1892, p. 3.

p. 44 **big-time—a name:** These are the words that James Bready used in an interview in December 1994.

p. 45 **"A club that is demoralized":** Hanlon was quoted in *The Sun* (Baltimore) on May 6, 1892.

p. 46 **Their remuneration would depend upon their efficiency:** This is verbatim from the paraphrase in *The Sun* (Baltimore), May 10, 1892, from which the account of the session in the Gibson House is drawn.

p. 46 **He had acquired his nickname:** Bready tells the story of Sadie McMahon's nickname in the 1984 edition of *The Home Team,* p. 114.

p. 46 **Indeed, he had apparently murdered a man:** The story of Carmen Malascalza's murder and John McMahon's trial is drawn from a Wilmington, Del., newspaper called *Every Evening,* May 10–11 and Oct. 1–2, 1888.

p. 47 **Later he claimed never to:** McMahon was quoted in *The Sun* (Baltimore), July 11, 1948, p. 2.

p. 47 **It was a record for batsmen:** The record of seven hits in a nine-inning game, which Robinson accomplished on June 10, 1892, was tied in 1975 by Rennie Stennett of the Pittsburgh Pirates.

p. 47 **With the Athletics he had been:** This story is drawn from a 1926 article about Wilbert Robinson in *The Elks Magazine.*

p. 48 **One day he was sitting on the bench:** This anecdote about McGraw comes from *The Great Baseball Managers,* by Charles B. Cleveland (New York: Crowell, 1950), p. 53.

p. 48 **It was never a game to him:** This insight is almost verbatim from *John McGraw,* by Charles C. Alexander (New York: Viking Penguin Inc., 1988), p. 106.

p. 48 **"A ballgame—any ballgame":** McGraw wrote this is an article intended for *Liberty,* but apparently never published, in the Arthur Mann papers in the Library of Congress.

p. 49 **Pittsburgh gave the Orioles $2,000:** Some accounts put the figure at $2,500.

p. 49 **"I had my eye on Kelly":** Hanlon was quoted in *The Sun* (Baltimore), Sept. 30, 1892, p. 6.

p. 49 **They added an "e":** This is from an interview I conducted with Mary G. Kelley, the ballplayer's daughter-in-law, at her home in Silver Spring, Md.

p. 51 **"Cy"—short for "Cyclone":** The nickname had started in 1892, according to *Cy Young: Baseball's Legendary Giant,* by Ralph H. Romig (Philadelphia: Dorrance & Co., 1964), p. 29.

p. 51 **Soon a compromise appeared:** As the meeting opened, the *Brooklyn Daily Eagle*—presumably privy to Charley Byrne's thinking—had predicted a compromise of five feet. This was in a front-page story on March 7, 1893.

p. 52 **"The change will not materially advantage":** This was an article by Chadwick in the *Brooklyn Daily Eagle* on March 8, 1893, p. 2.

p. 52 **"will possibly have the effect":** This was in *The Sporting News* on March 18, 1893, p. 2.

p. 52 **"He'd say maybe three sentences a season":** Jack Doyle, the Orioles' first baseman in 1896–97, was quoted in Bready's *The Home Team.*

p. 53 **"A ballplayer, to be successful":** Jennings was quoted in *Sporting Life,* May 25, 1912.

p. 53 **one of the most phenomenal stops:** This is verbatim from the *Baltimore American,* June 7, 1893, p. 3.

p. 54 **He would let the men mingle:** This is drawn from an article by Albert Mott, the Baltimore correspondent for *Sporting Life,* in early November 1895, in the Keeler scrapbook.

p. 54   **Not since 'ninety-one:** His streak of playing in 727 consecutive games was a record that stood until Everett Scott of the Boston Red Sox and the New York Yankees broke it in the 1920s.

p. 54   **Hanlon bought him cheaply:** The reports of the purchase price ranged from $800 to $1,000 to $2,500.

p. 55   **"I decided early in the game":** Hanlon was quoted in an unidentified clipping in a scrapbook compiled by Steve Brodie's family.

p. 55   **Frank Selee, Boston's easygoing manager:** This account of the Beaneaters' style and strategy is drawn from "Frank Selee, Dynasty Builder," by A. D. Suehsdorf, in SABR's *A Review of Baseball History,* 1985, p. 37.

p. 55   **The fence in right field:** These dimensions of Union Park were calculated by Lauren T. Zuckerman, a ballpark historian in Los Angeles, using old fire insurance maps. He calculates the left field fence at 310 feet.

p. 56   **nerve seeds that came:** These advertisements appeared in the *Baltimore American,* May 5–9, 1893.

p. 56   **When it came to science:** These examples of Baltimore firsts come from *The Amiable Baltimoreans,* by Francis F. Beirne (Baltimore: Johns Hopkins University Press, 1951), pp. 299–307.

p. 56   **"The game, like all things":** Hanlon was quoted in the *New York Sun,* republished in the *Morning Herald,* Aug. 17, 1897, p. 7. He was comparing scientific baseball at the time to ten years earlier.

p. 57   **He was jeered at:** What happened to Treadway is drawn from the *New York Sun,* Jan. 4, 1894, p. 8.

p. 58   **Hanlon had seen something in:** This is baseball researcher Al Kermisch's conclusion about Hanlon's view of Keeler.

p. 58   **"What's the matter?" Hanlon demanded:** This episode, including the dialogue, was recounted by Hughey Jennings in a 1926 column in the *New York World,* in the Keeler scrapbook.

p. 59   **"The Macon camp":** This is from *The Baltimore Orioles,* by Frederick G. Lieb (New York: G. P. Putnam's Sons, 1955), p. 45.

p. 59   **"This is a devil of an occupation":** Brouthers was quoted in the *Morning Herald,* April 8, 1894, p.3.

p. 59   **"Work, work, work, work":** Jennings was quoted in *Sporting Life,* July 5, 1902, p. 6.

p. 60   **Every evening and any day:** Much of this paragraph is drawn from "Hanlon's Heroes: Another Flock of Orioles," by Jim Miller, an amateur baseball historian and the executive vice-president of the New Orleans Saints in the NFL, in the *Orioles Magazine* that was distributed at Oriole Park at Camden Yards on opening day in 1994.

p. 60   **"would put the Princeton football eleven":** This is from *The Sun* (Baltimore), April 5, 1894, p. 6.

p. 60   **He did not hesitate to call:** This sentence and the next are almost verbatim from the *New York Sun,* respectively, on July 24, 1893, p. 8, and July 25, p. 3.

p. 60   **"He is eminently a just man":** Keeler was quoted in an unidentified clipping, apparently from a Brooklyn newspaper in late 1897, in the Keeler scrapbook.

p. 60   **"All wool and a yard wide":** Hanlon was quoted in the *Morning Herald,* April 1, 1894, p. 6.

p. 60 **Right field, when properly played:** This is from *Base-Ball: How to Become a Player,* by John Montgomery Ward, 1888, p. 116.

p. 60 **Willie had started playing right field:** Hanlon told this anecdote in Keeler's obituary in *The Sun* (Baltimore) on Jan. 2, 1923.

p. 60 **"I will make those Brooklyn people":** Hanlon was quoted in the *Morning Herald,* March 27, 1894, p. 6.

p. 61 **he stepped straight into each pitch:** This is close to verbatim from Arthur Mann's manuscript of *The Real McGraw,* by Blanche McGraw, p. 104, from the Arthur Mann papers at the Library of Congress.

p. 61 **In a corner of the dimly lit cellar:** The story of how Jennings stopped bailing out is drawn from Alexander, p. 37, and an article in *BonaVenture,* the college's student newspaper, on July 17, 1973, p. 4.

p. 61 **"At first it was an awkward manner":** Jennings was quoted in his obituary by Stoney McLinn, in an unidentified publication, in the Jennings file at the Hall of Fame.

p. 61 **"Why, he never touched me!":** Joe Kelley's dream is recounted in *The Sun* (Baltimore), April 7, 1894.

p. 62 **"Baseball, like everything else":** This was in the *Sunday Herald,* April 8, 1894, p. 3.

Chapter 4: Baltimore's Grandest Parade

p. 63 **had hit more home runs as a ballplayer:** Roger Connor's 138 career home runs stood as a record until Babe Ruth broke it in 1921.

p. 64 **good-naturedly wished each other misfortune:** This is almost verbatim from *The Sun* (Baltimore), April 19, 1894, p. 6.

p. 64 **"The Southern trip benefited the Baltimores":** Ward was quoted in the *Baltimore American,* April 19, 1894, p. 3.

p. 65 **Nobody before Hanlon:** Charles Alexander, on p. 327 of his McGraw biography, wrote, "Apparently until Hanlon came along, it had never occurred to anybody connected with the club that the appropriate colors for a team named the Baltimore Orioles should be those of a Baltimore oriole."

p. 67 **"For the time being, caste":** This is from the *Baltimore American,* April 20, 1894, p. 3.

p. 67 **"Beer, ginger ale, lemonade, cigars":** The shouts of the vendors were reported in the *Morning Herald,* April 20, 1894, p. 2.

p. 67 **the sausage-like sandwiches:** This derivation of what became known as hot dogs is described by H. L. Mencken in *Happy Days: 1880–1892* (New York: Alfred A. Knopf, 1940), p. 40.

p. 68 **"The only way I have ever managed to hit Amos":** Keeler was quoted in an unidentified clipping, in the Keeler scrapbook.

p. 69 **In the bleachers, the cranks rose:** "[W]hen enthusiasm got to work at their muscles and pulled them to their feet the surging throng rolled from one side to the other like 'fake' waves in a tank drama," the *Morning Herald* reported on April 20, 1894, p. 2.

p. 69   **And somewhere there is laughter:** This takeoff of "Casey at the Bat," published and first performed in 1888, appeared in the *Morning Herald,* April 20, 1894, p. 6.

p. 69   **"None of the boys will require larger sizes":** This was from *The Sun* (Baltimore), April 22, 1894, p. 7.

p. 69   **"That one series made the Orioles":** This was in an excerpt of McGraw's *My Thirty Years in Baseball,* published in the *New York Evening World,* Jan. 20, 1923, in the Keeler scrapbook.

p. 70   **Out along the York road:** This description of the Oxford House is drawn from the *Morning Herald,* April 23, 1894, p. 6, and reprinted in the *New York Clipper,* May 5, 1894. The article says that eleven Orioles stayed there but only names ten. York Road is now Greenmount Avenue.

p. 70   **"Aggressiveness":** McGraw wrote this in *My Thirty Years in Baseball,* p. 66.

p. 70   **"His skin is full of baseball":** This description of McGraw is from the *Morning Herald,* April 23, 1894, p. 6.

p. 70   **"Woe betide the player":** McGraw wrote this in his autobiography, in an excerpt in the *New York Evening World,* Jan. 20, 1923.

p. 70   **The champion Beaneaters, who:** To this day, fourteen runs still counts as the record for a ninth-inning rally.

p. 71   **Legend later had it:** This tale of Brouthers's 110-mile home run was written in an undated *I Remember Where . . .* column in the *Sun Magazine* in the vertical files at the Enoch Pratt Free Library.

p. 71   **"Oh yes it takes nerve":** Jennings was quoted in *The Sun* (Baltimore), June 27, 1903, p. 9.

p. 71   **"Then we'd go out to the ballpark":** This is from the McGraw article for *Liberty* in the Arthur Mann papers.

p. 71   **For hours they calibrated the chances:** In his *Liberty* article, McGraw claimed credit (with Keeler and Jennings) for inventing the squeeze play. But according to *The Dickson Baseball Dictionary, Hy Turkin's Baseball Almanac* says the play was first used by two Yale players in a game against Princeton on June 16, 1894, and was introduced to the major leagues in either 1898 or 1904.

p. 72   **"Batters of the new school":** Hanlon was quoted in the *Morning Herald,* May 28, 1894, p. 2. He was referring specifically to Keeler and utility infielder Frank Bonner.

p. 72   **"In addition to superior physical qualities":** This is from an editorial in the *Morning Herald,* June 10, 1894, p. 4.

p. 72   **the savage strikes:** Historian Eric Goldman wrote in *Rendezvous with Destiny: A History of Modern American Reform* (New York: Knopf, 1952), on pp. 52–53, "The 12 months that began in the middle of 1894 have been called the 'annee terrible' of the post–Civil War period, and the phrase is not overly dramatic for the record of savage strikes and brutal labor repression, deepening agricultural distress, and a national atmosphere of foreboding at the top and bitterness at the bottom."

p. 73   **Made of Italian marble:** The details about John von der Horst's burial vault were reported in *The Sun* (Baltimore), July 19, 1893, p. 8.

p. 73   **Lena, a family member:** She testified to this in the Circuit Court of Baltimore City on July 19, 1894.

Notes

p. 73 **Barely two weeks after the old man died:** Lena Wilkins filed her petition in court on July 20, 1894.

p. 74 **For a while it seemed:** This account of the Pullman strike almost stranding the Orioles is drawn from Jim Miller's article "Hanlon's Heroes: Another Flock of Orioles," in the *Orioles Magazine* that was distributed at Oriole Park at Camden Yards on opening day in 1994.

p. 74 **"You ought to go home":** Brodie was quoted in the *Washington Times,* according to the *Morning Herald,* June 19, 1899, p. 5. When this happened isn't clear.

p. 75 **"seem to think they are doing":** Hanlon was quoted in the *Morning Herald,* May 28, 1894, p. 2.

p. 75 **"Yes, those are the bruises":** Mrs. Mullane's July 7 testimony was quoted in the *Morning Herald,* July 9, 1894, p. 3.

p. 75 **By season's end the Orioles had spent:** This was the judgment of the *Morning Herald,* Sept. 13, 1894, p. 2.

p. 76 **An old black man stationed himself:** This anecdote comes from the *New York Evening Telegram,* republished in the *Morning Herald,* Aug. 17, 1894, p. 2.

p. 76 **the terror of visiting ballplayers:** These are the words that Johnny Evers used in describing Union Park's right field, in *Touching Second,* by John J. Evers and Hugh S. Fullerton (Chicago: The Reilly & Britton Co., 1910), p. 294. He also described the "rough and weedy" ground and the sloped fence.

p. 77 **"He knew his territory like a child its ABCs":** Brodie was quoted in *The Sun* (Baltimore) in Keeler's obituary, Jan. 2, 1923, p. 10.

p. 77 **Once, Willie and Brodie both went tearing:** This anecdote and the fact that Keeler could not be seen from home plate are from *The Sporting News,* Feb. 22, 1923. Hughey Jennings is quoted telling the same story in an unidentified newspaper story dated Nov. 12, 1928, in the Jennings file at the Hall of Fame.

p. 77 **His voice was rarely heard:** This is drawn from the description of Keeler in *Microsoft Complete Baseball,* the 1994 edition of the CD-ROM.

p. 77 **"It was all done for its psychologic effect":** McGraw wrote this in his article for *Liberty,* in the Arthur Mann papers.

p. 77 **as much for diversion as demonstration:** This is almost verbatim from the *Morning Herald,* Sept. 2, 1894, p. 11.

p. 78 **"Why, he is so fast":** This was quoted in an unidentified scrap of a clipping on a page marked "1894" in the Keeler scrapbook.

p. 78 **"Keeler had the best batting eye":** McGraw wrote this assessment of Keeler in his article in *Liberty.*

p. 79 **"Say, I think I'm the luckiest guy":** Keeler was quoted in an unidentified clipping in the Keeler file at the Hall of Fame.

p. 80 **"The success of the Baltimores":** The grain merchant and numerous other Baltimoreans were interviewed in the *Morning Herald,* Sept. 23, 1894, p. 11.

p. 81 **The shouts awakened the ballplayers:** This account of the Orioles' train trip back to Baltimore is drawn from the *Morning Herald* and *The Sun* (Baltimore), Oct. 3, 1894, p. 1.

p. 81 He was presented with a colossal glass bat: The bat, which the Frostburg, Md., team had won from the Cumberland team in 1882, was destroyed during a fire at Oriole Park in 1944.

p. 82 By five o'clock some five thousand cranks: The *Morning Herald* attributed these estimates to unnamed "persons accustomed to big crowds," on Oct. 3, 1894, p. 1.

p. 82 More than two hundred thousand people came out: This was the crowd estimate in *The Sun* (Baltimore), Oct. 3, 1894, p. 10.

p. 83 A precocious fourteen-year-old: This is according to *Mencken: A Life*, by Fred Hobson (New York: Random House, 1994), p. 50.

p. 83 The parade went on for miles: *The Sun* (Baltimore) estimated the length of the parade at five miles. The *Morning Herald* said two miles.

p. 83 Ugly on the outside: "For nearly fifty years the old hostelry at the top of Liberty street hill, so hideous outwardly and so charming within, has been a great deal more than a mere hotel; it has been one of the salient institutions of Baltimore—as much so, almost, as Lexington Market," H. L. Mencken, who'd eaten more than three thousand meals there, wrote in *The Evening Sun* on Feb. 15, 1932, as the Rennert was closing.

p. 83 "Glasses up," he ordered: This account is from *The Sun* (Baltimore), Oct. 3, 1894, p. 10.

p. 84 "If I could only get five minutes' rest": This unidentified Oriole, "upon whom the 'rooters' have showered an especially large share of attention," was quoted in the *Morning Herald* on Oct. 4, 1894, p. 2.

p. 84 the decision by Baltimore's management: Fred Lieb reported the doubling of ticket prices in *The Baltimore Orioles*, p. 56.

p. 85 "That agreement goes": The exchange between McGraw and Davis was reported in the *Morning Herald*, March 25, 1895, p. 2.

p. 85 "We play the series": Robbie was quoted by O. P. Caylor in the *Sunday Herald*, Aug. 18, 1895, p. 6.

Chapter 5: The Big Four

p. 87 Shortly before midnight: This account of the Union Park fire is from the *Morning Herald*, Jan. 15, 1895, p. 2. The account in the *Baltimore American* has Murphy already awake when the fire broke out, frantically trying to squelch it while shouting a warning.

p. 87 "The stands were burned": Murphy was quoted in the *Baltimore American*, Jan. 15, 1895, p. 3.

p. 88 "So you see it won't take": Keeler described his off-season in a letter from Brooklyn to the *Morning Herald*, dated Jan. 31 and published Feb. 2, 1895, p. 2.

p. 88 "We have had a prosperous winter": Kelley's letter was printed in the *Morning Herald* on Feb. 6, 1895, p. 6.

p. 88 Dan Brouthers, almost thirty-seven: This is what columnist O. P. Caylor reported in the *Morning Herald* on March 3, 1895, p. 6, though it may have been fanciful.

Notes

p. 89   **They prayed together every Sunday:** This is according to Al Kermisch.

p. 89   **(Willie and Hughey would double-date):** This is from an interview with Charles Keeler.

p. 89   **"The question that is always uppermost":** This is from McGraw's *My Thirty Years in Baseball,* p. 111.

p. 89   **The attendance had more than doubled:** The attendance at Union Park in Baltimore had grown from 93,589 in 1892 to 143,000 in 1893 to 328,000 in 1894, according to the 1997 edition of *Total Baseball.*

p. 89   **the $1,500 they had been paid in 'ninety-four:** This is according to a letter from Hanlon to August ("Garry") Herrmann on Jan. 23, 1906, in the Hanlon file at the Hall of Fame.

p. 89   **Would they not be earning five times as much:** According to historical data from the federal Census Bureau, the average wage earner in manufacturing earned $420 in 1893, $386 in 1894, and $416 in 1895.

p. 90   **"Players should remember":** This is from the *Morning Herald,* Feb. 10, 1895, p. 6.

p. 90   **He reminded them he had offered raises:** This account is drawn from *The Sun* (Baltimore), March 1, 1895, p. 6.

p. 90   **"Players always hold out":** This is from Hanlon's Jan. 23, 1906, letter to Herrmann.

p. 90   **Nary a cheer went up:** This sentence is almost verbatim from the *Morning Herald,* March 12, 1895, p. 6.

p. 91   **"Colluded . . . fraud":** These quotations are from the petition of Lena V. Wilkins, filed on Sept. 24, 1894.

p. 91   **He would say only:** This was reported in *The Sun* (Baltimore), Dec. 10, 1894, p. 10.

p. 92   **"He is of convivial habits":** Emma von der Horst's quotations are from her petition to Circuit Court No. 2 in Baltimore City, filed in Jan. 1895.

p. 93   **The simple wood-planked dressing room at Union Park:** This portrait of life in the Orioles' clubhouse is drawn from a feature in the *Morning Herald,* Aug. 11, 1895, p. 7.

p. 94   **on Twenty-fourth street:** According to James Bready, the address for McGraw and Jennings was 14 Twenty-fourth street, now W. Twenty-fourth.

p. 94   **"A band of comrades":** Jennings's reminiscences to the *Brooklyn Daily Eagle* were republished in *The Sun* (Baltimore) on June 27, 1903, p. 9.

p. 94   **"Teamwork was our middle name":** McGraw wrote this in *My Thirty Years in Baseball,* p. 68. The second part of the quotation is from the same book, excerpted in the *Evening World,* Jan. 20, 1923.

p. 94   **He would take a short quick chop:** This is almost verbatim from *Sporting Life,* Nov. 14, 1908, p. 6.

p. 95   **"Every boxman has a weakness":** Keeler was quoted in an interview, apparently with the *Brooklyn Daily Eagle* in 1897, in the Keeler scrapbook.

p. 95   **"I have never been able to find out":** Keeler's discourse on batting slumps was quoted in the *New York Sun,* in an undated clipping marked "1895" in the Keeler scrapbook.

p. 95   **"To think that so small a man"**: This statement from *Sporting Life* was republished in the *Morning Herald,* July 30, 1895, p. 6.

p. 95   **the rhythm and sound of the nursery rhyme:** This is suggested in a monograph on Keeler by John J. Rainey of Troy, N.Y., which is in the Keeler vertical file at Cooperstown.

p. 95   **He cried bitterly and shook:** This sentence and the next one are drawn from Frank Patterson, who covered the Orioles for *The Sun* (Baltimore), in an unidentified clipping the following year in the Keeler scrapbook.

p. 95   **"Even when the ball beat him to second"**: Bill Clarke was quoted on McGraw in the article on the Baltimore Orioles in *The Ball Clubs* (New York: HarperPerennial, 1996), by Donald Dewey and Nicholas Acocella, p. 12.

p. 96   **McGraw became known for holding baserunners:** The only instance in which Al Kermisch, the baseball researcher, has found direct evidence that McGraw held a baserunner by the belt came in an exhibition game against the minor league club in Erie. The player who unbuckled his belt has variously been said to be Pete Browning, Ed Delehanty, and Mike Kelly.

p. 96   **"Look here, old man"**: This back-and-forth between McGraw and Keefe is quoted in a *Boston Herald* clipping that Henry Chadwick pasted into his diary for July 23, 1895, in the Chadwick diaries at the New York Public Library.

p. 96   **One afternoon, playing in Boston:** This version of the anecdote is taken from Fred Lieb's *The Baltimore Orioles* (New York: G. P. Putnam's Sons, 1955), pp. 68–69.

p. 96   **"I think Mr. Kelley is the handsomest"**: This anecdote was in the *Boston Herald,* republished in the *Morning Herald,* Aug. 20, 1897, p. 7.

p. 97   **"What's the matter, Ed"**: This dialogue is from an article called "Golden Days of the Orioles," in *The Sun* (Baltimore), p. 1 of the features section, July 11, 1948. McMahon died in 1954.

p. 97   **The team had earned its name:** This is according to *Misfits! The Cleveland Spiders in 1899: A Day-by-Day Narrative of Baseball Futility,* by J. Thomas Hetrick (McFarland & Co. Inc., 1991), p. 2.

p. 97   **"Show me a team of fighters"**: This was quoted in an article on Tebeau by William McMahon in *Nineteenth Century Stars,* published in 1989 by the Society for American Baseball Research.

p. 97   **Hanlon had said that Charley Esper:** This anecdote comes from *The Sun* (Baltimore), Sept. 11, 1895, p. 6.

p. 99   **"There is not a man in the party"**: This is from the Oct. 8, 1895, account in the *Cleveland Plain Dealer,* p. 2.

p. 100   **"Can Anson act?"**: This is from O. P. Caylor's column in the *Sunday Herald* in Baltimore, Nov. 24, 1895, p. 9.

p. 100   **The chief kicker's face looked:** This is drawn, much of it verbatim, from O. P. Caylor's column in the *Sunday Herald,* Dec. 8, 1895, p. 5.

p. 100   **"Jack is quite a ballplayer"**: Keeler was quoted in O. P. Caylor's column in the *Sunday Herald,* Jan. 19, 1896, p. 4.

p. 100   **"He is one of our kind of men"**: Hanlon was quoted in the *Morning Herald,* Nov. 17, 1895, p. 4. The last part of the quotation is from an unidentified clipping in the Keeler scrapbook.

Notes

p. 101　**"We start south this year"**: Hanlon was quoted in the *Morning Herald,* Jan. 26, 1896, p. 4.

p. 101　**"I am very much in favor of a third term"**: Hanlon was quoted in the *Morning Herald,* Nov. 17, 1895, p. 4.

p. 101　**from sponge baths to:** This is according to Alexander's biography of McGraw, p. 49.

p. 102　**A six-footer seized Willie Keeler:** This anecdote, including the policeman's quotation, is from the *Morning Herald,* April 10, 1896, p. 6.

p. 102　**"Look here," Quarles said menacingly:** This was Kelley's account of the fight as told to the *Morning Herald,* April 11, 1896, p. 6.

p. 103　**"Schoolboys in the field":** This was from the *Morning Herald,* April 17, 1896, p. 6.

p. 105　**the most fervent left-handed compliments:** This phrase was O. P. Caylor's in a column in the *Sunday Herald* on Feb. 2, 1896. The incident against the Giants at the Polo Grounds happened near the end of the 1895 season.

p. 105　**"That old conquer-all spirit":** This is from the *Morning Herald,* May 6, 1896, p. 6.

p. 106　**"His appearance put new life":** This is from the *Morning Herald,* Aug. 26, 1896, p. 6.

p. 107　**"Three cheers for Hughey Jennings Bryan":** This quotation and the ensuing description are drawn from the *Morning Herald*'s account on Sept. 20, 1896, pp. 1–3.

p. 107　**Music Hall, on Mount Royal avenue:** This later became known as the Lyric.

p. 109　**"[H]e pitched very good ball":** This was from the Oct. 3 entry in a handwritten diary that Keeler kept from Sept. 27 apparently to Dec. 5, 1896. This was sent to me by John Clegg of Chagrin Falls, Ohio, a relative of Keeler's by marriage.

p. 109　**twenty-five cents for the bleachers:** This was reported in the *Morning Herald,* under the headline "Back to Popular Prices," on Oct. 4, 1896, p. 10.

p. 110　**"we expect to win it the first day":** This is from Keeler's diary for Oct. 6.

p. 110　**filled with champagne—fifteen bottles:** The *Morning Herald* reported that the cup held fifteen quarts. Keeler wrote in his diary that it held seventeen bottles and was filled and drained three times, though fifty-one bottles for a team of fourteen men or so seems unlikely.

p. 110　**Now Wee Willie Keeler had captured:** This is drawn from Lieb's history of the Orioles, p. 66, as is the judgment that the Orioles were the best team yet.

p. 111　**Ted Sullivan, the gruff old manager:** These facts about Sullivan come from an article on him by Harold Dellinger in SABR's *Nineteenth Century Stars* (SABR, 1989), edited by Robert L. Tiemann and Mark Rucker, p. 120.

p. 111　**"Today was one of the finest days":** These comments are from Keeler's diary for Oct. 22, 1896.

p. 111　**"It is a shame, after so many people":** Keeler's letter to Prof. James A. Diffenbaugh, the deputy collector of the Port of Baltimore, was published in an unidentified clipping in the Keeler scrapbook.

p. 111　**"you can't imagine how beautiful":** This is from Keeler's diary entry for Oct. 25, 1896.

p. 111   **"a board walk just like"**: Ibid., Oct. 27, 1896.

p. 111   **"Keeler alone was bored"**: Kelley's letter was quoted at length in a column by O. P. Caylor in the *Sunday Herald,* Nov. 15, 1896, p. 9.

p. 112   **"Bryan got it good and hard"**: This was in a letter that Kelley sent to Wilbert Robinson from Brussels, quoted in an unidentified clipping in the Keeler scrapbook.

p. 112   **"Amsterdam is a very pretty city"**: This is from Keeler's diary for Nov. 11, 1896.

p. 112   **"Your first glimpse of Paris"**: Keeler's description of Paris is from his diary entry for Nov. 16, 1896.

p. 112   **"one of the most gruesome places"**: Keeler described the Catacombs in his diary entry for Nov. 21, 1896.

Chapter 6: Individual Glory

p. 113   **As the band played the opening strains:** This paragraph is almost verbatim from the *Morning Herald,* April 23, 1897, p. 9.

p. 114   **KEELER, THE WONDER:** This headline is from an unidentified newspaper, in the Keeler scrapbook.

p. 115   **"Keeler is not a hard hitter"**: This is from an unidentified clipping in the Keeler scrapbook, early in the 1897 season.

p. 115   **He was a big left-hander:** This portrait of Killen is drawn from Robert L. Tiemann's profile of him in SABR's *Nineteenth Century Stars,* published in 1989.

p. 115   **He did not feel right:** This is Al Kermisch's conclusion. The *Morning Herald* reported that he was ordered to the bench.

p. 115   **"but he kept up his record"**: This was from the *Morning Herald,* June 17, 1897, p. 9.

p. 115   **"And I'll beat them, too"**: Killen was quoted in the *Sunday Herald,* June 20, 1897, p. 11.

p. 115   **The weak-kneed pitcher:** Part of this description of Killen's metamorphosis is verbatim from the *Baltimore American,* June 20, 1897, p. 13.

p. 115   **after forty-four games:** This is still the National League record for hits in consecutive games in a season—which is how the record is officially framed. Pete Rose tied it in 1978. Joe DiMaggio set the American League record in 1941, hitting safely in fifty-six consecutive games.

p. 116   **on Howard street:** No known photograph exists of The Diamond, which was located at 519 N. Howard Street.

p. 116   **One day, The Diamond's manager:** This account of the origin of duckpins at The Diamond is taken from *The Book of Duckpin Bowling,* by Henry Fankhauser and Frank Micolizzi (Cranbury, N.J.: A. S. Barnes & Co. Inc., 1969), pp. 17–18.

p. 116   **"Robbie was the sugar"**: McGraw wrote this in *My Thirty Years in Baseball,* p. 114.

p. 117   **handsome and roomy row houses, side by side:** McGraw lived at 2738 St. Paul and Robinson at 2740 St. Paul.

p. 117   **the daughter of a clerk:** Alexander, on p. 52 of his McGraw biography, described Minnie Doyle as the daughter of a retired clerk for the city's Appeals Tax Court. Bready, on p. 31 of *The Home Team,* described her as a printer's daughter.

p. 117   **On the same day as Kel's wedding:** Both Kelley and Jennings were married on Oct. 14, 1897. Kelley had announced his plans around the time of McGraw's wedding, while Jennings made his plans in September. The description of Elizabeth Dixon comes from an interview with Grace Doherty, the granddaughter of Hughey and Elizabeth Jennings, on April 24, 1997.

p. 117   **he had a sacrament:** This was James Bready's idea, offered in an interview.

p. 118   **he carried a looking-glass under his cap:** Umpire Burnham was the source of the story about Kelley carrying the mirror under his cap, according to the *Cincinnati Enquirer.* The same newspaper reported the tale of the mirror popping out of Kelley's pocket, at a game in early July 1897. These items were reprinted in the *Morning Herald,* July 9, 1897, p. 7.

p. 119   **"Yes, get out":** This is Doyle's version of what Jennings said, as he reported in an interview with the *Morning Herald,* May 25, 1899, p. 9.

p. 119   **"I got my Dutch up":** Stenzel was quoted in the *Pittsburgh Press,* as reprinted in the *Morning Herald,* Sept. 8, 1897, p. 5.

p. 119   **He was cold-blooded:** This is what James Bready said of Doyle, whom he interviewed.

p. 119   **"in a cowardly manner":** McGraw comment to *The Sun* (Baltimore), July 8, 1897, p. 6, was quoted in Alexander's *John McGraw,* p. 54.

p. 120   **When Willie returned to the diamond:** This story of the Keeler-McGraw fistfight comes from Bready's *Home Team,* p. 111. He left the detail of what McGraw said out of the book but related it in an interview, though he cautioned he had been told this story by Doyle, who disliked McGraw.

p. 120   **"What did you mean by cursing me":** This exchange is quoted on p. 54 of Alexander's biography of McGraw.

p. 120   **"At least ninety percent of the batsmen":** Mercer was quoted in the *Morning Herald,* May 27, 1897, p. 9.

p. 120   **When Chick Stahl hit a long fly:** This anecdote is taken (much of it verbatim) from *Touching Second,* by John J. Evers and Hugh S. Fullerton (Chicago: The Reilly & Britton Co., 1910), p. 294. It isn't clear if it happened in 1897 or 1898.

p. 122   **Joe, ordinarily known for:** In an interview with *Sporting Life,* Dec. 12, 1900, p. 2, Oriole groundskeeper Tom Murphy said: "When Corbett retired from the game on the plea that a finger on his pitching hand had been hurt by a batted ball, that he could not work, Hanlon became suspicious, and after investigation, came to the conclusion that it was Joe's heart, and not his hand, that caused him to quit."

p. 123   **"If Stenzel made the catch":** Ibid.

p. 123   **the smallest man in the big league:** This is according to the *Morning Herald,* Oct. 18, 1897, p. 5.

p. 123   **"We can count on our fingers":** This quotation from Keeler and those in the next two paragraphs are from the *New York Clipper,* April 9, 1898, p. 97.

p. 124   **"I would not care so much if":** Hanlon was quoted in the *Morning Herald,* March 12, 1898, p. 9.

p. 125   **"I would like to have a photograph":** Hanlon was quoted in the *Morning Herald,* April 4, 1898, p. 9.

p. 126   **"How do you like that throw, Kelley?":** The unidentified bleacherite was quoted in the *Morning Herald,* April 9, 1898, p. 9.

p. 126   **"I think we have the strongest team":** Hanlon was quoted in the *Morning Herald,* April 12, 1898, p. 13.

p. 126   **Mothers and wives and sisters and:** This description is drawn from *The Sun* (Baltimore), April 26, 1898, p. 12.

p. 127   **In Newport News, Hughey Jennings had hired a boatman:** The anecdote about Jennings visiting the USS *Maine* was reported in the *Morning Herald,* Feb. 20, 1898, p. 7.

p. 127   **With his speed, curves:** This is almost verbatim from the description by John Chidwick, the chaplain on the *Maine,* quoted in *A Ship to Remember: The Maine and the Spanish–American War,* by Michael Blow (William Morrow and Company Inc., 1992), p. 82.

p. 127   **looking as spruce as ever:** This is verbatim from the *Morning Herald,* April 18, 1898, p. 5.

p. 128   **"Keeler's presence makes":** This is from the *Morning Herald,* May 17, 1898, p. 5.

p. 128   **"I have yet to hear Mr. Hanlon":** McJames was quoted in *The Washington Post,* as reported in the *Morning Herald,* June 21, 1898, p. 9.

p. 129   **DOPEY BALL PLAYING:** This headline is from the *Morning Herald,* June 7, 1898, p. 9.

p. 129   **The receipts just about paid:** This sentence is almost verbatim from the *Morning Herald,* June 8, 1898, p. 9.

p. 129   **Hanlon was convinced he could hit .300:** This was Hanlon's assessment of Holmes to *The Sun* (Baltimore), June 9, 1898, p. 8.

p. 129   **"Oh! Ducky, you're a lobster":** The Associated Press quoted "a fan" in the grandstand. The quotation from the Tammany henchman was reported in the *Morning Herald,* July 26, 1898, p. 9.

p. 129   **"Well, I'm glad I don't have to work":** This is the version in *The Ball Clubs,* p. 345. The Associated Press version was, "Well, I'm glad I'm not working for a sheeny anymore." The *Morning Herald* reported Holmes saying, "Well, I am not working for a 'Sheeny,' anyway."

p. 129   **"Lynch, I want that man Holmes thrown out":** This is from the account in the *New York Sun,* July 26, 1898, p. 4.

p. 130   **"Holmes, Freedman wants you to get off":** Ibid.

p. 130   **"This man Freedman needs":** Hanlon was quoted in the *Morning Herald,* July 29, 1898, p. 7.

p. 131   **In front of the Gibson House:** This story comes from an unidentified 1898 clipping in the Keeler scrapbook.

p. 133   **It had been lucky to break even:** Hughey Jennings was the source of the financial results for 1897–98 in "Baltimore, a Pioneer in Organized Baseball," by John H. Lancaster, in *Maryland Historical Magazine,* Vol. 35, No. 1, March 1940, p. 42.

p. 133   **filled up with winning:** This is James Bready's phrase, in an interview, in trying to explain why attendance fell off.

p. 133   **"When it was seen that we should lose":** McGraw wrote this in his autobiography, p. 117.

p. 134   **"I am a Baltimorean":** Von der Horst was quoted in the *Morning Herald,* Oct. 21, 1898, p. 5.

Chapter 7: Syndicate Baseball

p. 137   **"There is no significance in the concurrence":** McKelway's oration was printed in his newspaper on Jan. 2, 1898, pp. 4–5.

p. 138   **Manhattan drew the rich and the poor:** This description of the differences between Brooklyn and Manhattan is drawn from an article called "The City of Brooklyn," by Julian Ralph, in *Harper's New Monthly Magazine,* April 1893, pp. 652–53.

p. 139   **His father was the president:** This is according to John Thorn, the noted baseball expert and the editor of *Total Baseball,* in an interview.

p. 140   **"There is nobody backing me":** Ebbets was quoted in the *New York Sun,* Jan. 4, 1898, p. 8.

p. 140   **"The illness of Mr. Byrne":** Ebbets was quoted in the *Brooklyn Daily Eagle,* Jan. 2, 1898, p. 22.

p. 141   **the prospect of Charley Byrne's passing:** "When it was realized, recently, that the recovery of Mr. Byrne was hopeless, Mr. Abell concluded that it was time for him to sell out. Then came the opportunity for Charley Ebbetts [*sic*] to step into the breach . . ." Chadwick wrote in *The Sporting News,* Jan. 15, 1898.

p. 141   **"The man who always tells the truth":** Ebbets was quoted in *Sporting Life,* Jan. 9, 1909, p. 6.

p. 141   **He persuaded two trolley companies:** This was reported in the *Morning Herald,* Feb. 2, 1899, p. 5. The dollar figure is from the *New York Clipper,* March 4, 1899, p. 12.

p. 142   **"there will not be a hundred people":** The ex-manager, Billy Barnie, was quoted in the *Brooklyn Daily Eagle,* Jan. 26, 1899, p. 12.

p. 143   **"We intend to improve the service":** Brown was quoted in the *Baltimore American,* Dec. 10, 1898, p. 1.

p. 143   **"but," he said emphatically:** This quotation from Alex Brown is from the *Morning Herald,* Dec. 9, 1898, p. 3.

p. 143   **The railroad's board of directors:** This is according to *History of the Baltimore and Ohio Railroad,* by John F. Stover (West Lafayette, Ind.: Purdue University Press, 1987), pp. 190–91.

p. 144   **During the winter of 'ninety-eight:** This paragraph and the next one are drawn from *Baltimore: The Building of an American City,* by Sherry Olson (Baltimore: Johns Hopkins University Press, 1980), pp. 238–40.

p. 144   **He had been spending a quiet winter:** Keeler's winter was described in *The Sun* (Baltimore), Dec. 14, 1898, p. 6.

p. 144   **Manhattan just before Christmas:** This description is drawn from the *New York Sun,* Dec. 22, 1898, p. 3, and Dec. 25, p. 3.

p. 146   **"No proposition whatever":** Hanlon was quoted in the *Baltimore American,* Dec. 16, 1898, p. 4. His quotation in the next paragraph is from the same source.

p. 146   **It had been his and Charley Ebbets's notion:** This was in a draft of McGraw's *Liberty* article, evidently written by Arthur Mann, at the Library of Congress.

p. 147 **"We have something which"**: Abell was quoted in the *Baltimore American*, Dec. 17, 1898, p. 1. Hanlon's quotation is from the same source.

p. 147 **"had little to say and"**: This is from *The Sun* (Baltimore), Dec. 17, 1898, p. 8. The other headlines were on p. 1 of the respective newspapers on the same day.

p. 148 **"I shall do nothing hastily"**: Von der Horst was quoted in the *Baltimore American*, Dec. 19, 1898, p. 10.

p. 148 **"the biggest sensation"**: McGraw wrote this in *My Thirty Years in Baseball*, p. 117.

p. 148 **"It is a matter of business"**: This was from a news article in the *Morning Herald*, Dec. 17, 1898, p. 1.

p. 148 **The arithmetic worked:** These estimates were published in the *Brooklyn Daily Eagle*, Feb. 3, 1899, p. 12.

p. 148 **"I will be right here"**: Robinson and McGraw were quoted in *The Sun* (Baltimore), Dec. 17, 1898, p. 8.

p. 149 **he would make no move:** This paraphrase of Hanlon's views is almost verbatim from the *Morning Herald*, Dec. 16, 1898.

p. 149 **"Mr. Hanlon will have just the same authority"**: Abell was quoted in *The Sun* (Baltimore), Dec. 17, 1898, p. 8.

p. 149 **Several days later, in Baltimore:** This account of the meeting is from the *Morning Herald*, Dec. 23, 1898, p. 9.

p. 150 **he was reportedly unwilling to give up half:** "While the story has not been verified as yet, it is known that Vonderhorst and Hanlon have become disgusted with the poor attendance of the cranks in Baltimore during the past season and have been trying to arrange deals with Brooklyn and Philadelphia for the transfer of the Orioles. They were not successful as neither Ebbets nor [Philadelphia owners] Reach and Rogers would agree to parting with half their holdings," the *Brooklyn Daily Eagle* reported on Oct. 24, 1898, p. 5.

p. 150 **"I am in full control"**: Ebbets was quoted in an interview with the *Brooklyn Daily Eagle*, Nov. 15, 1898, p. 10.

p. 150 **"I can say frankly"**: Keeler was quoted in an interview with the *Brooklyn Daily Eagle*, Dec. 23, 1898, p. 11.

p. 150 **Joe Kelley had just bought:** The address of his home, still standing, is 2826 N. Calvert St.

p. 151 **"I think the Baltimore people"**: Jennings was quoted in the *Brooklyn Daily Eagle*, Dec. 20, 1898, p. 11.

p. 151 **talked over the situation and:** This is almost verbatim from the *New York Clipper*, Jan. 14, 1899, p. 777.

p. 151 **"If we are to be the stars"**: McGraw, Kelley, and Jennings were quoted in the *Baltimore American*, Dec. 20, 1898, p. 4.

p. 152 **"Baseball players will be"**: Von der Horst was quoted in *The Sun* (Baltimore), Dec. 20, 1898, p. 10.

p. 152 **"out for money"**: Clarke was quoted in *The Sun* (Baltimore), Dec. 17, 1898, p. 8.

p. 152 **"whoever takes charge as manager"**: Hanlon was quoted in *The Sun* (Baltimore), Jan. 7, 1899, p. 6. He actually started as manager in 1892.

p. 152 **"I consider Baltimore":** Hanlon was quoted in *The Sun* (Baltimore), Jan. 2, 1899, p. 5.

p. 153 **"Well, if they will not sell":** McGraw was quoted in *The Sun* (Baltimore), Jan. 17, 1899, p. 6.

p. 153 **"He is only looking for prominence":** Von der Horst was quoted in the *Morning Herald*, Feb. 2, 1899, p. 5.

p. 153 **"A swelled head":** This was ascribed to "some of [Abell's] associates," unnamed but obvious, in a letter from Edward Connor, at Twenty-third street and Fifth avenue in Brooklyn, published in the *Eagle*, Jan. 28, 1899, p. 9.

p. 153 **"Upon him alone":** This letter from "One Crank" was published in the *Eagle*, Jan. 25, 1899, p. 12.

p. 153 **"Shameful that a man":** This letter, from "A Constant Reader," was published in the *Brooklyn Daily Eagle* on Jan. 26, 1899, p. 12.

p. 154 **"If selling beer were attended":** Von der Horst was quoted in the *Baltimore American*, Feb. 3, 1899, p.4.

p. 154 **"It is all politics":** Barnie was quoted in the *Baltimore American*, Feb. 3, 1899, p. 4.

p. 155 **"Are there absolutely":** This exchange between the newspaperman and Ebbets is from *The Brooklyn Daily Eagle*, Feb. 5, 1899, p. 30.

p. 155 **"Baseball is in as bad shape":** Ibid. The *Eagle* quoted Ward as saying "replace" instead of "place," which was probably an error.

p. 155 **Abell and von der Horst:** This is how Seymour put the proportions of ownership in *Baseball: The Early Years*, p. 305. The *Baltimore American* reported the same proportions (without specifying how Hanlon and von der Horst would divide their 50 percent) on Feb. 6, 1899, p. 10. The *Brooklyn Daily Eagle* reported on Feb. 5, 1899, p. 30, that Hanlon and von der Horst would own 50 percent, Abell 30 percent, Ebbets 11 percent and the Brooklyn ballclub's lawyers "and others" the remaining 9 percent.

p. 155 **"I never made any such promise":** This scene at the Broadway Central Hotel was reported in the *New York Sun*, Feb. 6, 1899, p. 5.

p. 156 **three pitchers who had won a total of:** According to *Total Baseball*, Harry Howell's record was 2–0 and McKenna's was 2–6 in 1898, their rookie season. But a profile of McGraw by Arthur Mann (in his Library of Congress papers) puts McKenna's record at 1–7. The third pitcher, Joe McGinnity, had gone 10–3 for Peoria in 1898 but had never pitched before in the National League.

p. 156 **"I am well satisfied":** McGraw was quoted in the *Morning Herald*, March 21, 1899, p. 9.

p. 157 **for $2,600:** This is according to the financial ledgers of the Brooklyn ballclub for the years 1897, 1899, and 1900, found for me at the Hall of Fame archives by librarian James L. Gates, Jr. It shows that Jennings was paid the same, and Kelley was apparently paid $2,800 as the captain.

Chapter 8: Business Beats Sentiment

p. 158 **Every evening Willie Keeler put on his best duds:** This paragraph is drawn, some of it verbatim, from the *Augusta Chronicle*, March 29, 1899, p. 2. I found this courtesy of Robert Keeler, an anthropology professor at Clackamas Community College in Portland, Ore., who kindly shared his notes with me. He isn't related to Willie Keeler but has conducted some research on him.

p. 158 **"Were it not for my connection"**: Hanlon was quoted in the *New York Clipper,* March 21, 1899, p. 71.

p. 158 **"I can tell better how they will work"**: Ibid.

p. 159 **A wit in the press box:** Frank Graham, in *The Brooklyn Dodgers: An Informal History* (New York: G. P. Putnam & Sons, 1945), attributes the name to "some press box nimble-wit."

p. 159 **"Why, we have done more"**: Jack Ryan, the new backup catcher—Bill Clarke had been sold to Boston—was quoted in the *Morning Herald,* March 24, 1899, p. 9.

p. 159 **"We are liable to surprise some people"**: McGraw was quoted in the *New York Clipper,* March 25, 1899, p. 71.

p. 159 **"My outfield will compare favorably"**: Ibid.

p. 160 **"But for his almost supernatural work"**: This is from the *Morning Herald,* April 4, 1899, p. 9.

p. 160 **The cranks in Augusta had never seen:** "Without a doubt, Keeler's work individually was the greatest ever seen on the Augusta grounds," the *Augusta Chronicle* wrote on April 4, 1899, according to notes taken by Robert Keeler.

p. 160 **he was the easiest kind of pitcher:** "Broadway Aleck" Smith, who caught McGinnity for most of 1899 in Baltimore, was quoted in *Sporting Life,* May 26, 1900, p. 5: "In many respects he is one of the most wonderful men I ever saw in the box. He can put a ball over the plate more times and with more ease than any pitcher I know of. He is the easiest kind of pitcher to catch. The ball settles in your gloves [*sic*] like a feather. Why, I could sit down in a rocking chair and catch McGinnity."

p. 160 **"Why no"**: McGinnity was quoted in the *Morning Herald,* April 7, 1899, p. 9.

p. 160 **"Why, this fellow must have"**: Hanlon was quoted in the *Morning Herald,* April 7, 1899, p. 9.

p. 161 **"If I were a cartoonist"**: Robinson was quoted in the *Morning Herald,* April 6, 1899, p. 9.

p. 161 **"It's no use, Mac"**: This anecdote is from *The Real McGraw,* by Blanche S. McGraw and edited by Arthur Mann (New York: David McKay Co. Inc., 1953), p. 120.

p. 161 **"I could not get him off the field"**: Murphy was quoted in the *Brooklyn Daily Eagle,* May 10, 1899, p. 14, which reprinted the item from a paper called the *Exchange.*

p. 162 **A better ballplayer had:** Keeler was the "greatest with the possible exception of Lou Gehrig, ever to spring from the sidewalks of Greater New York," *The Sporting News* wrote in a profile on Feb. 16, 1939.

p. 162 **"I have requested my friends"**: Willie's letter was published in the *Brooklyn Daily Eagle,* April 12, 1899, p. 18.

p. 163 **"half a mile from the diamond"**: This is from a letter signed "H.G.T.W.," published in the *Brooklyn Daily Eagle* on Jan. 25, 1899, p. 12.

p. 163 **the haunting odor of the hot dogs:** This is almost verbatim from a letter to the *Brooklyn Daily Eagle,* published on Sept. 2, 1945, from Robert Ryder, who also enclosed a drawing of Washington Park as he remembered it.

p. 163 **nothing in the annals:** This judgment is almost verbatim from the *Brooklyn Daily Eagle,* April 16, 1899, p. 10.

p. 165 **"As fine a game":** For both Hanlon and Ebbets quotations, Ibid.

p. 165 **"No arrangements will be made":** The telegram from Giants secretary H. A. Bonnell to Harry Bormann, the bookkeeper at the von der Horst brewery who was now the secretary of the Orioles, was quoted in the *Brooklyn Daily Eagle,* April 4, 1899, p. 6.

p. 165 **an incident in the Waldorf-Astoria café:** This story was recounted in the *Baltimore American,* March 7, 1900, p. 4.

p. 166 **Under any conditions he was a dangerous:** This sentence is almost verbatim from the *Brooklyn Daily Eagle,* April 26, 1899, p. 14.

p. 166 **"It will be a month":** Hanlon was quoted in the *Brooklyn Daily Eagle,* April 25, 1899, p. 6.

p. 167 **"We landed at the top":** Hanlon was quoted in the *Brooklyn Daily Eagle,* May 23, 1899, p. 14.

p. 167 **"Don't consent to deal":** The text of Jennings's telegram and his verbal explanation were published in the *Brooklyn Daily Eagle,* July 18, 1899, p. 6.

p. 168 **A newspaperman in Cincinnati noticed:** This observation on McGraw is originally from the *Cincinnati Enquirer,* quoted in the *Morning Herald,* July 1, 1899, p. 9.

p. 168 **He seldom got fooled by a curveball:** This assessment of McGraw's strengths at the bat is drawn, some of it verbatim, from the *New York Telegram,* quoted in the *Morning Herald,* Sept. 1, 1899, p. 9.

p. 169 **"The Baltimores are soaring":** This is from the *Boston Herald,* quoted in the *Morning Herald,* June 17, 1899, p. 9.

p. 169 **"We will be up there somewhere":** McGraw was quoted in the *Cincinnati Enquirer,* as reported in the *Morning Herald,* June 27, 1899, p. 9.

p. 170 **"Imagine my surprise":** McGraw was quoted in the *Baltimore American,* Aug. 4, 1899, p. 4.

p. 170 **He had promised not to use Baltimore:** Hanlon was quoted to that effect in *The Sun* (Baltimore) on Jan. 10 and again on Feb. 13, 1899.

p. 170 **"They own the two clubs":** McGraw was quoted in the *Baltimore American,* Aug. 4, 1899, p. 4.

p. 170 **"Certainly the public would take":** This is from an editorial entitled "Syndicates in Sport," in the *Baltimore American,* Aug. 6, 1899, p. 4.

p. 171 **"a torrent of indignant protest":** This is from *The Sun* (Baltimore), Aug. 5, 1899, p. 6.

p. 171 **He phoned McGraw in Philadelphia:** This was according to *The Sun* (Baltimore), Aug. 5, 1899, p. 6. The *Brooklyn Daily Eagle* reported that Hanlon sent a telegram.

p. 171 **"I opposed the deal":** Hanlon was quoted in the *Brooklyn Daily Eagle,* Aug. 5, 1899, p. 14.

p. 171 **"I only desire the good":** This is from a telegram that von der Horst sent, apparently to the *Baltimore American,* quoted in full in the newspaper on Aug. 6, 1899, p. 12.

Notes

p. 172 **"The system of team play"**: This was in the *Morning Herald,* Sept. 1, 1899, p. 9, in an article from St. Louis that was headlined BIRDS DEMORALIZED.

p. 172 **"If McGraw had not met with"**: Robinson was quoted in the *Morning Herald,* Sept. 6, 1899, p. 9.

p. 173 **"The Brooklyn players want to win"**: Hanlon was quoted in the *New York Sun,* Aug. 10, 1899, republished in the *Morning Herald,* Aug. 12, 1899, p. 9.

p. 173 **The fanatics at Washington Park**: "Here the crowd is fickle, hurling sarcasm when it is behind and cheering on the victors under all circumstances," the *Brooklyn Daily Eagle* reported on Aug. 10, 1899, p. 10.

p. 173 **"They don't like to be picked up"**: This was written by John B. Foster, the Brooklyn correspondent for *Sporting Life,* in the edition of June 15, 1901, p. 5.

p. 174 **"Brooklyn will win"**: Von der Horst was quoted in the *Brooklyn Daily Eagle,* Aug. 17, 1899, p. 10.

p. 175 **"the Dewey of managers"**: Ebbets and McCaffrey were quoted in the *Brooklyn Daily Eagle* account of the testimonial, on Oct. 22, 1899, p. 8.

Chapter 9: Survival of the Fittest

p. 178 **Every so often the door to the parlor**: This is drawn from the *Brooklyn Daily Eagle,* Dec. 17, 1899, p. 38.

p. 178 **used a front man**: This is from p. 218 in the uncorrected proofs of *The League That Failed,* by David Quentin Voigt, published in 1998 by Scarecrow Press Inc. of Lanham, Md., which he and his editor, David Biesel, generously shared.

p. 178 **Later he physically attacked**: This is according to "The Abominable Owner," an article on Freedman by Mark Alvarez in *Sports Heritage,* Nov/Dec 1987, p. 45.

p. 180 **"Syndicate ball and methods"**: Freedman was quoted in an interview with the *New York Journal* on Nov. 16, 1899, reprinted in full in *Sporting Life,* Nov. 25, 1899, p. 5.

p. 180 **"The Baltimore club is not for sale"**: Von der Horst was quoted in the *Morning Herald,* Dec. 12, 1899, p. 8.

p. 181 **Hanlon considered it the only logical**: This is nearly verbatim from the paraphrase in the *Brooklyn Daily Eagle,* Oct. 29, 1899, p. 11.

p. 181 **"Where have you been, Harry?"**: The text of this exchange between von der Horst and Brush is from the *Baltimore American,* Dec. 16, 1899, p. 4.

p. 182 **"I have no hesitation in saying"**: Ebbets was quoted in the *Brooklyn Daily Eagle,* Dec. 17, 1899, p. 10.

p. 182 **"Of course, if we get our price"**: Hanlon was quoted in the *Morning Herald,* Dec. 18, 1899, p. 8.

p. 182 **"than all the previous history"**: This is from a *New York Times* editorial on Dec. 31, 1899, p. 20.

p. 183 **"The United States the Envy"**: This headline was from *The New York Times* on Jan. 1, 1900, p. 2 of its Annual Financial Review and Quotation Supplement.

p. 184 **The duelling armies of angry men**: This account is drawn mainly from the *Baltimore American* of Feb. 4, 1900, p. 11, *The Sun* (Baltimore), and *Sporting Life.*

p. 185 **"Yes, the jig is up"**: McGraw was quoted in the *Morning Herald,* Feb. 16, 1900, p. 8.

p. 185 **"The local sentiment":** Von der Horst was quoted in *Sporting Life*, Feb. 3, 1900, p. 3.

p. 186 **"For the fourteen hundredth time":** Hanlon was quoted in the *Baltimore American*, March 4, 1900, p. 12.

p. 186 **"I have been in the baseball business":** Abell was quoted in the *New York Evening World*, March 8, 1900, reprinted the following day in *The Sun* (Baltimore), p. 6.

p. 186 **"I am against you now":** The argument between Dreyfuss and Abell was reported in the *Baltimore American*, March 9, 1900, p. 4.

p. 188 **"We got our price":** Hanlon was quoted in the *Baltimore American*, March 9, 1900, p. 4.

p. 188 **"When I put my signature":** Von der Horst was quoted in the *Morning Herald*, March 10, 1900, p. 8.

p. 188 **a short walk from the Music Hall:** This is verbatim from *The Home Team*, by James H. Bready, p. 19, except for "Music Hall" in place of "Lyric," the current name.

p. 188 **"The idea of going away":** Robinson and McGraw were quoted in the *Morning Herald*, March 12, 1900, p. 8.

p. 189 **"a last resort":** Hanlon was quoted in *Sporting Life*, April 7, 1900, p. 2.

p. 189 **St. Louis was a good thirty hours:** This is from an 1897 railway schedule provided by Anne Calhoun, the archivist at the B&O Railroad Museum in Baltimore. So is the time estimate of a trip from Baltimore to New York.

p. 189 **How could they risk:** This accounting is from *Sporting Life*, March 24, 1900, p. 7.

p. 189 **"Hello, Mac":** This exchange between Abell and McGraw is from the *Baltimore American*, March 24, 1900, p. 9.

p. 190 **an ardent admirer:** This description of Gompers and his comments are from *Sporting Life*, April 7, 1900, p. 5.

p. 190 **"The game is not benefited":** Ebbets was quoted in the *New York Clipper*, Dec. 30, 1899, p. 923.

p. 190 **"I am capable of being a success":** The text of Jennings's letter to Harry Merrill of Wilkes-Barre was published in *Sporting Life*, March 31, 1900, p. 2.

p. 190 **"The grab-all policy of the present magnates":** Jennings was quoted in *Sporting Life*, March 31, 1900, p. 2.

p. 190 **"Not that I don't like Brooklyn":** Keeler was quoted in *Sporting Life*, March 31, 1900, p. 6.

p. 191 **Shock, disgust, grief:** "Baltimore's hard tumble out of the National Baseball League shocked the loyal rooters yesterday," *The Sun* (Baltimore) began on March 10, 1900, p. 6. "Baltimore's fall into a minor league condition filled the loyal with absolute disgust."

p. 191 **a perfect shriek of feminine "No's":** This is verbatim from *Sporting Life*, April 21, 1900, p. 8.

p. 192 **"Baltimore is not a minor city":** This is from an editorial in the *Baltimore American*, March 10, 1900, p. 6.

p. 192 **"made to join company with Buffalo":** This was in the *Morning Herald*, Jan. 19, 1900, p. 8.

p. 194 **"It may be a benefit and"**: Keeler was quoted in *Sporting Life*, March 24, 1900, p. 6.

p. 194 **"I had no luck"**: Keeler was quoted about the beginning of the season in *Sporting Life*, Aug. 11, 1900, p. 5.

p. 194 **"When there was a chance to bring"**: Keeler was quoted in *Sporting Life*, Nov. 17, 1900, p. 1.

p. 196 **"the swell heads got done up"**: These are from a sketch of the mood in 1900 in *Sporting Life*, June 28, 1902, p. 1.

p. 196 **"The transfer of the Baltimore team"**: This harsh assessment was written in retrospect by John B. Foster, the Brooklyn correspondent for *Sporting Life*, June 28, 1902, p. 1.

p. 196 **"I don't like Brooklyn at all"**: Jennings was quoted in *Sporting Life*, Dec. 2, 1899, p. 2.

p. 196 **He had become accustomed to sitting:** This anecdote was told by George H. Koch of 312 Weirfield St., Brooklyn, in a letter published in the *Eagle* on Nov. 23, 1952.

Chapter 10: A Competing League

p. 197 **"We were expecting two or three brass bands"**: Keeler described the Cuban tour in *Sporting Life*, Nov. 24, 1900, p. 8.

p. 198 **"From the very start"**: Jennings was quoted in the *Morning Herald*, Dec. 14, 1900, p. 4.

p. 198 **"They're only bluffing"**: Ebbets was quoted in *Sporting Life*, Dec. 22, 1900, p. 3.

p. 200 **"The sentiment was missing"**: This is from McGraw's autobiography, p. 124.

p. 200 **They would get themselves ejected:** This is from *Baseball and the American Dream*, by Joseph Durso (St. Louis: Sporting News Publishing Co., 1986), p. 62.

p. 200 **"The American League was formed to protect"**: Johnson was quoted in the *Morning Herald*, Jan. 20, 1901, p. 4.

p. 201 **"Today marks the beginning"**: Sheriff Schwatka's remarks at the groundbreaking ceremony for American League Park were reported in the *Morning Herald*, Feb. 13, 1901, p.4.

p. 201 **"Today I break ground"**: This legend on the spade was reported in the *Morning Herald*, Feb. 12, 1901, p. 4.

p. 202 **"Should any other club dispute"**: McGraw was quoted in *Sporting Life*, Feb. 2, 1901, p. 5.

p. 202 **"The National Baseball League is"**: A Nov. 10, 1900, interview with McGinnity in the *South McAlester Daily Capital* in the Indian Territory (later Oklahoma) was republished in *Sporting Life*, Dec. 15, 1900, p. 5.

p. 202 **They huddled on a corner bench:** This scene is described in *The Real McGraw*, p. 145.

p. 203 **"A quarter century ago this sport"**: This is from an editorial in the *Morning Herald*, March 18, 1901, p. 4.

p. 203 **"Doesn't that make a crackerjack"**: Robinson was quoted in the *Morning Herald*, March 26, 1901, p. 4.

p. 203   **He had looked like a black man:** This account is from the *Morning Herald*, March 16, 1901, p. 4.

p. 203   **"He is a real Indian":** McGraw was quoted in *Sporting Life*, April 6, 1901, p. 4.

p. 203   **McGraw was no social pioneer:** This explanation for McGraw's attempt to represent Charley Grant, a black ballplayer from Chicago who was working as a bell-hop at the Eastland Hotel in Hot Springs, as an Indian is from Alexander's *John McGraw*, p. 75.

p. 203   **"get a Chinaman of my acquaintance":** Ibid., p. 76.

p. 204   **"You insulted the committee":** The conversation between Ebbets and Dahlen was quoted in *Sporting Life*, Dec. 15, 1900, p. 5.

p. 204   **"I do not know whether Keeler signed":** Ebbets was quoted in *Sporting Life*, Feb. 16, 1901, p. 3.

p. 205   **"one of the best cities":** Hanlon's comments were quoted in *Sporting Life*, May 5, 1900, p. 1.

p. 205   **"These magnates need":** Fielder Jones was quoted in the *Brooklyn Daily Eagle*, Feb. 16, 1901, p. 16.

p. 205   **"If ballplayers would have a little":** Hanlon was quoted in *Sporting Life*, April 26, 1902, p. 6.

p. 205   **"a home man":** This is from the *Brooklyn Daily Eagle*, March 27, 1901, p. 12.

p. 206   **the huge crowds and grandstand plays:** This is almost verbatim from the *Morning Herald*, April 27, 1901, p. 4.

p. 206   **Oriole Park:** At first the *Morning Herald* referred to the new ballpark as the York Road Park, but by August was calling it Oriole Park. It shared the site of the original Oriole Park, which the American Association team had used from 1889 to 1891, before Union Park was built. The new ballpark was also referred to as American League Park.

p. 208   **"The tighter the situation":** This comment about McGraw was made in the *Morning Herald*, June 18, 1901, p. 4.

p. 208   **"exercising an authority very similar to the Czar":** This description of Ban Johnson is from the *Morning Herald*, May 23, 1901, p. 4.

p. 208   **"It would not be so bad if":** McGraw was quoted blasting the umpires in the *Morning Herald*, May 20, 1901, p. 4.

p. 209   **"Of course, I know nothing about the rules":** Jennings was quoted in the *Morning Herald*, June 10, 1901, p. 4.

p. 209   **"Then, if, as I believe":** Jennings was quoted in *The Sun* (Baltimore), June 20, 1901, p. 6.

p. 209   **"I will go to Hanlon":** Jennings was quoted in *Sporting Life*, June 22, 1901, p. 5.

p. 210   **"He never intended to play with us":** Connie Mack was quoted in *Sporting Life*, June 29, 1901, p. 5.

p. 210   **"One would think that the American League":** Jennings was quoted in *Sporting Life*, July 7, 1901, p. 4.

p. 210   **"Now we have information he is":** Ban Johnson was quoted in *Sporting Life*, Aug. 3, 1901, p. 7. McGraw's retort is from the same source.

p. 211   **Connolly did not forget to shout:** This is verbatim from *The Sun* (Baltimore), Aug. 26, 1901, p. 6.

p. 212   **"I'll make a stab at it, Ned":** This anecdote was reported in the *Brooklyn Daily Eagle,* June 7, 1901, p. 13.

p. 213   **"The cranks want to see a team":** Keeler was quoted in the *Brooklyn Daily Eagle,* April 16, 1901, p. 13.

p. 213   **something like their old-time form:** This is verbatim from *Sporting Life,* Aug. 17, 1901, p. 8.

p. 214   **So why should anyone grouse if Brooklyn:** In 1895, when Ebbets prepared the schedule, Brooklyn played at home on Decoration Day, July 4, and Labor Day, according to the *Morning Herald,* March 1, 1895.

p. 215   **"three times as many as":** Ebbets spoke about his aversion to personal passes in an interview with the *Brooklyn Daily Eagle* published on May 10, 1907, meaning he might have given out even fewer than three by 1901.

p. 215   **a little man in little things:** This is nearly verbatim, only with the clauses reversed, from Thomas C. Rice's obituary of Ebbets in the *Brooklyn Daily Eagle,* April 19, 1925, p. 8A.

p. 215   **because Ebbets was a councilman:** The *Brooklyn Daily Eagle* reported on Sept. 8, 1899, p. 13, after Umpire Emslie had incurred the wrath of the Washington Park crowd and left the ballpark: "When the steps to the elevated station were reached, a rush was made by a number of men who believed they could wreak vengeance on the umpire on board the train unmolested by the police. But again Ebbets was too quick for them. Hustling Emslie up the stairs, he stationed himself at the foot and with the assistance of the police, held the crowd back until a train had come along and taken the umpire away."

p. 215   **he had never seemed all that happy in Brooklyn:** "Hanlon, although he had won two pennants in four years and had not been lower than third, never seemed to be completely happy in Brooklyn," Frank Graham wrote in *The Brooklyn Dodgers: An Informal History* (New York: G. P. Putnam & Sons, 1945), p. 12.

p. 215   **"He has done a great many good turns":** Hanlon was quoted in *Sporting Life,* Jan. 18, 1902, p. 9.

Chapter 11: Betrayals

p. 217   **"Give me time," Brush had written:** This letter, apparently written during the summer of 1901, was quoted in the *Morning Herald,* Dec. 10, 1901, p. 4.

p. 218   **Since coming to Pittsburgh he:** This is from a July 1908 article in *Baseball Magazine* called "Barney Dreyfuss—the Man," by Ralph S. Davis.

p. 218   **"An impracticable and wicked scheme":** This is from *Sporting Life,* Oct. 5, 1901, p. 1.

p. 219   **"All I want to see":** Freedman was quoted in *Sporting Life,* which published the stenographic minutes of the four-day meeting, Feb. 8, 1902, p. 21.

p. 219   **"I am against it":** Dreyfuss was quoted in the *Morning Herald,* Dec. 12, 1901, p. 4.

p. 220   **"Lead her around the hard 'bases'":** The Reverend C. F. Thomas, who performed the wedding, was quoted in *Sporting Life,* Jan. 18, 1902, p. 11.

p. 220   **"The Season has been one of":** This is from Goldman's written financial report to the directors for 1901, which is part of the Arthur Mann collection at the Library of Congress. A full list of salaries mentions, among other things, a payment of $140 to J. H. Anderson, apparently the baseball writer for the *Morning Herald,* without explanation. The attendance figure was cited in an exhibit in a report on organized baseball published by the House Judiciary Committee's subcommittee on the study of monopoly power, after hearings in 1951.

p. 220   **Sometime between noon and half past eleven:** This sentence is almost verbatim from an article called "Why Donlin Wasn't in Left Field," by James H. Bready, published in *The Evening Sun,* April 12, 1962, from which this account is drawn.

p. 221   **"We are catering to the public":** McGraw's telegram was quoted in the *Morning Herald,* March 15, 1902, p. 4.

p. 221   **He knew little about books:** Mahon said this about himself, according to an article in Baltimore's *Evening Sun,* Dec. 20, 1961.

p. 221   **"It isn't justice any of us want":** Mahon wrote this in the first of four installments of "The Autobiography of a Baltimore Boss," in *The Sun* (Baltimore), Oct. 1, 1922.

p. 221   **Joe Kelley secured an interest:** This sentence is nearly verbatim from *Sporting Life,* Jan. 18, 1902, p. 3.

p. 222   **"You know that is a big lot of money":** Keeler was quoted in the *Morning Herald,* Jan. 9, 1902, p. 4.

p. 222   **It had been a long time since Brooklyn:** John B. Foster, the Brooklyn correspondent for *Sporting Life,* wrote this on Jan. 18, 1902, p. 9.

p. 222   **"I was tempted to make a move":** Keeler was quoted in the *Morning Herald,* Jan. 9, 1902, p. 4.

p. 222   **"I am told by the newspapers":** Keeler was quoted in *Sporting Life,* Jan. 4, 1902, p. 2.

p. 223   **"He almost equals Carnegie":** The rooter's letter to the *Brooklyn Daily Eagle* was written on Dec. 20, 1901, and published the following day, p. 3.

p. 223   **"I expect to play ball for six":** Keeler's comment is from an interview in *The Sporting News,* excerpted in *The Sun* (Baltimore), Feb. 23, 1902, p. 6.

p. 224   **"At the present rate":** William F. H. Koelsch wrote this in his column from New York in *Sporting Life,* Nov. 8, 1902, p. 3.

p. 225   **"I do not say that it is a perfect team":** Hanlon was quoted in *Sporting Life,* April 19, 1902, p. 10.

p. 225   **"Jump, jump!":** This exchange was reported in *Sporting Life,* May 31, 1902, p. 2.

p. 225   **"Willie is studying up some new angles":** This rendition of Keeler's famous phrase was in *Sporting Life,* May 31, 1902, p. 11.

p. 226   **Bunts and line drives started coming in bunches:** This is almost verbatim from *The Sporting News,* June 7, 1902, p. 7.

p. 226   **With the speed of an automobile:** Ibid.

p. 226   **LEFT BRAINS IN THEIR BAT BAGS:** This headline is from the *Baltimore American,* May 15, 1902.

p. 227   **"The usual ragtime argument":** This is from the *Baltimore American,* June 29, 1902, p. 12.

p. 227 **$10,000 a year:** This is the figure as reported by *Sporting Life* and the *Baltimore American*. But the *Morning Herald* put his salary at "more than $10,000," and Seymour, p. 321, at $11,000.

p. 228 **"I am in love with this city":** McGraw was quoted in the *Baltimore American*, July 8, 1902, p. 11.

p. 228 **"I can't stand for Ban Johnson":** McGraw was quoted in the *Baltimore American*, July 9, 1902, p. 11.

p. 228 **"The muttering of an insignificant":** Ban Johnson was quoted in *Sporting Life*, July 17, 1902, p. 5. The next quotation from McGraw is from the same source.

p. 228 **"Looked at in a cold business light":** This is from the *Baltimore American*, July 8, 1902, p. 11.

p. 228 **"Well, you know, they are all out for the money":** McGraw was quoted in the *Morning Herald*, July 11, 1902, p. 4.

p. 229 **Kel had wired a Baltimore newspaper:** Kelley's telegram (from Baltimore) was published in the *Baltimore American*, July 16, 1902, p. 10.

p. 230 **"betrayers in high places":** This is from an editorial in the *Morning Herald*, July 17, 1902, p. 6.

p. 230 **"This is my home":** Robinson was quoted in the *Baltimore American*, July 18, 1902, p. 2.

p. 230 **Tom Murphy got down on his hands and knees:** This anecdote is from Bready's *The Home Team*, p. 111.

p. 231 **"Baltimore might be a good club":** Ban Johnson was quoted in the *Morning Herald*, Feb. 19, 1902, p. 4.

p. 231 **"One thing I would like to say":** Ebbets was quoted in *Sporting Life*, Sept. 6, 1902, p. 7.

p. 231 **Ebbets had made it clear that he:** Ebbets's preference for a "war of extermination" is a direct paraphrase from *Sporting Life*, Aug. 2, 1902, p. 4.

p. 232 **"We know each other's ideas":** Keeler was quoted in *The Sporting News*, in an interview republished in *The Sun* (Baltimore), Feb. 23, 1902, p. 6.

p. 232 **"Brooklyn suits me pretty well":** Keeler was quoted in *Sporting Life*, Sept. 13, 1902, p. 4.

p. 233 **Willie Keeler had some business of his own:** Much of this account of Keeler in Chicago is drawn from an undated article in the *New York Press*, probably from Jan. 1903, in the Keeler scrapbook.

p. 233 **a salary of $10,000:** Some accounts indicate that the $10,000 was made up of a salary of $8,000 and a bonus of $2,000, which would suggest that Keeler was paid only $8,000 in 1904.

p. 234 **"According to Jay":** This is from the *Record-Union* of Sacramento, Nov. 27, 1902, p. 2.

p. 234 **his salary-making arm:** This is verbatim from *The New York Times*, Jan. 6, 1903, p. 6.

p. 235 **"Sure," Willie replied:** Keeler and Ebbets were quoted in the *Brooklyn Daily Eagle*, Jan. 4, 1903, p. 6.

p. 235   **"No one blames Keeler":** This is from Brooklyn correspondent John B. Foster in *Sporting Life,* Dec. 27, 1902, p. 7.

p. 236   **the noisy, formidable machine:** Much of this description of the early X-ray machines comes from Nancy Knight, a Maryland-based radiology historian, in a June 1998 interview.

p. 236   **"I'd rather be on the slab,":** Keeler was quoted in the *Brooklyn Daily Eagle,* Jan. 6, 1903, p. 13, from which this story of his examination is drawn.

Chapter 12: Playing 'Til Dark

p. 238   **"We have been liberally treated":** Ebbets was quoted in *The New York Times,* Jan. 23, 1903, p. 10.

p. 238   **Within a year, he predicted:** Ebbets was quoted on interleague play in the *Brooklyn Daily Eagle,* Jan. 25, 1903, p. 6.

p. 239   **between 165th and 168th streets:** Columbia Presbyterian Hospital now occupies the site where Hilltop Park stood from 1903 to 1912.

p. 239   **a wild waste of brushwood and boulders:** This is almost verbatim from *The New York Times,* April 6, 1903, p. 6.

p. 240   **"I can make about two throws":** Keeler was quoted in *Sporting Life,* Aug. 29, 1903, p. 3.

p. 240   **After a game Willie took inconspicuous:** This anecdote and Keeler's quotation were reported in *Sporting Life,* July 11, 1903, p. 9.

p. 242   **That was McGraw's doing:** "[T]he Giant manager was assumed to be in full support of, if not the inspiration for, his boss's position: risk nothing and stay at the top," Benton Stark wrote in *The Year They Called Off the World Series: A True Story* (Garden City Park, N.Y.: Avery Publishing Group Inc., 1991), p. 167.

p. 242   **"Muggsy is afraid to play":** Griffith was quoted in *Sporting Life,* Oct. 1, 1904, p. 5.

p. 242   **"The spitball":** Chesbro offered what the headline called SECRET OF THE SPITBALL in *The Sun* (Baltimore), Feb. 4, 1905, p. 9.

p. 243   **On a wintry Sunday morning:** Much of this account is drawn, some of it verbatim, from *Baltimore Afire,* by Harold A. Williams (Baltimore: Schneidereith & Sons, 1954).

p. 244   **an attitude toward life:** "[T]rue, new buildings were to come, but something not built by hands was gone—the spirit of a colorful age, an atmosphere, an attitude to life as it was in the eighties, the nineties and before. All these did not return with reconstruction, nor will they ever come back," Meredith Janvier wrote in *Baltimore in the Eighties and Nineties* (Baltimore: H. G. Roebuck & Son, 1933), p. 296.

p. 245   **"The man with money to burn":** Von der Horst was quoted in *Sporting Life,* May 20, 1905, p. 9.

p. 246   **"It looks now as though he had made":** Hanlon was quoted in *Sporting Life,* March 25, 1905, p. 7.

p. 246   **"Economy is the watchword":** Ebbets was quoted in *The New York Times,* March 21, 1905, p. 12.

p. 247   **"I'm ready to sign":** This dialogue between Keeler and Farrell was reported in *Sporting Life,* Dec. 3, 1904, p. 5.

p. 247   **"Since they've settled up":** Keeler was quoted in *Sporting Life,* Dec. 3, 1904, p. 6.

p. 247   **"He's got a bad leg":** The unidentified ballplayer spoke of Keeler to John B. Foster of *Sporting Life,* Dec. 10, 1904, p. 6.

p. 248   **"I surely expect to play ball":** Keeler was quoted in *Sporting Life,* April 20, 1907, p. 11.

p. 248   **"G'wan with you":** This story is told in an unidentified clipping in the Keeler file at the Hall of Fame.

p. 249   **for that was what the newspapers had started to call:** *Sporting Life* used the term "Yankees" in the body of a story as early as May 20, 1905, p. 6. Lyle Spatz, chairman of SABR's baseball records committee, reports seeing it as early as 1904. He cites a report in the *The Sporting News* record book of 1937 that credits the coinage to Mark Roth of the *New York Globe* (later the Yankees' traveling secretary) and Sam Crane of the *New York Journal,* who had seen the Providence Grays of the early 1880s, also known as the Yankees. In *The New York Yankees: An Informal History* (New York: G. P. Putnam's Sons, 1943), Frank Graham gives credit for the name to Jim Price of the *New York Press.* The story of why Price chose the name is from Harvey Frommer's *The New York Yankee Encyclopedia,* Vol. I (New York: Macmillan, 1997), on p. 6.

p. 249   **"If it gets any smaller":** Graham, in *The New York Yankees,* p. 13, attributes this to Mark Roth of the *New York Globe.*

p. 249   **It was a declining twirler named Bill Hogg:** This account is from an article published in the *New York American* on July 16, 1908.

p. 250   **He had decided not to be found:** Charles Keeler, Willie's grandnephew, told me this story of how Keeler vanished when he was wanted as the Yankee manager. I've found no contemporary source, but versions are recounted in several secondary accounts of Keeler's career, including those in *Cooperstown: Where the Legends Live Forever,* by Lowell Reidenbaugh (St. Louis: Sporting News Publishing Co., 1983); "Kings of the Diamond," an article by Wendell Plumlee of *The Philadelphia Inquirer* in *Baseball Digest,* March 1979; and *Baseball's Best—The Hall of Fame Gallery,* by Martin Appel and Burt Goldblatt (McGraw-Hill Book Co., 1977).

p. 250   **The majority stockholders:** This account of the Brooklyn ballclub's stockholders meeting is drawn from the *Brooklyn Daily Eagle,* Nov. 13, 1906, p. 1.

p. 251   **"We intend to keep the team in Brooklyn":** Ebbets was quoted in the *Brooklyn Daily Eagle,* April 30, 1907, p. 2 in section II.

p. 251   **"The worst season in twenty-three years":** Ebbets was quoted in the *Brooklyn Daily Eagle,* Oct. 9, 1905, p. 12.

p. 252   **"This is a case of sour grapes":** Ebbets was quoted in the *Brooklyn Daily Eagle* on Feb. 20, 1907, p. 11.

p. 252   **Ebbets and Abell met through the night:** This account is drawn from a profile of Ebbets in *The New York Times* on Jan. 21, 1912, p. 1 of the Sporting Section.

p. 252   **all of it belonged to Brooklyn:** Actually, 1 percent of the ballclub was owned by Albert Wall, a lawyer for the ballclub, as the New Jersey representative required under that state's laws, according to the *Brooklyn Daily Eagle,* Nov. 3, 1907, p. 8. Charles Ebbets, Sr., owned 59 percent, Henry Medicus owned 29 percent, and Charles Ebbets, Jr., owned 10 percent. One percent was owned by Robert Wright, a Medicus associate.

p. 253   **"It injured my batting":** Keeler was quoted in *Sporting Life,* Dec. 5, 1908, p. 7.

p. 253   **"Yes, I am going to quit baseball":** Keeler was quoted in *Sporting Life,* Nov. 14, 1908, p. 7.

p. 253   **be hitting them "where they ain't" as usual:** This is the exact paraphrase that William F. H. Koelsch, the New York correspondent for *Sporting Life,* used in describing Keeler's letter, Feb. 27, 1909, p. 5.

p. 254   **That very night, a banquet:** This account of the banquet for Keeler is drawn from the *Plainfield Courier,* Feb. 23, 1910, p. 1, and *Sporting Life,* March 5, 1910, p. 15.

p. 254   **largely for the sake of old times:** This is the conclusion of Joe Vila, the long-time *New York Sun* baseball writer, in his obituary of Keeler on Jan. 2, 1923.

p. 255   **He held the season records:** Keeler still holds the major league record for singles in a season. But George Sisler surpassed him for the major league record for hits in a season when he hit 257 in 1920, and Rogers Hornsby took the National League mark with 250 hits in 1922. Keeler also had more than 200 hits and scored more than 100 runs for eight years in a row—another surviving record.

p. 256   **"New York's private world's series":** This phrase is from *The New York Times,* Oct. 10, 1921, p. 1.

p. 256   **"I want to see Mac win":** Keeler was quoted in a *New York World* report on Keeler's funeral, on Jan. 5, 1923.

p. 256   **The vague chest pains and:** This and the next sentence are almost verbatim from p. 14 of a thirty-page, typewritten biography of Keeler by Dr. John J. Rainey of Troy, N.Y., in the Keeler file at the Hall of Fame.

p. 257   **the thinner bat:** This was the explanation offered by Ruth biographer Robert W. Creamer, in an interview in December 1996. In his book, *Babe: The Legend Comes to Life* (New York: Simon & Schuster, 1974), Creamer wrote on p. 41, "His home run swing came from coordination and total commitment as much as it did from sheer strength."

p. 257   **A physicist explained that the Bambino:** This is Professor A. L. Hodges's explanation in the *Cleveland News-Leader,* quoted in an article entitled "A New Hero of the Great American Game at Close Range," in *Current Opinion,* Oct. 1920, p. 477.

p. 257   **schoolboys on a day's outing:** This is verbatim from *The New York Times,* Oct. 12, 1921, p. 11.

p. 258   **One day a gray-faced man:** This anecdote is from Keeler's obituary in the *New York Mail,* Jan. 2, 1923.

p. 258   **"Any man can be a good fellow":** Keeler was quoted in *Sporting Life* on Nov. 9, 1907, p. 4.

p. 258   **allergy to work:** Charles Keeler, in a May 1994 interview, said his great-uncle was "allergic to work."

p. 258   **Tom and Joe were living a few blocks away:** Tom and Annie Keeler lived at 544 Hart street, Joe and Sarah and their three children at 534 Kosciusko street.

p. 258   **"If we could collect four or five thousand":** This is from the solicitation letter (with August Herrmann's name typed in) signed by Ebbets, Abe Yager, William J. Granger, Leonard F. Wooster, and William A. Rafter, in the Keeler file at the Hall of Fame.

Notes

p. 259　**"The league owners, hard-hearted":** This is from the *New York Globe,* Dec. 17, 1921, from clippings lent by Charles Keeler.

p. 259　**"Charley, I'd like to get a little money":** Keeler is quoted in his obituary in the *New York World,* Jan. 2, 1923.

Epilogue

p. 261　**merchant prince:** This is the term that Francis E. Beirne used in *The Amiable Baltimoreans* (New York: E. P. Dutton & Co., Inc., 1951) to describe Hopkins, George Peabody, Enoch Pratt, and William T. Walters, the nineteenth-century Baltimoreans who became the city's cultural benefactors.

p. 262　**Enough branch factories went up:** This is drawn from Sherry H. Olson in *Baltimore: The Building of an American City* (Baltimore: Johns Hopkins University Press, 1980), p. 304.

p. 262　**"We've long looked forward":** The Gunther Brewing Co., Inc., ad ran in *The Sun* (Baltimore), April 15, 1954, p. 29. The ellipses are in the original.

p. 262　**"A wonderful, wonderful parade":** Blanche McGraw was quoted in *The Sun* (Baltimore), April 16, 1954, p. 1.

p. 263　**"I have seen those immortals":** James A. Newell wrote this in "Old Fan Salutes the New Orioles," in the *Baltimore News-Post,* April 15, 1954.

p. 264　**modern Walter Johnson:** This is how Hugh Trader, Jr., described Turley in the *Baltimore News-Post* on April 15, 1954.

p. 264　**"When he stopped Minoso":** Lane was quoted in *The Evening Sun,* April 16, 1954, p. 23.

p. 264　**"There's no science left":** This was in Red Smith's syndicated column, "Views of Sport," in *The Evening Sun,* April 14, 1954, p. 63.

p. 265　**He had made himself the wealthiest man:** Hanlon's worth and holdings were described by John Lancaster in "Baltimore, a Pioneer in Organized Baseball," in *Maryland Historical Magazine* in March 1940, p. 43.

p. 266　**"too many colored population":** This is quoted in *Never Just a Game: Players, Owners & American Baseball to 1920,* by Robert F. Burk (Chapel Hill: University of North Carolina Press, 1994), p. 209.

p. 266　**"There are many different kinds":** Hanlon was quoted in *Sporting Life,* May 20, 1905, p. 9.

p. 266　**"The father of modern baseball":** This is from Hanlon's obituary in *The Sun* (Baltimore), April 15, 1937.

p. 267　**Occasionally fewer than a hundred fans:** This is according to Bready, *The Home Team,* p. 34.

p. 267　**"about the worst baseball town":** Jennings was quoted in Lancaster, op. cit., p. 47.

p. 267　**infused a wonderful degree:** This is verbatim from *Sporting Life,* April 11, 1908, p. 10.

p. 267　**His first season he blew a whistle:** This anecdote about Jennings is from *Baseball's Best: The Hall of Fame Gallery,* by Martin Appel and Burt Goldblatt (New York: McGraw-Hill, 1977), p. 227.

p. 267   **the piercing cry—"Ee-yah!":** Jennings explained the origin of his famous phrase in the *Detroit Free Press,* reprinted in *Sporting Life,* Nov. 9, 1907, p. 4.

p. 267   **He was drinking too much:** This is according to Charles Alexander, the McGraw biographer, in an interview with the author, and to Al Stump's biography, *Cobb* (Chapel Hill: Algonquin Books, 1994), p. 308.

p. 268   **"Life is full of trials":** Jennings was quoted in *Sporting Life,* Dec. 21, 1907, p. 4.

p. 268   **"just to manage me":** McGraw was quoted in *Pope's Greatest Managers,* by Edwin Pope (Garden City, N.Y.: Doubleday, 1960), p. 108.

p. 268   **moody and distracted:** These are the words used by Charles Alexander in his McGraw biography, p. 270. This paragraph is drawn from his book.

p. 268   **"I owe baseball more than":** Jennings was quoted in an unidentified news clipping in his file at the Hall of Fame.

p. 268   **"Confidentially, I would suggest":** Hanlon's letter to August ("Garry") Herrmann on Jan. 25, 1906, is in the archives at the Hall of Fame.

p. 269   **When he left at last, he was given:** This is from an interview with Kelley's daughter-in-law, Mary G. Kelley, of Silver Spring, Md., in early 1995.

p. 269   **His wife would know he had stopped:** This is from Kelley's daughter-in-law.

p. 269   **Once he went to retrieve Babe Ruth:** This anecdote was told to the author by Mary Krause, Kelley's granddaughter.

p. 269   **Kel began to seem lonely:** Al Kermisch, who met Kelley around 1940, said in a 1995 interview, "I had the impression he was pretty lonely, [that] it had all passed him by."

p. 269   **"The first and the fifteenth":** Ibid.

p. 269   **New Cathedral Cemetery:** McGraw and Robinson are also buried in the cemetery that stretches between Edmondson Avenue and Old Frederick Road, near the southwestern edge of Baltimore.

p. 270   **"He is the incarnation":** This is from "Mister Muggsy," a profile in *The New Yorker,* March 28, 1925.

p. 270   **Nobody had a better feel:** Or so his wife believed. "He understood the entertainment aspects of baseball better than any other player, manager or club owner," Blanche S. McGraw wrote in *The Real McGraw,* edited by Arthur Mann, pp. 224–25. "He proved it by commanding maximum newspaper space, paid admissions, personal popularity and unpopularity."

p. 270   **Mac acquired Mose Solomon:** The story of Mose Solomon (unrelated to the author) was told by Louis Jacobson, now a colleague at *National Journal,* in "Will the Real Rabbi of Swat Please Stand Up?" in *The Baseball Research Journal* in 1989.

p. 271   **That night Mac and Robbie:** This account is drawn from Charles Alexander's version in his McGraw biography, p. 171 (based on the account of umpire Bill Klem, who was there), and Richard Goldstein's account (attributed to Wilbert Robinson, years later) in *Superstars and Screwballs: 100 Years of Brooklyn Baseball* (New York: Penguin Books USA Inc., 1991), p. 103.

p. 271   **could not bear to have his dignity violated:** This is from a Dec. 1996 interview with Jack Kavanagh and Norman Macht, who are writing a biography of Wilbert Robinson.

p. 271 **McGraw scorned the cork-centered ball:** The rubber-centered ball was replaced by a cork-centered ball during the 1910 World's Series. "With the new ball, batting averages, runs, and home runs per game skyrocketed in 1911," Dan Gutman wrote in *Banana Bats and Ding-Dong Balls: A Century of Unique Baseball Inventions* (New York: Macmillan, 1995), p. 153. Ty Cobb hit .420 and Shoeless Joe Jackson, as a rookie, hit .408—their highest averages ever. In response, pitchers developed the knuckleball and the scuffball. The subsequent banning of the scuffball and the spitball as well as the policy of replacing dirty baseballs are considered to have touched off the hitting boom of the 1920s.

p. 271 **"The very sight of a railroad":** McGraw was quoted in *Sporting Life,* June 8, 1907, p. 1.

p. 271 **"I wouldn't know what to do":** McGraw was quoted in *The Sporting News,* July 9, 1925, p. 1, cited in Alexander, p. 269.

p. 272 **being anything but a businessman:** This is drawn from the interview with Jack Kavanagh and Norman Macht, who cited a speech Robbie gave at a testimonial held for him at the Hotel Belvedere.

p. 273 **He wanted to snatch Hughey:** This is according to Graham's *The Brooklyn Dodgers,* p. 40.

p. 273 **self-important:** This is Richard Goldstein's word in *Superstars and Screwballs,* p. 124.

p. 273 **"This broken arm doesn't hurt":** Wilbert Robinson's words were heard by Ralph McGill of the *Atlanta Constitution,* Aug. 9, 1934, p. 1. After that Robinson added: "Maybe this broken arm will break the Cracker jinx also. I hope they can win." Then he called his wife, "Mary, oh Mary"—his last words.

p. 273 **And nobody played so many years:** This is according to Bready in *The Home Team,* p. 30.

p. 274 **He introduced enunciators:** These innovations were reported in *Sporting Life* on, respectively, Sept. 14 and Oct. 3, 1912.

p. 274 **He left it for Len Wooster:** This account and (shortened) dialogue are from Graham's *The Brooklyn Dodgers,* p. 33.

p. 274 **"At Ebbets Field":** The minister was quoted in *Sporting Life,* July 13, 1912, p. 4.

p. 274 **sporting in a fancy automobile, reveling in luxury:** This is almost verbatim from the account in the *Brooklyn Daily Eagle,* Nov. 3, 1919, p. 1.

p. 275 **misconduct with an unnamed woman in Albany:** This is verbatim from an eight-page segment of a longer manuscript, in a folder labeled "Ebbets story," in the Arthur Mann collection at the Library of Congress. Much of this paragraph is drawn from the same source.

p. 275 **"to recuperate":** This is from the *Brooklyn Daily Eagle,* April 25, 1923, p. 22.

p. 275 **"I doubt if you fully realize":** This is from a Dec. 22, 1923, letter from Charles Ebbets, Sr., in Clearwater, Fla., to Meier Steinbrink, a lawyer in Brooklyn. The letter was part of a petition filed by Charles Ebbets, Jr., in the probate case in Surrogate's Court in Kings County.

p. 276 **"No reasonable offer will be refused":** This is from the "Ebbets story" in the Arthur Mann papers, from which much of this account is drawn.

p. 277 **The price was $240,000:** Ibid. Newspaper accounts the following year put the price at $250,000.

Notes

p. 278   **"Rickey and Two Associates":** The headline, RICKEY AND TWO ASSOCIATES OBTAIN CONTROLLING INTEREST IN DODGERS, is from *The New York Times,* Aug. 14, 1945, p. 24.

p. 278   **Brooklyn Trust backed Walter O'Malley:** This is according to Tom Knight, the baseball historian of Brooklyn, in an interview on May 18, 1998.

p. 278   **"Thus the name of Charley Ebbets":** This is from the *Brooklyn Daily Eagle,* Aug. 13, 1945, p. 11.

p. 278   **He was not prone to sentiment:** "O'Malley was unquestionably a shrewd businessman unaffected by sentiment in his operation of the Dodgers," Neil J. Sullivan wrote in *The Dodgers Move West* (New York: Oxford University Press, 1987), p. 216, "but in the end he lacked the influence in New York to exert his will. In Los Angeles, O'Malley found that his interests fitted those of the city, which desired a major league baseball team and wanted also to dispose of the land at Chavez Ravine." In *Dodgers! The First 100 Years* (New York: Birch Lane Press, 1990), Stanley Cohen wrote on p. 97: "O'Malley had no background in sports. He was a businessman whose interest in baseball appeared to be strictly financial."

p. 278   **The quiet war went on:** This account of how O'Malley consolidated his control is drawn from *Bums: An Oral History of the Brooklyn Dodgers* by Peter Golenbock (New York: G. P. Putnam's Sons, 1984), pp. 249–51.

p. 280   **"Other teams were forced to":** This is from Daley's sports column in *The New York Times,* Oct. 14, 1957.

INDEX

Index

Index

Edison, Thomas, 35, 45, 236
Edward VII, king of England (Albert
    Edward, Prince of Wales), 23
Eisenhower, Dwight D., 264
Elberfeld, Kid, 249, 250, 252
Esper, Charley, 75, 78, 80, 97
Evers, Johnny, 5

Farrar, Reverend James, 274
Farrell, Frank, 239, 241, 239, 247–50,
    253, 254
Farrell, Duke, 63, 64, 167
Federal League, 258, 265–66
Fewster, Chick, 257
Fields, Mamie, 220–21
Fleischmann, Julius, 231
Fleischmann, Max, 231
Flick, Elmer, 196
Flushings (semipro team), 14
Foster, John B., 9
France, Joseph C., 229
Freedman, Andrew, 98, 101, 129–30,
    134, 146, 154, 165, 173–74, 188, 197,
    215, 227–29, 231, 246, 267, 270; N.L.
    cut to eight teams, 178–81, 187; N.L.
    syndicate proposal and, 217–19
Frisch, Frankie, 257

Gehrig, Lou, 271, 272
Gilbert, Pete, 46
Gilliam, Junior, 280
Gleason, Kid, 8, 75, 78, 85, 93, 94, 98,
    100, 202
Goldman, Harry, 200, 209–10, 220, 221,
    230, 231
Gompers, Samuel, 190
Gordon, Joseph, 239, 241
Gorhams (semipro team), 16
Goucher, Rev. John F., 66
Grant, Ulysses S., 63
Gray, Mary Jane, 111–12
Greeley, Horace, 80
Griffin, Mike, 31–32, 142, 157
Griffith, Clark, 202, 240–42, 249–50,
    254, 262
Griffith, Mrs. Clark, 262
Grove, Lefty, 262, 263

Hamilton, Billy, 30, 33, 122, 132, 164,
    255
Hanlon, Ned, 200, 201, 241, 267, 270; as
    Baltimore Terrapins owner, 265–66;

Brotherhood of Professional Base
    Ball Players and, 24, 25, 57, 64, 93;
    death of, 266, 269; described, 44–45,
    59, 60, 91, 128, 214–15, 265, 266,
    269; new A.L. organized, 202–5; as
    player, 24, 25, 44–45, 55, 57
Hanlon, Ned—Baltimore Orioles, 252,
    263–64; 1892 season, 43–45; 1893
    season, 50, 52–58; 1894 season,
    58–62, 64, 65, 71, 72, 74–76, 78–81,
    84, 94; 1895 season, 87–91, 93, 94,
    96–98; 1896 season, 100–101, 105–6,
    108–10; 1897 season, 113, 119,
    122–25; 1898 season, 123–26, 128–30,
    132, 134, 152; hired by von der
    Horst, 43–45; N.L. cut to eight teams,
    181, 182, 184, 186–88 ; Orioles–
    Trolley Dodgers merger, 145–55; as
    part owner, 50, 91, 165; player hold-
    outs, 88–90, 93, 123–26, 128; as presi-
    dent, 50, 155, 170, 192; strategies and
    tactics, 55–57, 59–60, 72, 79, 96, 195;
    trades and transfers made, 49–50,
    52–54, 57–58, 60, 93, 100–101, 113,
    123, 125, 129, 134, 145, 188, 189
Hanlon, Ned—Brooklyn Superbas, 265,
    273; 1899 season, 155–63, 165–71,
    173–75; 1900 season, 190–92, 194–95;
    1901 season, 202–5, 209, 211–16;
    1902 season, 222, 224–26; 1903 sea-
    son, 232, 235; 1904 season, 246; 1905
    season, 251; Ebbets conflict, 214–16,
    245–46, 250–52; Orioles–Trolley
    Dodgers merger, 145–55; strategies
    and tactics, 158, 195, 213; trades and
    transfers made, 157, 161, 167,
    169–71, 173–74, 197
Hanlon, Ned—Cincinnati Reds, 268;
    1906 season, 251–52; 1907 season, 265
Hanlon, Ned—Pittsburgh Pirates, 44
Hanna, Mark, 192
Harrison, Benjamin, 19
Hemming, George, 78
Herman, Babe, 281
Herrmann, Garry, 237–38, 268
Heydler, John, 9
Hinchman, Bill, 253
Hoffer, Bill, 262
Hogg, Bill, 249–50
Holmes, Ducky, 129–31, 156, 160, 165,
    171, 185, 187
Holmes, Oliver Wendell, 19, 266

Index

McGinnity, Joe, 185; described, 160,
207–8; with Giants, 229, 241; with
Orioles, 156, 160, 161, 168, 171, 174,
202, 203, 205, 207–8, 211–12, 224,
226, 228, 229; with Superbas, 195,
202

McGraw, Blanche Sindall, 219–20, 262,
270, 271

McGraw, John; career records of, 290; as
college coach, 61, 89, 169, 207; death
of, 272; described, 48, 61, 70, 77, 89,
94, 95, 104, 116, 119, 168, 169, 208,
213, 267, 269–72; The Diamond
(business), 116–17, 148–49, 192, 193,
200, 201, 221, 229, 272; marries
Blanche Sindall, 219–20; marries
Minnie Doyle, 117; new A.L. organized, 199–205

McGraw, John—Baltimore Orioles, 5, 7,
9, 200, 230, 242, 259, 263–64; 1892
season, 48; 1893 season, 54, 57; 1894
season, 61–62, 67–72, 74, 75, 77–80,
85, 94, 117; 1895 season, 88–90,
93–96, 98, 99, 117; 1896 season,
101–8, 111, 112, 117; 1897 season,
113, 115, 117, 119–20, 123; 1898 season, 117, 125, 127, 128, 131, 133;
1899 season, 117, 156–61, 165,
168–74, 176, 272; 1901 season, 117,
201–12; 1902 season, 221, 224,
226–28; N.L. cut to eight teams, 177,
182–86 ; holdout, 88–90, 93; Orioles–
Trolley Dodgers merger, 148–49,
151–53, 156; traded to Browns,
188–89; trades and transfers made,
169–71, 202–3

McGraw, John—New York Giants, 7–8,
227–29, 268, 273, 280 ; 1903 season,
241, 269; 1904 season, 242, 269; 1905
season, 269; 1907 season, 271; 1910
season, 254, 255; 1914 season, 273;
1921 season, 256, 257; 1923 season,
270–71; 1926 season, 270; 1927 season, 270; 1928 season, 270; 1932 season, 272

McGraw, John—St. Louis Browns, 117,
192–94, 200–201; traded from Orioles, 188–89

McGraw, Minnie Doyle, 117, 172

McGuire, Deacon, 174, 225, 232

McJames, Jimmy ("Doc"), 125, 128, 132,
213

McKeever, Ed, 9, 275–77

McKeever, Steve, 275

McKelway, St. Clair, 137–38

McKinley, William, 108, 112, 126, 158

McLaughlin, George, 277

McLaughlin, Hugh, 163–64, 180

McMahon, Sadie, 46–48, 61, 68, 70,
74–76, 78, 80, 93, 97–99, 271

McPhee, Bid, 229

Medicus, Henry, 245, 251

Meekin, Jouett, 63, 85, 173–74

Mencken, Charlie, 83

Mencken, Henry L., 83, 244

Mercer, Win, 120

Milwaukee Braves, 279

Milwaukee Brewers, 199, 209, 230

Minoso, Minnie, 264

Montreal Expos, 268

Morgan, J. P., 36, 37

Morse, Samuel, 56

Moses, Robert, 279

Moss, Clara Roberta, 4, 259, 260

Mullane, Tony, 75

Murphy, Tom ("Murph"), 71, 77, 87,
123, 161, 201–2, 205, 207, 230

Murphy, Yale, 63–64, 68

Mutrie, Jim, 28

National League, 9, 31, 44, 46, 50–51,
86, 130–31, 145–47, 197–99, 266, 276;
1893–1904 league standings, 283–87;
birth of, 19, 23, 158; Brotherhood of
Professional Base Ball Players and,
23–27; Brush Classification Plan, 23,
25; cut to eight teams, 177–89,
191–92, 196; merger with American
Association, 28; Peace Committee settles with A.L., 237–38; pitcher's box
moved, 51–52, 55–56; player signing
war with A.L., 202–5, 209, 224–25,
227–29, 231–33; player signing war
with American Association, 27–28;
Playing Rules Committee, 51–52;
reserve clause, 24, 179, 198, 200, 238,
265; syndicate proposed by Freedman, 217–19; *see also individual teams
and players*

Newell, James A., 263–64

New London Stars, 44

New York City: Brooklyn merged into,
137–40; described, 10, 137, 144–45;
Hilltop Park described, 233–39, 241;
Polo Grounds described, 29; *see also*
Brooklyn; *individual teams*

339